Domestic Interests and International Obligations

Domestic Interests and International Obligations

Safeguards in
International Trade Organizations

by

Irving B. Kravis

Philadelphia

University of Pennsylvania Press

7380
Printed in the United States of America

to

L. P. K.

Foreword

Sooner or later the day is bound to come when the United States will feel as close to its major trading partners of western Europe as many of the European countries now feel towards each other. In one way or another we shall be following the path toward broader international commitments that they have taken in the course of expanding intra-European trade and in moving towards the integration of national states into larger entities. Their experience in reconciling the conflict between these new international commitments and domestic interests that are adversely affected by them is therefore of great interest from the standpoint of the future development of American commercial policy.

A large part of this study is devoted to an examination of the nature of these commitments and of the manner in which domestic interests have been safeguarded in three purely European arrangements—the Organization for European Economic Cooperation's Code of Liberalization, the European Coal and Steel Community, and the European Economic Community. Considerable attention is given also to the General Agreement on Tariffs and Trade, which includes the United States and many other non-European countries.

These trading arrangements have not, so far as the author knows, been previously examined from this point of departure, and the author hopes that the individual chapters dealing with each of them will have some value for those interested in the organizations themselves rather than in the problem of reconciling domestic interests and international obligations. In this connection, however, it is necessary to bear in mind the fact

7

that our concentration on difficulties and their resolution often seems to lead us away from the positive aspects of the organizations under study. The exceptions and the escape clauses hold the center of our interest. Furthermore, our attention is focused almost exclusively upon the trade functions of these organizations, a restriction that is especially important in the cases of the European Coal and Steel Community and the European Economic Community. These limitations of purpose and scope must be remembered because we attempt not only to analyze the contents of the charters of our four organizations but also to describe and appraise the way in which they actually work. Our appraisals may therefore overlook or pass over lightly some of the genuine achievements of the organizations which a more comprehensive study would dwell upon.

Our purpose in making these remarks is merely to make clear our point of departure in evaluating the institutions studied herein. Apologies for concentrating on difficulties and exceptions are not necessary. In the first place, we have no desire to search out the weaknesses and failures of important and highly useful institutions simply in order to place them in an unfavorable light. Secondly, the pejorative connotation usually attached to "escape clauses," the kind of safeguard provision most in the public eye, is not justified in principle. Escape clauses and other safeguarding mechanisms are necessary elements of trade treaties and they can be fashioned so as to play a constructive role in the development of freer world trade.

The chapters other than those dealing with the four trading arrangements mentioned above are brief. An introductory chapter attempts to set out the problem of reconciliation as the author sees it, and three concluding chapters are devoted, successively, to a general outline of alternative safeguarding procedures, to reconciliation policy in Europe and America, and to implications for American policy. These chapters attempt to interpret and to draw certain inferences from the studies of the organizations. Some of the materials were drawn upon for an article which appeared in the March–April 1962 issue of the *Harvard Business Review*.

Virtually all the work was carried out in 1960–61 while the author held a Ford Foundation faculty research fellowship. The study benefited greatly from discussions with many busy and responsible officials who gave generously of their time; over a hundred officers of the four organizations and of the governments which participate in them were interviewed in Geneva, Paris, Luxemburg, Brussels, London, and The Hague. Messrs. Wilfred Beckerman, John Fay, and Joseph Mintzes in Paris were helpful in providing research facilities, and Baron Snoy and Mr. Paul Hatry of Brussels, Professors Raymond Vernon and Seymour Harris of Cambridge, Mass., and Professor Arthur Bloomfield of Philadelphia were among the nongovernmental readers of portions of the manuscript. The author is grateful to them, to the anonymous readers in official positions, to the officials who granted interviews or provided information through correspondence, and to the Ford Foundation, but of course the author alone is responsible for the views and interpretations found in the study. The author takes pleasure also in acknowledging his indebtedness to the library of the Organization for European Economic Cooperation, which has a splendid collection of materials on European integration and, what is equally important, an efficient and helpful staff.

Philadelphia, Pa.   April, 1962

Contents

Chapter 3

Chapter 4

PART I
The Safeguard Problem

Chapter I

The Conflict between Domestic
Interests and International Obligations

NATURE OF THE CONFLICT

TWO BROAD LINES OF DEVELOPMENT in the modern world have tended to create a conflict between the internal economic and social responsibilities of national states and their international obligations.

On the one hand, there has been a growth in the responsibility of the state for the economic and social welfare of its citizens. This has paralleled and been partly caused by the fact that larger and larger proportions of the population have become dependent upon the market economy. The fluctuations in the fortunes of groups of men in their capacity as producers thus no longer seem to depend to the same degree as in a past age upon natural factors; they now appear to depend upon the movement of markets which men think that governments should be able to control. Furthermore, modern means of communication and transportation have made possible the creation of more highly centralized markets, so that larger numbers of producers of a given product share common fortunes and are conscious of their common interests. The changes in communication and transportation have also increased the ease with which the government can in fact intervene in markets, enabling it to reach quickly into every corner of its territory and into every sector of its economy. The result is that there seems to be no segment of the population of a modern state which does not demand government intervention in its behalf when it is beset by economic adversity, however much its leaders may deplore the welfare state in principle and advocate *laissez-faire* in the abstract. The demand for succor is generally all the more potent politically when the difficulty can be ascribed to a foreign source.

On the other hand, the international obligations of the national states have increased because the same factors—the revolution in transportation and the growth of market interdependence—have operated across national boundaries as well as within them. The old shibboleths of sovereignty in the sense of the "unrestricted self-determination, by the individual state, of its external and domestic affairs"[1] are now less meaningful because almost any act of economic intervention by one state has repercussions on the economies of the others. The ways in which the United States disposes of its wheat surpluses, Japan of its textiles, Brazil of its coffee, and Russia of its tin are matters of international concern. Freedom of domestic policy is also limited in more pervasive ways; for example, the United States, whose monetary and fiscal policies long appeared impervious to balance-of-payments considerations has suddenly been made more conscious of the relation between its internal balance and its external balance. The result of this growing interdependence has been to make increasingly clear that many governmental tasks and objectives in the economic sphere are no longer within the competence of the national state. Governments have thus been forced into international cooperation to avoid economic anarchy and to pursue mutually desired ends.

Indeed, a serious question has been raised about the adequacy of the national state for the political and economic tasks that lie ahead. In this connection, it has been frequently

---

[1] K. Lowenstein, "Sovereignty and International Cooperation," *American Journal of International Law*, XLVIII (April, 1954), 243.

observed that the countries that have gone the farthest in accepting limitations upon their sovereignty are six nations in western Europe in which the inadequacy of the national state was vividly demonstrated in a brief span of years by depression, war, defeat, and occupation. The ties between nations will inevitably grow closer and the freedom of action of each be diminished, but the new rules and institutions which will govern their relations are still in the evolutionary stage.

The curtailment of freedom forced upon governments when pursuing certain domestic objectives through international agreements may limit them in serving the other interests of their domestic economies. The newly assumed international obligations are apt to be inimical to the interests of some groups, even though others or the economy in general may benefit. Or changing circumstances may bring about a situation in which international obligations stand in the way of measures that appear necessary or desirable in the interests of the economy as a whole.

The means of reconciliation in the trade area

Governments have sought to reconcile this conflict by means of safeguard clauses in treaties and agreements. The function of these clauses is to provide means of recourse or succor for domestic interests in case of need. Even the agreements that go farthest in the direction of limiting national sovereignty, such as those relating to the Common Market, contain safeguard clauses. Unequivocal commitments, without any avenue of recourse or succor, are rare if not nonexistent in peacetime international treaties and agreements dealing with economic problems.

While such safeguards may be found in treaties and agreements relating to a broad range of economic problems, our concern in this study is limited to their role in multilateral treaties and agreements dealing primarily with trading relations between nations. In particular, analyses are made in subsequent chapters of the safeguard provisions of the General Agreement on Tariffs and Trade (GATT), the Code of Liberalization of the Organization for European Economic Co-operation (OEEC Code), the European Coal and Steel Community (ECSC) and the European Economic Community (EEC). (The EEC is, of course, popularly referred to as the Common Market).

Of course, the very existence of such treaties or agreements affects the reconciliation of the conflict, particularly where the difficulty arises because some special interests are threatened or injured as a consequence of the international obligation. Indeed, it can be said that a major function of some of these trading arrangements, especially the less binding ones which really leave the power of decision to the governments, such as the OEEC Code and GATT, has been to organize external pressures to serve as a counterweight to the internal pressures of domestic interests for increased protection. More than one government has thus cited its international obligations—and the broad domestic interest in adhering to them—as grounds for resisting such domestic demands for intervention.

Before proceeding to the study of the safeguard clauses in the four organizations mentioned above, the nature of the safeguards should perhaps be made clearer. First we will consider what it is that safeguards are designed to protect, and second the means that are employed to achieve the desired protection.

What is safeguarded

Broadly speaking, safeguards in treaties and agreements

dealing with trade matters are designed to avoid one of three groups of contingencies : (1) injury to an industry or sector of the domestic economy; (2) interference with other governmental responsibilities or programs; and (3) failure of a signatory to receive the anticipated benefits.

For American commercial policy, it is clearly the first of these, injury to a particular industry or economic sector, that has been of primary importance. Only GATT, among the four trading arrangements analyzed in this study, clearly includes this type of safeguard, and it is in GATT as the result of American initiative. A comparable provision is either not found or found only in an attenuated form in the three other organizations in which the United States did not actively participate. The seemingly greater sensitivity of American industry to inroads from foreign competition as compared with the industry of European countries is a phenomenon to which we shall return in a subsequent chapter.

Treaties and agreements dealing with trade almost invariably attempt to safeguard the freedom of governments to fulfill their responsibilities in areas that transcend trade questions per se. For example, provisions are typically included to the effect that nothing in the agreement or treaty shall interfere with a signatory's freedom to take actions necessary for the protection of public health and morals and national security. Of course, there is the possibility that measures taken ostensibly for these reasons may really have a protective purpose, but charges of this nature have been relatively rare. More important in the actual operation or the trade treaties and agreements have been safeguards relating to government responsibilities in the areas of balance of payments, economic development, full employment, and agriculture. GATT contains safeguards for all of these purposes, and the other arrangements for all or most of them in one form or another. The balance-of-payments safeguards have easily been of the greatest practical importance in this group.

Safeguards against the failure to receive the anticipated benefits are usually confined to cases in which the absence of benefits can be ascribed to the actions of another signatory (e.g., dumping in the OEEC Code, GATT, and the EEC) or to the failure of another signatory to act (e.g., its failure to include exports important to the complaining country in its list of liberalized products under the OEEC Code). Such clauses may sometimes be invoked even when the party responsible for the absence of benefits is not in violation of the treaty or agreement. Perhaps the broadest clause of this character is found in GATT; it is designed to enable a country which finds that its benefits from the Agreement have been nullified or impaired for almost any reason to seek action to restore the "balance of benefits."

Safeguard methods

Without going into the details of the specific measures of safeguard that may be taken, it is possible to distinguish four broad approaches to the problem of providing safeguards. These are the methods of (1) frequent renegotiation, (2) advance exceptions, (3) derogations, and (4) adaptation.

The method of renegotiation restricts international undertakings to a short period of time, the understanding being that they will be renewed if all goes well or modified through negotiation if necessary. Of the trade arrangements covered in this study, only GATT includes a clear example of this technique. While the general obligations of GATT, such as most-favored-nation treatment and the avoidance of quantitative restrictions, apply indefinitely, the firm validity of tariff concessions has generally been limited to three-year periods. The disadvantage of the method of renegotiation is, of course, that it creates uncertainty about the future, and thus limits the value of the agreement. In the GATT context, however, this has been minimized by the fact that there have generally been relatively few actual changes in duties at the three-year intervals when renegotiation is permissible; the deterrent has been the necessity to offer compensatory concessions for those that are withdrawn. It might be stretching the term "renegotiation" too far to include under this method the technique used in the OEEC Code of permitting countries to withdraw products from the liberalized lists as long as they replaced them with other products to the extent necessary to maintain the prevailing target percentages for import liberalization. The method of renegotiation is not used in the ECSC and the EEC, although there are some matters left open for future negotiation, especially in the EEC. Perhaps the closest EEC approach to the method of renegotiation is the leeway left for the future determination of a limited number of external tariffs (i.e., those relating to third countries); however, once their levels are settled, it is intended that further changes will be made only in the course of reciprocal tariff concessions with third countries.

The second approach, the method of advance exceptions, is applied to sectors that are known at the time of drafting of the treaty or agreement to be exposed to injury if they are placed under the general rules that are being formulated. Consequently, the member state concerned receives an advance exception from all, or more usually, some of the rules on behalf of such sectors. The exception may be temporary or permanent. Each of the six member countries of the Common Market received special safeguards of this character for one or more particular situations under the treaties establishing the ECSC and the EEC. In the ECSC, for example, special provisions were made for the temporary protection of Belgian coal, which was known to be higher in cost and therefore unable to compete in the Common Market with French and German coal. In the OEEC Code, state-traded imports were excluded from the obligations to free trade of quantitative restrictions. Also, since the obligations were confined only to certain percentages of their private trade (from 50 to 90 per cent, at various times), the countries were able to withhold liberalization from the products that were most sensitive to import competition. In GATT, also, countries are free to refrain from making tariff concessions on items that are vulnerable to foreign competition, although the trading rules with respect to nondiscriminatory treatment and abstinence from quantitative restrictions apply in principle to all products. In arrangements which involve selection of individual products, such as the OEEC Code or GATT, future difficulties can be minimized by the avoidance of products that are characterized by declining demand. The earlier use by the United States of a growth criterion for the selection of products for the granting of GATT concessions would, for example, have avoided some of the escape-clause actions that were taken.[2]

The method of derogation is applied to circumstances that cannot be foreseen in terms of specifically identifiable situations but only in terms of general criteria to which it is expected or feared that future situations may conform. Such criteria, more or less detailed, are commonly designed to anticipate cases of balance-of-payments deficits or lack of adequate reserves, injury to particular industries, and shortages of supplies, among other types of difficulties. Sometimes there is, in addition, a broad clause providing for safeguard action in case of "serious difficulty" without specifying any particular source

---

[2] See my papers "The Growth Criterion for Tariff Concessions," *Quarterly Journal of Economics,* LXVI (May, 1952), 273–285; and "The Trade Agreements Escape Clause," *American Economic Review,* LIV (June, 1954), 319–338.

of the trouble, or a clause giving a broad grant of power which, while not referring specifically to safeguards, can be used for safeguard purposes if necessary. The EEC treaty, for example, contains both types of provisions; there is a safeguard clause limited to a transitional period which may be invoked if there are serious and persistent difficulties in any sector or region, as well as a permanent clause which authorizes any action consistent with the aims of the Community which is not specifically provided for in the Treaty. In GATT, a provision permitting waivers of obligations has been used as a general safeguard clause where other articles of the Agreement have not covered a desired exception. Generally, however, broad clauses of this character are interpreted as being reserved for unusual situations in which recourse to clauses of a more specific nature has been ruled out or exhausted, and the administrative mechanisms that control their use are usually designed so as to make their invocation more difficult. The method of derogation, which is generally the form of safeguard that is referred to when the term "escape clause" is used in discussions of commercial policy, is perhaps the most common type of safeguard. It is employed repeatedly in all four of the trading arrangements analyzed in subsequent chapters.

Still another approach to the safeguard problem, and perhaps both the most constructive and most uncommon one, is the method of adaptation or adjustment. In this approach, the changes that are imposed by the international trade obligations of the agreement or treaty are accepted, but at the same time an attempt is made to remove or ease the injury that is incurred by the people affected by the changes. Neither the OEEC Code nor the GATT contains such provisions. The ECSC treaty, on the other hand, broke new ground by providing for adaptation, or readaptation, as it is sometimes called. Under the ECSC, financial aid may be made available for workers affected by the functioning of the Common Market; the help may take the form of tideover allowances, resettlement grants, and support for retraining. Furthermore, financial aid may also be extended to new enterprises able to offer employment to displaced workers. The EEC treaty, signed by the same countries six years later, represents a considerable retreat from this position.

The functions of safeguard clauses

Having classified the scope of safeguard clauses, as the term is used in this study, a further word may be said about their functions. The function referred to earlier—that of reconciling domestic interests and international obligations—is largely economic in character. Safeguards serve to ease or to make unnecessary adjustments to new situations created either by the treaty or agreement itself or by economic changes during the course of its life span.

Safeguards also serve a political function, which explains why they occasionally figure so prominently in a treaty or agreement. Indeed, it is conceivable that a treaty or agreement may contain so many safeguard clauses that the exceptions to the rules of trade laid down by the document appear to be more numerous than the conformances. This was alleged, for example, with respect to the Havana Charter, and it may be true that its spiritual heir, GATT, contains sufficiently broad exceptions relating to underdeveloped countries so that in fact the commercial policy of such GATT signatories may not be seriously constrained by adherence to the Agreement. However it would be a misconception of political realities to assume that each signatory to a trade treaty or agreement enters the undertaking with the intention to work the exceptions for all they are worth.

The record of the four organizations reviewed in this study does not support the hypothesis of such a cynical approach upon the part of any important trading country. Rather, the safeguard clauses have been used for positive purposes. The insurance that they provide in connection with known trouble spots and against unanticipated difficulties enables countries to go farther in the direction of international cooperation than their domestic pressures and responsibilities otherwise would permit them to do. In the United States, for example, a safeguard clause has been the basis for the "no-serious-injury" promise, made by President Roosevelt and repeated more or less without qualification by his successors; this commitment smoothed the path for Congressional acceptance, tacit though it has been, of American participation in GATT. The advance fears of the dire consequences of arrangements involving freer trade are almost invariably exaggerated, and safeguard clauses serve the function of making agreement possible by allaying some of these groundless fears. Thus one of the chief authors of the European Common Market Treaty was speaking only half in jest when he said during the course of the negotiations : "Give them all the safeguards they want."

Controls over the invocation of safeguards

The confidence reflected in this remark is at least to some degree justified by experience. In fact, many safeguard clauses are never used; clauses that have never been invoked may be found in the charter of each of our four organizations. Nevertheless, there has been sufficient use of the others and there is sufficient opportunity for the use of all to raise the question of controls.

The controls over the invocation of the safeguard clauses,

which of course vary in detail from one treaty or agreement to another, include (1) the commitment of will and policy of each participating country, (2) the legal and moral controls imposed by the organization created by the treaty or agreement, and, underlying both of these, (3) the reciprocity that each country may expect from the others in the extent of its conformance or nonconformance.

With respect to the commitment of each country, it may be assumed that participation reflects the calculation that international cooperation in the form represented by the treaty or agreement is necessary to achieve an end or ends sought by the country. The participating countries therefore generally enter upon the new arrangement with the intention to adhere to the spirit of the undertaking. Of course, the extent of this spirit of commitment or "engagement," as one writer has called it [3] may vary from one participant to another. It may for example be deeper for the countries that were the main architects of the new scheme than for countries that felt obliged to join simply to avoid the greater disadvantages of being left out.

Each new trading arrangement draws its signatories together into a new society of nations with its own charter and, perhaps more important, its own ethos. The legal provisions controlling the invocation of safeguards vary within each treaty or agreement as well as from one treaty or agreement to another. They generally tend, for example, to be more lenient, in the sense of allowing more scope for unilateral action, for balance-of-payments safeguards than for others. It is with respect to those clauses over which the maximum controls are exercised that the most notable differences in administrative arrangements are found among the organizations. In GATT, for example, administrative controls consist

---

[3] E. Haas, *The Uniting of Europe,* London, 1958, p. 520. ff.

chiefly of procedures for consultation; the country seeking to apply the safeguard is almost always left free in the end to do as it wishes, subject only to the possibility of compensatory measures on the part of others affected by its action. In the Common Market, on the other hand, a number of the safeguard clauses require the assent of a supranational board for their application.

However, the ethos or moral climate of an organization also has much to do with the readiness with which countries seek to take advantage of safeguard clauses. In the earlier days of the OEEC Code, for example, an unusually strong feeling of solidarity among the member countries was an effective force in bringing about conformance to the spirit of the Code, although the Code imposed on no country an obligation which had to be regarded as having a clear priority over its national interests. This was due to a combination of circumstances unlikely to be matched again. To a common heritage, geographical proximity, and social and economic interdependence, were added a recent common experience of the ravages of war and a current common effort at recovery with the aid of a pool of American funds. The moral force toward conformance to the principles of GATT is less compelling; the community of nations represented there includes virtually as wide a spectrum as can be found. Nevertheless, no country likes to be placed in the position of having to explain to the others actions that appear to violate the letter or spirit of a treaty or agreement, and all are more or less sensitive to the candid criticisms that are offered in such cases in the working parties of GATT.

Where, as in the ECSC and EEC, a supranational board is in control of the application of certain safeguard clauses, the prevailing attitudes of the member countries work in another way to influence the extent to which the clauses are actually used. In practice the supranational boards must rely upon the member governments for concurrence and support in connection with a wide variety of matters, many of them not connected with safeguard questions, and they must therefore maintain close political rapport with the governments. The boards have thus been greatly influenced by the opinions of the governments in the use of their safeguard powers, and in some important cases they have hesitated to use their full legal authority. Hence, the substantial differences in the legal position regarding the invocation of safeguard clauses between the OEEC Code and GATT on the one hand and the ECSC and the EEC on the other hand are somewhat narrowed in actual practice, although the differences remain considerable.

Underlying both the country's will to conform and its responsiveness to the pressures of the others toward conformance is the realization that full, legally permissible use of safeguard clauses on its part is likely to invite other countries to do the same and thus to erode and finally perhaps to destroy the value of the international arrangement. GATT has tried to use the principle of reciprocity as a major means of control and guarantee. The basic notion is that the balance of benefits obtained by a country at the time of its original accession to GATT and with each subsequent expansion of reciprocal tariff concessions must be maintained. If, for any reason, including a safeguard measure by another signatory, a country finds that the balance of benefits has been altered in a manner which is unfavorable to it, it may seek redress. The balance of benefits is obviously difficult to measure, and countries have in fact enjoyed a certain leeway to invoke safeguard measures without bringing immediate retaliation; more extensive changes in concessions formerly granted have, however, generally required compensatory replacements in order to avoid the withdrawal of concessions by other parties.

The idea of reciprocity was used, somewhat differently, in the OEEC Code. Here the rule was that each member continued to enjoy the full advantage of the liberalization of the others under the Code even if it invoked a safeguard clause to withdraw some of the liberalization it was supposed to extend to the others. Given the strong group spirit that prevailed in the organisation, this principle, aside from being necessary to avoid a spiraling contraction of liberalization, served as a source of additional moral pressure upon a derogating country to conform to the Code as soon as possible.

The operation of the principle of reciprocity is more difficult to judge in the Common Market since the matrix of obligations is so much more complicated. Undoubtedly, extensive use of safeguards by one country would come at some cost in the continuous negotiations that are required about a broad range of issues, but the concessions granted for, say, the right of the French to give subsidies to paper producers, might relate to the choice of personnel for the supranational board or some other matter that has little direct connection with a trade question.

It is to be expected that different countries will react in different ways to the leeway provided by safeguard clauses. Of interest from this standpoint is the recent comment by the London *Economist* contrasting British and German attitudes in the course of a discussion relating to the possibility of British negotiations to enter the Common Market:

The fact is that good Europeans of Dr. Adenauer's circle, who like to consider themselves free trading liberals but are in many respects rather protectionist conservatives, have an instinctive urge to talk themselves into the acceptance of sweeping liberal and supranational principles; but they also have an instinctive trust, that if special difficulties should arise, their friends will show sufficient understanding not to insist on a contractual right to do them deliberate dirt.

By contrast Mr. Macmillan's ministers who call themselves Conservatives but are really free trading liberals, have an initial urge that works precisely the other way; they feel that they owe it to their titular respectability as Conservatives to examine every liberal utterance that could conceivably ever interfere with such vestiges of pragmatic conservatism as they still practise, and to insist on written escape clauses that would protect them against every dimly foreseen bogy which might ever arise in the dark. Europeans then naturally assume that Britain would stretch these legalistic escape clauses as far as they themselves are apt to stretch their looser ones.[4]

If the quick suspicion of the British that is referred to in the last sentence of the quotation exists—and this seems likely—it must be attributed to the bitterness over Britain's long ambivalence in its attitudes toward European integration. Such suspicion would hardly be justified by the British record of close adherence to the letter and spirit of its undertakings in GATT. If Britain's record in the OEEC Code is less impeccable, Britain's derogations still fell far short of those of France. France was inclined also to take more liberties with GATT. In the Common Market, on the other hand, France has resorted to safeguard measures to a lesser extent than Italy or Germany.

It is clear that the nature of the reconciliation of domestic interests and international obligations cannot be judged solely from the legal texts of multilateral treaties and agreements. The spirit of the organization established to administer the obligations and the circumstances of the participation of the individual countries greatly affect the outcome. In the chapters that follow, efforts are therefore made to place the use of safeguard clauses against the proper background in terms of the actual operating spirit and structure of the international organizations under study.

---

[4] May 13, 1961, pp. 662–663.

PART II
Safeguards in Four
International Organizations

Chapter 2

The General Agreement on Tariffs and Trade (GATT)

BACKGROUND

Origins

THE GENERAL AGREEMENT on Tariffs and Trade (GATT) came into existence on January 1, 1948, as a provisional measure pending the then expected ratification of the Havana Charter and the consequent establishment of the International Trade Organization (ITO).   When it became clear two or three years later that the United States, which had been the major instigator of the Havana Charter, would not ratify the Charter and that the ITO would not come into being, the provisional existence of GATT was indefinitely extended by common consent.   It has continued since as a makeshift international organization functioning in the name of the Contracting Parties [1] of GATT with a small secretariat. Beginning with 23 original signatories, GATT membership numbered between 30 and 35 during most of the years of its existence; more recently membership has climbed toward 40. Over 80 per cent of world trade is accounted for by the countries which are members of GATT.

An effort in 1954-55 to regularize the status of the organization by the creation of an Organization for Trade Cooperation foundered upon the same rock of Congressional

---

[1] Following GATT practice in its press releases, the term "Contracting Parties" with initial capital letters will be used here to refer to the signatories to the Agreement as an entity.

disinterest or hostility in the United States.[2]   The legal basis for American participation in GATT rests on the authority of the President of the United States under the Trade Agreements Act of 1934 to conclude executive agreements relating to trade and on his general power to conduct the foreign affairs of the United States.   Thus, GATT has neither required nor received Congressional approval.

The Agreement includes the essential obligations and rules governing trade that were in the Havana Charter, but it is not as extensive in coverage as the Charter; such matters as restrictive business practices, international commodity agreements, and the treatment of foreign investment are omitted. Tariff concessions negotiated at Geneva in 1947 between pairs of nations and automatically extended to all signatories were annexed to the Agreement.   These were supplemented by concessions resulting from four other negotiating sessions between 1949 and 1959, and still another round was in progress in the latter part of 1961.

Contents of the Agreement

The Agreement as it has evolved rests on four essential principles : (1) Trade should be conducted on the basis of nondiscrimination; that is, each signatory should give equal treatment to all of the other signatories.   (2) If protection has to be maintained on behalf of domestic industries, it should be through tariffs rather than through other devices.   (3) Countries are free to alter their commitments under prescribed procedures, but if such changes affect adversely the "balance of benefits" which any other signatory enjoys from the Agree-

---

[2] For the story of these events see W. Diebold, Jr., "The End of the I.T.O.," *Essays in International Finance,* No. 16, Princeton, 1952; and R. Vernon, "Organizing for World Trade," *International Conciliation,* November, 1955.

ment, compensation must be offered. (4) Consultation among the parties is relied upon to avoid damage to the trading interests of any signatory.[2]

In view of our subsequent need to cite specific articles of the Agreement, it may be worthwhile to describe the structure of the Agreement in a little more detail. The Agreement is divided into three parts. Part I contains only two articles, the first stating the essential obligation to accord most-favored-nation treatment to all other signatories and the second to give effect to the schedules of tariff concessions annexed to the Agreement. The basic purpose of the second part of the Agreement (Articles 3 to 23) is to set out supplementary trade rules, some of which are necessary to prevent the tariff concessions from being nullified by restrictive measures of other kinds. Perhaps the most important of these rules are those requiring the elimination of quantitative restrictions and providing that the treatment of imports with respect to internal taxes and regulations be no less favorable than that accorded to like domestic products (i.e., the "national treatment" clause). In addition to a number of other and generally more detailed rules, this part of the Agreement includes many of the exceptions and safeguards which will be discussed subsequently.

The obligations of the Agreement do not extend to the making of new tariff reductions, although a recently added provision of the Agreement (Article 28 bis) recognizes that "customs duties often constitute serious obstacles to trade" and provide for sponsorship of tariff negotiations by the Contracting Parties. Neither do the obligations of the Agreement prevent a signatory from increasing a duty on an item that has not been the subject of a concession (i.e., a reduction or bind-

---

[2] Cf. E. Wyndham White, *GATT as an International Organization* (Geneva, August, 1961).

ing against increase) in a negotiation with another GATT signatory.

The third part of the Agreement is given over largely to administrative matters. Since the Agreement was originally regarded as an interim measure, provisions for the management of the international relations to which it would give rise are limited. The Contracting Parties are to meet from time to time "for the purpose of giving effect to those provisions . . . which involve joint action and, generally, with a view to facilitating and furthering the objectives of this Agreement" (Article 25). Each country is to have one vote in such meetings, and decisions are generally to be taken by a majority of votes cast. The main exception to majority rule is the requirement of a two-thirds vote for granting waivers from the obligations imposed by the Agreement. The waiver clause, incidentally, has proved in practice to be a loophole in the pattern of obligations laid down in the Agreement second in importance only to the derogations permitted on balance-of-payments grounds. Provision is also made for the amendment of the Agreement and for the accession and withdrawal of signatories. Amendments for Part I and certain portions of Part III require unanimous acceptance by all contracting parties; amendments for other parts of the Agreement become effective, for those countries which have accepted them, when approved by at least two-thirds of the signatories (Article 30). Decisions concerning the accession of new signatories require a two-thirds majority (Article 32).

Administration of the Agreement

These brief provisions are virtually the only guidance given in the Agreement as to the manner in which the Contracting Parties are to discharge their joint responsibilities for interpreting and supervising the application of the rules set out in the Agreement. While annual sessions of the Contracting Parties soon became the rule, they were not frequent enough to meet all of these responsibilities. Intersessional provision had to be made, for example, for the investigation and the formulation of recommendations concerning requests relating to derogations from the Agreement or complaints regarding the nullification or impairment of benefits if undue delays were to be avoided. Accordingly, an intersessional committee was established in 1950; it was composed of 15 to 20 member countries, elected at each regular session so as to be representative both of the various geographical areas of the Contracting Parties and of the divergent stages of development and economic interests.[4] In 1960 this was replaced by a Council composed "of the representatives of Contracting Parties willing to accept the responsibilities of membership and to make arrangements for effective participation."[5] The functions of the Council are generally similar to those of the intersessional committee but it is given somewhat broader powers of initiative and decision making. However, final authority in all matters is retained by the Contracting Parties themselves; in the case of urgent issues that require their decision, the Council may call a special session or poll the parties by postal ballot.

The main function of the Council, like that of the intersessional committee before it, is to keep the affairs of the Contracting Parties moving. Most of the detailed technical work leading to decisions of the Contracting Parties is carried out by other subsidiary groups whose work the Council supervises. While use has been made of standing committees

---

[4] *Basic Instruments and Selected Documents,* Vol. II, p. 201. Hereafter, this series published by GATT will simply be referred to as *BISD* with volume or supplement number.

[5] *BISD,* Ninth Supplement, p. 7.

for some substantive matters, reliance upon *ad hoc* working parties has been more common. These groups, which are appointed in connection with derogations, complaints, and the wide variety of other technical matters that come before the Contracting Parties, thrash out the legal, economic, and political issues, and formulate recommendations for the plenary meetings. Their membership, which is suggested by the secretariat, usually includes the main countries and others known to have an interest in the problem in question. The broad membership of these groups and the fact that the persons present at their meetings speak as representatives of their countries mean that the recommendations of the working parties are almost invariably accepted by the plenary sessions. Occasionally, in disputes, use has been made of panels in which parties to the case are excluded from membership, although they are of course given an opportunity to express their views. Groups of experts have also been utilized from time to time; experts are free to express their own opinions, but their recommendations may not command the same ready acceptance as those of the other kinds of groups.

Where has the leadership come from in this group of 30 or 40 nominally equal countries, only loosely organized for the tasks at hand ? Some GATT countries, of course, tend to have more influence than others. This seems to derive almost as much from interest in the organization, as expressed in the willingness to provide adequate representation in Geneva, as from economic and political power. Of course, the powerful countries, especially the United States and the United Kingdom and the Commonwealth, carry great weight in GATT affairs, but so do others like India and Brazil by virtue of their representing a different segment of nations and of the interest in GATT that they have taken. Much of the driving force has, however, come not from a country or groups of countries, but from the executive secretary and his immediate associates in the secretariat of the Contracting Parties. This results both from the leadership vacuum created by the lack of organizational structure and from the effective personality of the man who has occupied the post of executive secretary during the entire life of the GATT.

Despite its somewhat unusual status, GATT has grown in stature and importance. This is probably attributable to two sets of circumstances. First, the very existence of a code of commercial conduct created a need for a mechanism through which disputes and problems arising out of the code could be worked out. On the one hand, countries with grievances sought a forum in which they could obtain redress, and on the other hand, countries which wished to seek relief from obligations that were multilateral in scope found it necessary to negotiate with the collective group to which the commitments had been made. The annual sessions of the Contracting Parties tended to bring together senior trade officials for meetings in which these and other trade problems could be discussed in a technically competent group, and encouraged the development of techniques of consultation and mutual adjustment.

The second factor that has brought GATT to the fore in recent years is the improvement of the balance-of-payments positions of most of the signatories and the consequent dismantling of quantitative restrictions that had been justified on balance-of-payments grounds. In the growing absence of quantitative restrictions, tariff concessions and the other protective devices controlled by GATT came to be more significant. In the words of one writer, "GATT's rules were becoming more relevant to the problems confronting trading nations."[6]

---

[6] Vernon, *op. cit.*, p. 190.

THE SAFEGUARD CLAUSES

The safeguard clauses of GATT may be considered under five headings.[7] Three of these—(1) emergency or short-run contingencies, (2) structural or long-run problems, and (3) defensive provisions for inequities resulting from practices of other members—are related to special sources of difficulty. The other two—(4) waivers granted to a member by the Contracting Parties and (5) certain clauses affording members the opportunity to revise or withdraw their GATT commitments —are general in character in that their availability is not limited to specified sources of conflict between national need and GATT obligation.

Emergency or short-run contingencies

The most important clauses covering emergencies or short-run contingencies relate to balance-of-payments difficulties (Article 12)[8] and to injury to the producers of particular products (Article 19).

Balance of payments. Despite the general prohibition of quantitative restrictions (Article 11), any contracting party may, according to Article 12, restrict imports in order to "safeguard its external financial position and its balance of payments." However, the restrictions may not exceed those necessary to forestall the imminent threat of, or to stop, a serious decline in its monetary reserves," or, if the country has very low reserves, to "achieve a reasonable rate of increase in its reserves." The determination of the International Monetary Fund is to be accepted as to what constitutes a serious decline, a very low

---

[7] The provisions of the Agreement have been changed through amendment from time to time. The version of the Agreement that is discussed in the following pages is, for the most part, that contained in *BISD*, Vol. III, which has been in force since 1957. Occasionally, reference will be made to provisions in effect earlier or later.

[8] One reader has questioned the inclusion of the balance-of-payments

level, and a reasonable rate of increase in monetary reserves (Article 15). The import restrictions imposed under Article 12 are to be relaxed progressively as soon as conditions warrant. Furthermore, the country applying the restrictions must attempt to avoid unnecessary damage to the interests of another member,[9] cutting off imports of commercial samples, reducing imports below the minimum quantities necessary to maintain trade channels, and interfering with patent, trademark, and copyright requirements. In more general terms, the signatories agree to give due regard to the need for external equilibrium in working out their domestic policies, and they recognize that in achieving this reconciliation it is desirable to avoid an uneconomic employment of resources,[10] and to adopt measures which expand rather than contract international trade.

On the other hand, a Contracting Party invoking Article 12 is permitted to give priority to imports of more essential products and it may not be required to withdraw or modify restrictions introduced under the article on the ground that a change in its domestic policies (whether intended to promote full employment or economic development) would make the restrictions unnecessary.

---

clause under the category of emergency or short-run contingencies, pointing out that there might be cases of countries which are chronically in balance of payments difficulties. In the present version of the Agreement, however, provisions for underdeveloped countries — those most likely to encounter chronic deficits — are placed in an entirely separate article. See pages 53–57.

[9] Also, according to an interpretive note (Annex I of the Agreement), an effort is to be made to avoid causing "serious prejudice" to exports of a commodity on which another contracting party is "largely dependent." *BISD*, Vol. III, p. 69.

[10] This undertaking, together with the commitment to avoid unnecessary damage to the interests of another member, has been interpreted as requiring a Contracting Party adopting import restrictions under Article 12 to minimize the incidental protective effects of the restrictions. Cf. *BISD*, Third Supplement, p. 171.

The individual signatory is the sole initial judge of the existence or nonexistence of the necessary conditions for the application of balance-of-payments restrictions, but fairly elaborate provisions for consultation serve to limit its freedom of action and to protect the interests of other contracting parties. In the first place, a country imposing new restrictions or substantially intensifying existing ones must consult with the Contracting Parties immediately after such action, or before, if it is practicable. The consultations are to cover the nature of the balance-of-payments difficulties (including both internal and external causes),[11] the available alternative corrective measures, and the possible effect of the restrictions on the economies of other signatories. Annual reviews of all existing balance-of-payments restrictions are to be held, involving consultations of similar scope. If consultations of either type reveal that the restrictions are not consistent with Articles 12 to 14 of the Agreement, the Contracting Parties are to advise the signatory concerned to make suitable modifications. If the deviation from the terms of the Agreement also involves damage or threat of damage to another signatory, the recommendations of the Contracting Parties for conformance to the terms of the Agreement are to specify a time limit. If the necessary changes are not made within the time given, the Contracting Parties may release the country whose interests are adversely affected from such of its obligations towards the offending signatory as they deem appropriate in the circumstances. The procedure of consultation, recommendation of conformance, and, if necessary, release of an injured party from certain of its obligations may be set in motion not only in connection with the initial notification of new restriction measures and the annual reviews, but at any time at the request of a signatory able to establish a *prima facie* case of violation and damage.

---

[11] *BISD,* Third Supplement, p. 173.

The quantitative restrictions introduced for balance-of-payments reasons are subject also to the general requirement that such restrictions be administered in a nondiscriminatory manner; that is, the application of the restrictions should distribute trade among other Contracting Parties in about the proportions that would have obtained in the absence of the restrictions (Article 13). However, Article 14 provides certain exceptions.[12] A country invoking Article 12 (or the similar balance-of-payments provisions for underdeveloped countries in Section B of Article 18 which will be described below) may deviate from the nondiscrimination rule by conforming its trade restrictions to the payments restrictions which it may be applying under Articles 8 and 14 of the Articles of Agreement of the International Monetary Fund. A member country applying import restrictions, either for balance-of-payments reasons or on grounds of its economic development program, may also depart temporarily from the nondiscrimination rule, with the consent of the Contracting Parties, with respect to a small part of its trade if the gains it thereby achieves "substantially outweigh" any injury to other members (Article 14, 2). Such a country may also direct its exports so as to increase its foreign currency earnings even if this involves a deviation from the nondiscrimination provisions (Article 14, 4).

---

[12] The provisions described in the text are those that took effect in February, 1961. (Cf. *Revised Provisions of Paragraph 1 of Article 14,* mimeo.) The earlier provisions permitted a country with difficult problems of postwar adjustment that had invoked Article 12 of GATT and Article 14 of the Articles of Agreement of the International Monetary Fund to deviate from the nondiscrimination principle by making its trade restrictions conform to its payment restrictions, by continuing restrictions in effect on March 1, 1948 even if discriminatory, or by relaxing restrictions in a discriminatory manner in order to increase total imports. (*BISD,* Vol. III, Art. 14, 1, b and c, and Annex J.) Such deviations were subject to review and consultation and, "in exceptional circumstances," to termination procedures by the Contracting Parties (*ibid.,* Article 14, 1, g and h).

In case of persistent and widespread application of the restrictions permitted under Article 12, which would indicate "the existence of a general disequilibrium which is restricting international trade," the Contracting Parties are to initiate discussions to consider the measures that might be taken either by the surplus or deficit countries or by an appropriate intergovernmental organization to remove the basic causes of the disequilibrium (Article 12, 5).

Escape clause for particular industries. The GATT provision for emergency action on imports of particular products, Article 19, is closely modelled on the escape clause included in United States trade agreements in the late forties by an executive order of the President and subsequently by act of Congress.[13] Under Article 19 a country may suspend an obligation or modify or withdraw a concession if : (1) there has been an increase in the quantity of imports; and (2) the increase is the result of (a) unforeseen developments and (b) GATT obligations; and (3) serious injury is caused or threatened to domestic producers of like or directly competitive products.[14] The protective action must be limited in extent and duration to that which is necessary to prevent or remedy the injury. While the invocation of the clause is unilateral, the invoking country must give written notice to the Contracting Parties and afford advance opportunity for consultation to the Contracting

---

[13] Congress first required the inclusion of such an escape clause when it extended the Trade Agreements Act of 1934 by means of the Trade Agreement Extension Act of 1951. Subsequent extensions of the law in the middle and late fifties altered the language of the American clause to make it easier for U.S. producers to obtain relief from the effects of U.S. trade-agreement concessions (see Chapter VII).

[14] Cf. U.S. Tariff Commission, *Procedure and Criteria with Respect to the Administration of the "Escape Clause" in Trade Agreements,* Washington, February, 1948 (processed), p. 5, and Contracting Parties to the GATT, *Report on the Withdrawal by the United States of a Tariff Concession under Article 19 of the General Agreement on Tariffs and Trade,* Geneva, November, 1951, p. 8.

Parties as an entity and to affected exporting members; in "critical circumstances, where delay would cause damage which it would be difficult to repair" consultation may be effected after action has been taken. Such consultations do not obligate the invoking country to alter its course of action. However, if agreement with other interested countries is not reached, the latter, after written notice and not later than 90 days after the invocation of Article 19, may suspend "substantially equivalent concessions or other obligations," subject to disapproval by the Contracting Parties.

The basis for this action by the affected members is different from that provided in the case of balance-of-payments restrictions; under Article 19, neither a violation of the Agreement by the country increasing its degree of protection nor injury suffered as a consequence by another member is a requisite condition for the suspension of obligations toward the protecting country by other affected members. The idea is that while any contracting party is free to act to protect its national interests by invoking Article 19, the other members are free to take action to restore the balance of benefits derived from GATT. The knowledge that such action may be taken is intended to serve as a restraining influence in the use of Article 19.[15]

Another safeguarding clause providing for emergency or short-run contingencies permits temporary export prohibitions or restrictions, despite the general obligation to avoid quantitative restrictions, in order to prevent or relieve critical shortages of foods or other essential products (Article 11, 2, a). A related clause leaves member countries free to take nondiscriminatory measures relating to the acquisition or distribution of products in general or local short supply (Article 20, j).

---

[15] *BISD,* Third Supplement, p. 180.

Structural or long-run problems

Among the clauses providing exceptions or escapes from the general commitments of the Agreement that are made necessary by structural or long-run factors are (1) those designed to reserve to the Contracting Parties freedom with respect to certain governmental functions that transcend questions of international trade such as public security and health, (2) those permitting preferential arrangements between certain groups of contracting parties, (3) those recognizing the conflict between free trade and domestic agricultural policies, and (4) those intended to give priority to the requirements of development programs over trade commitments.

Governmental functions. The security exceptions (Article 21) recognize that right of any signatory to take any action necessary to protect its "essential security interests" with respect to fissionable materials, traffic in arms, ammunition, and implements of war, and actions taken in time of war or other international emergency or in pursuance of its United Nations obligations for the maintenance of peace and security.

In addition, a series of general exceptions (Article 20, a to g) covers such matters as the protection of public morals and health, the export or import of gold or silver, products of prison labor, protection of national artistic or historical treasures, and conservation of exhaustible natural resources;[16] nothing in the Agreement is to be considered as preventing the adoption of measures relating to these matters, subject to the proviso that the measures not be applied so as to constitute "arbitrary or unjustifiable discrimination" between countries or a "disguised restriction" on trade.

A number of other clauses may be considered as providing

---

[16] Measures relating to natural resources must, however, be taken in conjunction with restrictions on domestic production or consumption.

exceptions in order to permit the contracting parties to fulfill their governmental functions; among these are the provisions which recognize the right of the member countries to pay subsidies exclusively to domestic producers (Article 3, 8, b), to levy upon imports charges equivalent to internal taxes on like products (Article 2, 2, a), to impose import and export restrictions necessary to regulate the classification, grading, or marketing of commodities in international trade (Article 11, 2, b), and to ignore with respect to governmental procurement the obligation to grant national treatment to the products of other contracting parties (Article 3, 8, a).

Preferential arrangements. The Agreement permits on the one hand the continuation of certain preferential arrangements existing at the time it was formulated, and allows on the other hand for the creation of new ones under certain conditions. Thus the general requirement to accord other signatories most-favored-nation treatment (Article 1) did not require the elimination of existing preferences among specified groups of countries and/or territories, including the British Commonwealth, the French Union, Benelux and territories of the Benelux countries, and the United States and its territories, Cuba, and the Philippines (Article 1, 2 and Annexes A to F). However, the margin of preference[17] may not exceed the maxima set forth in schedules attached to the Agreement; if not given in a schedule, the maximum margin is the differential existing on April 10, 1947 between the most favored nation and the preferential rates of duty (Article 1, 4).[18]

New preferential arrangements may be created under the

---

[17] Defined in absolute rather than relative terms. Cf. *BISD*, Vol. III, p. 65.

[18] The principle of taking the *status quo* as the maximum permitted deviation from the practices which the Agreement aims to establish may be seen also in the provisions governing mixing regulations (Article 3, 6) and screen quotas for movie films (Article 4, c).

terms of the Agreement in order to increase the freedom of trade through closer economic integration. Both customs unions and free-trade areas are regarded as serving this end. However, in order to forestall the possibility that new preferences not accompanied by genuine economic integration make a mockery of the most-favored-nation principle, it was necessary to define what was meant by a "free-trade area" and a "customs union." A free-trade area is defined as two or more customs territories in which duties and other restrictive measures are eliminated on "substantially all the trade between the constituent territories in products originating in such territories." Certain exceptions to the abolition of restrictions may, however, be permitted if necessary for reasons such as balance-of-payments difficulties or the carrying on of certain governmental functions that transcend questions of trade. A customs union must satisfy the same conditions, but in addition it involves the substitution of a single customs territory for two or more customs territories so that substantially the same duties and regulations are applied by each of the constituents to external trade (Article 24, 8).

By requiring that the removal in trade barriers within the free-trade area or customs union be nonselective, it was made more likely that the trade-creating effects would predominate over the trade-diverting effect.[19] Nevertheless, it was specified that the new units must serve the positive purpose of facilitating trade among the constituents and not the negative one of raising barriers to the trade of third countries with members of the new units. Thus, in the case of customs unions, the duties and other commercial regulations may not be "on the whole" higher or more restrictive than those of the constituent areas before the formation of the new grouping. If, in connection with a customs union, it is proposed to increase a rate of

---

[19] Cf. I. Frank, *The European Common Market,* New York, 1961, p. 137.

duty which has been reduced or bound under GATT, compensatory adjustments must be negotiated in terms of duties on other products,[20] due account being taken of the compensation afforded by reductions in the given duty made by other members of the proposed union (Article 24, 6).

Preferences enjoyed by a third party in trade with a country joining a customs union or free-trade area may not be extended so that the preferences are granted by all members of the new unit (Article 24, 9).

A contracting party that decides to enter into a customs union or free-trade area or into an interim agreement toward one of these ends must notify the Contracting Parties and make available the appropriate information necessary to enable them to make such reports and recommendations as they think proper. However, nothing is said at this point concerning the obligation of the participants in the proposed area or union to comply with such recommendations. Only in the event that the Contracting Parties find that an interim agreement is not likely to result in the formation of a customs union or free-trade area within a "reasonable" period, is it specified that the agreement may not be put into effect unless modified to conform to the recommendations of the Contracting Parties (Article 24, 7). On the other hand, as long as the arrangement will actually lead to the formation of a customs union or free-trade area within a reasonable period, the Contracting Parties have no option but to accept it.

The Contracting Parties may, by a two-thirds majority, approve proposals that do not fully meet the conditions stated above (e.g., on such points as the elimination of restrictions on "substantially all" trade, the treatment of third countries, and compensation for increased duties); provided that the proposals

---

[20] The provisions of Article 28 apply. See below, page 58f.

will lead to the formation of a customs union or free-trade area (Article 24, 10).

Agricultural policies. The ordinary obligations of the Agreement would expose a contracting party supporting domestic agricultural prices and/or incomes—and most or virtually all the signatories were, and are engaged in such programs in one form or another—to the danger that imports might undermine the domestic support program. Thus an exception is made to the prohibition of quantitative restrictions where import restrictions on agricultural or fisheries products are necessary to the maintenance of certain types of support programs (Article 11, 2, c). To be eligible for this exception, the governmental measures relating to a particular product which is either like an imported product or a direct substitute for it must operate to restrict marketing or output of this domestic product or to eliminate a temporary surplus of it through distribution to certain groups of domestic consumers free or at prices below the current market level. (Similar provisions apply to imported products of which the domestic production is negligible when the products are necessary for the production of an animal product which is the object of a program to restrict output). The decision to invoke this exception rests solely with the individual contracting party, but the latter must give public notice of the quantity or value of the quotas.[21] Moreover, the restrictions must not reduce imports relative to domestic production below the proportion "which might reasonably be expected . . . in the absence of restrictions." In applying this principle, the contracting party is to give due regard to the proportion during "a previous representative period and to any special factors which may have affected or may be affecting the trade in the product concerned."

---

[21] A GATT working party stated that this provision should be interpreted as requiring that a copy of the notice be sent to the Contracting Parties. *BISD,* Third Supplement, p. 190.

Not strictly limited to agricultural products or necessarily related to agricultural support programs are provisions concerning intergovernmental commodity agreements and exports of materials essential for a domestic processing industry. Nothing in the Agreement is to be construed as preventing the adoption or enforcement of measures taken to carry out the obligations of a commodity agreement which has been submitted to the Contracting Parties and not disapproved by them or which conforms to criteria which have been submitted to the Contracting Parties and not disapproved by them (Article 20, h). Nor is the Agreement to be interpreted as preventing a contracting party from restricting exports in order to assure a domestic processing industry of "essential quantities" of a material the domestic price of which is held below the world price as part of a governmental stabilization plan; however, such restrictions may not operate so as to increase the exports of or the protection afforded to the domestic industry and must conform to the rules relating to nondiscrimination (Article 20, i).

Economic development. The broad loopholes provided by Article 18 in favor of governmental assistance to economic development are justified on the ground that the attainment of the objectives of the Agreement[22] will be facilitated by economic development. Accordingly, three sets of temporary deviations are permitted for contracting parties with low standards of living and in early stages of development, which will be referred to here as "underdeveloped countries" although this term is not used in the Agreement. The exceptions relate to the

---

[22] These are stated in the Preamble to be the conduct of trade and economic relations so as to raise standards of living, ensure full employment and growth in real income, develop full use of world resources, and expand the production and exchange of goods. The Agreement is designed to contribute to these objectives by reciprocal and mutual arrangements to reduce trade barriers and eliminate discriminatory treatment.

application of quantitative restrictions for balance-of-payments purposes when difficulties arise because of high import demands generated by development programs (Section B), the modification or withdrawal of a concession in order to promote the establishment of a particular industry (Section A), and measures not permissible under other provisions of the Agreement, to promote the establishment of particular industries (Section C). In addition, a contracting party not characterized by a low standard of living and an early stage of development but which is "in the process of development" is also permitted to take exceptional measures to encourage the establishment of a particular industry (Section D).

The exceptions permitting quantitative restrictions for balance-of-payments reasons, set forth in section B of Article 18, closely parallel the terms of Article 12 which are available to all countries. The relatively minor differences reflect the fact that Article 18 is concerned with long-run problems while Article 12 deals with, hopefully, short-run problems. Thus the reference in Article 12 to an "imminent" balance of payments threat is deleted, and consultations are called for at two-year intervals instead of annually.[23] The most important substantive difference is the addition of a clause that permits an underdeveloped country to withdraw from the Agreement within 60 days instead of the usual six months (Article 31) if it finds that releases granted to other members as a result of its balance-of-payments restrictions adversely affect its development program (Article 18, 12, e).

The terms of the provisions relating to the modification of concessions also have their analogue in other clauses of the Agreement open to all contracting parties,[24] but once again

---

[23] Cf. *BISD*, Third Supplement, pp. 183–184.
[24] Art. 28, discussed below.

they provide for easier exceptions than are generally available to other members. An underdeveloped country may at any time enter into negotiations for the modification of a concession in order to promote the establishment of an industry. It must negotiate both with the original recipient of the concession and with other substantially interested countries. If agreement, which presumably would be concerned primarily with compensatory adjustments, is not reached within 60 days the underdeveloped country may refer the matter to the Contracting Parties. If the Contracting Parties find that the underdeveloped country "has made every effort to reach an agreement and that the compensatory adjustment offered by it is adequate" the latter is free to make its modifications if it puts its compensatory measures into effect at the same time. If the Contracting Parties do not find that the compensation offered is adequate but find that the underdeveloped country has "made every reasonable effort to offer adequate compensation," the underdeveloped country is still free to proceed with the modification but the other interested countries are in this case at liberty to modify or withdraw "substantially equivalent concessions" initially negotiated with the underdeveloped country involved.

It is expected that the provisions of Sections A and B will "normally be sufficient to enable contracting parties to meet the requirements of their economic development." However, there may be circumstances, Article 18 states, in which these provisions will not permit an underdeveloped country to grant the "assistance required" to promote the establishment of particular industries. In such cases, Section C provides, the underdeveloped country is to notify the Contracting Parties of its difficulties and of the specific measure affecting imports which it proposes to take. Presumably, the latter will involve the impairment of a tariff concession or other obligation, perhaps through quantitative restrictions, since modifications and withdrawals are covered by the provisions of Section A. The measure is not to violate the rules governing nondiscrimination, and it must conform to certain other rules laid down in connection with balance of payments derogations such as those relating to the maintenance of trade channels, samples, copyrights, etc.

If the Contracting Parties do not request consultation within 30 days the underdeveloped country may put the measure into effect, and even if consultation has been requested the underdeveloped country may apply the measure after 90 days whether the Contracting Parties have given their concurrence or not. (If the industry involved has already started production, the underdeveloped country may act to prevent imports from rising "substantially above a normal level" even before these time limits have expired).

If the proposed measure affects a product that is the subject of a concession, the underdeveloped country is required to negotiate with the affected countries. The Contracting Parties are to give their concurrence to the measure if they are satisfied that no alternative action consistent with the Agreement is practicable to achieve the developmental purpose sought by the underdeveloped country, and if agreement has been reached in the consultations. In the absence of agreement they may nevertheless concur if they think that the underdeveloped country has made "all reasonable efforts" to reach agreement and that "the interests of other contracting parties are adequately safeguarded" (possibly through compensatory concessions given by the underdeveloped country or through the withdrawal of concessions by the affected country or countries).

If the underdeveloped country takes advantage of its right to adopt the proposed measure without the concurrence of the Contracting Parties, the balance of benefits principle comes into play; that is, any member substantially affected by the action may withdraw equivalent concessions from the under-developed country.

A contracting party which is not underdeveloped (that is, which is not characterized by a low standard of living and early stage of development) but which is "in the process of development" is also permitted, under Section D of Article 18, to apply special measures not consistent with other provisions of the Agreement in order to promote the establishment of a particular industry. The provisions of Section D are generally similar to those of Section C except that the concurrence of the Contracting Parties is required before the special measures may be introduced. However, the scope of the measures possible under Section D may be broader; since Sections A and B do not apply to developing countries, the latter would have to use Section D if they wished to apply a measure that an underdeveloped country is permitted to adopt under Section A or B (for example, a modification of a concession in order to promote the establishment of a particular industry).

Waivers

Sweeping powers to waive "in exceptional circumstances not elsewhere provided" in the Agreement any obligation undertaken by members are conferred upon the Contracting Parties by Article 25, 5. Such decisions must, however, be taken by a two-thirds majority of the votes cast and the majority must comprise more than half of the Contracting Parties. The Contracting Parties may also, by the same voting arrangements, establish "categories of exceptional circumstances" to which other voting requirements for the granting of waivers may apply.

Freedom to alter commitments

Certain provisions give contracting parties some freedom to modify, limit, or withdraw some or all of their undertakings under the Agreement.

Thus, a regular procedure is provided by Article 28 for the modification of concessions through negotiation and agreement. Such modifications have been generally permitted at three-year intervals; in the present version of Article 28 such intervals date from January 1, 1958.[25] This periodicity represents a compromise between the indefinite validity of concessions and freedom to alter them at any time. The former would have permitted renegotiation of concessions only by special exception granted by the Contracting Parties and was considered too rigid; the latter would deprive members of any assurance with respect to the continuance of concessions and would be too chaotic. During each three-year "open season" the negotiations for modifications are to be carried on with the country to which the concession was originally granted and with other principal suppliers. In the negotiations, which may lead to compensatory adjustments relating to other products, the parties involved are to try to maintain "a general level of reciprocal and mutually advantageous concessions not less favorable to trade" than the former arrangements. If agreement cannot be reached, the country initiating the negotiations is free to modify the concession, but the other affected parties

---

[25] Substantially the same pattern of three-year freezes of concessions was achieved under earlier versions of the Agreement, sometimes as in the original draft by direct provision but mainly through declarations of the Contracting Parties to the effect that they would not seek to modify or to cease to apply the concessions annexed to the Agreement until a specified date, usually three years into the future. The declarations were binding only for the nations that agreed to accept them, but the obligation to avoid reopening a concession did not apply for concessions granted to GATT members that had not themselves accepted the same obligation. See, for example, *BISD,* Vol. II, pp. 30–31.

are, in accordance with the balance-of-benefits principle, at liberty to withdraw substantially equivalent concessions originally negotiated with the initiating country. Such compensatory withdrawals must be made within six months of the original modification, and they require written notice to the Contracting Parties.

In addition the Contracting Parties may, by a two-thirds vote, set periods for the modification of schedules other than the three-year intervals mentioned above. They may also, "in special circumstances" authorize a contracting party to enter into negotiations for the modification of a concession at a time other than that provided for the other members (Article 28, 4). In these special negotiations, the Contracting Parties may play a somewhat larger role in bringing about a settlement; if the negotiating parties do not reach agreement, the Contracting Parties are to submit their views in order to assist in a solution. Also, the initiating party is not free to modify the concession if the Contracting Parties conclude that it has "unreasonably failed to offer adequate compensation."

Finally, Article 28 provides that a contracting party may, at the beginning of one of the three-year intervals dating from January 1, 1958, reserve the right for the duration of the next period to modify any or all of its concessions according to the same procedures that are available at the beginning of the period (Article 28, 5).

The individual signatories also have some limited freedom with respect to the country coverage of the obligations assumed under the Agreement. Thus, under Article 35 a contracting party has the option of not applying Article 2, which gives effect to the schedules of tariff concessions attached to the Agreement, or the Agreement as a whole with respect to any contracting party with which it has not entered into tariff negotiations. A member may also withdraw any concession initially negotiated with a country which has not become or ceased to be a contracting party (Article 27). Finally, a contracting party may withdraw from the Agreement upon six months notice (Article 31).

Defensive measures

A number of safeguards relating to the effects of the actions of other contracting parties may be found in the Agreement. In a sense the releases and opportunities for compensatory withdrawals of concessions afforded to members bearing the effects of the escape actions described in the preceding pages fall in this category. Further provisions of this defensive character are scattered throughout the Agreement. Mention may be made of the provision for antidumping duties and countervailing levies with respect to subsidies (Article 6) and of special duties or penalties for deceptive marks of origin (Article 9, 5). There are, however, also some major provisions designed to assure equitable treatment of each member at the hands of the others.

Basic reliance is placed in this connection upon consultation between the contracting parties. "Each contracting party shall accord sympathetic consideration to, and shall afford adequate opportunity for consultation regarding, such representations as may be made by another contracting party with respect to any matter affecting the operation of this Agreement" (Article 22). If a member does not obtain satisfaction through such consultations, it may request the Contracting Parties to take the matter up with the other members involved. In addition to this general provision, consultation is specified at a number of points in the Agreement; besides those already mentioned, Article 2, 5, for example, provides for consultation and negotiation where a member feels that product is not receiving the benefits expected when a concession was received for the product from another member. Again, a signatory granting a subsidy is obliged to discuss with another member whose interests are seriously prejudiced or threatened by the subsidy the possibility of limiting the subsidization (Article 16, 1).

Perhaps the most general provision of a defensive character is Article 23, dealing with nullification or impairment. If a signatory considers that any benefit accruing to it under the Agreement is being nullified or impaired or that the attainment of an objective of the Agreement is being impeded by (1) the failure of another member to carry out its obligations, (2) the application of any measure by another member, whether in conflict with the Agreement or not, or (3) any other situation, it may make written representations or proposals to the party or parties involved. If no satisfactory adjustment is achieved by this means, the Contracting Parties are to investigate and to make a recommendation or to give a ruling on the matter, even going so far as to authorize the complaining party to suspend concessions or obligations with respect to the other members involved. In the latter event, however, the country against which action has been taken is free to withdraw from the Agreement upon 60 days notice.

Article 23 is a safeguard clause of an extensive character. It goes beyond guarding a signatory against injury and provides protection against the failure to derive the anticipated benefits from the Agreement. This protection is not limited to situations in which the lack of benefit can be attributed to some action of another signatory, whether in violation of the Agreement or not; it applies under circumstances that are very broadly defined. Here again, the underlying notion is that the balance of benefits must be maintained.

Balance-of-payment derogations

During the first dozen years of the existence of GATT, about two-thirds of its members maintained quantitative restrictions on imports for balance-of-payments reasons under Article 12,[26] and all but two or three of these took advantage of the provisions of Article 14 to apply their restrictions in a discriminatory fashion, usually to the detriment of dollar goods. Since the list of countries invoking Articles 12 and 14 included virtually all of the major trading countries of western Europe, these derogations had the effect of nullifying to a considerable extent the benefits that the United States and other dollar-area countries might have derived from the Agreement. This fact was widely noted in the United States and appears to have been an element in the opposition, or at least in the lack of more vigorous support, first for the Havana Charter and later for the proposed Organization of Trade Cooperation, and, indeed, for GATT itself. The American attitude seems not to have been without some basis in European thinking; for example, the Executive Secretary of GATT recently surmised that at the time the GATT clauses were written some European countries ".. were actuated by a certain cynicism as to the probability of the quantitative restriction ban becoming effective if only because of the prevailing belief that balance-of-payments difficulties would continue indefinitely . . . ."[27]

---

[26] Article 12 originally governed balance-of-payments derogations of all countries, but when the revision of Article 18 came into effect in October, 1957, the balance-of-payments derogations of underdeveloped countries were covered by Section B of the revised article. At that time, the required consultations for derogating underdeveloped countries were placed on a two-year rather than on an annual basis.

[27] E. Wyndham White, *Europe in the GATT,* GATT, Geneva, 1960.

Despite the reservations induced by such considerations, the United States maintained a relatively liberal import policy while accepting the discriminatory restrictions of the western European countries. This, together with other policies of the United States, notably foreign aid, helped European reconstruction and the restoration of monetary reserves to a level which made possible the reestablishment of a multilateral system of trade and payments.

The role of GATT in these events is not easy to assess. The existence of GATT and its promise of future benefits to American trade once European currencies were restored may have made it more feasible for the successive American administrations to maintain the policies referred to despite the scepticism about GATT. It is difficult, however, to avoid the impression that the cold war had more to do with the maintenance of such policies than the prospective benefits that might flow from GATT.

Perhaps more credit can be assigned to GATT for the dismantlement of the balance-of-payments restrictions by the European and other countries. Certainly, the balance-of-payments deviations from the obligations of the Agreement were kept under constant review in accordance with the provisions of the Agreement. The annual reports on balance-of-payments restrictions, while eschewing criticism of individual countries, often stressed the need to minimize the protective effects of import restrictions and to avoid falling into permanent reliance upon restrictions as a solution to balance-of-payments difficulties.[28] At the same time, they attempted to set forth the positive case for the liberalization of trade in terms of the situation of the moment.

The consultations and the discussions leading to the formulation of the annual reports provided an opportunity for

---

[28] See, for example, *BISD*, Fourth Supplement, p. 53.

the representatives of signatories not applying balance-of-payments derogations, particularly the United States and Canada, to press for full compliance with the Agreement. When around 1952 or 1953 the dollar and gold holdings of nondollar countries began to improve, these pressures became more difficult to resist.

At any rate the process of reducing import restrictions, aside from the intra-European program of trade liberalization within the framework of the OEEC, made a slow beginning at this point.[29] Not all countries shared in the increases in reserves, and those that did tended to relax restrictions on products that would lower domestic costs of production, such as industrial raw materials, rather than on an across-the-board basis.[30] Dollar liberalization in particular tended to be restricted to raw materials and other essential commodities; manufactured products were less favored, and agricultural products still less.[31] The movement toward the elimination of restrictions quickened after the reestablishment of convertibility for most of the important trading currencies at the end of 1958. However, two years later no fewer than 17 contracting parties still maintained import restrictions on balance-of-payments grounds, with 11 of them exercising some degree of discrimination among various sources of supply.[32] The November, 1960, report of the Contracting Parties on the discriminatory application of import restrictions questioned the justification of some of these derogations and urged all the signatories applying them to eliminate them quickly.[33] It should be added that most of the 17 countries that still

[29] *BISD*, Second Supplement, p. 40. See also GATT, *Review of Import Restrictions under Articles 12: 4 (b) and 18 (b)*, Geneva, 1949.

[30] *BISD*, Fourth Supplement, p. 50.

[31] *BISD*, Fifth Supplement, p. 63.

[32] *BISD*, Ninth Supplement, p. 63.

[33] *BISD*, Ninth Supplement, p. 66.

maintained import restrictions at the end of 1960 were under-developed countries; Austria, Denmark, Finland, Turkey, and Greece were the only European countries in the list.

Emergency action for particular products

Article 19, the "American escape clause", was invoked by the United States in 13 cases up to June, 1961, representing a more extensive use of the provision than that of all the other signatories combined. Germany invoked the clause in favor of hard coal and Australia in favor of printed cotton textiles and casual footwear; Greece (apples and electric refrigerators), Canada (strawberries), and Austria (porcelain) were the other countries that took escape action.[34]

However, the 13 cases in which the clause was actually used by the United States represented only a small fraction of the 125 that were investigated for possible escape action by the U.S. Tariff Commission, and only about one-third of the instances in which the Commission recommended to the President that the escape clause be invoked. For both the investigated cases as a whole and the 13 in which the President actually invoked the escape clause, the list of products was dominated by commodities which accounted for small money values of imports. Among the products for which the escape clause was actually invoked, the value of imports was largest for lead and zinc ($306 million in 1957), watches ($71 million in 1953), and bicycles ($21 million in 1954). The other commodities for which escape action was taken, including the widely publicized case relating to women's fur felt hats and hat bodies generally involved imports amounting only to one or two million dollars per annum.

---

[34] *GATT, Analytical Index of the General Agreement (Revised)* (Geneva, 1959), pp. 88–89.

The hat case is of particular interest because it gave rise to a report of an *ad hoc* working party [35] which affords an insight into the application of Article 19 in actual practice. The working party was appointed to report on the case because Czechoslovakia, one of the principal suppliers, disputed the right of the United States to invoke Article 19.

There was little disagreement that American imports of women's fur felt hats and hat bodies had increased substantially in 1949 and the first half of 1950 over both the immediately preceding years and the prewar period. It was agreed also that the increase in imports was related to a change in fashion in favor of hats with special finishes such as velours, and that most of the imports consisted of these newly favored styles. The dispute centered on the other conditions requisite for the application of Article 19: specifically, whether, as the U.S. claimed and Czechoslovakia denied, the increase in imports resulted from unforeseen developments and were causing serious injury to the American producers.

With respect to the first issue, Czechoslovakia argued that the change in fashion which led to the increase in imports, despite duties which even after the concession amounted to 50 per cent ad valorem, could and should have been foreseen in advance. The U.S. negotiators should have known at the time of the Geneva negotiations in 1947 that velours were then fashionable in Paris and should have drawn the inference that this style change from plain hat bodies would spread to other countries. Furthermore, the change in fashion in the American market could not only have been foreseen in this manner, but it was even deliberately planned in advance; Czech and Italian exporters with the aid of selling organiza-

---

[35] *Report on the Withdrawal by the United States of a Tariff Concession under Article XIX of the General Agreement on Tariffs and Trade,* Geneva, 1951.

tions in the United States and of American milliners created the demand for the new designs. The working party concluded, however, that "the United States negotiators in 1947 could not reasonably be expected to foresee that this style change in favor of velours would in fact subsequently take place, and would do so on as large a scale for so long a period as in fact it did." The style change was unfavorable to American producers because the special finishes required more labor than the production of plain-finished hat bodies, and the high level of American wages was not matched by correspondingly high output.

The American claim of serious injury rested on output and employment figures. No data were available regarding financial results of the industry. The production of women's hat bodies represented about 25 to 30 per cent of the industry's total output, with the remainder accounted for by men's hat bodies. Domestic production of women's hat bodies in the late forties was only a little more than half of the prewar level. (Domestic consumption had declined to about the same extent.) Production in 1949 and in the first half of 1950, when imports were increasing, declined below the 1948 levels by 10 and 18 per cent, respectively. Employment in the production of women's hat bodies could not be estimated separately; in the industry as a whole, there had been declines below the 1945 level of 1 per cent in 1948 and 15 per cent in 1949. It was difficult to ascertain to what extent the decline was due to the downward trend on the men's side of the business, but the Tariff Commission concluded that a "considerable part" was attributable to increased imports of women's hat bodies. A large majority of the employees were skilled workers with dependent families and were concentrated in two New England cities, and declining employment would create difficult social problems.

Drawing upon the arguments of the Czechoslovak representative, but not repeating them all or confining ourselves to them, the weaknesses in the United States case may be summarized as follows:

1. No evidence was submitted to show that financial losses had been suffered by the domestic hat firms. If they had been injured to the extent of encountering losses, nothing was said about it.

2. No clear link between increased imports and serious injury to workers was established. Even if the connection between imports of women's hat bodies and employment in a hat industry in which 70 to 75 per cent of production represented men's hat bodies had been more rigorously demonstrated, that in itself would have shown only "displacement," and not "serious injury" of workers. Of course, it could be argued that the involuntary displacement of workers from an industry, especially if on a large scale, constitutes serious injury, but it seems reasonable to inquire into the new circumstances in which the workers find themselves before deciding whether they have been seriously injured or not. There was little evidence on this point in the hat case. The most relevant fact seems to have been that total unemployment had increased in the two cities where hatmaking was predominant. However, there seemed to be little correlation between the movement of total unemployment and changes in employment in hatmaking in the two cities.

3. There was a significant improvement in the position of the American industry in the latter half of 1950, with the result that production for the year as a whole was no lower and even higher than that of the preceding years. While the post-Korea boom affected the entire economy at this time, there is also some evidence that the domestic firms had begun to adapt themselves to the new styles.

The working party held that the data on the last half of 1950 were irrelevant since they had become available after the investigation of the Tariff Commission and the working party was called upon to determine whether serious injury or a threat thereof "could be considered to have existed" at the time of the investigation. However, these figures led the working party to suggest that the difficulties in the industry were temporary and that producers might be able to dispense with the additional protection in the near future. The position should be kept under review, especially since, in any case, Article 19 provides for action that is essentially of an emergency character which should be of limited duration. No time limit had been set in the American action, mainly on the ground that renewals would have required the repetition of the entire procedure set forth in the American regulations. It was also mentioned that compensatory adjustments were contemplated for two affected parties, and that the future restoration of the concession would call into question the continuation of these adjustments. The working party nevertheless took the position that the concession should be restored as soon as possible. In the actual event, the United States subsequently used the renegotiation procedures of Article 28 to withdraw the items from its schedule of concessions.

With respect to the validity of the American invocation of the clause, the working party based its findings mainly upon the displacement by imports of domestic production and upon the admittedly inconclusive statistics on employment and unemployment. The working party summed up its position by stating that while the available data supported the view that increased imports had caused or threatened some adverse effects upon domestic producers, it was not clear whether or not the degree of the untoward effects could be described as "serious injury." Such a decision is "essentially a matter of economic and social judgment involving a considerable subjective element," and the U.S. authorities had better facilities for obtaining the necessary bases for forming such a judgment. "Further, it is perhaps inevitable that governments should on occasion lend greater weight to the difficulties or fears of the domestic producers than would any international body, and that they may feel it necessary on social grounds . . . to afford a high degree of protection to individual industries which in terms of cost of production are not economic." However, the U.S. did not have to prove the existence of serious injury conclusively; since the issue was whether the U.S. had violated Article 19, it was entitled to the benefit of any reasonable doubt.

In short, the working party accepted the primacy of the judgment of the country invoking the escape clause rather than attempting to make a fully independent assessment of the applicability of its provisions to the case at hand. The result seemed to underline the unilateral character of the escape provision in Article 19, and thus the outcome of this early case may have something to do with the fact that none of the subsequent invocations of Article 19 was challenged.

Preferential arrangements

The important new developments in connection with preferential arrangements included the establishment of the European Coal and Steel Community, the European Economic Community, the European Free Trade Area, and the Latin American Free Trade Area. The first of these clearly failed to meet the criterion of covering substantially all trade, required by Article 24 of the Agreement for new discriminatory arrangements in the form of free-trade areas or customs unions. It thus could not be considered as an arrangement anticipated by the Agreement, but had to be treated by waiver as an exception *sui generis* to the most-favored-nation provisions of Article 1. The others were regarded, not without some reservations, as falling under the terms of Article 24.

The formation of the European Economic Community (EEC) raised understandable fears on the part of a number of the trading partners of the six members of the EEC (the Six), which were exacerbated by the history of the unsuccessful efforts to establish trading arrangements that would encompass a wider circle of European nations. It is therefore not surprising that the Treaty of Rome (signed in March, 1957) was submitted to a close and rather critical evaluation when the Contracting Parties reviewed it in accordance with their prerogatives under Article 24. To some extent the critical stand taken by certain GATT signatories may have served tactical purposes since a number of significant details of the common external tariff had not yet been settled and, perhaps more important, since the Treaty left a considerable range within which the new arrangements could in fact operate in a liberal or protective fashion.

Even after allowance is made for such factors, however, there remains a hard residue of doubt about certain aspects of the new Treaty and the new Community from the standpoint of the Agreement and individual contracting parties. Some features of the Treaty are difficult to reconcile with the Agreement and there is an apprehension that the Treaty opens the door to a policy of the exchange among the Six of mutual benefits at the expense of third countries. Substantively the most serious issues relate to agriculture and to the treatment of underdeveloped countries and territories.[36]

The consistency of the Rome Treaty with the provisions of

---

[36] For a summary of the arguments pro and con see *BISD*, Sixth Supplement, pp. 68–109.

the Agreement is, perhaps, most vulnerable to challenge with respect to its provisions for the association with the Common Market of the overseas territories and former territories of the six member countries. Briefly, the Treaty provides duty-free access to the Common Market for the products of the territories, although it permits the territories to levy duties either for development or fiscal reasons on products coming from the Six (subject only to the requirement that equal treatment must be extended to all members of the EEC). Areas that formerly enjoyed a preferred position only in the market of the mother country (to use a convenient if outdated term) were thus given a privileged position in the markets of the other member countries as well. This extension of preferences appeared to be inconsistent with the provisions of Article 24, 9, and was clearly detrimental to the interests of other underdeveloped countries and territories, many of which had been able to develop and hold important markets which now, in becoming part of the Common Market, were being transformed into privileged areas for competitors. Furthermore, this diversion of trade would be accompanied by a concentration of investment in the former colonial areas, thus making it more difficult for other underdeveloped areas to attract capital.

In discussions with the Contracting Parties, the EEC defended the association of the overseas areas on the ground that the arrangements constituted a free-trade area, although they had not been so described in the Rome Treaty. The view was not accepted by most of the representatives of the countries on the GATT working party that studied the question.[37] They were of the opinion that the barriers which the overseas areas were permitted to put on goods coming from the Common Market placed the association outside the definition of a free-trade

---

[37] *Ibid*, 91–96.

area as defined by Article 24. The reply of the EEC was that
the fiscal duties which the territories were permitted to levy
should not be considered since they were nondiscriminatory
and compensated by internal duties, and the protective duties
would cover only 1.4 per cent of the trade between the European and overseas territories. In response to the claim of the
others that the protective duties could be expected to increase
as industrial development accelerated in the overseas territories,
the EEC argued that even if the proportion of protected trade
rose as high as 20 per cent, 80 per cent liberalization would
meet the criterion of Article 24 that "substantially all" trade be
free and even if, as was not anticipated, a still higher proportion
of trade was protected, the European Economic Community
could apply to GATT for a waiver. The others, dissatisfied
with the method of computing the percentage and particularly
at the omission of trade restricted by quotas, remained of the
view that the requirements of Article 24 had not been satisfied
and that the association constituted an extension of existing
preferential systems contrary to Article 1, 2 of the Agreement.[38] However, in the pragmatic method that is typical of
the working of GATT, it was agreed to concentrate future
consideration on the practical effects of the association on the
trade of third countries in such products as cocoa, coffee,
bananas, oilseeds and vegetable oils, wood and timber,
tobacco, hard fibers, cotton, sugar, and tea.

With respect to agriculture, the representatives of the
countries other than the members of the EEC recognized the
large area of discretion which the Rome Treaty left open for
the implementation of its agricultural provisions. However,
the majority were of the opinion that the measures set forth

---

[38] Another argument which commanded less support was that the
Agreement did not permit the same countries to participate both in a
customs union and in a free-trade area simultaneously, but either in one
or the other. *Ibid.,* p. 90–91, 104–107.

in the Treaty, including minimum prices, long-term contracts, countervailing charges, and a common organization committed to a guarantee of the standard of living of producers, "carried a strong presumption of increased external barriers and a substitution of new internal barriers in place of existing tariffs and other measures." [39] If these fears were justified, the new organization would not fulfill the purpose for which the Agreement recognized the validity of customs unions, namely to facilitate trade among its constituent units and not to raise barriers to trade with third countries (Article 24, 4).

Other issues raised in the discussions related to the nature of the obligations imposed upon the EEC members by Article 24, 6 to provide other GATT members with compensatory adjustments for any duties increased in the course of forming the customs union and to the consistency of the Rome Treaty provisions for common quantitative restrictions with GATT obligations to avoid quantitative restrictions except in circumscribed conditions. In connection with the latter point, particular concern was expressed at the possibility that a member of the Six would impose balance-of-payments restrictions not justified by its own balance-of-payments position. [40]

The Contracting Parties concluded, at the end of 1958, that it was premature to complete the examination of the Rome Treaty and that both the examination and the legal questions involved should be postponed without prejudice to the rights of the Contracting Parties under Article 24. Beyond this the main result was an agreement to utilize consultation procedures under Article 22, particularly with respect to the "specific and practical problems" arising in the trade relations of third countries with the EEC. [41]

---

[39] *Ibid.,* p. 88.

[40] For a discussion of this problem, see I. Frank, *op. cit.,* pp. 246–249.

[41] *BISD,* Seventh Supplement, pp. 69–71.

Once again the Contracting Parties as an entity seems to have avoided a direct challenge to the unilateral interpretation of the Agreement by major powers. However, the alternative course would have been quite drastic. The political and psychological commitment of the members of the EEC was so extensive and a reopening of the terms of the Treaty so cumbersome and dangerous to the whole enterprise, that the most practical avenue for the Contracting Parties was to press for appropriate policies under the Treaty rather than for changes in it. Perhaps they went as far as was possible for the moment along these lines. Article 24 itself does not provide them with a great deal of support other than ensuring their right to information. The Contracting Parties could make recommendations to the EEC to bring this or that policy in line with the requirement of the Agreement, but, except to the extent that the transitional arrangements of Treaty justified its treatment as an interim agreement, nothing in Article 24 requires the EEC to heed such recommendations. Individual members of GATT could presumably find recourse to the provisions of Article 23 dealing with nullification and impairment facilitated in such circumstances, but if GATT was to survive such actions could not be encouraged.

Some of the issues that gave rise to disagreements in GATT discussions of the Rome Treaty arose also in the deliberations of the working party appointed to examine the Stockholm Convention (signed November, 1959) establishing the European Free Trade Association (EFTA or the Seven).[42] There was concern, for example, about the possibility that the preferences enjoyed in the British and Portuguese markets by areas associated with these countries might be extended to other members of the EFTA. Unlike the EEC arrangements, the Stockholm Convention did not provide for such an exten-

---

[42] *BISD*, Ninth Supplement, pp. 70–87.

sion directly, but some countries felt that the same result might follow indirectly. The abolition of drawbacks on trade between members of the EFTA, for example, might encourage a firm in Britain producing for export to another member country to use materials from sources enjoying preferential treatment, whereas before the formation of EFTA the existence of the drawback would put nonpreferential sources of materials on an equal footing in this respect.

With respect to quantitative restrictions also there were differences of opinion between the members of the new unit and the other contracting parties, but they do not appear to have been as sharp as those that arose in the examination of the EEC. Unlike the EEC members, the EFTA countries accepted the principle that quantitative restrictions imposed for balance-of-payments reasons would have to be justified in terms of the balance-of-payments position of the individual country rather than in terms of its membership in a group of countries, one or more of which had balance-of-payments difficulties. However, the EFTA members argued that they were entitled to remove these restrictions as well as others (such as those on the exports of products in short supply under Article 11) among themselves without eliminating them against third countries. They also felt that a member of a free-trade area could, if it were justified in invoking quantitative restrictions for balance-of-payments reasons, apply them only to third countries and not to other members. Other countries were of the opinion that Article 24 contained nothing that relieved members of a free-trade area from the obligation to apply quantitative restriction in a nondiscriminatory manner.

However, it was the agricultural provisions of the Stockholm Convention that raised the most serious doubts about its consistency with the Agreement. Agriculture was excluded from the general obligation placed by the Convention on the

EFTA members to eliminate barriers to trade. Owing to this exclusion, the other GATT signatories contended, it could not be maintained that duties and other restrictive regulations were being eliminated on "substantially all trade"; consequently, the EFTA could not qualify as a free-trade area under Article 24. The seven EFTA members considered that the bilateral agricultural agreements between members provided for in the Convention facilitated the expansion of trade in agricultural products. They argued that the trade conducted under these agreements should be included, to the extent that it represented trade freed of barriers, in determining whether duties and other restrictions had been eliminated on "substantially all trade." The reply was that the agreements that had been concluded to date had provided for the removal of tariffs only in the case of a small number of products. Furthermore, the removal was only to be effected by one member, an arrangement that did not conform to Article 24. This and other provisions of some of the agreements, particularly non-tariff provisions that seemed intended to increase the share of one of the members in the market of another, were regarded as violations of the most-favored-nation principle of GATT. Particularly when account was taken of the inclusion in EFTA of countries that were not signatories of GATT, some thought that the Stockholm Convention could be considered under Article 24 only by invoking the provisions of Paragraph 10 relating to free-trade areas or customs unions that do not fully comply with the other clauses of Article 24. Others took the view that the provisions of Article 24 were not applicable and that the EFTA countries should seek a waiver.

Since the EEC had not been challenged—beyond verbal brickbats in committee—for arrangements that on the whole may well have represented a greater departure from the terms of the Agreement than EFTA was proposing, it was not to be expected that the Contracting Parties would take any formal action that would call the provisions of the Stockholm Convention into question. Despite the candid criticisms expressed in the working party, the Contracting Parties in effect accepted the Stockholm Convention by adopting conclusions that paralleled those taken in connection with the Rome Treaty. The Contracting Parties stated their decision not to avail themselves of their prerogative to make recommendations to the EFTA countries, but, in view of the unresolved legal and practical issues, reserved their rights under Article 24.[43]

The provisions of Article 24 were called upon also in connection with the proposed establishment of a Central American free-trade area and with the plans for a Latin American free-trade area laid down in the Montevideo Treaty. Neither of these proposals was as fully developed as the EEC or EFTA scheme. In connection with the first, the Contracting Parties recognized the right of Nicaragua to claim the benefits of Article 24, subject to review after five years.[44] This action was taken under Paragraph 10 of Article 24, indicating that the Contracting Parties did not consider that the proposed free-trade area met the conditions required by the Agreement. Apparently the difficulty arose from the fact that the Central American treaty proposed to apply free-trade-area treatment not to all goods but only to a specified list. The Montevideo Treaty (signed in February, 1960), which was also a list type of arrangement, was the subject of a declaration similar to those relating to the Rome Treaty and the Stockholm Convention.[45]

---

[43] *BISD*, Ninth Supplement, pp. 20–21

[44] *BISD*, Fifth Supplement, pp. 29–30. Article 24 had been invoked earlier by Nicaragua in connection with a free-trade area to be established with El Salvador (treaty signed in March, 1961). *BISD*, Vol. II, p. 30.

[45] *BISD*, Ninth Supplement, pp. 21–22, 87–94.

Economic development

Aside from the restrictions imposed by underdeveloped countries for balance-of-payments reasons, the most extensive use of Article 18 was made by Ceylon.[46] The Government of Ceylon sought to promote the sale of certain locally produced industrial products by requiring importers to purchase a specified quantity of the domestic product as a condition for obtaining a license to import a given amount of the like foreign good. The "standard ratio," which determined the proportion between the local and imported products that the importer was required to maintain in his purchases, was fixed from time to time in the light of the relationship between domestic production and domestic consumption. No restriction was placed on the quantity imported as long as an importer fulfilled the obligation to purchase the prescribed proportion of the corresponding local product. Nevertheless, the scheme was considered to conflict with the provisions of Article 11 of the Agreement which prohibited quantitative restrictions, and Ceylon was held to require releases from its obligations under that article to the extent that they could be justified by the provisions of Article 18 dealing with exceptions for development reasons.[47]

In the dozen years of the existence of the GATT, Ceylon sought and obtained such releases for products falling under about 40 different tariff classifications. Many but not all of the

---

[46] Under the older version of Article 18, which was in effect until October, 1957, any contracting party, regardless of its stage of development, was given the opportunity to obtain relief from certain of its obligations in the interests of its economic development or reconstruction. A few European countries, including Norway, Denmark, Greece, and Italy, made notifications under these provisions. For the most part, however, it was concluded that the derogations involved were covered by Article 12 relating to balance-of-payment difficulties. (For an early report on the use of Article 18, see *Report of Working Party on Article 18,* September 9, 1948, GATT Document CP. 2/38.)

[47] *BISD,* Vol. II, p. 67.

items could be produced out of locally available materials and almost all could be placed under the heading of light industry.[48] When the items were the subject of a concession under the Agreement, Ceylon had to negotiate with the countries chiefly affected by the increase in protection.

Ceylon claimed that the releases were sought only as a last resort when other measures of sales promotion of local products had proved inadequate. The need for import controls arose, it was alleged, because of consumer prejudice against local products; this attitude could be overcome if the domestic industry could be assured of a part of the market for a brief period of years. Such assurance was particularly necessary, in addition to tax exemptions and governmental capital contributions, to induce private investment in the industries which the government had designated for development by private capital. The other conceivable measures, such as tariff protection, tariff quotas, or subsidies, would either prove too uncertain in providing the new firms a foothold in the domestic market or would create difficult administrative problems for Ceylon. Sometimes it was claimed that the domestic product was or soon would be equal in quality to the imported good, and, occasionally, that it would be no higher in price.

The early releases stipulated a maximum quantity of domestic output that could be used in calculating the standard ratio. Usually, the maxima were established at the rather ambitious production targets set by Ceylon, and therefore did not constitute an effective limitation on the degree of restriction actually introduced by Ceylon. In the middle fifties, when the output of Ceylon with respect to certain of the items involved seemed capable of approaching the level of total consumption,

---

[48] The products included plywood panels, leather goods, cotton textiles, rubber products, paper, ink, nails, screws and certain other iron and steel products, batteries, razor blades, electric light bulbs, toothbrushes, dried fish, and aluminum hollow ware and foil.

the releases began to specify also the maximum standard ratio, thus in effect ensuring that a certain proportion of domestic consumption would be satisfied out of imports. Ceylon accepted this arrangement stating that it welcomed some imports to act as a stimulant to the improvement of efficiency and quality by local producers.[49]

Some further stiffening of the attitude of the Contracting Parties toward the use of domestic-import ratios as a means of furthering Ceylon's development program was evident when the new version of Article 18 governing releases for development reasons came into effect in October, 1957. In connection with one application or another, questions were raised on each of the points with respect to which Article 18, 16 provides for consultation—viz., the purpose of the proposed measure, the availability of alternative measures under the Agreement, and the possible effects on the commercial and economic interests of other signatories. With respect to purpose, doubts were raised that, taking the output and price effects of the proposed measures together, there would be any improvement in the real standard of living. The availability of alternative measures under the Agreement, especially means of increasing tariffs, was consistently pressed upon Ceylon; protection through tariffs was preferred not only because tariffs would avoid the element of compulsion of the domestic-import ratio technique but also because the Agreement specified that Section C of Article 18 was to be invoked only in exceptional circumstances where no other measure under the Agreement would serve the purpose. Finally, some of the products with respect to which Ceylon sought releases were exported by signatories which were themselves underdeveloped, a factor which made particularly pertinent the requirement that the interests of other members be taken into account.

---

[49] Cf. *BISD,* Fifth Supplement, p. 92.

Cases in which Ceylon revised downwards its suggested maximum standard ratio or withdrew notifications after preliminary consultations became somewhat more frequent.[50] Thus in 1959 a panel considering additional notifications submitted by Ceylon expressed itself as follows :

The Panel is under the impression that more intensive efforts could be made by the Ceylon Government to explore the possibility of using other permissible measures under the General Agreement for the purpose of achieving its objective. The Panel has found it difficult to recommend the granting of some of the releases requested. The Panel also wishes to place on record its doubts as to the validity of the argument put forward by Ceylon that the quantitative restriction of imports would not have the effect of raising domestic prices as would be the case if increases in customs tariffs were resorted to in order to assist the domestic industries concerned.[51]

On this occasion the panel also stated its opinion that future releases should be on the basis of "lower working" standard ratios which could be reconsidered and increased if subsequently warranted rather than as in the past on the basis of maximum standard ratios which were high enough to cover all possible contingencies. For two categories, aluminium foil for packing and asbestos cement products, the panel could not see its way clear to recommending the grant of the releases

---

[50] When Ceylon complained that the stipulations in the releases regarding maximum domestic availability went beyond the conditions prescribed in Article 18 in that they tended to limit domestic production, it was agreed not to include them in future releases. The purpose of the stipulations, it was explained, had not been to limit the development of the local industry but to ensure that the Contracting Parties would have the opportunity to review the need for restrictions when the industry had reached a level of production at which its initial difficulties had been overcome. The latter purpose was subsequently served by a provision in the releases to the effect that, should domestic production exceed a specified level, the maximum standard ratio would be revised so as to ensure that imports could compete with the production in excess of the stated level. *BISD*, Seventh Supplement, pp. 77–78.

[51] *BISD*, Eighth Supplement, p. 91.

requested. However, when Ceylon persisted in pressing its requests, they were granted at the next session though at ratios below those originally put forward by Ceylon. Although it was thought that Ceylon could find a remedy through other measures consistent with the Agreement and although it was doubted that the proposed measures would solve the difficulties even if as alleged they were caused by "the so-called traditional consumer resistance to domestic products prevailing in Ceylon," there was no conclusive evidence that the releases would materially injure the interests of other contracting parties and, "having regard to the general philosophy underlying Article 18 . . . Ceylon should be given the benefit of the doubt. . . ."[52]

The provisions of Article 18, other than those relating to balance-of-payments restrictions, were invoked in few other instances. Ceylon was permitted to impose quantitative restrictions in connection with an agreement with three petroleum companies to build a refinery, subject to the condition that the new refinery would not be permitted to sell its products at prices above the landed costs in Ceylon of like products.[53] India sought stand-by authority to reimpose quantitative restrictions on grinding wheels over a ten-year period in order to give the industry assurance for further investment and development, but such authority was granted only for three years.[54] Cuba obtained a five-year release that enabled her to impose import quotas on fibers of henequen and sisal to permit the development of agricultural production to a point where the Cuban product could withstand world competition;[55] originally requested for a ten-year period, the release was extended for five years in 1955 and, partly on the grounds of the political events which had disturbed the economy, for a further period of

[52] *BISD,* Ninth Supplement, pp. 98–99.
[53] *BISD,* Fourth Supplement, pp. 30, 36–37.
[54] *BISD,* Vol. II, pp. 52–54.
[55] *Ibid.,* pp. 50–51.

three years in 1960.[56] A release granted in connection with Haiti's tobacco monopoly was later deemed to have been unnecessary on the ground that the Haitian measures did not actually conflict with the provisions of Article 11.[57]

The relatively infrequent use (aside from Ceylon) made of the provisions of Article 18 other than those relating to balance-of-payments problems cannot be ascribed to obstacles put in the way of their application by the manner in which the Contracting Parties administered them. There do not appear to have been any instances in which an underdeveloped country failed to receive the necessary concurrence of the Contracting Parties or was found to have offered inadequate compensation, although in a few instances, proposals to invoke Article 18 were withdrawn after preliminary discussions.

As in the cases involving the use of the escape clause (Article 19) and the customs union and free-trade-area provisions (Article 24), the resolutions and decisions relating to economic development reveal a rather permissive policy on the part of the Contracting Parties when they were confronted with the actions of a signatory that were difficult to reconcile with the Agreement. Reliance seems to have been placed upon candor in working-party discussions and reports as a means of exerting pressure on the country concerned to modify its practices in the direction of closer conformance to the Agreement. This was particularly evident in the case of Ceylon, perhaps because Ceylon provided the most frequent opportunity; in this instance, GATT pressures may have had a modicum of success in leading to a less restrictive policy.

Waivers

The major uses of waivers were to permit certain new

---

[56] *BISD,* Ninth Supplement, pp. 100–101.
[57] *BISD,* Fourth Supplement, pp. 38–41.

preferential arrangements, to resolve difficulties connected with balance-of-payments problems, to reconcile the conflict between agricultural protection and the provisions of the Agreement, and to permit tariff reforms or other changes to be put into effect promptly while the normal procedures for negotiating the changes were being carried out. Waivers were also employed to extend deadlines of various types, and for various other minor purposes.

Preferential treatment. Waivers involving the establishment of new preferential arrangements were granted to further economic development, to promote economic integration, and to take account of changes in the political status of certain areas.

Although the provisions of Article 18 enable an underdeveloped country to seek relief from its obligations under the Agreement, they do not provide an opportunity for a more advanced country to extend aid to a less advanced one through giving the latter a privileged position in its markets. Since the Contracting Parties were willing to recognize that preferential customs treatment was a legitimate means of providing assistance for the development of underdeveloped areas and since no other provision of the Agreement authorized increases in margins of preference for such purposes, the waiver device had to be employed to this end. Such waivers usually contained the basic notion that the specially authorized trade arrangements had to be structured so that the benefits accrued to the underdeveloped country, and it was commonly stipulated that injury to other signatories be avoided. Procedures involving prior notification, consultation, and, if necessary, negotiations with other interested signatories relating to increases in preference margins were designed not only to minimize the possibility of injury but also to control the extent of the increases in preferences. Other means of control consisted of limitations on the duration of the waivers and the requirement of annual reports.

Waivers permitting duty-free or other preferential treatment to certain products entering relatively developed countries from territories, former territories, or protectorates were granted in the following cases :[58]

	Date of decision	Issue	Page
1	September 8, 1948	Vol. II	9
2	October 26, 1951	Vol. II	10
3	October 24, 1953	2d Suppl.	18
4	November 19, 1960	9th Suppl.	40
5	November 19, 1960	9th Suppl.	39

Metropolitan Country	Territory, Former Territory, or Protectorate
1. United States	Marshall, Caroline, and Marianas Islands
2. Italy	Libya
3. Australia	Papua–New Guinea
4. Italy	Somalia
5. France	Morocco

A waiver broader in scope but generally of the same category was granted to the United Kingdom on behalf of the more than 50 dependent territories that were under its jurisdiction as of March 5, 1955. The underlying principle was that the United Kingdom should be permitted to find solutions for the problems of these areas by measures which it was permitted to apply under the Agreement, on behalf of its domestic industry and agriculture. Thus a broad range of permissible measures was opened, including not only increases in margins of preference beyond the limits permitted by the Agreement for products imported into the United Kingdom from the territories, but also, on terms equivalent to those available or in effect for domestic products, subsidies, countervailing and

---

[58] Later decisions modified those referred to in lines 2 and 3 ; see *BISD,* Fourth and Eighth Supplements.

antidumping duties, and escape-clause action (i. e., invocation of Article 19). However, no benefits could be derived from the waiver by the industries or exports of the United Kingdom or any other area except the dependent territories. It was limited to colonial products which depended wholly or to a large extent upon the United Kingdom market; it included a "limited range of agricultural and forest products, mostly tropical or subtropical in character, and a limited range of processed goods, based on local supplies of these primary products." Since the terms of the waiver did not specify particular products, prior concurrence of the Contracting Parties was required for any measures that established or increased a margin of preference beyond the limits permitted by Article 1. The usual arrangements regarding annual reports and consultations and compensatory negotiations were included, and special provision was made for the settlement of disagreements regarding injury or compensation.[59] At the time that the sixth annual report was made (November, 1960), the waiver had been invoked only to raise the most-favored-nation rate of duty for bananas and lime oil, although its use for a third product was contemplated.[60]

The principle of aid to a less developed country in the form of preferential treatment by a more developed country was involved also in the relations between the Union of South Africa and the Federation of Rhodesia and Nyasaland when the Federation succeeded to the rights and obligations under the Agreement which had formerly pertained to the Government of Southern Rhodesia and, with respect to Northern Rhodesia and Nyasaland, to the Government of the United

[59] *BISD,* Third Supplement, pp. 22–25, 131–139.
[60] *Sixth Annual Report (1960) on the Use of the Waiver by the United Kingdom,* November 4, 1960, GATT document L/1341, and preceding reports in the series.

Kingdom.[61] South Africa had accorded duty-free entry to almost all products from Northern Rhodesia since the beginning of the century, and had granted similar treatment to Southern Rhodesia under the terms of a customs-union agreement that had been approved by the Contracting Parties. Nevertheless, the trade agreement between the Federation and South Africa negotiated in 1955 represented an extension of preference margins in that the preferences extended by South Africa to the entire Federation were not generally reduced to the lowest margin accorded to any constituent territory. However, preferences in general were reduced by the Agreement, and, considering the economic difficulties that would have ensued had the minimum preference principle been followed, the Contracting Parties waived the provisions of Article 1.[62]

At the expiration of the five-year term of the initial agreement, the two parties wanted to conclude a new agreement that would accelerate the economic development of the Federation by widening the range of products benefiting from preferences in the South African market. Other features of the agreement, including the possibility of increases in preference margins for some South African products in the Federation, the reciprocal exemption of the two countries' exports from balance-of-payments import restrictions, and the freedom of the two countries to increase preferences further during the life of the agreement, roused objections from the other signatories. Increased preferences for South African products could not be justified on economic development grounds, they felt, and there was no GATT precedent for the discriminatory application of balance-of-payments restrictions in order to

---

[61] Cf. *BISD*, Fourth Supplement, pp. 17–20, 72–74; Ninth Supplement, pp. 51–53, 231–236; and references cited therein.

[62] A trade agreement between the new Federation and Australia was readily found acceptable by the Contracting Parties since most of the preferences enjoyed by the constituent territories were eliminated and only a few extended to the entire Federation.

encourage economic development. They were opposed to future increases in preferences without a procedure for notification, consultation, and negotiation.

The agreement that was actually concluded in 1960 and the waiver granted by the Contracting Parties represented a compromise between these positions. Although preferences were extended to some new products, there was a considerable overall narrowing of preferences between the two countries. Future increases in South African preferences to the Federation were possible but were to be confined to "a strictly limited number of cases" and were subject to procedures for notification, consultation, and negotiation, although these procedures were less restrictive in certain respects than those usually specified in such waivers. The waiver made no reference to the clause in the trade agreement providing for reciprocal exemptions from balance-of-payment import restrictions.

A preferential arrangement of an entirely different character that required a waiver from the most-favored nation obligations of the Agreement (Article 1) was the European Coal and Steel Community (ECSC). As already noted, the ECSC could not qualify as a customs union or free-trade area under the provisions of Article 24 chiefly because it was confined to coal and steel and thus fell far short of covering "substantially all trade." A number of considerations were set out as the bases for the decision giving the waiver, among which were:

1. The new organization had objectives which were consistent with those of the Agreement.

2. The realization of these aims, if accompanied by appropriate trade policies by the ECSC, could benefit other Contracting Parties by increasing supplies of coal and steel products.

3. The ECSC had undertaken to take account of third-country interests, to further the development of international

trade, and to ensure that "equitable prices" are charged by its producers in external markets.

4. The ECSC member states proposed to harmonize their customs duties on coal and steel on a lower and less restrictive basis than previously applicable.

The waiver authorized the member states of the ECSC to act as though they constituted a single contracting party as concerned their obligations under the Agreement with respect to coal and steel. Specifically, they could eliminate or reduce tariffs among themselves without extending the same treatment to other signatories, and they could impose quantitative restrictions on other contracting parties without imposing them on other ECSC members, provided that the restrictions were otherwise levied in accordance with the provisions of the Agreement. This principle was specifically noted in connection with the right to invoke certain safeguard provisions of the Agreement such as emergency protection of the imports of a particular product (Article 19) and restrictions to relieve critical shortages of essential products (Article 11).[63]

In view of the difficulties expected for the Belgian coal industry in the new Community, Belgium was released from the obligations of Article 11 and was permitted to maintain or institute quantitative restrictions on coal "to the extent necessary to avoid sudden and harmful shifts in production" for a maximum of seven years from the establishment of the common market for coal.

The waiver required annual reports from the members of the ECSC during the five-year transitional period provided in the Treaty. The discussions of the reports reflected some of the concerns that other signatories had felt with respect to the new Community from its very beginnings.[64] The major issue

---

[63] *BISD,* First Supplement, pp. 17–22, 85–93.
[64] *BISD,* successive supplements from the second to the seventh.

arose out of the feeling on the part of certain European countries, notably those of Scandinavia, and to a lesser extent of overseas signatories such as India, that the common market was partly responsible for the restoration of a steel cartel that was maintaining export prices above those prevailing within the Community. Owing to this effect of the common market in minimizing competition among the national producers—an effect which placed the steel-consuming industries outside the Community at a competitive disadvantage since the Community was their major source of steel—the consuming countries were being deprived of benefits that the ECSC was supposed to confer on third countries. The representative of the High Authority of the ECSC claimed, however, that export prices had not gone beyond the limits of the "equitable prices" mentioned in the Treaty and in the waiver, and that the High Authority's powers to regulate monopolistic practices were confined to the internal market unless "equitable" export prices were exceeded. The debate then turned upon the question of whether the appropriate basis for gauging the equitability of prices was the internal price level of the Community, as the other contracting parties claimed, or the frequently higher prices prevailing in other markets, as the ECSC representative argued.

If steel prices occupied the center of the stage in these sessions, they did not monopolize it. Austria's fears for her small, specialized steel industry, which depended upon Community markets, received attention. Partly in this connection, dissatisfaction was expressed with the rate at which the new Community was leveling down external duties, and, subsequently, at the ECSC interpretation that the "harmonization" of external tariffs did not require uniformity among the members of the EEC in their external tariffs. There were complaints also concerning coke prices and the supplies of coke and of steel scrap made available by the ECSC to countries that had formerly relied upon ECSC-member countries for such materials.

It is not unlikely that the claims of the other contracting parties, that the conditions upon which their governments had agreed to the waiver were not being satisfied to the proper degree or with appropriate speed, helped to ameliorate some of the practices of the Community's steel producers, the member governments, and the ECSC which were the subject of the complaints and criticisms.

Another set of special circumstances that required a waiver from the most-favored-nation principle of Article 1 arose when the Saar was transferred from France to Germany under the provisions of a Treaty concluded in October, 1956. The fulfillment of the customs-union features of the European Economic Community would eventually include the Saar, France, and Germany in a single customs territory, but meanwhile a waiver was necessary to permit Germany to accord certain Saar products duty-free treatment during a three-year transitional period before the Saar would become part of German customs territory. After this transition period, the waiver also provided for the continuance of duty-free treatment in trade between France and the Saar.[65]

Mention may also be made of waivers to Article 1 freeing the United Kingdom from the obligation to extend to Commonwealth countries or territories increases in certain types of duties, subject to the proviso that the incidental establishment or increase in a margin of preference would not be likely to lead to an increase in the volume of trade from Commonwealth areas at the expense of imports from other sources.[66] The reason given for seeking the waivers was that the United

---

[65] *BISD*, Sixth Supplement, pp. 30–31.

[66] *BISD*, Second Supplement, pp. 20–22, 96–101; Third Supplement,

Kingdom wished to be free to increase protective duties on certain products without formally altering its traditional policy of free entry for most Commonwealth goods. Since the products involved were of little or no interest to Commonwealth suppliers, the incidental increase in preference margins would be purely technical.[67] The waiver was used to increase a number of duties, including certain fresh and preserved fruits and vegetables, certain flowers, foliage and nursery stock, and antimony.[68]

Balance of payments. Although the provisions permitting derogations on balance-of-payments grounds, Articles 12 and 18, might seem broad enough to cope with this source of difficulty in meeting the obligations of the agreement, waivers proved necessary in two sets of circumstances. The simpler of these, in some respects, was represented by the cases of three South American countries whose balance-of-payments position entitled them to impose quantitative restrictions but who preferred to levy higher duties instead. The other and in some ways more troublesome circumstances arose when it became obvious that restrictions imposed on balance-of-payments grounds were no longer justifiable on this basis but that countries were unwilling or unable to dispense with the protective effect that the restrictions afforded to certain industries. Agriculture in particular appears to have been protected under this guise, and some countries demanded and received continued protection for their agriculture through waivers.

---

pp. 25–26, 139–141. The first of these sources refers to a waiver granted in October, 1953, relating only to items that had not been the subject of a GATT concession by the United Kingdom; the second relates to an extension of the waiver in March, 1955, to include tariff concession items.

[67] GATT document L/115, August 28, 1953.

[68] Annual reports on use of waiver by the United Kingdom; e.g., *Seventh Annual Report (1960)*, GATT document L/1342, November 4, 1960.

When Peru,[69] Chile,[70] and Nicaragua[71] encountered balance-of payments difficulties in 1958 and 1959, they chose to increase customs duties or to levy tariff surcharges rather than to impose new quantitative restrictions as provided for in Article 18. Since temporary increases in tariffs could be deemed less detrimental to trade than quantitative restrictions, the provisions of Article 2 were waived to permit the increase in connection with items on which GATT concessions had been granted. Higher customs duties, in the opinion of some observers, had the advantage of minimizing chances of corruption in administration. Peru's waiver also included a release from the most-favored-nation requirements of Article 1 in order to permit her to avoid applying the surcharges to products covered by bilateral agreements with neighboring countries.

The countries receiving the waivers were to use them in a manner that would avoid "unnecessary damage" to the interests of other signatories and the impairment of regular channels of trade. They were also to accord sympathetic consideration to representations from affected parties; if the ensuing consultations did not lead to agreement, the Contracting Parties could ultimately, if they found the measures taken under the waiver "unduly restrictive" and the cause of "serious damage" to a complaining signatory, release the complainant from appropriate concessions to the country having received the waiver.

The waivers were limited in commodity coverage, and the maximum extent of the increases in duties or surcharges was specified. All were of less than three-years' duration, although the two that would have expired by the time of writing (mid-1961) were extended for one-year periods.[72] It may not prove

---

[69] *BISD,* Seventh Supplement, pp. 37–39; Eighth Supplement, pp. 56–58.
[70] *BISD,* Eighth Supplement, pp. 29–31.
[71] *Ibid.,* pp. 52–56.
[72] *BISD,* Ninth Supplement, pp. 38, 45.

easy to induce the countries involved to dispense with the additional measure of tariff protection represented by the increased duties or surcharges, especially in view of Brazil's earlier success in sharply increasing its tariffs within the scope of exceptions made by the Contracting Parties. (See page 107.)

The problem relating to the removal of the protection provided by balance-of-payments restrictions began to be faced when, toward the middle fifties, notable improvements became increasingly evident in the balance-of-payments position of a number of countries that had long invoked quantitative restrictions on balance-of-payments grounds. The general consensus that emerged was that certain "hard core" cases which had benefited from what was euphemistically referred to as the "incidental protection" of the balance-of-payments restrictions would require the further protection of import controls during a transitional period in order to enable them to make the adjustment to living without the aid of any restrictions.

Since no provision of the Agreement justified quantitative restrictions on such grounds, even temporarily, the possibility of an amendment to the Agreement was considered. However, the fact the problems at issue were essentially temporary in character weighed against the idea of amendment. Yet, since the difficulties were faced by more than one country, it seemed desirable to deal with them by means of a general rule rather than by a series of waivers. Accordingly, it was decided to use the authority provided in Article 25, 5, i to define these difficulties as a set of "exceptional circumstances" in which the Contracting Parties would by a majority vote waive the obligations of Article 11 to permit the temporary maintenance of import restrictions, where necessary to overcome transitional problems, even after they were no longer justified on balance-of-payments grounds.[73]

---

[73] *BISD*, Third Supplement, pp. 38–41, 191–195.

However, the decision, which was taken on March 5, 1955, and referred to as the "hard core" decision, provided that certain conditions would have to be met before the Contracting Parties would apply it to a given case. The country concerned would have to ask for the waiver before its entitlement to restrictions on balance-of-payments grounds ended, and the restrictions which it desired to continue would have to have been in force continuously since January 1, 1955. Furthermore, the waiver would be granted only if the sudden removal of the restrictions would cause serious injury to a domestic industry that had received incidental protection from it, and if no other "practicable" measures consistent with the Agreement would permit the industry to adapt itself to the situation created by the end of restrictions. The applying country would have to undertake a policy for the progressive relaxation of the restrictions and for their elimination in "a comparatively short period of time." The restrictive effect of the derogation thus authorized could not exceed that of the original balance-of-payments derogation. The restrictions would have to be administered in such a way that the share of imports in the total market would not fall below the average of the three preceding years and the other contracting parties would be given a "fair and reasonable" share in the market. The derogation would not be granted for more than five years, and the Agreement's requirement of nondiscriminatory application of quantitative restrictions would not be waived. Annual reports and review were provided, and the right of other signatories to seek recourse under the nullification and impairment provisions of Article 23 was reserved.[14]

---

[14] The decision originally set the end of December, 1957, as the time limit for applications for the waivers, but a series of one-year extensions kept open the possibility of new applications. *BISD,* Ninth Supplement, pp. 35–36.

For some time before the "hard-core" decision was taken, Belgium had maintained quantitative restrictions that were no longer justified by its balance-of-payments position, and the Belgian Government now sought to place itself upon a firmer legal footing by obtaining a waiver for a broad range of agricultural products under the terms of the decision. Belgium claimed that of the alternative measures it might take, subsidies would be too costly and increased duties were ruled out by its membership in the Benelux customs union. In view of the limitations on Belgium's freedom of action imposed by her participation in Benelux, the Contracting Parties extended the maximum period of five years permitted by the "hard-core" decision for another two years with respect to restrictions that Belgium might not be able to terminate by the end of the five-year period (the extension being made directly under the authority of Article 25, 5).[75]

The annual reviews brought considerable criticism at Belgium's slow progress in the elimination of the restrictions permitted under the waiver, and at the failure to submit a detailed program of import liberalization. Five years after the waiver had been granted, a large number of items were still under controls, and some of those that had been freed were newly subjected to variable import levies. The levies could have the effect, a working party pointed out, of nullifying or impairing the benefits that the other signatories could expect from the removal of the restrictions. The fear was expressed that Belgian agricultural policy was one of self-sufficiency; a rise in farm rents during the period the waiver had been in effect might be a reflection of the government's policy of supporting farm prices at too high a level.

The Belgian representative affirmed his government's intention to move ahead with import liberalization in keeping with

---

[75] *BISD,* Fourth Supplement, pp. 22–26, 102–110.

its obligations. The waiver related only to quantitative restrictions, and the import levies did not conflict with GATT obligations. Not self-sufficiency but an equitable income for producers was the aim of Belgian policy. Land values had risen as a result of increased demand for building sites.

It is difficult to avoid the impression that one of the working parties was well justified in its fear that the hard-core decision might prove "an ineffective method of dealing with transitional measure of protection for agriculture after balance-of-payments difficulties have disappeared."[76]

Perhaps, however, it was the rigorous terms of the "hard-core" decision rather than the lack of scintillating success in its application to Belgium that accounted for the fact that no other country tried to use its provisions. For example, when Luxemburg, associated with Belgium in an economic union, requested a waiver for agriculture at the same time that Belgium did, Luxemburg based its request directly on Article 25, 5 on the ground that the problems involved were "structural" rather than temporary.

The Luxemburg waiver[77] was based upon the frankly avowed desire of the country to protect its agriculture. Despite "highly unfavorable natural factors," Luxemburg regarded it as essential to maintain agricultural production and took the position that the removal of the restrictions that had been imposed on balance-of-payments grounds would cause serious injury not only to agricultural producers but also to its national interests. Anyway, it was argued, no appreciable benefits would accrue to other signatories in the event of the abolition of the restrictions; the trade of Luxemburg would in

---

[76] *BISD,* Sixth Supplement, p. 137. Perhaps the most comprehensive review of the problem relating to Belgium's use of the waiver may be found in the Ninth Supplement, pp. 236–243; see also reports in the Fourth, Fifth, and Seventh Supplements.

[77] *BISD,* Fourth Supplement, pp. 27–29.

any case be small since the population numbers only 300,000. Furthermore, the country's Benelux partners, the Contracting Parties who were chiefly affected, had expressly accepted the maintenance of the restrictions. On these bases, a working party concluded that Luxemburg was a special case, and that no precedent would be created for other countries in granting the waiver.[78] The Contracting Parties accepted the recommendation and Luxemburg was released from its obligation under Article 11 to avoid quantitative restrictions.

The waiver was limited to specific products listed in an annex, and Luxemburg was required to make annual reports on the administration of the restrictions. The waiver decision noted undertaking of the Luxemburg Government to make its agriculture more competitive and to relax the restrictions as far as "practicable." The question of the waiver was to be reviewed in 1960 in the light of the progress made by that date. When the time for review came, it turned out that, while there had been some improvement in agricultural efficiency, the position with respect to the need for the waiver had changed but little. No liberalization measures had been taken during the initial period of the waiver, but the representative of Luxemburg informed the review working party that his Government was prepared to withdraw restrictions on two categories immediately and on a few others in the course of the next few years. The other members of the working party pressed for more rapid removal of the restrictions and the next review was set for the end of 1965 or earlier if a Contracting Party requested it.[79]

Germany was another country which at a relatively early

---

[78] *BISD,* Fourth Supplement, pp. 110–113. The Danish representative on the working party did not associate himself with the conclusion that there were exceptional circumstances prevailing in connection with the agriculture of Luxemburg that justified resort to Article 25, 5. (See *ibid.,* p. 111.)

[79] *BISD,* Ninth Supplement, pp. 255–259.

date moved out of a balance-of-payments position that justified quantitative restrictions. When after formal action by
the International Monetary Fund, the Contracting Parties
decided in June, 1957, that Germany was no longer justified
in maintaining import restrictions for balance-of-payments
reasons, Germany sought to maintain many of the restrictions
on other grounds. Germany based her case both on legal and
economic arguments. The basis of the German legal case was
the fact that Germany was required under the Torquay
Protocol to apply Part II of the Agreement (which contains
the obligation to avoid quantitative restrictions) only to the
fullest extent not inconsistent with legislation existing at the
time of the protocol (April 21, 1951). Germany claimed that
its marketing laws in existence on that date relating to cereals,
meat, fat, and sugar required import restrictions, and that
these laws thus took priority over the Agreement. Economically, the sudden removal of restrictions on certain products,
both in the agricultural and industrial fields, would cause
serious injury which could be avoided only if the import
controls were removed gradually.

Both lines of argument were greeted with scepticism by
other signatories. Most members of the working party which
considered the case were of the opinion that the German laws
were not mandatory upon the executive, and that only mandatory requirements imposed upon the executive by domestic
legislation were entitled to take precedence over the Agreement; the German representative denied the latter as well as
the former.[80]

From an economic standpoint, the German representative
stated that certain policies of other countries had adverse
effects on Germany's ability to abolish import restrictions on

---

[80] *BISD,* Seventh Supplement, pp. 99–107.

industrial products. He mentioned in this connection the existence of monopolies or export taxes for raw materials, and stated that a number of signatories, by invoking the right given by Article 35 to withhold the application of the Agreement from other signatories in certain circumstances (i.e., Japan), had distorted competition and made liberalization of some products more difficult. With respect to agriculture, he challenged the realism and pertinence of GATT principles, and argued that either through measures partly consistent with GATT rules or through waivers, countries had generally preserved their agriculture and protected it against foreign competition. The "world-wide application of export subsidies of all kinds to agricultural products" helped to make import controls necessary in Germany and also in other countries. Furthermore, the German Government could not take any action with respect to agricultural import restrictions owing to the uncertainties created by the free-trade-area negotiations and the pending formation of a common agricultural policy in the EEC. More generally, it should be remembered that Germany still had a balance-of-payments problem in that its balance with the dollar area was becoming more passive even if there were considerable surpluses in trade with other European countries.

The restrictions which the German Government wished to maintain covered 379 food and agricultural products and 165 industrial products which in the aggregate had accounted for about one-sixth of German imports in 1956. This represented a 75 per cent reduction in restrictions toward the dollar area, and in addition discriminatory features of certain remaining quotas were to be ameliorated or eliminated. These proposals were widely regarded as falling far short of what could be expected of a country in Germany's strong financial position, particularly since some of the liberalization measures were to take effect only after a two-year delay.[81]

The outcome was that Germany made some significant concessions, especially in the industrial area.[82] Under the authority of Article 25, 5, the Contracting Parties granted Germany a waiver (in May, 1959) from the prohibition of quantitative restrictions in Article 11, citing but not endorsing the German legal and economic arguments for maintaining restrictions. Annexes to the waiver contained schedules of products to be liberalized on successive dates over the ensuing three years, and other lists for which Germany could retain restrictions. Germany was to keep the latter under constant review so as to afford increasing access to German markets through liberalization as soon as possible. The decision, which reserved the rights of affected parties to seek recourse to the nullification and impairment procedures of Article 23, was effective for three years. Annual reports and reviews on progress in relaxing or eliminating the restrictions were stipulated.

The reviews indicated that Germany was meeting the promised deadlines the products on the liberalization schedules, but that she was taking virtually no action to remove the restrictions that the waiver permitted her to maintain. Despite the promise to liberalize as soon as possible, there was no evidence, the review working party stated, that serious consideration had been given to the removal of restrictions in the agricultural sector. The representative of Germany stated that in view of the failure to find a solution for the agricultural problems faced by other countries as well as by Germany, his government could give no assurance concerning the date by which the restrictions currently in force (late 1960) could be eliminated.[83]

---

[81] *BISD*, Sixth Supplement, pp. 55–68.
[82] *BISD*, Eighth Supplement, pp. 31–50.
[83] *BISD*, Ninth Supplement, pp. 243–254; also Eighth Supplement, pp. 160–163, 167–172.

Nevertheless, the vigorous criticisms of German policy within GATT may have strengthened the bargaining positions of some agricultural exporters such as New Zealand and Denmark so that they fared better than they might have otherwise in bilateral negotiations with Germany.

Agriculture. A number of the waivers described in the foregoing sections have served to protect agriculture, but there remains to discuss the important waiver granted for this purpose to the United States.

The need for the waiver arose out of a change in domestic legislation. Section 22 of the Agricultural Adjustment Act had, since 1935, provided for fees or quantitative restrictions when found necessary by the President to prevent imports from interfering with the government's agricultural programs. The conflict with Article 11 of the Agreement, which permits quotas only if the programs involve controls over the domestic production or marketing of the products, was resolved when in 1948 Congress amended Section 22 to make clear the priority of the GATT commitment.

However, a few years later (1951) Congress reversed the priorities and declared that no international agreement should be applied in a manner inconsistent with Section 22. Thus, regardless of the provisions of the Agreement, the President was henceforth required to impose restrictions, in the form either of fees or quantitative restrictions, upon imports to the extent necessary to prevent imports from rendering ineffective or materially interfering with an agricultural program, or from reducing substantially the amount of any product processed in the United States from an agricultural commodity which is covered by such a program. The fees imposed may not exceed 50 per cent *ad valorem* and the limitation of imports may not reduce their quantity below 50 per cent of the import level during a representative period determined by the President. The President's action, except when taken provisionally in emergencies, is to follow an investigation by the Tariff Commission which is to be made after due notice and opportunity for hearing to the interested parties.

Compliance with the revised law placed the United States in violation of its GATT obligations, a fact which was formally noted by the Contracting Parties each year [84] until the waiver was granted in March, 1955. The waiver decision [85] summarized Section 22, deplored the circumstances that made it necessary for the United States to impose restrictions that impaired concessions and impeded the attainment of the objectives of the Agreement, and released the United States from its obligations under Articles 2 (in connection with the fees) and 11 (in connection with the import limitations) to the extent necessary to avoid conflict with the actions that the United States Government is required to take under Section 22. Conditions and procedures attached to the waiver require notification by the United States to the Contracting Parties of any investigation or decision and provide other contracting parties with the right to make representations regarding the domestic details of the program that are relevant to the trade restriction. In addition, annual reports and reviews are specified, and the United States is obligated to remove or relax each restriction permitted under the waiver as soon as circumstances permit. [86] The other signatories retain their rights to take recourse to Article 23, which would permit them to restore the balance of benefits. [87]

The United States successfully opposed some proposed amendments which would have limited the waiver to a fixed period of time and restricted it to products currently under

---

[84] See, for example, *BISD,* Vol. II, pp. 16–17.

[85] *BISD,* Third Supplement, pp. 32–38.

[86] *BISD,* Third Supplement, pp. 141–146.

[87] See above, p. ?? ff.

quantitative control, with an assurance of sympathetic consideration for future cases as they arose. The United States sought a blanket waiver for all items subject to Section 22 even though for many such products restrictions were placed on domestic marketing (e.g., wheat, cotton, and peanuts) and import restrictions thus could have been justified under the terms of Article 11, c. Apparently the American administration wished to be in a favorable position to meet any Congressional query about the legal status of Section 22 in view of obligations assumed under the Agreement. The American representative was unable also to accept as a condition of the waiver an undertaking by the United States Government to adopt measures that would remove the underlying causes of the situation that necessitated import restrictions.

At the time the waiver was adopted (March, 1955) import controls were in effect on cotton, wheat, dairy products, peanuts, oats, rye, and barley; and fees were imposed on filberts, almonds, flaxseed, linseed oil, and peanut oil. At the end of 1960, controls were effective with respect to cotton, wheat, dairy products, peanuts and peanut oil, and tung nuts and tung oil; and flaxseed and linseed oil were subject to fees.[88]

The annual reviews were generally the occasion for rather candid criticisms of American agricultural policy and the application of pressure for the amelioration of its impact upon international trade. It was pointed out that the high level of support prices maintained by the United States Government was the principal factor contributing to the need to maintain restrictions; high prices kept the domestic market out of balance by stimulating production and discouraging demand. The lowering of support levels that had taken place, while in the right direction, was less than adequate, and in the absence

---

[88] For this and other information cited in connection with the annual reviews, see *BISD,* Fourth to Ninth supplements inclusive.

of plans for more drastic measures the fear was expressed that the need for import restrictions would continue indefinitely. The controls for dairy products, where the United States had actually increased support prices, were subject to especially sharp criticism. United States attempts to dispose of its surpluses overseas, while carried out with care, had nevertheless sometimes caused disruption of normal trade and created problems for other producing countries.

Most of all, there was a theme of disappointment that the United States, rather than exercising leadership in the removal of quantitative restrictions, had obtained a waiver from its GATT obligations to impose restrictions of its own. Other governments, it was said, were also under constant pressure to follow protectionist policies; an appropriate American example would place them in a better position to resist and to move towards the elimination of import restrictions. The American waiver, some held, "had caused more serious damage to the fulfillment of the objectives of the General Agreement than any other single factor."[89] It was difficult for some countries to understand why the United States was unable to devise a system to protect low-income farmers without disrupting world trade. There is little doubt that the need to seek the waiver greatly weakened the American position in GATT affairs and in trade matters generally.

Tariff revision. Waivers were granted to a number of countries to enable them to put into effect tariff changes immediately without waiting for the completion of the consultations and negotiations normally required (Article 28) before such changes can be made.

Perhaps the most sweeping waiver of this type was that accorded to Brazil in November, 1956.[90] Like a number of

---

[89] *BISD*, Ninth Supplement, p. 261.
[90] *BISD*, Fifth Supplement, pp. 36–38, 122–125.

other Latin American countries, Brazil found herself in the position of being a low-tariff country by virtue of a combination of long-standing specific duties and confronted at the same time by an upward spiral of world prices. Brazil combined a move to restore the protective element in its tariff with proposals to ameliorate its sytem of exchange control, which involved multiple exchange rates, and to eliminate certain discriminatory or otherwise undesirable features of its import controls, customs regulations, and internal taxes. Brazil gave assurances that the new tariff would not result in a "significant increase" in the costs of imports, nor change the pattern of imports, nor reduce the volume of trade. On this understanding, the Contracting Parties waived the provisions of Article 2, 1 to the extent necessary to permit Brazil to put the new tariff into force immediately upon its enactment.

It was provided, however, that Brazil would undertake negotiations as soon as possible after the new tariff was enacted to establish a new schedule of concessions, which would be put into effect no later than a year after the enactment unless this period was extended upon the request of the negotiating countries. Until the new concessions came into effect, other signatories would be free to cancel concessions originally negotiated with Brazil (subject to the right of other parties affected by these concessions to obtain compensation). If another country considered that the situation resulting from the negotiations was unsatisfactory, the Contracting Parties would authorize the suspension of the mutual obligations under the Agreement between that party and Brazil. At the conclusion of the negotiations also, any country with a substantial interest in any concession modified or withdrawn in the negotiations was entitled to withdraw substantially equivalent concessions initially negotiated with the party having made the modification or withdrawal.

In actuality Brazil, while actually removing quantitative restrictions, established very high and restrictive rates in the new tariff, and carried out the required negotiations from these levels. Nearly a score of signatories were involved, and three years rather than one were required for the process. Most of the new concessions were put into effect in August, 1960, but negotiations had to be reopened for a few concessions which the Brazilian Congress did not approve.[91]

New Zealand,[92] Turkey,[93] and Greece[94] also received waivers authorizing the imposition of revised tariffs before the normal processes or renegotiation of concessions had been completed. For some of these countries domestic law required the application of new rates immediately after legislative approval, the purpose being to avoid the disruption of markets that might occur if the details of tariff changes were divulged in advance. These waivers contained provisions designed to protect the interests of other signatories similar to those of the Brazilian waiver.

The possibility of speculative disruption of markets also led to a waiver permitting Cuba to impose quantitative restrictions between the time a new tariff schedule became effective and the conclusion of negotiations, in which it was understood that Cuba would seek increases in the duties on many of the items bound under GATT.[95] The Cuban controls, the waiver specified, were not to restrict the import of any product below the average for the three most recent years.

Miscellaneous uses of waivers. Perhaps the most frequent single use of waivers was to extend various time limits speci-

---

[91] *BISD,* Eighth Supplement, pp. 164–167; Ninth Supplement, pp. 36–38.

[92] *BISD,* Sixth Supplement, pp. 34–35; Ninth Supplement, pp. 42–45.

[93] *BISD,* Ninth Supplement, pp. 49–51.

[94] *BISD,* Eighth Supplement, pp. 51–52; Ninth Supplement, p. 40.

[95] *BISD,* Sixth Supplement, pp. 27–28.

fied in the Agreement. Such waivers were common, for example, in connection with the provision of Article 19, 3, limiting the possibility of withdrawal of equivalent concessions to a period of 90 days following the invocation of the escape clause in the same article.[96]

Other administrative or technical questions that were adjusted through the use of waivers included the release of New Zealand and Czechoslovakia from the obligation of Article 15, 6 for signatories not members of the International Monetary Fund to sign special exchange agreements with the Contracting Parties.[97] In the same category might also be placed certain waivers which released a country from a legal tangle but involved no derogation from the principles of the Agreement. One such waiver enabled Greece to raise specific duties in view of the effects of inflation in having reduced their effect[98] and another permitted Finland to alter its specific duties to take account of a devaluation of its currency.[99]

Waiver policy. Viewed in the most favorable light, the Contracting Parties' policy in extending waivers was based on the notion that the provisions of the Agreement should be waived when they stood in the way of some measure which, while inconsistent with the provisions, would promote the objectives of the Agreement. For example, the waivers to permit the extension of preferential arrangements in order to promote economic development and partial economic integration could be explained in these terms.

Embodied in the waivers were the general principles of equity and control found throughout the Agreement. Efforts were consistently made to protect the interests of the other parties through provisions relating to "sympathetic considera-

---

[96] *BISD,* Eighth Supplement, p. 179; Ninth Supplement, p. 267.
[97] *BISD,* Third Supplement, pp. 42–44.
[98] *BISD*, Second Supplement, pp. 24–25.
[99] *BISD,* Third Supplement, pp. 28–29, 126–127.

tion," consultation, negotiation, and, sometimes, the adjudication of disputes by means established by the Contracting Parties. The basic principle underlying these provisions was to enable other parties affected by the waiver to take action to ensure that the balance of benefits from the Agreement would be preserved. The control aspects were represented by reporting requirement, provision for periodic review, and, usually, the limited duration of the waiver, or sometimes the understanding that the exceptional measures were to be progressively eliminated.

There are some signs of a tendency to amass and invoke precedents in the granting of waivers. Thus in the consideration of the proposed revision of the trade agreement between South Africa and the Federation of Rhodesia and Nyasaland, precedents of other waivers were cited to press the requirement of prior notification and consultation in the event of increases in preferences and to reject the use of quantitative restrictions in a discriminatory manner as a means of promoting economic development.[100] In the case of the waiver for Luxemburg agriculture, the opposite concern, namely, to avoid establishing a precedent, was evident.

Despite some efforts to fit the problems that arose into categories provided by the Agreement or created through the waiver procedure on grounds of consistency with the objectives of the Agreement, a number of the waivers that were granted would be difficult to justify under any principle except that of political expediency. The overriding pressure of national interests, regardless of irreconcilability with the Agreement, was most clearly apparent in connection with the protection of agriculture. Of the waivers granted on behalf of agricultural products, including those to the United States, Luxemburg, Germany, and Belgium, only in connection with

---

[100] *BISD,* Eighth Supplement, pp. 158, 159.

the last was any effort made to treat the exception as falling under general rules. And while the Belgian case was pushed into the category created by the hard-core decision, it did not fit very well and the subsequent experience was not encouraging. It is not surprising therefore, that the "guiding principles" adopted by the Contracting Paries for the consideration of waivers relate solely to the protection of the interests of other parties and procedures for control and include no references to criteria upon which waivers should be granted or withheld.[101]

General safeguard rules thus did not obviate the need for the Contracting Parties to recognize through waiver actions that the principles of the Agreement had to take second place when they came into direct conflict with a strong domestic interest of any country, large or small.

Freedom to alter commitments

The "open-season" negotiations under Article 28 provide the signatories opportunities at three-year intervals to alter any concessions that may have given rise to difficulties for domestic interests. Early in the history of GATT, France came to one of these negotiations with a list of items numbering in the hundreds, but generally countries have sought to renegotiate relatively few items. For example, at the time of the Geneva negotiations in 1961, the American delegation was faced with requests for changes in concessions to the United States or in concessions in which the United States had a substantial interest from about a score of countries. Generally the amount of U.S. export trade involved was very small, exceeding $10 million with respect to only four of the countries. Furthermore, these cases included not only "open-

---

[101] *BISD,* Fifth Supplement, p. 25.

season" negotiations but also some negotiations under the "special-circumstances" provision of Article 28, 4 and under waivers granted to individual countries providing for the use of Article 28 procedures.[102] The deterrent to a larger volume of renegotiations is the experience in the French and other cases that modifications are expensive in terms of the compensatory concessions that other countries demand as the price for agreement to the desired changes.

The Contracting Parties have not thus far been called upon to "assist in a solution" or to judge the adequacy of compensation in the "special circumstances" negotiations of Article 28, 4.[103]

Although not specifically provided for by the Agreement, GATT practice has permitted "rectifications," which are minor changes that do not affect the substance of the tariff concessions. Rectifications do not require formal negotiation or compensation, but they are subject to the review of the Contracting Parties, and occasionally a working party has concluded that proposed "rectifications" actually represented "modifications."[104]

The right to refrain from applying the Agreement to certain countries has been invoked in a number of instances. Cuba exercised this right with respect to more than a dozen countries, and Indian and Pakistan with respect to South Africa.[105] The most important use of this provision, however, related to Japan. Many signatories withheld GATT treatment from Japan after its accession in 1955; five years later there were still more than a dozen in this position, including

---

[102] U.S. Delegation, *Status of Article 28 Negotiations for Which the U.S. Delegation in Geneva Is Responsible,* July 5, 1961 (mimeo.).

[103] See above, p. 59.

[104] *BISD,* Vol. II, p. 145.

[105] GATT, *Analytical Index of the General Agreement (Revised),* Geneva, April 1959, pp. 125–126.

the United Kingdom, France, Australia, and the Benelux countries.[106]

Four countries, Syria, Lebanon, Liberia and China, have invoked their right to withdraw from the Agreement,[107] and three others, Republic of Korea, the Philippines, and Colombia negotiated but never completed their accession to the Agreement. A number of signatories acted under Article 27 to withdraw concessions negotiated with one or more of these countries.[108]

Defensive measures

The defensive measures open to a signatory include the right to take unilateral action against dumping or subsidization and the right to seek redress from the Contracting Parties in case of nullification or impairment of benefits from the Agreement. The latter covers, of course, a much broader range of situations and falls more directly within the purview of the Contracting Parties. The claims that have been brought may be considered under four headings according to whether they involved allegations of increased duties, quantitative restrictions, discriminatory treatment, or increased subsidies. Before turning to these cases, however, a word should be said about antidumping and countervailing duties.

Antidumping and countervailing duties. Because the details of these cases generally do not come before the Contracting Parties, information about them is not centrally available. Fortunately, however, a recent survey by the GATT secre-

---

[106] *Survey of the Seventeenth Session of the Contracting Parties to the GATT,* Press Release GATT/553, November 28, 1960 (mimeo.), p. 12

[107] GATT, *Analytical Index,* p. 114.

[108] The first two countries withdrew under the terms of Paragraph 5 of the Protocol of Provisional Application; the others under the provisions of Article 31.

tariat gives some indiction about the extent to which such measures are employed.[109] As of 1958, a score of GATT signatories had legislation or administrative regulations providing for duties against dumped or subsidized products, but less than half of them were actually making use of the provisions. Five countries had antidumping duties in force, and three had countervailing duties in effect. The Union of South Africa and the United States were on both lists, with the former making the most extensive use of antidumping duties (more than a score) and the latter the most extensive use of countervailing duties (a dozen). Generally, the laws and regulations of the countries using antidumping and countervailing duties conformed to the terms of the Agreement (Article 6), although the United States did not require injury by the subsidized import as a condition for the levy of a countervailing duty.

Only one complaint relating to antidumping duties has been brought before the Contracting Parties,[110] and with the possible exception of the two countries mentioned above these defensive measures do not appear to have been widely employed.

Quantitative restrictions. Among the cases involving claims of nullification or impairment of benefits, two based on the imposition of new quantitative restrictions led to formal action by the Contracting Parties. Paradoxically, in view of its basic opposition to quantitative restrictions in principle, the United States was cast in the role of defendant.

In one of the cases, Czechoslovakia charged that the United States administration of its export license system did not

---

[109] GATT, *Anti-Dumping and Countervailing Duties*, Geneva, July, 1958; and *Additions and Corrections to the Report of the GATT Secretariat of July 1958*, Geneva, November, 1959 (mimeo.).

[110] See below, p. 127f.

conform to the provisions of Article 1 of the Agreement.[111] The incident that brought the charge was the refusal of the United States to issue export licenses for certain mining equipment ordered by Czechoslovakia, a country that had recently come under Communist rule. The United States refusal was based on the supposition that the equipment, though ostensibly for coal mining, was actually intended for the mining of uranium.

The withholding of the export license was justified, the U.S. maintained, under the terms of the national-security provisions of Article 21, b, 2 relating to implements of war and other materials for the supply of a military establishment. In their decision, the Contracting Parties, reluctant to place too broad an interpretation of the national-security exceptions, avoided any reference to Article 21; they simply rejected the contention of Czechoslovakia that the United States had failed to meet its obligations under the Agreement.[112]

The other case, which was not contested, concerned restrictions on imports of dairy products imposed by the United States first under Section 104 of the Defense Production Act and subsequently under Section 22 of the Agricultural Adjustment Act. The Contracting Parties recognized in October, 1952, that the restrictions had caused serious damage to a number of signatories and declared that the injured countries were justified in invoking the provisions of Article 23, 2 under which the Contracting Parties may authorize a signatory to suspend the application of specified obligations or

---

[111] *BISD*, Vol. II, p. 28; United Nations Office at Geneva, Information Center, Annecy Press Release No. 42, June 8, 1949.

[112] This case might also have been considered in a section devoted to the use of safeguards relating to the military and other functions of government (see above, p. 48f). While there are undoubtedly many controls on trade for these reasons, their necessity does not seem to be challenged; in any case, the task of assembling information about them would be formidable.

concessions to another signatory that is not fulfilling its obligations.[113] Nevertheless, the Contracting Parties counseled the affected countries to delay such action in order to give the United States the time it requested in order to rectify the situation through the repeal of Section 104. A year later, the offending legislation had not yet been repealed, and the Netherlands asked the Contracting Parties to authorize the suspension of its obligations to the United States to the extent necessary to permit the restriction of imports of American wheat flour to 57,000 metric tons during 1953, a reduction of approximately 15,000 tons from the import rate then current. While the working party that examined this request did not consider it unreasonable in view of the damage caused to the dairy industry and to the over-all Dutch effort to stimulate exports to the United States, it recommended a 60,000 ton limit.[114] The Contracting Parties acted in accordance with this recommendation; subsequently similar authorizations were granted to the Netherlands annually until 1959.[115]

Increased customs charges. The United States was involved also in one of the cases of alleged impairment of benefits resulting from increased customs charges or duties. Once again there was no dispute about the facts of the case. The United States had increased its duty on dried figs under the provisions of Article 19 relating to emergency action on imports of particular products. Turkey, as one of the countries with a substantial interest in this action of the United States, availed itself of its right to withdraw substantially equivalent concessions which it had granted to the United States. Turkish duties on a range of products, including mainly iron, office furniture, office machines, and refrigeration equipment were

---

[113] *BISD,* Vol. II, pp. 16–17.
[114] *BISD,* First Supplement, pp. 32–33, 62–64.
[115] BISD, Second to Seventh Supplements, inclusive.

raised. The Contracting Parties formally stated (in November, 1952) that they did not disapprove of these modifications by Turkey.[116]

Belgium also withdrew a concession in response to the American use of Article 19, but in this instance, involving hatters' fur, the United States restored the concession and Belgium terminated its compensatory measure.[117]

Two complaints related to increased import duties were lodged against Greece. One, brought by the United Kingdom, concerned increases in the coefficients that Greece applied in converting metallic drachmae rates of customs duties into paper drachmae rates. The conversion rates had been bound for items on the schedule of concessions that Greece had granted in the Annecy and Torquay negotiations, and the Greek Government agreed that the increases, which were put into effect in July, 1952, and which varied according to product from 10 to 100 per cent, were not consistent with its GATT obligations. Acute financial difficulties required such action as an emergency measure, but the Greek Government assured the GATT complaints panel late in 1952 that the increases would be withdrawn before July, 1953. The United Kingdom accepted this settlement of the case, which was duly carried out.[118]

A more complicated complaint against Greece, brought by France with the support of the United Kingdom, alleged that a special "contribution" levied by Greece on certain imports was inconsistent with Article 3, 2 since no corresponding charge was levied on like domestic products. The Greek delegation argued that the contribution represented a charge imposed on foreign exchange allocated for commodity imports

---

[116] *BISD,* First Supplement, pp. 28–30.
[117] GATT, *Analytical Index* . . ., p. 89.
[118] *BISD,* First Supplement, pp. 23, 51–53; Seventh Supplement, p. 69.

equivalent to a multiple currency practice. The GATT complaints panel recognized that if it was a multiple currency practice and if it was in conformity with the Articles of Agreement of the International Monetary Fund—questions which the IMF would have to settle—it would fall outside the scope of Article 3. The question would remain, however, whether the Greek measure constituted frustration by exchange action of the provisions of Article 3, in which case it would fall afoul of Article 14, 4. The case was not made simpler by the fact that the "contribution" which was the subject of the complaint had undergone substantial change since it was first introduced in November, 1951. The legal issues, which were posed by the GATT panel near the end of 1952, were never formally resolved, since Greece terminated the charges after the devaluation of the drachma in April, 1953.[119]

In another case, France was called to account for a special compensatory tax on imports which she defended as a temporary and transitional device to facilitate the removal of quantitative restrictions on commodities liberalized under the OEEC program for the freeing of trade. The French representative claimed that France was not obliged to take the liberalization measures as far as its GATT obligations were concerned (since the restrictions in question represented balance-of-payments derogations permitted by Article 12), and the tax was levied (in April, 1954) only on the products which had been voluntarily liberalized in the OEEC framework.[120] Nevertheless, the Contracting Parties decided (in January, 1955) that the tax increased customs charges beyond the maximum rates bound under Article 2 and raised preferences beyond the maximum margins permitted under Article 1 (since

---

[119] *BISD*, First Supplement, pp. 48–50; Seventh Supplement, p. 69.

[120] The rates of the tax varied from 7 to 15 per cent, and less than 8 per cent of total French imports were subject to the tax. Cf. GATT document L/412, September 28, 1955.

the tax was not levied on imports from the French Union). Thus the action of the French Government provided adequate grounds for any signatory whose trade was adversely affected to propose compensatory action under Article 23 for the approval of the Contracting Parties. Furthermore, the Contracting Parties expressed regret that France had imposed the tax without first presenting the case to them for consideration. The Contracting Parties took note of the reductions in the tax already effectuated for a number of goods and of the undertaking of the French Government to remove the tax as soon as possible. They recommended that France take steps to reduce the discrimination against the trade of signatories whose exports were subject to the tax but to which the liberalization measures did not apply (i.e., the non-OEEC countries). The French Government was called upon to report the measures taken to implement its undertaking and the recommendation in three months, and the matter was to be reviewed at the next session of the Contracting Parties.[121]

The question was re-examined at two subsequent sessions, meeting at approximately annual intervals. Each time the Contracting Parties noted some progress in reductions and removals of the tax, but expressed their disappointment at the lack of more rapid progress and at the absence of measures to improve the position of signatories whose exports were subject to the tax but not included in the liberalization measures.[122] It was not until August, 1957, about three years after Italy filed the complaint, that the tax was abolished and replaced by levies on foreign exchange which technically fell under the jurisdiction of the IMF rather than of GATT.[123]

A variation upon the theme of impairment as a result of

---

[121] *BISD,* Third Supplement, pp. 26–28.

[122] *BISD,* Fourth Supplement, pp. 20–21; Fifth Supplement, pp. 27–28.

[123] *BISD,* Seventh Supplement, p. 68; and GATT document L/671, September 9, 1957.

increased customs charges was seen in a complaint about the failure to fulfill a promise to reduce duties. Such a case was brought before the Contracting Parties by Benelux against Germany. The two parties agreed that German promises to reduce duties on cereal starch and potato flour to the level of the Benelux tariff formed part of the balance of concessions negotiated at Torquay in 1951. A major obstacle to the fulfillment of the promises appears to have been the direct and indirect effects of the price-support scheme for cereals maintained in Germany, and negotiations between the two countries, including discussions between the industries concerned, were unsuccessful in resolving the issue. Alternative suggestions were advanced by the Germans, but were not accepted by the Benelux countries. The GATT complaints panel, at its first hearing of the case, concluded that there was little prospect that the German Government would be able to reduce the tariffs to the Benelux level in the immediate future. Its chairman invited the two countries to resume discussions in order to attempt to reach a solution on the basis of an "alternative but constructive" offer from Germany; if such a solution could not be found, the panel would have to adjudicate the dispute. The outcome was agreement on a plan by which the German delegation agreed to "request the Federal Government to propose to Parliament" to grant tariff quotas at the Benelux duty level on potato, corn, and wheat starches for a three-year period. The path was also opened to negotiations on tariff reductions for rice starch and starch derivatives. The Benelux countries reserved the right to bring the case before the Contracting Parties again if the proposals were not approved by the German Parliament or if the concessions were withdrawn after the three years specified in the German offer.[124]

---

[124] *BISD,* Third Supplement, pp. 77–80.

Discrimination. Charges of discrimination seem to have been the most common ground for complaints relating to nullification or impairment of benefits. In some instances, the discrimination that was alleged related to the treatment of domestic products relative to imported goods; in other instances, it concerned treatment of imports from alternative foreign sources.

A case in the former category which dragged on for a decade before settlement involved Brazil. Brazil had legislation dating from 1945 which taxed foreign products more than like domestic products. Since this law predated the Agreement and since the equal-treatment obligations (Article 3) were in Part II, which had to be applied only to the fullest extent not inconsistent with existing legislation, the 1945 discriminatory taxes were beyond the reach of the Agreement. However, the same could not be said for new discriminatory taxes and increases in the old rates levied by a 1948 law. The controversy centered on the increases. While the taxes on both domestic and foreign goods were increased, the differential of 100 per cent between the two tax rates was generally retained, with the result that the absolute differences in the levels of taxation were greatly enlarged. For example, the 1945 law had imposed taxes of 3 cruzeiros on domestic and 6 cruzeiros on imported liqueurs, whereas the rates under the new laws were 18 and 26 cruzeiros, respectively. Most of the members of the GATT working party that examined the case were of the opinion that Article 3 prohibited any increase in the absolute difference between the tax on a domestic product and that on a foreign product, while the Brazilian representative claimed that the provision applied to the proportionate difference. Other issues that came into the debate turned on the language of Article 3, 1 specifying that the tax and other treatment of foreign and domestic products should not be such as "to afford protection to domestic production." On this basis, the Brazilian representative argued that the new law could not be said to be incompatible with the provisions of Article 3 unless it could be shown that its effect had been to increase protection and unless damage to other signatories could be demonstrated. Article 3, he claimed, did not apply where there were no imports or imports were small. In the case at hand, none of the contracting parties was "either greatly interested or affected by the levy of these internal taxes." However, most of the members of the working party took the position that, in view of the trade potential for other signatories as exporters were there equal treatment, the provisions of Article 3 were applicable to all cases, whether imports were nonexistent, small, or substantial. The issue seemed close to settlement the following year (1950) when the Brazilian Government placed a draft law before its legislature that went a long way toward satisfying the GATT working party which examined it. The law would have removed all but a few of the recent increases in indiscriminatory taxation on products imported from GATT members.[125] Despite repeated prodding from the Contracting Parties,[126] however, it was not until August, 1958, that the discriminatory taxes were actually abolished.[127]

A charge of discrimination in favor of a domestic product was sustained also in connection with special credit facilities provided by the Italian Government to farmers for the purchase of domestically produced agricultural machinery. The United Kingdom, in 1957, claimed that the failure to extend similar credit advantages to purchasers of imported machin-

---

[125] *BISD,* Vol. II, pp. 181–188.

[126] *BISD,* Second Supplement, pp. 25–26; Fourth Supplement, pp. 21–22; and Fifth Supplement, p. 37 (paragraph c).

[127] *BISD,* Seventh Supplement, p. 68.

ery was discriminatory in the sense outlawed by Article 3. The Italian delegation argued that Article 3 was limited to measures governing trade (presumably, therefore, excluding finance), and that the article did not prevent a signatory from taking measures to promote economic development and to increase employment. Furthermore, credit facilities to purchasers had a smaller effect on the conditions of competition than subsidies to producers which were specifically exempted from the strictures of Article 3. The panel examining the case rejected all the Italian contentions. The provisions of Article 3 refer to laws, regulations, and requirements *affecting* internal sale, purchase, etc., and not only to laws, regulations, and requirements which directly governed the conditions of purchase or sale; therefore, it could be inferred, financial arrangements were within the purview of the article. As for the promotion of economic development and employment, other measures were permitted by the Agreement for such purposes. Indeed, if the object was to promote economic development through encouraging increased use of machinery by small farmers, it was difficult to see why the credit facilities should not be extended to purchases of all equipment regardless of origin. If, on the other hand, the real though unstated objective was to protect the Italian farm machinery industry, other methods were, again open under the Agreement. In fact, the industry already had the benefit of a 32 per cent tariff. Finally, the panel held that the exemption for production subsidies could not be extended to subsidies for purchasers. The panel also concluded that British exports had been adversely affected. As a result of these considerations, the Contracting Parties formally recommended to the Italian Government that it "consider the desirability" of eliminating the adverse effects of imports by extending the same credit facilities to agricultural machinery produced by other signatories as was given to

Italian machinery.[128] Agreement between the two countries was reached in 1958 on the basis of this recommendation, but the United Kingdom reinstated its complaint in September, 1960, on the ground that the Italian Government subsequently introduced legislation extending the discriminatory administration of the rotating fund for farm machinery for five years beyond 1964.[129]

Another dispute centering around a charge of discrimination arose when in July, 1949, Australia withdrew a subsidy from sodium nitrate, of which Chile was the principle supplier, while continuing to subsidize ammonium sulphate, some of which was produced domestically. The subsidies, which were paid both on the foreign and domestic products, had been instituted during wartime and had been in effect in 1947 when Australia agreed to set the duty on sodium nitrate in GATT negotiations with Chile. The reason given for maintaining the subsidy on ammonium sulphate was that users of this fertilizer would have been prevented by domestic price controls and long-term contracts from recouping the rise in costs through price increases whereas the agricultural producers who used sodium nitrate were no longer subject to price controls. The working party that reviewed the case concluded that Australia could not be considered to have failed in fulfilling its obligations under the Agreement. The Australian action violated neither the most-favored-nation requirement of Article 1 nor the national-treatment obligations of Article 3; these clauses both referred to "like products" whereas the two fertilizers were directly competitive but not alike. Nevertheless, the group concluded, the Australian measure had nullified or impaired the 1947 tariff concession (i.e., the binding of the duty) granted to Chile

---

[128] *BISD*, Seventh Supplement, pp. 23, 60–68.

[129] *GATT*, document L/1294, September 16, 1960.

since the action of the Australian Government in disturbing the competitive relationship between the two fertilizers could not reasonably have been anticipated by the Government of Chile at the time of the negotiations. The Australian Government, faced with the wartime shortage of fertilizers, grouped the two products together and treated them uniformly, and Chile thus had reason to assume that equal treatment would be continued. The Australian representative took issue with this conclusion; he claimed that the practice of GATT negotiations showed that if a country wished to assure itself of a certain treatment apart from the rates of duty and going beyond what is required by the Agreement, it must seek the objective as a matter of negotiation in addition to the negotiations relative to the duties. Nevertheless, Australia heeded the recommendation made by the Contracting Parties (in April, 1950) on the basis of the working party's report that she take steps to remove the competitive inequality between the two fertilizers.[130]

The nullification or impairment of a concession as a result of unanticipated changes in competitive relationships also figured in a dispute concerning the treatment of Norwegian sprats and herrings by Germany. Equality of customs treatment for these products with sardines had been guaranteed by notes exchanged between Norway and Germany in the 1920's. At Torquay (1951), Norway obtained concessions which resulted in German duties of 20 and 25 per cent and, while there was no written commitment, proceeded on the assumption that the equality of customs treatment with sardines would be continued. Shortly thereafter, however, Germany began to apply a 14 per cent duty on sardines, partly on the basis of a prewar concession to Portugal. Germany also liberalized imports of sardines from the OEEC in connection with the OEEC program of trade liberalization, but continued

---

[130] *BISD,* Vol. II, pp. 188–196.

import restrictions for sprats and herrings. Finally, the manner in which Germany levied a charge on imported sprats and herrings equivalent to the German turnover tax operated to the disadvantage of the Norwegian product relative both to sardines and to German preparations of sprats and herrings. The GATT panel which investigated the Norwegian complaint concluded that the evidence was not sufficient to show that the German Government had failed to carry out its obligations to accord most-favored-nation treatment generally (Article 1, 1) and specifically in the administration of import restrictions (Article 13, 1). This finding was based largely on the fact that the obligations referred to relate to "like products" whereas the German delegation at Torquay consistently treated sprats, herrings, and sardines as if they were separate products and that this was clearly understood by the Norwegian delegation. However, the panel recognized that Norwegian acceptance of this treatment rested on the assumption that customs equality would be maintained. Therefore, the actions of the German Government in disturbing the competitive relationships among the various species, which were considered by many interested parties as directly competitive, impaired the benefits accruing to Norway under the Agreement. Hence the panel considered that the Contracting Parties ought to recommend that Germany remove the competitive inequality that had been established. Such a recommendation was made (in October, 1952),[131] and Germany subsequently agreed to seek legislation to reduce its duties on the Norwegian products to 15 per cent and to maintain in future tariff alterations the ratio represented by the 15 per cent duty on these products and the 14 per cent duty on sardines.[132]

Another case involving the charge of discrimination be-

---

[131] *BISD*, First Supplement, pp. 30–31, 53–59.
[132] GATT, document G/52, October 5, 1953.

tween various foreign sources of supply related to a special levy imposed by Belgium on foreign goods purchased by public bodies when the country of origin did not have a system of family allowances that met specified requirements. Upon investigating a complaint by Norway and Denmark, a GATT panel determined that the 7.5 per cent levy represented an internal charge (within the meaning of Article 3, 2) rather than an import charge equivalent to an internal tax (covered in Article 2, 2), since it was imposed not at the time of importation but when the purchase price was paid and not on imports as such but only on imports purchased by public bodies for their own use. Since internal charges are specifically covered by the most-favored-nation requirement (Article 1, 1), the fact that Belgium had granted an exemption to another country whose family allowance system did not fully meet the established requirements justified Norway and Denmark in seeking similar treatment. The same exemption also disposed of the argument that the Belgian law made the imposition of the charge mandatory, and that the entire matter fell outside the scope of GATT since, at the time, Belgium was permitted to observe Article 1 only "to the fullest extent not inconsistent with existing legislation." Accordingly, the Contracting Parties recommended (in November, 1952) that Belgium remove the discrimination complained of, a recommendation which was carried out by a new Belgian law about 16 months later.[133]

The discrimination issue played a role also in a sharp controversy between Sweden and Italy over the application of Swedish antidumping regulations to imports of Italian nylon stockings. The dispute concerned both the consistency of the Swedish antidumping measures (decreed in May and October, 1954) with the requirements of the Agreement and

---

[133] *BISD*, First Supplement, pp. 59–62; Second Supplement, p. 18; Seventh Supplement, p. 68.

the factual data used in determining whether Italian producers actually were dumping stockings in the Swedish market. The Swedish regulations subjected imports entered at prices below certain "basic" prices established in the decrees to an antidumping inquiry; if the goods were found to be entering below their "normal value" as defined in the Agreement (Article 6), a countervailing duty was levied upon them. A central theme of the Italian complaint against the basic price system was that it discriminated against low-cost producers. The official character of the basic prices was apt to influence unduly the decisions of customs officials with regard to the determination of normal value, and the system would tend to develop into one in which minimum prices would be imposed for the admission of goods. Furthermore, the products of low-cost producers were subjected to uncertainties and delays that were not encountered by shipments of high-cost products. The GATT panel which reviewed the case concluded that the basic price system was not necessarily inconsistent with the most-favored-nation clause or with the requirement that normal value be used in antidumping procedures if, as the Swedish representative stated, the basic prices were fixed so as to be no more than the actual market price of the lowest-cost producer. However, the panel considered that in actual practice the administration of the system could easily conflict with these obligations of the Agreement. Constant supervision of the system would be required to avoid turning it into a general protection against low-cost producers; the basic prices had to be kept under continual review and alleged cases of dumping adjudicated in a matter of days after the arrival of the goods. Apart from the legal issues, there was the question of whether Italian commercial interests had been injured and the benefits accruing to Italy thereby impaired. Italian exports had decreased appreciably under the new regulations, but, since irreconcilable figures on Italian costs of production were advanced by the Swedish and Italian representatives, the existence or non-existence of dumping could not be ascertained. The panel suggested that the Contracting Parties recommend that Sweden improve the administration of its antidumping system so as to minimize delays and other impediments to the export of Italian nylon stockings to Sweden, and also that the two governments arrange for a Swedish inquiry to clarify the disputed facts about Italian costs. The Contracting Parties made these recommendations (in February, 1955), and about six months later Sweden abrogated the antidumping regulations that were the subject of the complaint.[134]

Subsidies. A case involving the charge of impairment as a result of export subsidies was brought by Australia against France early in 1958.[135] Australia claimed that as a result of subsidies on exports of wheat and wheat flour which were inconsistent with the provisions of Article 16, 3, French exports displaced Australian products particularly in traditional Australian wheat-flour markets in Ceylon, Indonesia, and Malaya. French exports of wheat and flour were organized in connection with a scheme to stabilize domestic prices and returns to producers; payments were made to exporters to cover the difference between the domestic and the lower world wheat price and additional bonuses were paid in connection with flour exports. These payments were made by a government organization which controlled the production, collection, storage, domestic sale, and exports and imports of cereals. About one-third of the funds of the organization were obtained from government sources and the rest from a special

---

[134] *BISD,* Third Supplement, pp. 81–91; Seventh Supplement, p. 69. The same dispute was carried on in the framework of the OEEC, where it took a similar course. See below, Chapter III.

[135] *BISD,* Seventh Supplement, pp. 22–23, 46–60.

tax and from revenues derived from above-quota deliveries of grain by farmers. The GATT conciliation panel thus concluded that the export subsidies were partly financed out of public funds and hence fell within the purview of Article 16, 3.[136] This clause, however, outlaws subsidies only when granted in such a manner as to obtain a "more than an equitable share" of world exports, and the panel had to determine whether the French subsidies had had this effect. While the French share in world exports had fluctuated very widely in the interwar and postwar years,[137] beginning in 1954 it rose to higher levels than in previous years. The absolute and relative gain was associated with prices that were on the whole lower than those of other exporting countries. Indeed, the price for wheat flour barely exceeded that charged for wheat, compared to the 30 to 50 per cent differential between wheat and flour export prices maintained by major exporters such as Australia, Canada, and the United States.[138] Thus, while the panel recognized the difficulty of defining an "equitable" share, it concluded that the subsidy arrangements had contributed "to a large extent" to the increases in French exports and that the "present" share (around 7.5 per cent for wheat and 9 to 10 per cent for wheat flour) "is more than equitable." It concluded also that Australia had suffered direct damage from the displacement of its wheat flour by French exports in southeast Asian markets and indirect damage with respect to its milling and transport business. In keeping with

---

[136] The panel was guided at this point by the interpretative note to Article 16, 3 in the Agreement. See *BISD*, Vol. III, p. 72.

[137] French wheat with its high moisture content, the panel observed, was not capable of being stored for long periods. Furthermore, storage and drying facilities were inadequate. Thus it was inevitable that a substantial part of any sizable surplus would have to be placed on the world market.

[138] However, the panel noted that other European countries followed the French practice; Germany, for example, actually exported flour at lower prices than wheat.

the suggestions of the panel, the Contracting Parties therefore recommended (in November, 1958) that the French Government alter the system of payments to exporters so as to avoid the adverse effects on world wheat and flour markets and particularly on normal Australian exports of wheat flour to southeast Asia.

The complaints record

On the whole, the record of the Contracting Parties in coping with complaints about the nullification of impairment of benefits is brighter than the waiver record. Defensive measures in the form of compensatory withdrawal of concessions were permitted in a few instances to restore the balance of benefits after a signatory had increased the degree of protection through the invocation of a safeguard clause. More often, however, the disputes were related not to formal use of safeguard mechanisms but to practices that allegedly represented violations of the Agreement. In such cases the ability of GATT to elicit and to expose the facts to public view often went far toward producing a settlement. Perhaps also the interests that the defendent countries had at stake in these instances were less essential than those that were involved in the situations in which safeguard clauses were formally invoked. For these or other reasons, the success of GATT in achieving settlements that avoided the further contraction of trade was notable.

EVALUATION

The GATT approach

GATT, as a member of its secretariat observed, is better

equipped for conciliation than for condemnation. The efficacy of the organization has consisted in bringing the senior trade officials of the various countries together to discuss problems and controversies that arise under an agreement that contains a set of trading rules and obligations but which provides no means of strict enforcement. The emphasis has been on finding *ad hoc* solutions through negotiation and compromise rather than on the strict interpretation and application of the legal terms of the Agreement.

This emphasis on conciliation, on moderation, and on reasonableness finds its reflection in the elaboration at almost every turn of procedures providing for consultation. So important has this feature been in the actual operation of GATT that the Contracting Parties have not been content to provide in Article 22 a blanket commitment to "accord sympathetic consideration to" and to "afford adequate opportunity for consultation regarding, such representations as may be made by another Contracting Party with respect to any matter affecting the operation of this Agreement," but have specifically provided the rights of consultation and negotiation for affected parties in connection with many decisions regarding the application of safeguard clauses and waivers.

The stress on the satisfaction of the parties to the Agreement rather than upon the strict conformance to the terms of the Agreement has led to a tendency to consider only those violations of the Agreement that are the subject of complaint by one of the signatories. Furthermore, the terms of the settlement of disputes by the parties thereto have usually been accepted without further inquiry with respect to their conformance to the provisions of the Agreement. If all parties are satisfied, the coals are not raked over. This forms a marked contrast [139] to the independent efforts of the central organizations of the coal and steel community and of the Common Market to exercise surveillance over conformance to treaty rules and to examine in this light any agreements that may be reached between the countries in community matters.

Permissive policy with respect to safeguards

The policy with respect to the application of GATT obligations that emerges from this approach has a highly permissive character. No country has in actual practice been rigidly bound by GATT rules; the exceptions have been significant and both authorized and unauthorized in character.

There are a number of legal avenues of escape from commitments that prove embarrassing. The most widely used, though declining in importance at least for the developed countries, has been the clause permitting quantitative restrictions for balance-of-payments reasons. The United States has not resorted to this safeguard, but it has invoked the Article 19 escape clause more than any other country. The periodic opportunity to renegotiate concessions has also served as a means of revising commitments with respect to specific commodities, and a number of countries have used their right to withhold GATT treatment from Japan. Perhaps a score of urgently desired exceptions that could not be justified under any of the regular safeguard provisions of the Agreement were legalized by means of the waiver procedures. In some instances, a country's desire for increased protection was satisfied by the successful search for a measure that achieved the desired result without technically violating the Agreement;

---

[139] Though not one necessarily unfavorable to GATT, considering the differences in the circumstances.

the French substitution of a tax on foreign exchange for its special tax on imports seems to be a case in point.

Beyond these legally sanctioned exceptions and releases from obligations, there were some cases in which countries were formally judged to be in violation of the Agreement. These included, for example, American import restrictions for agricultural products, Greek increases in import duties, and Brazilian discrimination against imported products through internal taxation.

However, the Contracting Parties never hastened to condemn, particularly so long as there was a prospect of obtaining conformance to the Agreement through pressure or negotiation. Thus, there were instances in which signatories were known to be in violation of the Agreement but in which no formal action was taken. For example, a number of western European countries which were generally quite conscientious about their GATT obligations were slow to remove quantitative restrictions after they could no longer be justified on balance-of-payments grounds.

A strong investigative and enforcement arm of the Contracting Parties might have brought forward other cases. For example, a question is raised by the failure of the underdeveloped countries to make more extensive use of the provisions of Article 18 other than those relating to balance-of-payments derogations. One possible explanation is that the balance-of-payment loopholes are adequate for their needs and desires. Another is that there are a number of deviations from the rules of the Agreement which would be revealed were the trading practices of some of these countries exposed to the bright light of world interest that has illuminated the details of the trading practices of the advanced trading countries. (Account must also be taken of the inclination of many underdeveloped countries to regard GATT as unsuited to their needs and to hold it partly responsible for their failure to share more fully in the great expansion of world trade in the last 10 or 15 years.)

In short, there are few contracting parties which at one time or another have not found it necessary or convenient to circumvent a GATT obligation. Conflicts between pressing national interests and GATT obligations have generally been resolved in favor of the former, whether the domestic interest grew out of a single sector or pertained to the economy as a whole. This permissiveness of the GATT applies to small as well as to large countries. Luxemburg and Belgium as well as Germany and the United States obtained waivers on behalf of agriculture, and Central and South American countries as well as European countries were permitted to enter into new preferential arrangements that may not have conformed strictly to the requirements of the Agreement.

Furthermore, in a number of cases the exception or suspensions have in effect represented a permanent adaptation of GATT obligations to the domestic interests involved, with little prospect for eventual adaptation in the opposite direction. This seems most clearly the case with respect to the difficult and intractable problem posed for the Contracting Parties by agricultural protectionism, but it is true also outside of the agricultural area as, for example, in a number of the instances in which the United States has invoked the Article 19 escape clause. The point does not apply, of course, in the important group of cases related to balance-of-payments difficulties.

Achievements of GATT

Nevertheless, after all has been said about the consistency with which GATT obligations tend to be shrugged off in case of necessity, there remain to be described substantial achievements of GATT.

No small part of these accomplishments stems from the annual, or more recently, semiannual, meetings of senior trade officials in the plenary sessions of the Contracting Parties. The personal working relationships that have emerged from these contacts have helped to smooth the settlement of frictions and disputes relating to trade matters. More importantly, perhaps, they have promoted an understanding of the positions of other countries and a sensitivity to their needs and interests that help in the avoidance of frictions and disputes. The existence of personal ties also makes more unpleasant the task of explaining or defending the position of a country which has taken a measure that cannot be justified in terms of the Agreement. Thus the GATT process of eliciting the facts and exposing them to public view serves not only to help an injured party obtain remedies, but also to restrain the adoption by individual governments of measures that would embarrass them upon exposure.

Indeed, an important aspect of the GATT contribution is that it provides a means by which the pressures of the community of nations may be brought to bear upon governments to adhere to rules of good conduct in international trade relationships. It is true that GATT principles give way if pressure from a domestic source is strong enough, but the existence of GATT has shifted the yielding point away from protectionism by better organizing the external pressures. Governments seeking to promote freer trade can point to the basic principle of the balance of benefits that underlies GATT, and thereby hope to mobilize domestic interests that would be adversely affected by a contraction of trade against those seeking greater protection.

In point of fact, however, the balance-of-benefits principle has not and probably cannot work on the small scale but only on the large. The signatories have not, in general, played a tit-for-tat game in response to derogations from obligations involved in the safeguard and waiver actions. Thus, for example, only in two instances was retaliatory action taken in the more than dozen cases in which the United States invoked the Article 19 escape clause and only one country took such action in response to the American use of its agricultural waiver. Again no signatory accepted the virtual invitation to seek compensation formally issued by the Contracting Parties in their decision condemning the French special import tax. This indicates that a government is left with some leeway to increase protectionism, if it is so inclined, without losing off-setting benefits. However, this is true only to a limited degree; more extensive changes in tariff commitments, such as, for example, those involved in the establishment of the Common Market, require new negotiations to restore the balance of benefits.[140]

The actual effect of GATT upon the conduct of commercial policy by the signatories is thus significant.[141] If they have not been led to strict conformance to all the rules of the Agreement and to indefinite adherence to all tariff commitments, they have at least been induced to avoid measures that hurt others without helping themselves very much. Disputes have thus been minimized, and when they have arisen they have been successfully settled; hence, a series of mutually retaliatory measures that would contract trade has been

---

[140] This may apply more to the advanced trading countries than to underdeveloped countries; it could be argued, for example, that Brazil was able to increase tariff protection and thereby altered the balance of benefits in her favor.

[141] Tangible evidence of GATT influence was recently provided, for example, by the close attention given to the GATT rules in the drafting of the treaties establishing the European Economic Community and the European Free Trade Area.

avoided. These are notable achievements in themselves, for they represent the establishment of an ordered world where a jungle might otherwise exist.

The accomplishments of GATT go beyond this, but they become more difficult to gauge. To some extent, the existence of GATT has hastened the termination of certain trade restrictions, notably those maintained for balance-of-payments reasons, which countries had avowed were temporary. To some degree, the existence of GATT has served as a means of slowly chipping away at the barriers to international trade, and, perhaps equally important, restraining the erection of new ones.

Chapter 3

The OEEC Code of Liberalization

THE ORGANIZATION FOR EUROPEAN Economic Cooperation (OEEC) was established as the means by which the western European countries could work together to further their individual efforts towards postwar economic recovery. Formed under the stimulus of General Marshall's famous invitation of June, 1947, to the European countries to agree among themselves on a program by which the United States could best help European recovery, the OEEC directed major efforts toward the freeing of intra-European trade. To this end, it worked simultaneously for the reestablishment of a multilateral payments system and the elimination of quantitative restrictions on trade.

The reduction of quantitative restrictions would have been largely meaningless if foreign exchange were not made available to firms desiring to import goods freed of quotas. The OEEC commitments to liberalize trade therefore included the obligation to allocate foreign currency for payments on liberalized imports. As a result, the willingness and ability of countries to liberalize was closely linked to the development of a multilateral payments system. While the trade and payments program of the OEEC thus went hand in hand, we shall be concerned here only with the trade program.[1]

---

[1] The payments aspects are fully treated in R. Triffin, *Europe and the Money Muddle,* New Haven, 1957. For an earlier discussion of both programs, see W. Diebold, Jr., *Trade and Payments in Western Europe,* New York, 1952. A more detailed analysis of the earlier stages of the trade liberalization program may be found in F. Boyer and J. P. Sallé,

The program of trade liberalization got under way in the latter half of 1949. The first steps were a general agreement to work for the progressive elimination of quantitative restrictions on intra-European trade, an undertaking for the unilateral liberalization of quotas by the countries "as fully as their economic and financial position permits . . .," [2] the negotiation of reciprocal reductions in restrictions, and the substitution of global quotas open to all OEEC members for existing bilateral quotas. These measures were followed before the end of the year by the decision to remove restrictions on at least 50 per cent of imports on private account from other member countries in each of three categories—foodstuffs and fodder, raw materials, and manufactured goods.[3] In the next year trade liberalization was extended to the 60 per cent level and a start was made in the liberalization of invisibles.

The accumulating body of decisions on trade liberalization was consolidated and elaborated into a Code of Liberalization, which came into force in September, 1950, when the Euro-

---

"The Liberalization of Intra-European Trade in the Framework of the OEEC," International Monetary Fund *Staff Papers,* IV (February, 1955), No. 2, 179–216. For the more general aspects of the OEEC, an authoritative review of the Organization's structure and powers has been provided by A. Elkin, the head of its legal division, in the *European Yearbook,* IV (1958), 96–140.

[2] OEEC, *Acts of the Organization,* Vol. V, p. 65, Decision of Council, July 4, 1949.

[3] The limitation, throughout the history of the OEEC, of the liberalization requirements to private trade reduced the real significance of the program, particularly in the agricultural sector where state trading was important for a number of the countries. The percentage of 1952 imports (of all categories) from OEEC countries subject to state trading was 34 per cent for France (although France was exceptional in that state trade covered mainly nonagricultural products), 10 per cent for Germany, between 6 and 8 per cent for Norway and the United Kingdom, between 2 and 4 per cent for Switzerland and Sweden, and 1 per cent or less for other countries. The average for all OEEC countries was 7 per cent. OEEC, *Sixth Annual Report,* Paris, March, 1955, Vol. I, p. 133. See also M. Ouin, "State Trading in Western Europe," *Law and Contemporary Problems,* XXIV (1959) 398–418.

pean Payments Union began operations. Like the other decisions affecting trade and payments, the Code was put into effect by the Council of the OEEC, the governing body of the organization.[4] The Code was changed from time to time as new decisions with respect to trade liberalization were taken by the Council. The last collated version of the Code, which was published in July, 1960,[5] is the form upon which most of the following discussion is based. The Code of Liberalization, as it affected commodity trade, passed into limbo at the end of September, 1961, with the replacement of the OEEC by the Organization for Economic Cooperation and Development (OECD), in which the United States and Canada became full members.

The Code itself contained only a commitment to 75 per cent liberalization; subsequent Council decisions to raise liberalization to the 90 per cent level were regarded, for reasons that will be mentioned, as more provisional, and were not incorporated into the Code.[6] Current invisibles were

---

[4] The Council, "composed of all the members," is "the body from which all decisions derive." Article 15, *Convention for European Economic Cooperation,* Paris, April 16, 1948. The Council met almost every week, usually at the official but sometimes at the ministerial level. Elkin, *op. cit.,* p. 103.

[5] OEEC, *Code of Liberalization,* Paris, July, 1960.

[6] The 75 per cent level for total private imports was accompanied by the requirement to liberalize at least 60 per cent in each of three categories—food and fodder, raw materials, and manufactured goods. The 90 per cent level for total private imports brought the obligatory liberalization in each of these categories up to 75 per cent.

For most countries the percentages of liberalized trade were calculated on the basis of the relative importance of various goods in their 1948 imports on private account. The question has sometimes been raised as to the significance of liberalization percentages for the middle and late 1950's calculated on a 1948 base. An inquiry by the Steering Board for Trade indicated that when the 1957 percentages were calculated on the basis of the 1957 relative importance of imports, the results for total imports, raw materials, and manufactured goods differed only slightly from the percentages calculated on the 1948 base. In the food and fodder category, however, the differences were more notable; for four of the seven countries for which data by categories were available,

treated separately in the Code and capital movements were the subject of a separate Code [7] which was put into effect in 1959. For both current invisibles and capital movements, many governments stipulated a number of reservations exempting themselves from the obligation to apply the general commitment for liberalization to specified types of transactions. The safeguard clauses and many other provisions governing current invisibles and capital movements were parallel to those that applied to commodity trade. It was anticipated that the OECD would continue the work of the OEEC with respect to the liberalization of current invisibles and capital movements, but that trade obligations would revert to the province of GATT.

The freedom of the OEEC countries to reduce trade restrictions among themselves while maintaining them against outside countries could be justified in the light of their obligations as members of the International Monetary Fund only as long as they were in balance-of-payments difficulties. When, at the end of 1958, most of the OEEC countries made their currencies convertible, they were put under pressure to end discrimination in their programs of trade liberalization. In most cases considerable progress had already been made in liberalizing imports, particularly from the outer sterling and the dollar areas.

SAFEGUARD CLAUSES

The general philosophy underlying the OEEC liberalization program was to dismantle the restrictions in successive stages.

---

the figure on the 1957 base was about 10 percentage points below that on the 1948 base, and in one instance it was over 30 percentage points lower (Steering Board document dated June 30, 1959). Furthermore, some countries would have been below the required percentages had the reference date been 1957.

[7] OEEC, *Code of Liberalization of Capital Movements,* Paris, 1960.

Thus, with respect to commodity trade, the Code called for the progressive elimination of quantitative restrictions on imports "as fully as their economic and financial position will permit, and taking account of similar efforts made by other member countries" (Article 1). Target dates for the achievement of 60 per cent liberalization and of 75 per cent liberalization were also established (October, 1950, and February, 1951, respectively).

The language of the general commitment just quoted makes it clear that no country assumed an international obligation which it had to regard as taking a clear priority over its national interests. It was obliged to eliminate quotas only as "fully" as its "economic and financial position" would "permit," and to give due attention to reciprocity in determining its course of action.

Three grounds were provided for relief from the specific commitments for 60 and 75 per cent liberalization (Article 3). In the first place, a country did not have to meet these targets if its "economic and financial situation" justified the failure to liberalize to the full extent of the target percentages (Paragraph a). Secondly, a country could withdraw measures of liberalization already taken if they resulted in "serious economic disturbance in the member country concerned" (Paragraph b). Third, if a country's balance-of-payments position "develops adversely at a rate and in circumstances which it considers serious in view of the state of its reserves," it could temporarily suspend the liberalization measures which it had taken in conformance with the Code (Paragraph c). In such a situation, special attention was to be given to the effect on the balance of payments of "specifically European" factors, but these did not have to be considered "essential" in the case of a country whose balance-of-payments was "fundamentally influenced by its relations with nonmember countries." Prior to the replacement of the European Payments Union (EPU) by the European Monetary Agreement (EMA) at the end of 1958, the deficit of the country in the EPU rather than the broader balance-of-payments criteria just mentioned was the controlling consideration in this safeguard clause.

Derogations under any of the paragraphs of Article 3 were subject to the condition that the escape measures not only be nondiscriminatory among member states, but also that they be designed so as to "avoid unnecessary damage which bears especially on the commercial and economic interests of another member country" (Paragraph e). In the case of derogations for balance-of-payments reasons, certain guiding principles were to be followed to ensure that such damage be avoided or minimized; for example, the economies in the use of foreign exchange were to be spread over as wide a range of commodities as possible (Section II bis).

Another basis for escape from the 60 and 75 per cent targets was introduced with the advent of the EMA and of currency convertibility for many member countries. This clause provided for derogation if a country's commitments under other international agreements required it to extend the liberalization measures to third countries and if the country "fears that such an extension would cause it, in view of the state of its reserves, serious balance-of-payments difficulties endangering the maintenance and development of . . . measures of liberalization" (Article 2 bis and Article 4).

In addition to the 60 and 75 per cent targets, the Code contained a common list of products which all countries were to free from quota restrictions in the course of achieving the specified degrees of liberalization (Article 4 bis). This list of commodities, which included textiles, agricultural products, chemicals, hides, and timber and paper (Annex A, Section III), was agreed upon in 1951 at a time when the OEEC was hesitating between the pursuit of liberalization in terms of percentage targets and liberalization in terms of economic sectors. Influenced by the current discussions of European integration on a sector by sector basis, the common list was intended to encourage the development of a single European market and to promote intercountry equity with respect to the commodity coverage of liberalization measures. A country that had invoked escape clauses on grounds of unfavorable economic or financial position (Article 3a) or on grounds of balance-of-payments difficulties (Article 3c) was not obliged to free the goods on this list. A country that had not invoked these safeguard clauses could withhold liberalization of one or more of the listed items if "sufficient reasons of national importance or equity justify such a course" (Article 5). Actually, the common list provision proved to be a dead letter, although it remained officially part of the Code. France, which had approved the Council decision establishing the common list did not liberalize some of the items on it (cheese, dried figs, and printed textiles) and certain other countries also failed to comply fully. With the movement to 90 per cent liberalization, the common list receded in importance, and it appears to have been ignored by common consent.

By the time the 75 per cent level of liberalization had been reached, some of the low-tariff countries of the OEEC, notably Denmark, had come to feel that further progress in the development of intra-European trade required the reduction of tariffs in order to translate the removal of quantitative restrictions into actual increases in trade. Hence, when 90 per cent liberalization was finally adopted by the OEEC the safeguard provisions were broader. The decision, in addition to providing avenues of escape on balance-of-payments grounds similar to those in the Code itself, specified "reasons of national importance or equity" as justifications for the failure of a country to adopt or maintain measures of liberalization beyond the 75 per cent level required by the Code itself.[8] Thus a country that found itself deprived of the reciprocal benefits that it might expect from other countries' liberalization, whether due to high tariffs of the other countries or to other factors, could invoke this clause.

The 90 per cent decision was accepted only for 18 months and, while subsequently renewed, was technically provisional in character; thus, the 90 per cent liberalization level was never incorporated in the Code.

The Code permitted derogations in certain cases as measures of defense against harmful actions taken by other members or against the harm that followed from the failure of other members to take certain actions. In general, these defenses took the form of exempting the injured member from the obligation to adhere to the commitment to nondiscriminatory treatment of other members. Relief from the nondiscrimination rule was provided if "a country considered that it is being denied the benefits which it could reasonably expect to derive from the liberalization of trade" because its exports are hindered or blocked by obstacles placed in their path by another member or because commodities that are important in its export trade are not included in the liberalization measures taken by another country (Article 9). A country would be exempted from the requirement of nondiscriminatory treatment also if it "suffers any prejudice as the result of dumping" by another member (Article 10).

In addition to the possibility of the use of the escape clauses, the countries were accorded freedom to withdraw the liberali-

[8] OEEC, *Acts of the Organization,* Decision of Council, July 19, 1956, Vol. XVI, p. 681. The original 90 per cent decision also required countries to remove 10 per cent of the restrictions on private imports in force as of June 30, 1954. This does not seem to have created difficulty for any of the countries.

zation of one product by substituting for it the liberalization of one or more other products, provided that the minimum required percentage of liberalization was maintained. This freedom was limited in principle by the consolidation provision which was intended to bind the countries to maintain the liberalization of the specific commodities that they had freed of quotas in the course of meeting the Code requirement of 60 per cent liberalization in each of three commodity categories (Article 11). The purpose of this provision was to protect exporters from arbitrary changes in the list of liberalized commodities. Deliberalization of consolidated commodities was supposed to be permissible only through the use of one of the escape clauses. For this purpose, one of the bases of derogation provided in Article 3 could be used; in addition the obligation to maintain the liberalization of a consolidated commodity could be waived if "special difficulties due to defense preparations, including those resulting from shortages of raw materials, justify such action" (Article 11).

In the last years of the Code, therefore, each country could consider that the status of import commodities with respect to liberalization commitments fell into three different categories. Each country supposedly[9] had least freedom with respect to those commodities which it had notified the OEEC as comprising the 75 per cent level of liberalization since these were subject to the consolidation provision. Secondly, there were the commodities in the 75 to 90 per cent *tranche* which could be withdrawn by notification without the invocation of an escape clause, provided that substitutions were made. Further-

[9] The word "supposedly" is used because the attempt to enforce the consolidation commitment was abandoned after France and the United Kingdom refused to include all the formerly liberalized items in the restoration of liberalization following their invocation of the balance-of-payments escape clause. However, the consolidation provision was never officially rescinded, and a number of the smaller countries tried to live up to the obligation.

more, if substitutions were inconvenient, broader escape clauses were available for these commodities than for those in the first group. Finally, there were commodities with respect to which the country had complete freedom to maintain quantitative restrictions because they did not have to be liberalized in order to reach the target level of 90 per cent of 1948 trade on private account. This afforded a significant area of protection, which naturally tended to be reserved for those industries that needed it most. In some countries where state trading accounted for a significant share of 1948 imports of foods and feeding stuffs, liberalization of 75 per cent of 1948 imports on private account (all that was required when the 90 per cent level on total imports on private account went into effect) left ample room to protect the products which might have caused difficulties had imports been freed.

USE OF THE SAFEGUARD CLAUSES[10]

Almost every member country of the OEEC invoked some escape clause in the Code of Liberalization or in a Council decision relating to liberalization on some occasion. By far the most common basis for derogation was the balance-of-payments position.

One group of cases simply involved delay in the achievement of a higher level of liberalization newly agreed upon. Norway and Denmark postponed the attainment of the target levels at the 60 per cent, 75 per cent, and 90 per cent rounds; the Netherlands and Germany on the occasion of the establishment of the 75 per cent level; and Austria, Benelux, France, Switzerland, and the United Kingdom when 90 per cent

---

[10] This summary is based chiefly on OEEC *Acts of the Organization*, Vols. 9–19.

liberalization was agreed upon." The bases for a number of these postponements were balance-of-payments grounds, although the delays in the 60 and 75 per cent cases were technically based on Article 3a, which contains only the broader reference to the "economic and financial position" of a country.

The aftermath of the Korean War, with its adverse consequences for the payment balances of many countries, brought a whole series of derogations. A majority of the countries, including Germany, the United Kingdom, and France, invoked safeguard clauses in 1951 and 1952. The German balance-of-payments crisis developed in the later part of 1950, and Germany suspended her measures of liberalization early the next year. The United Kingdom invoked Article 3c at the end of 1951 and did not return to full compliance with OEEC liberalization commitments until mid-1954. France had the worst record of derogations among the large countries. She invoked Article 3c early in 1952 and did not withdraw its invocation for three years, although she did take some steps to ease restrictions before the end of this period. France again resorted to the safeguard clauses in 1957 when she suspended liberalization entirely; she resorted liberalization at the 90 per cent level on January 1, 1959, when the Common Market actually began to operate.

Another group of cases related to countries that were regarded as having "structural" deficits—Greece, Iceland, Turkey, and Spain. These countries were treated as special cases, being granted exemptions or waivers during much or all of

---

" In some cases the safeguard clause was invoked because a country felt it could not achieve the liberalization target in one of the three import categories. Benelux, for example, established the 90 per cent over-all level, but felt unable to reach the 75 per cent liberalization that the 90 per cent decision required for agricultural products. Steering Board document dated April 23, 1956.

the period of their association with the OEEC. Each was involved in a joint program of action with the OEEC in which the Organization provided financial aid and technical advice to aid in the achievement of the internal financial stability that was necessary to enable it to meet its liberalization commitments.

Virtually no use was made of the escape clause in Article 3b which provided for derogations in case of "serious economic disturbance." Apparently, this was due in no small part to the fear that the establishment of a precedent involving the use of this clause might open up a Pandora's box in the form of escape actions on behalf of a whole series of individual industries in various countries. The clause was actually invoked by Ireland in 1952 when that country withdrew liberalization of motor truck bodies and certain yarns. The argument for these actions was not impressive and the Council decision, taken on the basis of the recommendations of the Steering Board, was to deny the validity of the case for motor truck bodies and to permit withdrawal of the yarns with the proviso that other commodities be substituted for them in order that the then required 75 per cent level of liberalization be maintained. The decision, which Ireland accepted, thus avoided reference to Article 3b. The use of 3b was avoided also by Norway, which refrained from the liberalization of tankers on balance-of-payments grounds. (Tankers constituted 13 per cent of Norway's 1948 imports on private account.)

There were a few escape actions on grounds of "national importance" or "equity," bases of derogation which were provided in the Council decision relating to 90 per cent liberalization. The "national importance" justification was cited by Switzerland in its derogation of the obligations to liberalize the food and fodder category to the 75 per cent level. Switzerland took the position that the protection of its agriculture was required by two of its basic national policies: (1) the maintainance of a balance between the rural and urban elements in its economy, and (2) the maintainance of an adequate food supply independent of external sources of supply in order to support its position of permanent neutrality and independence. Switzerland had instituted a three-phase system of import controls for fruits and vegetables, the continuation of which made the derogation necessary. Imports were unrestricted during the season in which there was no home production, then admitted in reduced amounts as home production began to come to market, and finally suspended altogether during the season in which home production could satisfy demand. Thus, the system guaranteed market priority to home production and allowed imports to satisfy the balance of demand. While the Organization conceded the right of Switzerland to invoke the escape clause, there was concern about the requirement in the clause that the derogating country take steps for progressive liberalization. Since the Swiss declared that their policy was not to encourage the expansion of home production except as a result of increasing productivity, it was anticipated that imports would benefit from the growing market for fruits and vegetables that might be expected to accompany the rise in Swiss incomes. The Organization accepted this prospect as meeting the requirement of progressive liberalization, especially as there was some evidence of increases in the importation of vegetables. It was suggested that the system be extended to all member countries on a nondiscriminatory basis, that the authorities of the exporting countries be consulted on the timing of the three phases, and that Switzerland undertake not to administer the system less liberally as time progressed. The Swiss accepted these suggestions.

The most important case involving the notion of equity was brought up by Denmark. Throughout most of the period of

the liberalization program Denmark felt that certain circumstances operated to deprive her of the reciprocal benefits that
she might legitimately expect. One key element was that the
processed agricultural products which were important among
her exports were often excluded from liberalization, sometimes
by virtue of being in the state trading sector and in other cases
simply as a result of being left unliberalized. In addition, the
high tariffs maintained on these products by certain countries
prevented the Danes from benefiting from increased trade even
when liberalization was extended to them. These factors
played a role in the invocation by Denmark of escape clauses
in 1951 and they were the main basis for Denmark's refusal
to move to 90 per cent liberalization on grounds of lack of
"equity." Denmark's complaint was never really satisfied,
although she eventually met the obligation to liberalize to the
90 per cent level.

The Organization had more success in settling a number of
cases in which countries invoked or threatened to invoke an
escape clause as a measure of retaliation against another
country. Sweden, for example, withdrew liberalization of nylon
stockings from Italy on grounds of dumping, invoking the provisions of Article 10. After an investigation which included a
study by independent experts, the Steering Board found that
the Swedish charge was not justified and Sweden withdrew
her invocation of Article 10.[12] In another case Switzerland
placed quotas on automobiles and certain other French goods,
retaliating under Article 9 for the alleged failure of France to
extend the benefits of liberalization to her. At the urging of the
Steering Board, the matter was settled by bilateral negotiation.

All in all, the number of derogations over the 10 or 12 years
of the liberalization program appears to have been quite

---

[12] This case, like some others, was also considered in GATT. See
Chapter 2.

modest. Certainly, little or no use was made of most of the safeguard clauses; only the balance-of-payments basis was employed with any frequency. We shall consider the significance of this fact after examining the way in which the escape clauses were administered.

ADMINISTRATION OF THE SAFEGUARD CLAUSES

Member countries were generally free to invoke the safeguard clauses by unilateral action. While the mechanisms called into play by such a step varied somewhat according to the provision invoked, they usually included the requirement of notification of the derogation to the Organization with a statement of the reasons therefore, review by the Organization both upon initial notification and at periodic intervals thereafter, and the search for measures—some recommended to the country involved and others to its sister nations—to make it possible for the country to meet its liberalization obligations at the earliest possible moment.

Following the extensive use of the balance-of-payments escape clause in 1951 and 1952, a series of amendments was adopted designed to bring the use of this basis for derogation under greater control. Henceforth, countries invoking Article 3c were to endeavor to restore liberalization at least to the 60 per cent level within 12 months, and to the 75 per cent level in 18 months. More systematic procedures were also established for the reporting by the derogating country of its past measures and future plans for the restoration of liberalization, including internal measures necessary to achieve balance-of-payments equilibrium; the strengthened clauses also dealt with review and recommendations by the Organization.

Another set of amendments adopted in 1954 was designed to ensure that the burden of derogations did not fall too heavily upon any one country or any one economic sector. Three principles were established to guide countries derogating on balance-of-payments grounds : (1) The trade restrictions should not reduce imports of a limited range of commodities to a very low level, while imports of other goods were left at a high level. (2) Restrictions on imports not kept at a high level should be as uniform as possible. (3) The sector of imports which had never been liberalized should not receive more favorable treatment than the sector for which liberalization was suspended. These principles made it difficult or impossible for a country to confine new restrictions mainly to luxury products.

The Organization could, in principle, disapprove the invocation or continued use of a safeguard clause. In such an event the country would have been required forthwith to conform to the Code or other Council decision regarding liberalization. In actual fact, however, disapproval authority rested with Council, the decision-making body of the Organization, which functioned according to the unanimity principle.[13] Since each member country was represented on the Council, it had in effect the power to veto a decision unfavorable to it. However, this power was seldom, if ever, used. The whole philosophy of the members of the OEEC was to avoid having matters come to the point of a Council vote unless unanimous agreement had been attained.

The efficacy of the Code did not rest, therefore, upon binding legal commitments which the countries were not free to waive in actual practice. Rather it rested upon reciprocity and self-interest and, on the basis of these motives, upon arrangements that were designed to enable the Organization and member countries, functioning both individually and through

---

[13] For a discussion of the unanimity rule in the OEEC, see Elkin, *op. cit.*, pp. 115–123.

the Organization, to bring pressure on any given country to live up to the spirit of the Code.

A key role in this process was played by the Steering Board for Trade, which was established in 1952 as a restricted technical committee. This group was given broad responsibilities for reporting to the Council on trade matters; it was responsible for the first and perhaps most important stage of the process of review and examination of the cases involving derogations, and for the formulation of the appropriate recommendations to the Council. The Steering Board consisted of seven members "chosen by reason of the knowledge they have of problems of commercial policy and of the personal standing which they have within the Organization or in their respective countries." They were appointed by the Council from persons nominated by the countries for one-year terms subject to reappointment (Article 35). Each member designated an alternate, subject to the approval of Council.

As the system actually worked out, the Steering Board was characterized by continuity of membership, two members having served during the entire period of its existence, and others for long periods. While each member was supposed to serve in his capacity as an expert, care was taken to spread the appointments of members and alternates among different countries. A national of each of the four large large countries of the OEEC (France, Germany, Italy, and the United Kingdom) was always to be found among its members, as was a Scandinavian; a Belgian chaired the group throughout its existence, giving it distinguished leadership. The members were high-level officials of their governments, usually in residence at their respective capitals rather than in Paris. The work of the Board was organized for its meetings by the alternates, who were usually members of their country's permanent delegation to the OEEC, and therefore resident in Paris. Staff work was provided by the Trade and Payments Division of the Secretariat.

The small size of the Steering Board, its semipermanent membership and expert character—all similar to the Managing Board of the European Payments Union[14] established a couple of years earlier—gave it advantages over both the plenary groups and the *ad hoc* restricted groups that had been used to cope with trade questions in the early stages of the trade liberalization program. Its size and continuous membership enabled it to provide effective leadership. Its expert character gave it a certain degree of independence and yet the governmental connections and experience of its members prevented them from departing from the political realities of a given situation. The Steering Board obviously could not function by issuing orders to a derogating country, or even by recommending that the Council issue orders. However, while chary of directives, the Board did not hesitate to diagnose a situation with a degree of candor which would have been impossible for a representative body. For example, in reporting upon the French invocation of Article 3c in 1957, the Board said :

to reimpose quantitative import restrictions cannot, under any circumstances, provide a lasting solution to France's present difficulties . . . the sole remedy for such difficulties is a vigorous policy of reform based on measures to restore internal financial stability. Import restrictions, on the other hand, although they may be a palliative, may well increase the gravity of the problem by accustoming producers to the idea of artificial protection, by contributing to a rise in prices, and by rendering the necessary adjustments more difficult. In particular, the Steering Board cannot rule out the possibility that

---

[14] For an appraisal of the role of the Managing Board, see R. Triffin, *op. cit.*, pp. 177–179.

the administration of restrictions may be influenced by protectionist pressures.[15]

The work of the Steering Board involved frequent consultations with the trade officials of each country, but for the most part its written statements were confined to reports to the Council. Occasionally, however, it communicated its views directly to the country concerned. On one instance, for example, the Steering Board instructed its chairman to write to the minister of commerce of one of the Member countries to the effect that machinery, omitted from a recently announced list of liberalized products, should have been included both to conform to the recommendations of the OEEC, and to serve the best interests of the country's stabilization program.[16]

While the Steering Board tried to influence derogating countries to meet their over-all liberalization obligations under the Code, it was perhaps more effective in influencing the way in which derogating countries managed their import programs within a given degree of restrictiveness. The Steering Board sought, with considerable success, to ensure equitable treatment for all parties affected by deliberalization measures and to obtain adherence to the principles established to guide countries derogating for balance-of-payments reasons. Thus, in the French case cited above, the Board made suggestions to the French Government, which were favorably received, regarding the treatment of goods in transit at the time the new restrictions were announced, of pending import applications, and of outstanding contracts.

In many instances the Steering Board was the focal point for working out compromises, sometimes involving the attempt

---

[15] *Interim Report by the Steering Board for Trade to the Council* (Document dated June 24, 1957).

[16] Steering Board document dated June 13, 1960. The reply of the minister stated that the liberalization of machinery had been withheld pending a tariff revision, and that it would be announced shortly.

to minimize the degree of departure by a particular country from the obligations of the Code, other times involving the settlement of disputes between two countries related to the liberalization program of one of them or to the import program of a derogating country.

The Steering Board's assessment of the merits of a particular case tended to have great weight in the political arena of the Council. Its recommendations appear to have been regarded with respect by the large as well as the small countries and the Council appears never to have rejected a unanimous proposal of the Board. If the Board did not achieve quite the prestige and authority of its older sibling, the Managing Board of the EPU, it should be remembered that the Steering Board, unlike its brother financial board, had no financial credits to advance. Also, matters of trade touched sensitive political nerves in every country in the form of interest groups in commerce, industry, agriculture, and labor, while the financial problems dealt with in the EPU concerned mainly central banks, and were more technical and remote from the public. This sensitivity of trade questions to the political situation explains why the effectiveness of the Steering Board diminished after the split between the Six and the Seven.

A parallel Committee for Invisible Transactions carried out the same functions with respect to current invisibles and capital movements as the Steering Board did for commodity trade. Liberalization of the invisibles proceeded on an item-by-item basis; this was in contrast to the technique of the commodity Code which, by operating in terms of percentage tranches, left each country free to choose its own combination of items. Thus, individual countries often found it necessary to enter reservations with respect to particular invisibles, and there were many more reservations attached to the decisions liberalizing the invisibles than to those governing visibles. However, the reservations were subject to annual review "directed to making suitable proposals designed to assist member countries to withdraw their reservations" (Article 24 bis). The work of the Committee for Invisibles consisted much more in trying to do away with these "escapes in advance" than in coping with invocation of the actual escape clauses in the Code. Indeed, possibly because of the existence of these reservations, escape clauses were less frequently invoked in the case of invisibles than with respect to commodity trade. By 1960 most of the reservations regarding current invisibles had been withdrawn and liberalization was nearly complete, the main remaining restrictions being in the fields of insurance and transportation.

EVALUATION

The strategy of the OEEC liberalization program can be said to have been marked by three key elements : the principle of reciprocity, the use of time to buy conformance, and the effective organization of community pressure to obtain conformance.[17]

The principle of reciprocity was a foundation stone in the entire process of the liberalization of trade and payments in western Europe. Without the expectation that other countries would increase their imports from it, no country would have been able or willing to go so far so rapidly in dropping trade barriers. As already noted, failure to obtain real reciprocity was one of the grounds which a country could use to obtain relief from its liberalization obligations. On the other hand, the Code set forth the principle that a country invoking a safeguard clause would as long as it conformed to the notification and reporting procedures that were established,

---

[17] For an evaluation of the OEEC from a more general standpoint, see Elkin, *op. cit.*

continue to enjoy the benefits of liberalization by the other countries (Article 6). This principle of nonretaliation was necessary, of course, to avoid a spiral of increasing restriction following the invocation of a safeguard clause by any one country. It may also have served, in view of the emphasis on reciprocity in the program, to increase the pressure on members to avoid derogations or to limit their duration.

If each stage of liberalization had been delayed until every country was politically and economically prepared to accept it, the process of liberalization would have been very slow indeed. Therefore, at each point, the decision was made to move ahead with the liberalization program even though it was understood that some countries would have to invoke an escape clause to postpone their adherence to the new measures. The focus of effort then turned upon the attempt to get the lagging countries, who meanwhile benefited from the increased liberalization of the others, to attain the liberalization to which they had agreed in principle. The same tactic of gradualism in righting matters was applied to withdrawals of liberalization, whether for balance-of-payments reasons, lack of reciprocity, or other reasons.

The power that can be exerted by the pressures of other countries varies with such factors as the number of countries included in the group, their feeling of solidarity, and the size of the country whose affairs are involved. A number of elements combined to give the OEEC countries an unusually strong feeling of solidarity. Among them were a common heritage, geographical propinquity, and social and economic interdependence. More specifically, their recent common experience in sharing first the ravages of war, then the common objective of postwar reconstruction, and, to some extent, a common pool of resources in the form of American aid, developed an *esprit de corps* that remained a binding force until the issue of European integration brought about the split between the Six and the Seven. The result was that community pressure was an effective force in bringing about conformance to the Code of Liberalization.

Small countries obviously felt this influence more strongly than large countries. Their loyalty to the Organization and their adherence to its rules may also have been enhanced by the way in which it strengthened their position *vis-à-vis* the larger countries. In addition, the governments of small countries, perhaps more than those of large countries, sometimes found it convenient to cite international obligations under the Code to domestic interests pressing for protection. Finally, certain small, or at least less-developed, countries which lacked an experienced civil-service staff trained to cope with economic problems turned to the OEEC for advice and guidance. They received technical aid from the OEEC secretariat and advice from the experts of the more advanced countries who served on the various OEEC committees and boards concerned with trade, payments, and other technical matters.

Even the large countries could not be indifferent to the continued criticism of their policies in the OEEC. At the very least, a large country, such as France for example, was led to modify its programs so as to ease the impact of its restrictionist measures upon one country or another that claimed it was bearing an undue portion of the burden. It is a more open question whether France, which utilized the escape clauses more than any other large country, was led to adopt more liberal policies as a result of its membership in the OEEC. There is some, but far from unanimous, opinion in OEEC circles that the OEEC process of review and examination— i.e., "confrontation"—did have such an effect. In this view, the existence of the OEEC as a forum for mutual evaluation and criticism sometimes helped the technicians to persuade political leaders to take measures that might be unpopular at home, but which were necessary for balance of payments or other external reasons.

There appears to be little doubt, however, that the most effective work of the Organization in influencing the policy of member countries occurred in those cases in which the Organization was able through the European Payments Union or the European Fund to provide financial aid to a country. The most important recent illustration was the occasion in early 1958 when the Organization joined the International Monetary Fund and the United States Government in advancing credits of $655 million to France after receiving explicit undertakings from the French Government to adopt fiscal and monetary measures that would curb inflation and bring about a balance-of-payments equilibrium. The improvement in the French position enabled France to withdraw her 1957 invocation of safeguard clauses and to establish liberalization at the present 90 per cent level by January 1, 1959, when the first tariff reductions in connection with the establishment of the Common Market became effective. While the immediate initiative and the basic formulation of the reform program seem to have been purely French, the continual criticisms in the OEEC of French policies may have helped induce the French decision to embark upon this course; at the minimum, the OEEC confrontations made the French clearly aware of the kinds of measures that they would have to propose in order to obtain the financial support necessary to start a stabilization program. In other cases where the extension of financial aid was contingent upon commitments with respect to financial stabilization and eventual trade liberalization, such as Iceland and Spain, the formulation of the program seems to have been less unilateral.

It is notable that little need was felt to provide for hardships suffered by particular industries in the course of liberalization. There is no reference in the Code to the possibility of the expansion of some industries within each country and the contraction of others as a consequence of the growth of international specialization that might be expected as a result of the freeing of trade. Neither is there any reference to the problems of adjustment on the part of individual firms and workers. The safeguard clauses that come the closest to providing lines of defense for particular industries [18] were not drafted so as to encourage their use for such a purpose. One cited "national importance" and the other a "serious economic disturbance in the member country concerned" as grounds for derogation; neither was expressed in terms of hardship or damage to a particular industry and, as we have seen, their invocation to this end was discouraged and, in the main, avoided.

How may the absence of a concern about injury to domestic industries be reconciled with a genuine intention to make trade freer? The question is the more pertinent since there is little evidence of repeated or extensive complaints by business groups in any country about the effect of the trade liberalization program upon their interests. Nowhere, for example, is found the story of the political mobilization of forces pro and con that characterizes the successive renewals of the Reciprocal Trade Agreements Act in the United States.

There are several ways of explaining this. Perhaps the best explanation lies in economic expansion. There is no denying that in the circumstances of 1948–50 a substantial restoration of trade was possible before very much damage was done to well-established industries. Subsequently, the large increases in real output and in the absorption of real produce in the

---

[18] Aside from those related to defense against unfair practices such as dumping.

OEEC countries [19] afforded a further opportunity for the expansion of trade without driving local industries out of business. These factors seem to have been counted on by at least some of those responsible for the establishment and development of the program.

In addition to the impact of general economic expansion, there is some evidence of a tendency for a pattern of specialization to develop in terms of types of products within broad branches of industry rather than specialization in terms of whole branches.[20] The relative stability of the industrial structure in the various countries thus may tend to conceal the increased specialization that might have occurred.

Another facet of the explanation, at least for a number of countries, was the widespread recognition in business and labor as well as in government circles of the national advantage in the pursuit of a policy of trade reciprocity in western Europe. In these situations the government was able to press business to adapt itself to forthcoming measures of liberalization, either by shifting the alternative lines of production or lowering costs to meet foreign competition. A common technique was to increase import quotas gradually, with the consequence that the quotas eventually became so generous that *de facto* liberalization was in fact achieved. Sometimes the final step of formal liberalization was delayed or avoided in order to maintain the right to protect the domestic industry in case of need; in other cases, particularly for the Scandinavian countries, the motive in delaying formal liberalization was to retain bargaining power *vis-à-vis* the import quotas and tariffs of the other member countries.

---

[19] For the OEEC countries as a whole, industrial production rose by 75 per cent between 1950 and 1960. *OEEC Statistical Bulletins, General Statistics,* November, 1960, Part II, p. 2.

[20] See below, Chapter 5.

However, while a number of the marginal industries that had sprung up in various countries under the isolation of the war and immediate postwar periods—the "ash-tray" industries as the Danes called them—quickly fell by the wayside with the first breath of international competition, other casualties of the liberalization program appear to have been quite infrequent. The margins of protection that were left were sufficiently high to minimize the possibility of injury to a given industry in a given country. First, the quotas in the unliberalized sector still were available to protect the most vulnerable industries. Secondly, protection was afforded by tariffs, which were not only reduced by the OEEC trade liberalization program, but were in some cases, including Norway, Switzerland, Denmark, and Spain, actually revised upwards to take account of the possible effects of the removal of quotas. Thus a hard core of protection remained which the liberalization program never touched, and this, too, helps to account for the relative smoothness with which it worked despite the absence of broad safeguards for specific industries.

While this limitation must be recognized and while it was a factor which helped to turn the movement toward a single European market into another channel, there can be little doubt that the OEEC was effective in the dismantling of quantitative restrictions over private trade between its members.[21] Aside from the rising liberalization percentages, which are not without their misleading aspects, intra-OEEC trade expanded more than the trade of the OEEC members with outside countries.[22]

---

[21] There is wide agreement on a favorable evaluation of the OEEC trade liberalization program. See, for example, Boyer and Sallé, *op. cit.,* pp. 201–207, and I. Frank, *The European Common Market,* New York, 1961, pp. 68–71.

[22] OEEC *Statistical Bulletins, Foreign Trade,* Series A, October, 1960, pp. 3–4.

In any case the ingenuity and inventiveness of those responsible for the work of the OEEC produced techniques that are worth the study of persons concerned with the design of international economic arrangements.[23] In particular the formal freedom to invoke safeguard clauses unilaterally was linked to the effective organization of community pressure for adherence to commitments. An important role in process was played by restricted semipermanent committees composed of high-level men drawn from governments, but acting independently in their capacity as experts. The most efficacious pressures on individual countries were exerted when financial aid was linked directly to trade practices. Progress was hastened by willingness to allow some countries more time than others to reach a desired goal, even though the laggards recieved the immediate benefits of the measures taken by those who met the commitments promptly. The device of making commitments to liberalize more binding for a basic tranche of imports, of permitting easier escape measures for other tranches and of allowing countries freedom to continue restrictions on a segment of their imports, clearly watered down the effectiveness of the program. It seems probable, however, that this was the price that had to be paid for agreement, and for the progress that was achieved.

---

[23] Cf. other evaluations in Political and Economic Planning, *European Organisations*, London 1959, pp. 43–126; and Triffin, *op. cit.*, pp. 246–251.

Chapter 4

The European Coal and Steel Community

BACKGROUND

LIKE THE OEEC, the European Coal and Steel Community (ECSC) had its genesis in a statement by a minister of foreign affairs. In May, 1950, Robert Schuman, French Minister of Foreign Affairs, proposed on behalf of his government that French and German production of coal and steel be placed under a common authority in an organization open to the participation of other European countries. His declaration left no doubt of the political inspiration that motivated the proposal. Faced with the inevitability of German economic revival and rearmament, the path chosen by the French was intended to put an end to Franco-German hostility by binding the two countries together in the key industries that provide the sinews of war. The pooling of the coal and steel industries, Schuman said, would make war between France and Germany "not only unthinkable, but materially impossible." It would represent "the first concrete groundwork for a European federation indispensable to the preservation of peace." However, the economic aspects of the proposal were important ends in themselves and not merely the means through which political objectives were to be achieved. Schuman spoke of the need for the modernization of production and the improvement in the quality of output, of the ferment that would be introduced by the establishment of a larger community, and of the rationalization of production and increased productivity that could be obtained through planned investment and the use of funds to facilitate the reconversion of industry. There

167

were also more immediate French economic interests underlying the plan—notably the French reliance upon Ruhr coal,
and perhaps less pressing, the prospects of overproduction in
steel and the need for export markets.[1]

The French proposals, which reflected the thinking of Jean
Monnet, fell upon soil that had been prepared by a widely
supported movement for the political and economic integration of western Europe. The Federal Republic of Germany in
particular welcomed the French initiative because the proposal would serve some important objectives of German
policy. The German Government sought to identify Germany
closely with western Europe as an equal partner with the
other major powers; here for the first time since the end of the
war, a major Allied power was offering the Germans genuine
political equality. The coal-and-steel pool would also hasten
the end of Allied controls over Germany industry. Once
German assent was secured, the French were eager to avoid
the dilution of the supranational character of the projected
organization. They requested prior acceptance of the principles of the Schuman statement by the other governments
invited to join the negotiations. England refused, owing
mainly to an unwillingness to enter any European arrangement that departed from the unanimity principle of the OEEC
and thus involved a surrender of sovereignty.[2] Germany, Italy,
the Netherlands, Belgium, and Luxemburg quickly accepted,
and the Treaty was negotiated in a remarkably short time,
considering the enormous complexity of the matters with
which it was concerned and the range of policy questions that

---

[1] The quotations from Schuman's speech are taken from his preface to
P. Reuter's authoritative *La Communauté Européenne du Charbon et de
l'Acier*, Paris, 1953. For an extensive account of the origins of the Coal
and Steel Community, which has been drawn upon here, see W. Diebold,
Jr., *The Schuman Plan*, New York, 1959. For the early history of the
ECSC, see also E. B. Haas, *The Uniting of Europe*, London, 1958.

[2] Diebold, *op. cit.* pp. 48–60.

had to be decided. The implementation of the proposal of May, 1950, required a set of documents running to more than 130 printed pages. The treaty contained 100 articles and the important Convention Containing the Transitional Provisions, almost a treaty in itself, took more than 30 articles. There were, in addition, four protocols, including one on the code of the court of justice, and an exchange of letters between France and Germany relative to the status of the Saar. All these documents were ready for signature in April, 1951, and the Treaty and related instruments were forwarded to the countries for ratification. Ratification was accorded in all the countries by comfortable legislative margins, although not without vocal opposition, and the 50-year Treaty came into force in July, 1952.

The common market

The Treaty provides for the establishment of a common market in coal and steel through the elimination of quantitative restrictions and tariffs. A single Community-wide market, which is open to buyers and sellers from all member countries on equal terms, is encouraged through the prohibition of state subsidies and the outlawing of discriminatory practices by coal and steel enterprises. The common market is sought as the means of achieving a more rational distribution of production, economic expansion, and rising standards of living. The interests of consumers as well as of producers are taken into account; thus, the institutions of the Community are charged with ensuring regular supplies for the common market at the lowest possible prices. All these and related objectives are to be pursued "while safeguarding the continuity of employment and avoiding the creation of fundamental and persistent disturbances in the economies of member states" (Article 2).[3]

The Community is to achieve its purposes as much as possible through informing, persuading, and mediating on the one hand, and through the provision of financial assistance on the other hand. Although it is equiped with considerable direct powers, it is to "take direct action with respect to production and the operation of the market only when circumstances make it absolutely necessary" (Article 5).

The Treaty does not, however, make a clear and unambiguous choice between reliance on the market mechanism and *dirigisme*. In the view of one authority, this matter can only be determined by the context of the times in which the Treaty is applied.[4] In the opinion of another, the Treaty takes competition as the starting point, but provides for intervention in order to make sure that competition is "fair" and to avoid the undesirable social consequences that unfettered competition might produce (e.g., with respect to the regularity of employment and wage levels).[5] For the promotion of competition, heavy reliance is placed upon the requirement of price publication and the principle of nondiscrimination. The first half-dozen years of operation of the common market in coal and steel seemed to indicate a desire on the part of the Community authorities to promote competition, but they do not appear to have had any great success in leading reluctant industries to change long-established patterns.[6]

---

[3] This and subsequent quotations from the Treaty and the Transitional Convention are based on an English translation published by the High Authority of the Coal and Steel Community.

[4] P. Uri, cited in A. Philip, "Rapport Presenté au Nom du Conseil Economique," *Communauté Européenne du Charbon et de l'Acier*, Conseil Economique, Etude et Travaux No. 21, Paris, 1952, p. 116.

[5] Reuter, *op. cit.*, pp. 141–145.

[6] L. Lister, *Europe's Coal and Steel Community* (New York, 1960), pp. 403–405.

Institutions of the Community

The Community is partly supranational and partly intergovernmental. Its supranational features may be summarized
as follows: (1) Important powers, such as the authority to
define and enforce rules of "fair" competition and the right
to impose production quotas in times of oversupply and
rationing in times of undersupply, have been transferred from
the governments to the Community. (2) Many of these powers
give the Community direct access to business enterprises. (3)
Certain limits are placed upon the freedom of governments to
exercise their powers even in some areas which were specifically left reserved to their jurisdiction; thus, in the field of
transportation, generally a matter for national rather than
Community competence, nondiscriminatory rates must be
extended to coal and steel shipments regardless of country of
origin or destination. (4) The Community is independent of
the governments which created it in a number of important
respects in addition to those already mentioned; for example,
it is financially independent and also the institutions of the
Community can amend the Treaty without formal reference
to the governments.

The intergovernmental aspects of the Community have, as
we shall see, emerged more strongly than might have been
anticipated from an analysis of the Treaty. They stem largely
from the ability of the governments through the Council to
check the exercise of power by the Community and from the
broad political and economic authority of the governments to
influence the environment within which the coal and steel
industries operate. In general, the supranational powers of the
Community are more notable with respect to enterprises; its
powers over the governments are relatively weak.

The institutions of the Community include a High

Authority, a Special Council, a Court of Justice, and a Common Assembly. The provisions governing the two latter institutions were subsequently revised so as to enable them to serve the European Economic Community and the European Atomic Energy Community (Euratom) as well as the Coal and Steel Community. In addition, a Consultative Committee, consisting of 30 to 51 members, equally divided among experts chosen from producers, workers, and dealers and consumers, serves in an advisory capacity to the High Authority; the High Authority is obliged to consult the committee in certain circumstances.

Executive functions in the Coal and Steel Community are vested largely in the High Authority. The nine members of the High Authority are chosen for their "general competence," and they are to "exercise their functions in complete independence, in the general interest of the Community." They are neither to "solicit nor accept instructions from any government or from any organization." Each signatory agrees to respect the "supranational character" of their functions and "not to seek to influence the members of the High Authority in the execution of their duties" (Article 9). The members serve six-year terms, which after the initial period are staggered so that one-third of the membership is renewed each year. The governments and the remaining members alternate in the designation of new members (Article 10). The High Authority takes its decisions by vote of a majority of its members (Article 13). It may issue *decisions,* which are "binding in all their details"; *recommendations,* which are binding with respect to objectives but leave the choice of means to those to whom the action is addressed; or *opinions,* which are not binding (Article 14). The functions of the High Authority presume a high level of *expertise* on the part of its members. In addition to ordinary executive duties, it is called upon to act as banker, arbitrator, judge, and quasi-legislator.[7] However, virtually all of its actions are subject to the checks of the other institutions of the Community, and these, perhaps, should be described briefly before discussing the powers of the High Authority.

The Council is composed of one representative from each country who must be a member of his country's government. This body was added to the original French plan, largely upon the initiative of the Dutch and the Belgians, to provide a check on the powers of the High Authority.[8] The Council is also given the task of "harmonizing the action of the High Authority and that of the governments which are responsible for the general economic policy of their countries" (Article 26). In most cases where its agreement is required, the Council may give its concurrence to a proposal of the High Authority by an absolute majority of its members, including at least one from a major producing country.[9] This type of majority is generally required also for other kinds of Council

---

[7] Cf. Reuter, *op. cit.,* pp. 83–84, and H. L. Mason, *The European Coal and Steel Community,* The Hague, 1955, p. 74. There is some disagreement with respect to the legislative functions of the High Authority. The French negotiating delegation considered that the Treaty itself fulfilled the legislative function and that the duties of the High Authority were confined to the development of administrative regulations to apply the Treaty. On the other hand, it has been argued that the scope left by the Treaty in some areas, as for example in the definition of unfair pricing practices, is so broad that the task of interpretation of them is at least partially legislative. See *Rapport de la Délégation Française sur le Traité et la Convention Signés à Paris le 18 Avril 1951,* Paris (undated), p. 23; and Mason, *ibid.*

[8] Reuter, *op. cit.,* p. 52; Diebold, *op. cit.,* p. 63.

[9] The treaty does not actually use the phrase "major producing country" but refers to countries producing at least 20 per cent of the Community's output of coal and steel. Only France and Germany met this criterion. (After France ceded the Saar to Germany in 1957, the criterion was changed to one-sixth in a special treaty modifying the Treaty of Paris in this one respect.) If there is an even division of votes and the High Authority persists in placing the matter before the Council, the representatives of both major producers must assent.

decisions (Article 28). In certain cases, however, unanimity or, less frequently, a two-thirds or five-sixths vote is specified.

The Assembly apparently was added as something of an afterthought on the part of the French. It is not clear whether the motive was to create at least in rudimentary form a European parliament that would provide a future source of support for the development of European integration, or merely to offset the criticism that the proposed institutions would represent a supranational technocracy beyond democratic control.[10] In any case, the Assembly is a relatively weak parliamentary body which has few legislative powers and none whatsoever in the key area of finances. Aside from the right to question the High Authority (Article 23) and the requirement of its approval of amendments to the Treaty under one of the procedures for making amendments (Article 95), the only power accorded the Assembly by the Treaty is the right—too drastic to be of great use—to force the resignation of the High Authority as a body by passing a motion of censure against its general report by a two-thirds vote (Article 24).

It has been suggested that the weakness of the Assembly and the consequent need to reply upon other checks on the powers of the High Authority account in part for the extensive powers given to the Court of Justice.[11] The function of the Court is to protect the rights of individuals against illegal acts, particularly by the High Authority, and to maintain the balance of powers specified in the Treaty among the several institutions of the Community and between the Community and the governments.[12] Disputes between the states about the

---

[10] Reuter, *op. cit.*, p. 52; Diebold, *op. cit.*, pp. 62–63, 601–603.

[11] Mason, *op. cit.*, p. 40.

[12] M. Lagrange, "Le Rôle de la Cour de Justice des Communautés Européennes," *Les Problèmes Juridiques et Economiques du Marché Commun*, Colloque des Facultés de Droit, Lille (Juin 1959), Paris, 1960, pp. 41–53.

provisions of the Treaty also fall within the jurisdiction of the Court.

The Court may annul decisions and recommendations of the High Authority "on the grounds of lack of legal competence, major violations of procedure, violation of the Treaty, or of any rule of law relating to its application, or abuse of power" (Article 33). Such annulment may be the consequence of an appeal by a state or the Council or an enterprise, but the latter has the right of appeal only against individual decisions and recommendations affecting it which involve an abuse of power.[13] The right of appeal extends to a "tacit negative decision presumed to result" from a failure of the High Authority to act (Article 35).

Furthermore, there are important kinds of cases in which the Court is not limited to questions of law but is permitted or even obliged to consider questions of fact or economic circumstance. These cases include those involving allegations of abuse of power or misapplication of the Treaty, fines against enterprises, sanctions against states, dissolution of combinations, and the existence of a fundamental disturbance of sufficient importance to warrant special measures. Perhaps the extent to which the Court may be concerned with substantive economic matters explains why the Treaty, by not requiring a legal background for the judges, permits the governments to appoint persons wiith qualifications in other fields, such as economics and business as well as jurists.

Grounds of abuse of power provide the most readily available basis for appeals involving conflicts of interest between

---

[13] Reuter points out that individuals or firms may be able to circumvent the limitation on their right to appeal by refusal to execute a general order of the High Authority. This is the case since any penalty imposed by the High Authority is subject to an appeal to the Court in which the petitioners may contest the legality of the High Authority's decision or recommendation which they have allegedly violated. (Article 36.) Reuter, *op. cit.*, p. 90.

the Community on the one hand and individuals, firms, or governments on the other.[14] The concept of abuse of power (*détournement de pouvoir*) was taken from French administrative law; French practice would oblige the Court not only to examine the objective circumstances but also the motives of the High Authority.[15]

The Court may, at the request of the High Authority or of a government, also annul the resolutions of the Assembly and of the Council, but such appeals are limited to "grounds of lack of legal competence or major violations of procedure" (Article 38).

The balance of power

In this set of institutions, it is the High Authority that is without question placed in the role of leader in the operation of the Community and in the formulation of its policy. While subject to rather extensive powers of review by the Court, the High Authority is armed with an impressive array of powers. Some of them it can exercise without any reference to the Consultative Committee or the Council; with respect to others, it must first consult the Consultative Committee or the Council or both; and with regard to a third group of powers, it must obtain the agreement of the Council before exercising them.[16]

The High Authority need not defer to any other institution before using its powers to gather information and issue studies

---

[14] Reuter, *op. cit.*, pp. 90–92.

[15] The French *"détournement de pouvoir"* refers to an act that although within the legal competence of the executor is really undertaken to achieve a purpose other than that authorized by law. Cf. G. Bebr, "The European Coal and Steel Community: A Political and Legal Innovation," *Yale Law Review*, LXIII (November, 1953), 30.

[16] For a fuller account than the summary which follows, see L'Institut des Relations Internationales de Bruxelles, *La Communauté Européenne du Charbon et de l'Acier*, Paris, 1953, pp. 35–53.

and forecasts, to tax coal and steel production within certain limits, to borrow money, to lend money to coal and steel enterprises, to review proposed investment projects of coal and steel enterprises and forbid them access to sources of finance external to the firm, to forbid discriminatory practices and to fine violators, and to prohibit agreements and combinations that do not satisfy certain conditions set forth in the Treaty. In addition, after consultating the Consultative Committee and/or the Council (but without the obligation to obtain their consent), the High Authority may authorize compensation schemes,[17] finance readaptations, define and administer rules regarding "unfair" competitive practices and prices, and fix maximum or minimum prices. In general, financial measures beyond certain limits specified in the Treaty require the agreement of the Council; this is true, for example, of the establishment of the production tax at a rate higher than 1 per cent, and of the use of Community funds for research, for compensation schemes, or for aid to industries related to coal and steel but not actually within the jurisdiction of the Community. Council consent is necessary also for sanctions against the governments and for the exercise of an emergency powers to impose production quotas in cases of oversupply and rationing in cases of undersupply, although the High Authority is somewhat less restricted by the need for Council agreement in the last regard than in the others. As might have been expected from the high cyclical variability of the coal and steel industries, the use of the emergency powers has been an important issue at several points in the brief history of the Community.

Despite this rather formidable list of powers, the precise role of the High Authority could only be determined in the actual operation of the Community. The Treaty provided a

---

[17] Programs in which firms with low costs are taxed to provide subsidies for firms with high costs.

complex structure of power relationships, which, while specifying some general principles and a number of particulars as
well, fell far short of defining the relationships precisely. More
perhaps than many constitutions, the Treaty left the path
open for the several institutions of the Community, the
governments, and the Community's economic interest groups
to work out their own power relationships with rather broad
limits. While these relationships seem to have varied somewhat
from time to time, and may shift again in the future, it
appears that the High Authority has emerged somewhat
weaker relative to the other foci of power than may have been
expected when the Treaty was drafted. There are many
reasons for this, a number of them inherent in the basic
political and economic circumstances of the Community and
its members states.[18]

One proximate cause is the policy of the High Authority
itself. While the High Authority has sometimes acted or tried
to act decisively and while it has consistently defended its
supranational powers in principle, it has tended to follow a
cautious policy in practice. This has involved on the one hand
a rather narrow interpretation of the powers given to it by the
Treaty, and on the other hand efforts to obtain prior agreement and consent from the Council, the governments, and the
economic interest groups concerned, even where it clearly had
the power to act alone. This course can be defended on many
grounds. It has helped to win the confidence of the business
community; it has enabled the High Authority to avoid the
burdensome and intricate task of closely regulating these
complex industries when it was trying to establish the common market and to encourage entrepreneurial initiative after

---

[18] Cf. G. Bebr, "The Balance of Power in the European Communities,"
European Yearbook, Vol. V, The Hague, 1959, pp. 53–75.

many years of government control and cartelization.[19] The High Authority also had to tread carefully with respect to the governments. The governments, through the Council, could prevent the High Authority from exercising some of its key powers, particularly those most useful in emergency situations. In still other areas, including, for example, the implementation of the provisions regarding the mobility of labor, the Treaty left matters largely to the governments to settle rather than for the High Authority to determine. Finally, the limitation of the Community to coal and steel made the Community particularly dependent upon the goodwill and cooperation of the governments. After all, the coal and steel industries had to function in an economic environment which the governments and not the High Authority had the power to influence and alter; exchange rates, money, wages, prices, taxation, foreign trade, and economic growth all represented areas in which government policies inevitably would have important influences upon the coal and steel industries even if these industries were not made the specific objectives of national action. In pursuit of its national objectives, a country could easily find itself frustrating the Community's policy with respect to the coal and steel industries. An illustration of this is provided by the efforts of governments, particularly of France and Germany, to prevent coal and steel prices from increasing in order to help in their fight against inflation. The High Authority complained of the interference of the governments repeatedly, saying on one occasion :

Although Community prices are free, Governments have on a number of occasions, without raising the matter in the Council and without possessing direct powers of their own, exerted considerable influence on them, especially during boom periods. The enterprises are not, of course, legally obligated to respect their Governments' wishes in these

[19] Cf. Diebold, *op. cit.*, pp. 610–619.

matters, but it is often very difficult to do otherwise within
the national economy. This is a serious problem inasmuch as
the long-term expansion of an industry in a given country
may be gravely prejudiced if the industry is called upon to
make sacrifices which are not asked of its competitors in the
Common Market.[20]

Perhaps the basic fact that has molded the establishment of
the actual power structure of the Community is that the
national governments have retained the hard core of political
power even in matters that relate directly to coal and steel.
They have been generally unwilling to surrender policy-making functions in the economic sphere to the High Authority.
As this fact became clearer, membership on the High
Authority became less attractive and it was more difficult to
find men of the same stature as the first presidents (Jean
Monnet and René Meyer) to serve on it. At least in the three
large countries of the Community, the path to the political pin-
nacle for an able and influential political figure continues to lie
along national lines; membership on the High Authority is not
a stepping stone near the top. Although some distinguished
men have served on the High Authority, it might have been
able to take a stronger stand had it had more members of the
first political rank.

The power of the governments in the affairs of the Community have been most directly exercised through the Council.
While the Treaty gives the Council as such the power of
initiative in relatively few cases, the High Authority policy of
consulting the Council on all important matters, whether
required in the Treaty or not,[21] the Council's power over

---

[20] The quotation in the text is from the High Authority's *Eighth
General Report,* p. 13. See also the *Fifth General Report,* pp. 106–108,
129; and *Sixth General Report,* Vol. II, p. 62. Hereafter the general
reports of the High Authority will be referred to solely by number, as for
example, *"Fifth Report."*

[21] Cf. *Sixth Report,* Vol. II, p. 15, for a statement by the High
Authority of this policy.

certain key High Authority actions, and the Council's primacy in the important areas left to the governments have served to enhance its relative position in the power structure of the Community. The result has been to moderate the supranational character of the Community in the direction of an intergovernmental organization. After the advent of General de Gaulle to power in 1958, France, the original advocate of supranational powers, opposed supranationalism and stressed the intergovernmental aspects of the Community.

One authority has pointed out that the Treaty makes a distinction between the governments and the Council, assigning certain powers to the former and others to the latter.[22] Furthermore the Treaty permits the Council to take binding decisions without reference to governments for approval. The distinction between the Council and the governments may prove important, since it provides a means by which a government may concur in a given Community action without having to place the matter before its parliament.

While the Council has limited the exercise of the supranational powers of the High Authority in the coal crisis and in other situations,[23] there are, as in the OEEC situation, strong constraints upon the freedom of a government to press its own views against the sentiments of the others :

the essence of the Council's conception of its own role is not only harmonization of national with High Authority policy, but the attainment and maintenance of consensus among its own members. Consequently, it does *not* regard itself as a continuing diplomatic conference, whose members are free to dissent and to block joint action. While the ministers frequently arrive with firm instructions, it is the essence of the Council's

---

[22] Reuter, *op. cit.*, p. 63.

[23] However, Mason reports that Council functioned in the first few years as an instrument through which the range of *de facto* powers of the High Authority was extended. *Op. cit.*, p. 51.. Cf. also Haas, *op. cit.*, p. 490.

code that these may eventually be changed or even disregarded under the pressure of other views. National interests are also compromised; they are never maintained in the face of the "atmosphere of cooperation" which prevails. Two techniques for achieving this atmosphere are singled out by M. Rey: the tendency of the Benelux delegations and to conciliate clashing French and German aspirations and the determination not to adjourn until unanimous consent has been obtained. These techniques tend all the more to be successful since members of the High Authority attend and participate in almost all sessions of the Council.[24]

This happy situation has not always been maintained, for it was often easier for the members of the Council to agree to reject proposals of the High Authority or to restrain the High Authority from policy making in a given area[25] than to find solutions which they could all support. Thus the High Authority recently complained that:

where the Governments have had to try to reach agreement by the traditional rules of international negotiation it has often proved extremely difficult to work out a solution which meets the requirements of the Treaty. Thus, it is disappointing to note that two years after the expiry of the transition period, the distortions resulting from differences in rate-making procedure for transport by road and by inland waterway have still not been eliminated, and that no solution has been found to the problem of publication of transport rates.

Again, there is the case . . . of making a start on the introduction of freedom of movements for workers within the Community. The agreement [among the governments] duly came into force—after one or two hitches—within a reasonably short space of time. But the matter has been handled so gingerly that the practical effects of the measures adopted are Nevertheless, the description of the functioning of the Council almost negligible.[26]

---

[24]Haas, *op. cit.,* pp. 490–491. M. Rey was the Belgian Minister of Economic Affairs and the Belgian representative in the Council.

[25] *Eighth Report,* p. 12.

[26] *Ibid.,* p. 12.

quoted above undoubtedly reflects important factors that have influenced the course of events. The member governments had a strong political commitment to the Community, and however the views of individual governments may have shifted with respect to its supranational character there appears to have been little serious consideration of the withdrawal of support in any member country. The frequent contacts of the ministers in Council meetings and of high-ranking civil servants in the subordinate bodies (which were developed to negotiate solutions that the ministers could ratify)[27] promoted a close cooperation which, if not successful in breaking new grounds for economic integration, ensured the smoother functioning of the measures of integration unequivocally required by the Treaty.

Of the other institutions of the Community, the Court has been the most important. Some of its earlier decisions tended to restrict the High Authority to the powers literally enumerated in the more explicit clauses of the Treaty and to deny it powers that might have been inferred from the more general clauses stating purposes and objectives.[28] A narrow interpretation of the High Authority's powers was involved, for example, in the Court's decision at the end of 1954 rejecting the right of the High Authority to permit enterprises to deviate from published prices within small percentage margins. Generally, however, the Court has upheld the actions of the High Authority, perhaps because the latter was usually inclined to follow a limited interpretation of its powers. In one case, indeed—that involving steel scrap[29]—the Court ruled against the High Authority not because it had exceeded its powers, but because it had delegated rather than exercised them. The High Auth-

---

[27] Cf. Haas, *op. cit.*, pp. 491–492.

[28] Haas, *op. cit.*, pp. 472–475.

[29] See below, p. 223f.

ority's practice of obtaining approval from the governments
(through Council) of most of its important measures whether
required by the Treaty or not also tended to eliminate an
important potential source of Court challenges to its actions.
Since most of the conflicts of interests involving governments
were thus resolved through negotiation before action was taken
by the High Authority, the cases coming before the Court
tended to relate mainly to the interests of particular economic
and social groups[30] rather than governments, the more so
because the Court has tended to interpret the right of appeal
broadly. The High Authority lost a few cases on grounds of
violation of procedure and of misapplication of the Treaty,
but it did not suffer any reverses on grounds of abuse of power.
The Court has made little use of its powers to enter into substantive economic considerations, and has leaned toward an
objective interpretation of the concept of abuse of power.[31]

The Assembly has been a livelier and more influential body
than might have been anticipated from a reading of the
Treaty. Through its committees, it has been in continual contact with the work of the High Authority, and has tended to
throw its influence toward integration and supranationalism.
The High Authority, conscious of the Assembly's position as
the only institution of the Community that can claim to have
a representative character, has sought the support of the members of the Assembly in influencing public opinion and possibly
government policy[32] and has, in some areas such as labor and
investment policy, been influenced by strongly held views of
the Assembly.[33] Early in 1962 the 142 members of the Assembly were still being chosen by the parliaments of the member
states from among their number, but there was growing pres-

---

[30] Lagrange, *op. cit.*, p. 46.
[31] *Ibid.*, p. 46.
[32] Cf. Haas, *op. cit.*, p. 479.
[33] *Ibid.*, pp. 71, 89–90, and 477–478.

sure to use the alternative method provided in the Treaty of direct universal suffrage under conditions to be determined by each country.

The provisions of the Treaty designed to safeguard various economic interests may be considered at several levels. There are first the transitional arrangements designed to ease the adjustment to the common market. These are set forth in a Convention Containing the Transitional Provisions appended to the Treaty. For the permanent period there are several types of safeguards. Probably the most important is a general escape clause making the High Authority the competent source for the granting of relief and providing for appeal to the Court in case of refusal by the High Authority to give satisfaction. Secondly, relief is provided for a country or economic sector in certain hardship situations such as may exist when rivals have a competitive advantage based on factors other than superior productivity, such as low wages or the ability to engage in price discrimination (dumping). Also, emergency provisions are included in the Treaty for a "manifest crisis" owing to a decline in demand and for a "serious shortage" of a product falling within the jurisdiction of the Community. In addition, as has already been noted, the states retain considerable powers to cope with difficulties that may arise.

Transition safeguards

The Convention set a transition period of five years duration, beginning with the date of the establishment of the common market in coal (Section 1, 4), which turned out to be February 10, 1953.[34] The Convention laid down the general

---

[34] The common market for iron ore and scrap also opened on that date, and the common market for steel began on May 1, 1953.

principle that the essential measures required to create a common market were to come into effect with the opening of the transition period (Sections 8, 9, and 11); that is, nondiscriminatory pricing was to be required, and export and import duties, quantitative restrictions, subsidies, and special charges were to be abolished. However, a major purpose of the Convention was to smooth the transition to the common market by providing for gradual adjustment to the new conditions so as to avoid sudden and disruptive changes. Thus, the organs of the Community were empowered to grant many temporary exceptions from the principles of the common market; indeed, these provisions made it possible, if it seemed desirable, to maintain the *status quo* for the moment in a given economic sector. But both the underlying premise and the explicit requirement of the Transition Convention were that this breathing period was to be used to make the necessary adjustments so that the need for exemptions and special aids would have passed by the end of the transition period. Some of the provisions designed for these purposes were general in character; others were intended specifically to protect certain interests from difficulties that appeared likely or possible. The specific provisions included not only measures on behalf of the coal industry and others on behalf of the steel industry, but also safeguards for at least one potential problem industry (specifically named) for four of the signatories.[35]

Distortions of competition. As a general precaution, the High Authority was instructed to examine with the governments the extent to which existing statutory or administrative measures created discrepancies between two or more member countries that could endanger competitive conditions in the common

---

[35] And of the other two, Germany was the beneficiary of a special clause concerning trade with East Germany, and the Netherlands shared in the special arrangement regarding Benelux imports of steel from third countries. See pp. 194 and 193 respectively.

market or in export markets. If the High Authority found that there were such differences, which might for example arise from the price fixing of by-products outside the jurisdiction of the Community or from different ways of financing social security, it was to "propose" the necessary measures to the governments concerned (Section 2, 4). The weak powers of the High Authority in this area (a "proposal" is not binding upon the governments) reflects the basic axiom underlying the negotiation of the Treaty to the effect that the Six were adequately homogeneous in the essential factors that affected competitive conditions,[36] and that it was mainly future distortions that had to be guarded against.[37] The preliminary findings of the High Authority supported the notion that existing differences among the six countries would have but limited effects in distorting competition in the common market. It was stated, for example, that government price controls had waned to a degree that neither the by-products of the coal and steel industries nor their raw materials (including gas and electricity) were being marketed at prices very different from those that would have been established by the free play of competitive forces.[38]

Readaptation. More positive powers were given to the High Authority to extend technical and financial assistance in order to facilitate the readaption of workers thrown out of employment and of enterprises obliged to cease or to modify their operations as a result of the opening of the common market

---

[36] Cf. Reuter, *op. cit.*, pp. 276–278.

[37] This was the purpose of Article 67; see page 202f.

[38] Haute Autorité, *Exposé sur la Situation de la Communauté*, 10 Janvier 1953, Luxembourg, 1953, pp. 85–92. As between Great Britain and the Six, on the other hand, it was claimed that substantial differences existed. Thus, the gap between coal prices in Great Britain and in the Community was explained largely in terms of the freedom of British coal from excise taxes and social security charges, burdens which Community coal had to bear.

(Section 23). The High Authority "at the request of the governments concerned and under the conditions specified below, must help to protect the workers from the burden of readaptation and assure them productive employment, and may grant nonrepayable assistance to certain enterprises" (Section 23, 1). In addition to loans or guarantees of loans to finance approved programs of readaptation of enterprises, outright grants could be made to enterprises forced to cease activities in connection with the expansion of production elsewhere in the Community (Section 23, 5). For the most part, however, grants were intended to help workers; the High Authority was to make contributions to (1) payments to tide workers over until they found new jobs, (2) the costs of technical retraining, and (3) resettlement allowances (Section 23, 4). Agreement of Council was required to relieve the governments of the obligation to contribute at least equal sums where grant aid was given and also to extend the aids to the two years following the end of the transition period (Section 23, 6 and 8).

Safeguards for coal. Special provisions for coal were intended to avoid sudden and "harmful" shifts in production or increases in prices. The High Authority was authorized to permit zonal pricing, which involves freight absorption by the seller and automatic alignment of prices within a given geographical region, and, more generally, to control the differences in the prices that an enterprise charged differently situated groups of buyers in the common market (Section 24, 3, a). The High Authority could also permit the continuation or creation of national compensation schemes in which low-cost mines are taxed in order to subsidize high-cost mines (Section 24, 3, b). These provisions served to enable the High Authority to avoid a sharp and chaotic break with the past at the time the common market was opened.

Forward-looking transitional measures for coal were also

included, the objective being to modernize and reorganize sectors of the Community's coal industry known to have high costs so as to enable them to compete in the common market by the end of the transition period. The High Authority was instructed to impose a compensation levy of not more than 1.5 per cent on the coal production of countries whose average costs per ton were less than the weighted average for the Community as a whole (i. e., on German and Dutch mines). The proceeds of the levy, which was to be reduced by 20 per cent of the initial ceiling each year, were to be used to enable Belgian coal and coal from the Sulci mines of Italy to meet competition on the common market. Governments of the recipient countries had to provide subsidies at least equal in amount to the proceeds of the levy (Section 25).

The Community subsidies in the case of Italy were to be limited to two years, after which it was expected that investments in process would have enabled Sulci coal to meet the competition of other Community coal. In addition, the High Authority was empowered to permit the Italian Government to maintain tariffs on Community coke, although the levels of such duties would have to be reduced progressively by stipulated percentages and finally eliminated by the end of the transition period (Section 27).

The Community's subsidies to Belgian mines were designed to achieve three purposes : (1) to reduce Belgian coal prices as close as possible to common market prices and over the course of the transition period to the expected costs of production at the end of the transition period (Section 26, 2, a); (2) to subsidize coal for the Belgian steel industry to offset any competitive disadvantage of that industry arising from high-cost coal (Section 26, 2, b); and (3) to cover 80 per cent of the difference between the delivered price of Belgian coal and other Community coal for such exports of Belgian coal as the

High Authority found necessary to meet the requirements of the Community (Section 26, 2, c).

Belgium was also given the option of an alternative course of action; she could isolate her coal market from that of the rest of the Community, subject to the control of the High Authority (Section 26, 3). In this case, the High Authority could recommend reductions in Belgian coal production of not more than 3 per cent per annum.[39] The right to keep Belgian coal out of the common market was limited to the transition period, although the High Authority with the concurrence of Council could grant two one-year extensions in "exceptional circumstances not now foreseeable" (Section 26, 4). After the integration of Belgian coal into the common market, the Belgian Government could be permitted to subsidize coal even after the end of the transition period. However, such subsidies were subject to the control of the High Authority and, with respect to over-all tonnage, of the Council, and they would have to be reduced as rapidly as possible (Section 26, 4).

France also was the beneficiary of specific safeguarding provisions for its coal industry. The decline in its coal production was to be limited to one million tons per annum (equivalent to about 2 per cent of French output when the Treaty was drawn up).[40] In order to effectuate this guarantee, the measures to prevent sudden shifts in production referred to above (i. e., those in Section 24) could be supplemented by a special levy imposed by the High Authority. The levy could not exceed 10 per cent of producers' receipts on those net deliveries to France which were in excess of 1950 net deliveries, up to the

---

[39] In the event of a downturn in Community production, Belgian output could be further reduced by the percentage decrease in Community production.

[40] In the event of a decline in Community production, French output could be further reduced by the percentage decrease in Community production.

amount of the decrease in French production. The proceeds
were to be used to reduce the prices of French coal (Section
28).

Safeguards for steel. For the steel industry, the Transitional
Convention provided the Community with sweeping powers to
protect firms and workers from shifts in production during the
transition period. Protection was to be extended to enterprises
which met difficulties connected with the opening of the common market but which would be able to meet competition
after suitable measures of adaptation. Also, care was to be
taken to avoid shifts in production that would lead to the displacement of more workers than could benefit from the readaptation provisions discussed above (i. e., Section 23). In
either of these cases, the High Authority was to give priority
to the use of appropriate provisions of the Treaty; specifically
mentioned in this connection were the use of indirect means to
stabilize markets (Article 57), emergency powers to apply production quotas (Article 58) or to establish rationing (Article
59), and the right to ease the ban against purely local price
reductions (Article 60, 2, b). If these measures "cannot be
applied,"⁴¹ the High Authority was authorized to resort, in
order of preference, to limitations upon the net increase in the
deliveries from one region of the Community to another, the
establishment of minimum prices, the imposition of production
quotas (except for exports), and the authorization to a member
state to impose on imports from third countries entering via

---

⁴¹ The Convention did not specify any criteria for the phrase "cannot
be applied." Some writers appear to interpret the clause to refer to cases
where the regular Treaty measures could not be applied in the sense
that they would be inadequate to cope with the situation. (Cf. Reuter,
op. cit., p. 299, and L'Institut des Relations Internationales de Bruxelles,
op. cit., p. 106.) The language seems also to cover the situation in which
the High Authority could not obtain Council agreement (in the cases in
which it is required). The provisions of Articles 57 to 60 are treated
more fully below.

another member state the same degree of protection as that imposed on its direct imports from third countries[42] (Section 29, 1). Technical criteria for the application of these provisions were to be worked out in the preparatory period between the time the Treaty became effective and the common market opened (Section 29, 2), and if the necessary adjustments could not take place in the transition period because of shortages of materials or of finances or for unforeseen reasons the provisions could be applied after the end of the transitional period (Section 29, 3).

These broad provisions made it less necessary to provide special safeguards for the steel industries of individual countries than was the case with respect to coal. There were, however, some clauses of a limited character relating to Luxemburg and Italy. In the case of Luxemburg, the High Authority was instructed to apply the general safeguard provisions for steel (see previous paragraph) so as to take account of the dominant role of the steel industry in the economy of the principality and of "the necessity for preventing serious disturbances" to the special position of Luxemburg steel in Belgian markets owing to the existence of the Belgian-Luxemburg Economic Union. Aside from this general commitment, the High Authority was empowered to use its own funds if necessary to aid the Luxemburg steel industry (Section 31).

For Italy, as in the case of coke, there was a provision authorizing the High Authority to permit tariffs against Community steel with the proviso that the rates diminish progressively and be eliminated entirely by the end of the transition

---

[42] Limitations of deliveries required only consultation with the Consultative Committee and Council; the other three measures required consultation with the Consultative Committee and the agreement of Council. The power to impose production quotas in Section 29 may have been regarded as necessary to supplement similar powers in Article 58 because the latter cover only the case of a "manifest crisis" due to a "decline in demand."

period. Italian steel was also protected by a provision which prevented other Community producers from aligning their prices for sales on the Italian market with those of Italian producers; reductions in prices below the enterprise's basing point plus freight to the Italian market or below the level established by third-country steel in the Italian market required the authorization of the High Authority and the agreement of the Italian Government (Section 30).

Other safeguards. The High Authority had the power to permit the continuation of subsidies to and of special charges on coal and steel products in effect at the time the High Authority assumed its functions (Section 11). It was also given the authority to deal with the diversion of trade with third countries and of foreign-exchange earnings from one member country to another (Sections 19 and 18).

Several miscellaneous types of safeguarding clauses round out the list for the transition period. Perhaps the most important one was designed to protect other members from third-country steel entering via low-tariff Benelux. The Benelux countries were permitted to maintain their low tariffs for third-country steel, but imports from non-Community sources in excess of domestic requirements were to be dutiable at higher rates. The quotas for low-duty imports were to be established in agreement with the High Authority which had the power, if certain difficulties arose, to apply temporary controls to deliveries from Benelux to the other member states. The Benelux obligation to maintain the tariff quotas did not extend beyond the transition period, but it was anticipated that external tariffs would be "harmonized" at that time. To facilitate harmonization, the Benelux countries were to increase their customs duties by as much as two percentage points if the High Authority in consultation with the other governments found it necessary (Section 15).

Safeguard clauses were inserted for transport also (Section 10). The High Authority was empowered, upon the recommendation of experts, to modify the requirement of international through tariff rates (i. e., degressive with total Community distance), if necessary to avoid "serious disturbances in the field of transport." For the same reason, the High Authority could permit the gradual modification, rather than require the immediate abolition, of special rates in the interest of one or several coal or steel enterprises. Finally, it could exempt Luxemburg, whose railroads were heavily dependent upon steel traffic, from applying the Treaty's transport principles at least until the governments could agree on what, if any, special measures were necessary.

Finally, a special provision stated that coal and steel trade between West Germany and East Germany was to be "regulated by the Government of the Federal Republic in agreement with the High Authority" (Section 22). Aside from this, there was no safeguarding clause either in the Treaty or in the Convention which was explicitly included for the benefit of Germany.

Permanent Safeguards

General safeguard clause. The most general safeguard clause for the permanent period is found in Article 37. According to the terms of this article, a member state that considers that an action by the High Authority or its failure to act is "of such a nature as to provoke fundamental and persistent disturbances" in its economy, may appeal to the High Authority. The High Authority, after obtaining the opinion of Council, has to determine whether it accepts the view of the member state. If it does, it must "decide on the measures to be taken, under the terms of the present Treaty, to correct such a situation while at the same time safeguarding the essential interests of the Community." If it rejects the member state's claim, the latter may appeal to the Court. As already noted, the Court has the power to review the substantive aspects of the case. Should the Court sustain the member state's appeal, the High Authority must "decide, within the framework of the Court's judgment, the measures to be taken" under the terms of the Treaty to correct the situation while "safeguarding the essential interests of the Community."

The right to initiate action under the article and the right to appeal to the Court if satisfaction is not obtained from the High Authority are given to the member states. No provision is made for complaint or appeal by private interests,[43] presumably because the disturbances contemplated affect the entire economy of a country rather than one or a few enterprises alone.

A first reading of the article seems to call to mind a situation in which a member state, dissatisfied with the action or inaction of the High Authority, seeks redress, first from the High Authority itself and then if necessary from the Court. It is possible, however, that the High Authority may have followed the course that the member state complains about because, under the normal functioning of the Treaty, the High Authority had no power to pursue a more vigorous line of action. Thus, in the actual event, on the first and only occasion in which Article 37 was invoked (the Belgian coal crisis discussed below), the High Authority had been unable to obtain the

---

[43] When the use of Article 37 by the High Authority in December, 1959, in connection with the Belgian coal crisis (see below) was challenged in the Court by two German coal organizations, the Court upheld the argument of the attorneys for the High Authority that a suit from nongovernmental sources was inadmissable. *Mémoire en Défense,* Court of Justice, Affaires nos. 2–60 and 3–60–15, September 30, 1960. Some of the ensuing arguments for the broad interpretation of Article 37 may be found in this document.

Council agreement required by the Treaty for emergency measures to cope with the disturbances to the economy of a member state. In circumstances such as these, the complaint of the member state initiating action does not necessarily imply criticism of the High Authority.[44]

The fact that the High Authority's action or failure to act need merely be "of such a nature as to provoke" the disturbances implies that the disturbances may only be feared or threatened rather than actual.[45] The key phrase "fundamental and persistent disturbances" is not defined, and the High Authority has to determine whether a given set of circumstances warrant this description. Presumably the terms "fundamental" and "persistent" exclude purely cyclical difficulties, and it may be assumed also that the troubles must be widespread rather than confined to one or a few firms, but beyond this the matter is largely one of judgment.[46] If a decision of the

---

[44] Indeed, it has been argued that if the High Authority were at fault, other provisions of the Treaty providing for appeal to the Court (Articles 33 and 35) would suffice. Cf. L. Janz, "Article 37 du Traité," High Authority Document 7789/59f, November 19, 1959 (mimeo.).

[45] Reuter, *op. cit.,* p. 245.

[46] In addition to making these points the *Mémoire en Défense* cited above referred to Section 26 of the Transitional Convention. The first paragraph of this section set a maximum limit of 3 per cent (more if over-all Community production declined) on the annual reduction in coal production that would have to be borne by Belgium in the event that the High Authority was called upon to make determinations relating to Belgian output. (See above, p. 190.) The *Mémoire* inferred from this that the drafters of the Treaty felt that a larger reduction would "strike a serious blow against the whole Belgian economy" (*ibid.,* p. 33). Earlier, Reuter had suggested that such analogies for the type of situation that might call Article 37 into play might be found in the transitional provisions (*Op cit.,* pp. 245–246).

The *Mémoire* relied both on objective fact and upon responsible supporting opinion to establish the existence of serious disturbances to the Belgian economy. In the first category, it cited the decline in production, the increases in unemployment and stocks, and the social unrest as evidenced by strikes in connection with the difficulties. In the second category, it made reference to the views of the Assembly and of certain member governments as expressed in official documents.

High Authority on this point is challenged before the Court, the Court is faced with the choice of accepting the High Authority's interpretation of the meaning of "fundamental and persistent disturbances" and its judgment with respect to their existence or nonexistence in a given situation, or of substituting its own interpretation and judgment for those of the High Authority.

There is doubt also about the nature of the remedies permitted by the article. One authority has argued that the stipulation to the effect that the corrective measures be "under the terms of the present Treaty" restricts the High Authority to relief measures provided elsewhere in the Treaty.[47] However, what are generally found elsewhere in the Treaty are either (1) clauses clearly intended to cope with Community-wide difficulties and thus providing Community-wide remedies or (2) safeguards that are quite specific as to the circumstances that warrant their use.[48] Thus, on such a literal interpretation, the High Authority would be armed with but a limited arsenal of powers to cope with the situation. The measures that it could take, which might include such steps as the lending of money, the authorization of compensation programs, and the easing of its price rules, would probably prove inadequate to cope with a critical disturbance in the economy of a member country. On this basis, the article would add little to the Treaty; thus the authority cited holds that its main effect is to assure a "second reading" of the case by the High Authority and to open the matter up for Court review of law and fact.[49]

---

[47] Reuter, *op. cit.,* p. 246.

[48] The specific safeguards, including readaptation measures and relief against unfair competition, and the Community-wide measures, including the emergency powers, are discussed in the next sections.

[49] Reuter, *op. cit.,* p. 246. An even more restrictive view, advanced by the plaintiffs in the case cited in a previous footnote holds that the article requires that some specific action or the omission of some specific action on the part of the High Authority literally "provoke" — that is,

On the other hand, several lines of argument can be advanced in support of a broader interpretation of the powers conferred upon the High Authority by Article 37. There is, in the first place, the principle of a reasonable and useful interpretation of legal texts, which is found both in national and international law and which the Court followed in other cases. The narrow interpretation does not conform to this principle because it makes Article 37 largely superfluous. Even if the strict interpretation is confined to the powers granted to the High Authority and stress is placed on the additional scope given to the Court, the usefulness of the article on this interpretation is marginal. The states have ample recourse to the Court in other articles, and if the High Authority is granted no additional powers why is a special and extended jurisdiction for the Court necessary? The ability of the Community to cope with fundamental disturbances in the economy of a member state would not be improved by the broader jurisdiction of the Court unless the Court is expected to initiate relief measures not specifically provided for in the Treaty. But this would, of course, transfer executive powers from the High Authority to the Court, and the article clearly states that it is the High Authority that is to decide on the measures to be taken. It seems more reasonable to consider that the inclusion of matters of substance as well as questions of law within the competance of the Court in connection with Article 37 represents an intention to put the Court in the position of a counterweight in view of the undefined powers granted to the High Authority to deal with a situation in which the normal functioning of the Treaty provokes a fundamental disturbance in the economy of the state.[50]

---

cause — the disturbances. This view implies that the High Authority would be powerless in the face of disturbances created by external conditions, such as structural economic changes.

[50] *Mémoire,* p. 47.

The broad interpretation tends to be supported also by the injunction to the High Authority to "correct such a situation while at the same time safeguarding the essential interests of the Community." Of course, this could be regarded as a warning to the High Authority to bear in mind the interests of the Community as a whole in applying the weak powers it derives from other articles (i. e., the lending, compensation, and pricing remedies referred to above) to help an individual member state. On the other hand, most of these provisions already contain allusions to the over-all purposes of the Treaty, and the general terms of reference of the High Authority also make such an admonition superfluous. The alternative interpretation is that the intent of the language just cited is to empower the High Authority to act as an arbiter, balancing the over-all interests of the Community and the adverse repercussions of the common market upon the economy of a member state[51] particularly for difficult situations not specifically anticipated in the Treaty.

Once it is admitted that Article 37 confers additional powers upon the High Authority, it is hard to avoid the conclusion that the grant of power is very broad indeed. The article places no limits upon the scope of the measures that may be taken by the High Authority, either by cross references to powers granted in other articles or by other means unless we return to the phrase "under the terms of the present Treaty." Even if we reject the restrictive interpretation of these words discussed earlier, they may still be construed as placing certain limitations upon the scope of the remedial measures. For example, they may lend support to the notion that the articles reserving

---

[51] Cf. Janz, *op. cit.* The view that the effect of Article 37 was to place the High Authority — and upon appeal, the Court — in the position of arbiter between the Community and a state suffering fundamental disturbances was held by the French delegation which negotiated the Treaty. Cf. *Rapport de la Délégation Française,* pp. 42–43.

certain powers to the states should take primacy over any attempt by the High Authority to infringe upon such areas under Article 37. Less reasonably, perhaps, it might be argued that the words limit the High Authority to the techniques accorded it within the Treaty; in any case this would not be much of a limitation if the impressive array of weapons, always circumscribed in the clauses in which they are granted to the High Authority, were considered available under Article 37 without qualification, and if they were available only with the same qualifications we would be back to the restrictive interpretation. Aside from the need to avoid infringement upon the powers reserved to the states and the general statements of the aims of the Community and the mission of the High Authority, the Court seems to have been given little guidance in limiting the powers of the High Authority granted by Article 37 unless it chooses to deny that any have been granted.[52] The potential power of the High Authority under the article is all the greater since it is required only to consult the Council, not to obtain its consent, for the corrective measures it proposes once Article 37 is invoked by a state.

Relief for certain hardship situations. The Treaty recognizes the possibility that certain types of situations might develop which would cause difficulties for a particular country or sector, and it instructs or authorizes the High Authority or the High Authority and Council to provide relief in such circumstances. Among the difficulties for which more or less explicit

---

[52] There is also the question of what parties have the right of appeal to the Court in connection with the measures taken under Article 37. The article refers only to the right of appeal of a member state when the High Authority has refused to recognize the existence of the situation in which disturbances are present or may be provoked. The *Mémoire* referred to in the previous footnotes argues that since the function of the High Authority contemplated by the article is to arbitrate between various public interests in the Community, it follows that other states or Council have the right of appeal but not private parties (*Mémoire*, pp. 7–10).

provision is made in the Treaty are those arising from foreign competition, competitive disadvantages within the common market other than those based upon lower productivity, and the technological displacement of workers.

In connection with the difficulties arising out of trade with third countries, the High Authority is "empowered to take any measures in accordance with this Treaty," bearing in mind the objectives of the Community and the obligations of the member states to live up to their agreements with third countries[53] (Article 74). The difficulties may arise as a result of (1) dumping or other practices condemned by the Havana Charter; (2) advantages derived by firms in third countries based on competitive conditions contrary to the provisions of the Treaty; and (3) the importation of one of the Community's products into one or more of the member states "in relatively increased quantities and under such conditions that these imports inflict or threaten to inflict serious damage on production, within the common market, of similar or directly competitive products." However, quantitative restrictions may be recommended in the second type of situation only with the concurrence of Council and in the third source of difficulty only under emergency conditions.[54]

---

[53] The High Authority may not take any action concerning commercial policy toward third countries which exceeds "the powers which the member States are free to exercise under the international agreements to which they are parties" (Article 71). Future agreements, however, are subject to the scrutiny of the High Authority for consistency with the Treaty (Article 75).

[54] That is, "only under the conditions set forth in Article 58." Article 58, which is discussed in the next section, provides for the establishment of quotas on production when the Community is faced with a "period of manifest crisis" due to a decline in demand. Article 58 requires the agreement of Council for its use, but it is not clear from the language of Article 74 whether the High Authority, once having obtained the approval of Council for the use of Article 58, is then free to recommend quantitative restrictions on its own authority or whether it must obtain Council consent for them also.

Another basis for protection against injury from third-country trade is to be found in the commitment of the member states to "lend each other the necessary assistance in the execution of measures recognized by the High Authority as being in accordance with this Treaty and with existing international agreements" (Article 71). The High Authority is empowered to propose the methods by which this mutual assistance is to be undertaken. Presumably, this involves mainly the coordination of commercial policy measures for such purposes as ensuring the effective control by a given member state over its imports from third countries and the avoidance of the diversion of third-country trade from one member to another. The High Authority also has the power to control quantitative restrictions on exports and imports (Article 73), and maximum and minimum tariffs may be established by unanimous action of Council upon a proposal of the High Authority (Article 72). While the High Authority has other emergency weapons against imports, such as the right to fix minimum prices within the common market (Article 61) and the authority to permit or to establish compensations mechanisms (Article 53),[55] its control over commercial policy is relatively weak. "Unless otherwise provided in this Treaty, the responsibilities of the governments of the member States for commercial policy shall not be affected by the application of this Treaty" (Article 71).

Protection against competition within the Community, except for the transitional period, would of course have been inconsistent with the establishment of the common market. However, the willingness to establish a common market was, as we have seen, predicated upon the assumption that competitive conditions in the various member states were suffi-

---

[55] It may fix minimum prices and authorize compensation programs after consultation with the Consultative Committee and Council, but it needs the unanimous agreement of Council to use Community funds for compensation schemes.

ciently similar so as to make it unlikely that serious inequities would result. But it was recognised that even if this assumption was valid as of the time of the Treaty negotiation, the competitive positions of the coal and steel industries in the several countries would inevitably be affected by actions in the broad spheres of economic policy that remained under the control of each government, including such key areas as exchange rates, transport, prices, taxes, and wages. Therefore, it was felt necessary to include special provisions to guard against the possibility that the action of a government might lead to the "impairment" of the conditions of competition (Article 67). Protection against competition within the Community based upon "abnormally low wages" was also stipulated (Article 68).[56]

The provisions concerning the impairment of competition relate primarily to actions of a member state that may "provoke a serious disequilibrium by substantially increasing differences in costs of production otherwise than through variations in productivity." If such measures produce "harmful effects" for the member state's own coal or steel enterprises, the High Authority may authorize the government to grant subsidies to such firms in amounts and under conditions agreed upon by the High Authority and the government. This possibility is open also in the case of a variation in wages or working conditions which would have harmful effects, even if it is not the result of a government action (Article 67, 2).

In the case where the actions of the state have harmful effects on the enterprises of another member country, the High Authority "may address a recommendation to the said State with a view to remedying these effects by such measures as that State may consider most compatible with its own econo-

[56] Cf. L'Institut des Relations Internationales de Bruxelles, *op. cit.*, pp. 110–123, for a discussion of Articles 67 and 68.

mic equilibrium." In other words, the High Authority may require the government to take measures to offset the impairment in competition that its action has caused, but the choice of the measures is left to the government (Article 67, 2).

The foregoing provisions relate to an action of a member state that has the effect of *increasing* the differences in costs of production, and appear to deal with general governmental actions affecting all industries within a given country rather than to action directed specifically to the coal and steel industries.[57] Normally, the High Authority would not find it necessary to intervene with respect to measures that have the effect of *reducing* the differences in the costs of production. However, if the reduction is achieved by means of measures that confer special advantages or place special burdens upon coal or steel enterprises in comparison with other industries in the same country, as for example different social charges or other forms of differential taxation, the High Authority is given the right to make recommendations that it thinks necesary [58] (Article 67, 3). In this, as in its other actions relating to the impairment of competition, the High Authority must consult the Consultative Committee and Council but it need not obtain their consent.

The provisions regarding the impairment of competition (Article 67, 2 and 3) also apply to harmful effects produced by changes in the financing of social security or in unemploy-

---

[57] Reuter, *op. cit.,* p. 195.

[58] The reference to the possible existence of special aids and charges in Article 67, 3 appears to be inconsistent with the seemingly sweeping prohibition of them in Article 4. Reuter suggests that Article 4 is not intended to outlaw all such aids and charges but only those that have the distortion of competition as their purpose. Thus, special provisions for the financing of social security in the coalmining industry would be consistent with Article 4 if adopted for social reasons but inconsistent with it if adopted in order to influence competitive conditions within the Community (*op. cit.,* p. 195).

ment compensation provisions and by a variation in wages (Article 68, 5).

While both wage policy and the methods of fixing wages and social benefits are left to the sovereignty of the member states, the High Authority may intervene in order to prevent "wage dumping" (the term is not used in the Treaty) or the improvement of competitive positions through wage cuts. Under the first heading, if the High Authority finds that one or more enterprises are charging prices that are "abnormally low" as a result of wages that are "abnormally low," it is to instruct the enterprises (or the government, if the latter is responsible for the maintenance of the low wage level) to make the necessary adjustments (Article 68, 2). While the term "abnormally low" is not defined either in connection with prices or wages, it is specified that the wages are to be judged with reference to the wage level of the region.

With respect to improvement of competitive position through wage cuts, if the High Authority finds that a reduction in wages (1) entails a decline in the standard of living, and (2) "is being used as a means of permanent economic adjustment by enterprises or as a means of competition among enterprises," it is to recommend compensation to the workers involved. However, exceptions are made to this rule. Wage decreases that result from a decline in the cost of living presumably would not meet the above criteria, and they are specifically excluded from the provisions of the article. Wage reductions in connection with a deflationary policy adopted by the government in order to re-establish its external equilibrium are also excepted; if a deflationary policy creates difficulties for the coal or steel industries, the provisions of Article 67 dealing with the impairment of competitive conditions may be applied. Finally, a wage decrease "intended to correct abnormal increases previously granted under exceptional circumstances which no longer apply" is excluded from consideration.

Apart from low wages, the Treaty places a general ban on "unfair competitive practices" (Article 60, 1). Specific mention is made of temporary or local price manipulation for the purpose of acquiring a monopoly within the common market, but otherwise the definition of the term is left to the High Authority under the sole restriction that it must consult the Consultative Committee. The broad prohibition of price discrimination found in the early clauses of the Treaty (Articles 3, b and 4, b) is specifically applied to price discrimination based on the nationality of the buyer and to pricing practices relating to payment of freight costs. In the latter connection, the High Authority is, first, given the power to prevent an enterprise from choosing an "abnormal" basing point (Article 60, 2, a)—that is, presumably one that is far from the seller's locus of production and close to the basing point used by a competitor.[59] Secondly, the High Authority is empowered to control the amount by which the method of quotation may involve a reduction from the equivalent basing-point price (Article 60, 2, b). Decisions on these questions (i.e., methods of price quotation) must be taken "when they appear necessary to avoid disturbances in all or any part of the common market, or disequilibria resulting from a difference between the methods of quotation used for a product and those used for its raw materials." However, enterprises remain free to align their prices to third-country quotations, though the High Authority must be notified of such transactions and may curb them in case of abuse.

Another source of potential difficulty that is provided for in

---

[59] *Rapport de la Délégation Française,* p. 109. However, price alignment downward to match but not to undercut competitor's delivered prices is permitted (Article 60, 2, b.). Upward price alignment is not allowed.

the Treaty is the displacement of workers through technological progress. "If the introduction of technical processes or new equipment, within the framework of the general objectives laid down by the High Authority, should lead to an exceptionally large reduction in labor requirements in the coal and steel industries, making it especially difficult in one or more areas to re-employ the workers discharged," the High Authority may grant nonrepayable assistance to tide workers over until they can find new jobs, help them meet resettlement expenses, and help finance technical retraining (Article 56). Such aid is to be conditional upon payments at least equal in amount by the interested government, but Council may waive this requirement by a two-thirds vote. The High Authority may also grant or guarantee loans to help finance installations that will provide employment for the displaced workers either in industries falling within its jurisdiction or, with the agreement of Council, in a different industry. The High Authority can exercise these powers with respect to readaptation only upon the request of a member government and after consulting the Consultative Committee.

There was, it will be recalled, a somewhat similar readaptation provision [60] in the Transitional Convention which was intended to cope with the displacement of workers as a result of the introduction of the common market. The rather sudden shift from a situation of coal shortage to one of oversupply between 1957 and 1959, owing to structural changes in the energy market,[61] called attention to a gap in the range of safeguards provided by the Community arrangements. Neither the section of the Transitional Convention nor the article of the Treaty dealing with readaptation covered the case of labor displacement arising from structural changes in the market.

[60] Section 23; see above, p. 187f.
[61] See below, p. 237f.

Accordingly, the High Authority proposed the amendment of the Treaty to remedy this deficiency. The final outcome in March, 1960, was a new section of Article 56 which provides additional grounds for readaptation assistance. Such aid may now be extended also if "profound changes in the marketing conditions of the coal mining or of the iron and steel industry, not directly connected with the introduction of the Common Market, make it necessary for certain enterprises permanently to discontinue, curtail, or change their activities." The amendment was the first to be adopted by the procedure of *"petite revision."*[62]

There are other situations for which the language of the Treaty might support special measures. For example, a loophole is left for limited exceptions by the High Authority to the general principle of nondiscriminatory transport rates (Article 70). However, those discussed above seem to have been the ones that were most clearly designed as safeguards and will probably prove to be the most important.

Emergency Provisions. The responsibility of the institutions of the Community for the welfare of the workers and enterprises in the coal and steel industries is not, however, limited to sources of difficulty affecting only one country or region or only one or a few firms. Rather, the general spirit of the Treaty is to place broad responsibility for the welfare of the industries upon the institutions of the Community. Thus, an attempt was made to endow it at one writing with specific powers to replace the analogous powers which the individual governments, each in accordance with its own pattern of legal evolution, had acquired over the years. This involved, on the face of the matter, a grant of broad powers to the High

---

[62] See below, p. 214f. An earlier version of the amendment, restricting its scope to the coal industry and its duration to three years upon the insistence of Council, was rejected by the Court.

Authority, or to the High Authority and Council, to meet difficulties imposed by unusual economic conditions. These include controls over production and prices and the ability to call into play certain financial mechanisms. In addition, recourse is provided to a general grant of authority to deal with situations not expressly provided for in the Treaty.

With respect to production, the High Authority is enjoined to use the indirect means at its disposal before resorting to direct action (Article 57). Cooperation with governments to influence consumption, intervention on prices, and action with respect to imports are specifically mentioned in this context. The High Authority has other indirect means of influencing production, such as through its investment policy (Article 54) and its market and planning studies (Article 46), but they are generally more appropriate for long-run than for short-run policy.

More drastic measures are provided in the case of a decline in demand if the High Authority thinks that the Community is faced with a "period of manifest crisis" which cannot be met by indirect methods (Article 58). The nature of the "manifest crisis" is not specified in more detail than that it be associated with a decline in demand and be one that confronts the Community as a whole. Presumably such a crisis exists if the quantities offered for sale exceed those demanded for more than a temporary period whose expiration is foreseeable, and in the opinion of one writer, even if the excess supply is due to growth in capacity rather than to a decline in the absolute level of demand.[63]

If the High Authority recognizes the existence of a crisis, it is obliged to proceed to the establishment of production quotas. For this, it requires the consent of Council. Council may, in the absence of an initiative of the High Authority,

---

[63] Reuter, *op. cit.*, pp. 241–242.

compel the latter to take action, though only if Council is unanimous. In any case, the method of determining the quotas is left entirely to the High Authority. The quota system must, however, satisfy certain conditions : it must be "equitable," take account of the principles stated in the opening articles of the Treaty, and be based on studies made in conjunction with the enterprises and their associations. The High Authority may place levies on tonnages produced in excess of quotas; the proceeds would be used to support employment in firms whose production is below the authorized level. The High Authority may impose fines on enterprises exceeding their quotas up to the value of their excess production. The system of production quotas is to be accompanied, if necessary, by import restrictions.[64] The quotas may be ended by the High Authority unless Council vetoes this action by a unanimous vote, or by the proposal of a member government unless Council rejects termination by a majority vote. It has been suggested that production quotas were made easy to abolish because they were in bad repute owing to their frequent use by cartels.[65]

In the opposite case, where the Community faces a serious shortage of coal or steel, the High Authority, after consulting the Consultative Committee, calls the matter to the attention of Council.[66] Unless Council decides otherwise by a unanimous vote, the High Authority is to make proposals to cope with the situation (Article 59, 1). On the basis of these proposals, Council, by unanimous vote, is to establish consumption priorities and to allocate supplies among (1) the coal and steel industries, (2) exports, and (3) other consumption. The

---

[64] As authorized in Article 74. See above, p. 201.

[65] Reuter, *op. cit.*, p. 242.

[66] If the High Authority fails to act and a member state calls the matter to its attention, Council may recognize the existence of a serious shortage, but unanimous action is required.

priorities thus established are to be the basis for obligatory production schedules that the High Authority is to draw up for the enterprises after consultation with the latter (Article 59, 2).

If Council fails to reach a unanimous decision, the High Authority is to allocate the available supplies among the member states "on the basis of consumption and exports and independently of the place of production." Each member state is to ration the supplies awarded to it, but it may not alter the prospective deliveries to other Member states, and it must consult the High Authority upon the quantities assigned to exports and to the operation of the coal and steel industries. If a state devotes less to exports than the amount included in the basis for the allocation among the states, or if it causes a decline in the production of a scarce product by reducing the allocation intended for the coal and steel industry, the country's share may be reduced in the next round of allocations (Article 59, 3). In any event, the responsibility for the equitable distribution of the supplies earmarked for the coal and steel industries remains with the High Authority (Article 59, 4). The High Authority may levy fines up to twice the value of the "production or deliveries prescribed which are not executed or are diverted from their proper use" (Article 59, 7).

Exports by the member states to third countries may also be placed under restriction by the High Authority or, provided that it is unanimous, by Council (Article 59, 6).

The difference in the procedures for coping with emergencies related to oversupply and those growing out of a shortage—notably the larger role of Council and the governments in the latter situation—has been explained by the fact that rationing in a period of shortage has broader effects upon the economic sectors outside of the jurisdiction of the Coal and Steel Community than production quotas in a period of overproduction.[67]

While the direct powers granted the Community with respect to production are intended mainly for emergency situations, the direct powers accorded with respect to prices are designed mainly to enable the institutions of the Community to promote competition in the coal and steel industries. However, there are some price powers—specifically, the authority to establish minimum and maximum prices—that are more relevant to short-run emergencies than to the long-run maintenance of competition. Indeed, the High Authority can establish minimum prices only if it finds that manifest crisis exists or is imminent; in addition, it must determine that such a decision is necessary to attain the general objectives of the Community (as stated in Article 3) (Article 61, 1, b). This crisis power of the High Authority, unlike the authority to establish production quotas, is not contingent upon the agreement of Council; both Council and the Consultative Committee must, however, be consulted both respect to the advisability of the step and the price level to be determined. In the absence of an initiative from the High Authority, Council may, by unanimous vote, request the High Authority to establish minimum prices.

While the same administrative arrangements are provided for the establishment of maximum prices, the latter are not directly linked to the rationing authority in connection with a serious shortage in the way in which minimum prices and production quotas are connected. The High Authority is to establish maximum prices simply if it finds that they are necessary to attain the general objectives of the Treaty (as stated in Article 3), especially the establishment of the lowest prices consistent with meeting amortization costs and provid-

[67] *Rapport de la Délegation Française,* p. 163.

ing a normal return on capital (Article 3, c).

The High Authority is also empowered to establish minimum and maximum export prices, but while the administrative arrangements are similar, its powers are circumscribed by the conditions stipulated in its grant of power (Article 61, 1, c). Such action may be taken only if it appears necessary because of dangers to the enterprises resulting from market conditions or if it seems needed to encourage international trade and to ensure equitable prices for foreign markets. In addition, price limits over exports are not to be established unless they can be effectively supervised.

Other safeguards. Aside from transitional subsidies and financial support for readaptation, the Treaty does not authorize the High Authority to use Community funds to succor firms or groups of firms suffering hardships. The purposes for which the High Authority is permitted to spend Community money (other than to meet the operating expenses of the Community's institutions), such as the support of investment programs (Article 54) and financial aid to technical and economic research (Article 55), would generally provide little direct or immediate aid to enterprises in difficulty. There is, however, one weapon in the financial sphere which the High Authority may conceivably use for short-run aid : this is its right to authorize or establish compensation schemes by which enterprises with high costs are subsidized from funds raised from enterprises with low costs. This appears to be the device referred to in the language of the Treaty which states that the High Authority may authorize or establish "financial arrangements common to several enterprises" on the conditions that they be necessary to attain the objectives of the Community (as stated in Article 3) and compatible with the provisions against restrictive agreements (Article 65) (Article 53). Specific reference is made to the possibility of authorizing such an arrangement in order to prevent the price of coal from being established at the level required by the production costs of the highest-cost mines whose output is temporarily needed to supply the Community (Article 62). The High Authority can authorize a "financial arrangement" after consultation with Council and the Consultative Committee, but it needs the unanimous consent of Council to establish one itself. The individual governments may also maintain mechanisms of this type, but they must be reported to the High Authority, which has the right to order them altered, if necessary, to conform to the Treaty (Article 53).

Finally, there is near the end of the Treaty a catch all grant of power to the High Authority, subject to the unanimous consent of Council. The High Authority is empowered, in all cases not expressly provided for in the Treaty, to make any decision or recommendation that is necessary to fulfil one of the purposes of the Community (as set forth in Articles 2, 3, and 4) (Articles 95, 1). The uses to which this clause could be put are virtually impossible to enumerate. It has, for example, been cited in order to permit the use of Community funds for financing coal stocks and aiding unemployed miners in the Belgian coal crises.[68] However, the requirement of unanimous consent of Council enables each member government to exercise a veto over the use of any residual powers that this provision might imply.

Perhaps mention should be made also of the related provision, found in the same article, which permits minor amendment of the Treaty by the institutions of the Community without action of the member states *qua* individual governments. Such amendments are to be proposed jointly by the High Authority and Council, the latter acting by a five-sixths majority. They are subject to a conforming opinion by

---

[68] See below, pp. 242f. and 247.

the Court, which may review questions of fact as well as of law, and to approval by the Assembly which must act by a vote of three-quarters of the votes cast and two-thirds of its membership (Article 95, 4). The amendments may be proposed if there is a need for a change in the rules by which the High Authority exercises the powers conferred upon it owing either to unforeseen difficulties in the operation of the Treaty or to profound changes in economic or technical conditions directly affecting coal and steel markets. The amendments may not modify the objectives of the Community (set forth in Articles 2, 3, and 4) or the power relationship between the High Authority and the other institutions of the Community (Article 95, 3).

It was under this process of *"petite revision"* that the Treaty was amended to include a safeguard that had not originally been provided—that is, readaptation aid by the Community in circumstances of structural changes in the coal and steel markets.[69]

USE OF THE SAFEGUARD CLAUSES

Transition period

Many of the precautionary provisions of the Transitional Convention never had to be applied. This was true, for example, of the production safeguards for French coal (Section 28) and Luxemburg steel (Section 31). Others, such as the

---

[69] See page 208. The Court rejected one version of this amendment mainly on the ground that its limitation to the coal industry was discriminatory in contravention of Article 4 and because the possible need to extend the amendment beyond the three year period for which it was proposed would weaken the position of the High Authority *vis-à-vis* the Council and the Assembly (Cour de Justice des Communautés Européennes, *Recueil de la Jurisprudence de la Cour,* Vol. V (1958–1959), pp. 553–562, Luxembourg, 1960). These limitations were removed from the version of the amendment that was finally approved.

temporary tariffs that Italy was permitted to apply on Community coke (Section 29, 2) and steel (Section 30, 1) were gradually eliminated during the transitional period in the manner anticipated by the Transitional Convention. On the whole, the broad program of transition to a common market appears to have worked smoothly, with the notably exception of Belgian coal.

Transitional Convention safeguards. The Belgian problem brought into play a number of the precautionary provisions of the Transitional Convention. First, the High Authority imposed the compensation levy, required by the Convention (Section 25), on the coal production of low-cost countries for the benefit of producers in high-cost countries. Beginning with an initial rate of 1.1 per cent and reduced to a rate of 0.3 per cent in successive stages, the levy had yielded about $57 million by the time it was ended in December, 1957; more than 90 per cent came from German mines and the balance from Dutch mines. The money was distributed to Belgian and Italian mines, with the former receiving nearly 90 per cent of the total. A small part of the sum paid to Belgian producers was to compensate Belgian exporters of coal to other Community countries (mainly the Netherlands, also Italy and Germany) for 80 per cent of the difference between the delivered Belgian price and the local price of delivered coal (Section 26, 2, c). The great bulk of the grants to Belgian mines was to offset the difference between the price of Belgian coal and other Community coal in the Belgian market, and thus to avoid either a decline in the receipts for the Belgian mines or the isolation of the Belgian coal market from that of the rest of the Community (Section 26, 2, a). An important reason for protecting the receipts of the Belgian producers was to enable them to invest in modernization as part of a broader program of reorganization of the Belgian coal industry that was supposed to make the Belgian mines competitive without the aid of subsidies by the end of the transition period. In view of this objective, the scheme of subsidization, originally applied to all coal and to all producers in Belgium, was made selective, first by eliminating certain types of coal which did not require subsidies and secondly by eliminating producers at both cost extremes—that is, those with such low costs that they could already meet competition, and those with such high-cost installations that they had little prospect of becoming competitive.[70] The High Authority supported the modernization program also through loans for the construction of pit-head power stations; $14 million had been advanced for this purpose by the end of the transition period.[71]

In addition to these measures, the High Authority permitted the Belgian Government to pay supplementary subsidies (Section 11) beyond the matching grants it had to make for the Community subsidies described above and to establish a compensation scheme involving only Belgian mines (Section 24, 3, b). In all, the Belgian Government paid out direct subsidies to the coal industry of $140 million, and various indirect subsidies, such as support from the public treasury for miners' social security, came to another $200 million.[72] These figures were somewhere in the vicinity of 5.5 and 8 per cent, respectively, of the market value of Belgian coal output.[73]

Despite the closing down of some uneconomical pits and an

---

[70] The experience with the compensation levy is summarized in the *Sixth Report*, pp. 27–48.

[71] *Eighth Report*, p. 44.

[72] The figures refer to the calendar years 1953 to 1957 inclusive and are derived from "Subsides Directs et Indirects Spécifiques à l'Industrie Charbonnière Belge," *Etudes*, 1961, No. 2, Ministère des Affaires Economiques.

[73] Based on a five-year output value of $2.5 billion calculated by multiplying the production figures by an assumed average price of $17 per ton. See *Eighth Report*, pp. 381, 400–401.

improvement in productivity, Belgian coal was little, if at all, closer to being able to compete in Community markets at the end of the transition period than at the beginning. Belgian coal costs at the end of 1957 were 40 per cent above the average for the rest of the Community and nearly 50 per cent above the costs of the Ruhr.[14] Underground output per manshift, though higher by 9 per cent in 1957 than in 1952 in absolute terms, was 75 per cent of the Community average in 1957 as compared with 76 per cent in 1952.

Under the boom conditions that characterized the coal market during most of the transitional period, the millions of dollars of Community and Belgian subsidies provided the margin by which many high-cost mines were able to carry on as usual. Production in the high-cost mines of the south declined by less than 10 per cent between 1952 and 1957,[15] and little was done to develop the rich Campine fields with a view to their use to replace the output of the uneconomical mines in the south. The High Authority was inclined to blame the Belgian Government for not carrying through a more vigorous reorganization program, and particularly for not pressing further with "negative rationalization," meaning the closing down of high-cost mines.[16] The Belgians felt that the primary object of the High Authority's policy had been to reduce costs, and that, owing to the energy shortage in the Community and the consequent need to import large quantities of foreign coal, the High Authority had not systematically pressed for a reduction in Belgian production.[17] In any

---

[14] *Sixth Report,* Vol. II, p. 40.

[15] *Sixth Report,* Vol. II, p. 45.

[16] *Sixth Report,* Vol. II, p. 46.

[17] This argument is strongly hinted at in an earlier version of the Belgian memorandum of November 21, 1959, relative to the invocation of Article 37, but it is not contained in the version reproduced in the documents of a case before the Court of Justice. See footnote on page 250 below.

case, the problem of Belgian coal became more troublesome than ever when the boom conditions in the coal market terminated at about the same time that the transition period drew to its close. Thus the Community was left to grapple with a problem industry largely upon the basis of the provisions of the Treaty itself.[78]

The experience with the smaller problem posed by Italian coal was only slightly better. The compensation payments were extended over a two-year period as provided in the Transitional Convention and a re-equipment program was carried out. Between 1952 and 1957 output per manshift rose by more than 50 per cent, but government subsidies were still necessary after the end of the transition period.

In the coal industries of France, Germany, and the Netherlands, subsidies, special charges, and compensation programs existing at the time the common market was opened were generally permitted to continue but were subjected to gradual dismantling. Of these temporary exceptions, the French subsidies were probably the most important from a quantitative standpoint : they amounted to perhaps 4 per cent of the market value of French coal output in 1953 and were gradually reduced to negligible amounts by the end of the transition period.[79] Special charges on the German coal industry in the form of reduced prices for certain consumers and a compensation arrangement in the Netherlands by which all consumers paid the same price for a given grade of coal regardless of origin or destination were terminated well before the end of the transition period.

Another transitional safeguard clause that was invoked in order to avoid disturbance to existing arrangements in the

---

[78] See above p. 207f.

[79] Subsequently, however, the losses of the nationalized mines were offset in effect by increases in "capital" contributed by the French Government.

Community's coal markets was the authorization of zonal pricing. The Treaty forbids price discrimination in general terms (Article 4, b) and purely local price discrimination in specific terms (Article 60, 1), but the High Authority used its special authority under the Transitional Convention (Section 24) to permit certain surplus-producing regions to align their prices for sales in their customary market areas. For example, coal from the Saar and from Lorraine could continue to be sold in southern Germany at prices comparable to delivered prices of Ruhr coal and in western France at prices competitive with those of British and Polish coal. The temporary continuation of these reduced delivered prices for entire zones was deemed necessary to avoid sudden shifts in production or large increases in prices. The arrangements were modified as time went on, especially when the situation was changed by the introduction of international through-transport rates. They were terminated by the end of the transition period.

The transitional precautionary measures invoked in the case of steel were less extensive than for coal, probably because there was, with the exception of Italy, no major sector of the industry with exceptionally high costs. The High Authority used the power given it in the Transitional Convention to permit Italy to levy duties on Community steel (Section 30, 1) and to forbid other Community producers from aligning their prices with those of Italian steelmakers (Article 30, 2).[80] The duties were gradually eliminated, and the vigorous modernization program successfully pursued during the transition years enabled the Italian steel industry, protected by the freight costs encountered by other Community steel in reaching the Italian market, to carry on without tariffs.[81]

---

[80] Community producers were, however, allowed to align prices with third-country quotations on the Italian market.

[81] However, at the end of the transition period the Italian steelmakers sought to retain their full geographical protection. In response to their

Another safeguard clause invoked during the transition period with respect to steel was the provision permitting the Benelux countries to import their domestic requirements of third-country steel at their pre-Community rates of duty with the understanding that imports in excess of domestic requirements would be subject to higher duties. The tariff quota arrangements appear to have worked satisfactorily until they were replaced at the end of the transition period by a "harmonized" but not equal common tariff. The basic rates of the harmonized tariff were the Benelux duties plus two percentage points, but France was permitted to supplement these rates by one point and Italy by two to four points.[82] The supplements for France and Italy corresponded to the "geographical protection" afforded them by transport costs from the Benelux countries; that is, tariffs above the Benelux levels by these amounts would not induce indirect imports from third countries.

The most general precautionary clause for steel provided in the Transitional Convention (Section 29) was never used, but it is of interest because the High Authority was required as one of its first tasks to establish "technical criteria" for its invocation. The provision, it will be recalled, requires the High Authority to prevent two types of "shifts in production" arising out of the introduction of the common market: (1) those that would create difficulties for enterprises which would

---

request to forbid price alignment by other Community producers under powers given the High Authority by the Treaty (Article 60, 2, b), the High Authority placed the volume of such alignments on the Italian market under observation. It subsequently concluded that the practice was not quantitatively important, and denied the request. *Eighth Report,* pp. 182–184.

[82] *Sixth Report,* Vol. I, pp. 82–83. Actually France and Italy were permitted to levy duties slightly above their harmonized rates on some products for a limited period. These were duly suppressed within the time limits established, and France, moreover, renounced the geographical protection referred to above. *Ninth Report,* p. 58.

be viable after a period of adaptation to the common market; and (2) those leading to the displacement of more workers than could benefit from the readaptation provisions of the Convention. The High Authority in carrying out this responsibility did not go beyond the language of the Convention with respect to the second type of shift in production. As concerns the first, it specified that there would have to be "a perceptible falling off" of production in any unit ranging from a country to an important sector of an enterprise, provided that the decline relate to normal production and that it upset the equilibrium of the territory or organization concerned. From the standpoint of the enterprise itself, the key question was whether the continuity of activity of the enterprise was likely to be jeopardized, and in considering this question the social aspects, especially the effects on the workers, had to be taken into account along with the technical and economic factors.[83] Perhaps it was well that the transition period was marked by prosperous conditions in the steel industry, for these criteria seem to have left the door wide open for almost any firm in difficulty to make a case for help. The High Authority's stress on the need to preserve flexibility and on its willingness, in response to views expressed in the Consultative Committee and in Council, to take account of the individual circumstances of particular cases seem to confirm the impression that the safeguarding clause was very broadly construed.

Readaptation measures, which also played a small role during the transition period, will be considered in a later section.

Treaty safeguards. Some safeguards provided in the Treaty itself were invoked during the transition period, although the most important uses of the precautionary clauses of the Treaty

---

[83] *The Establishment of the Common Market for Steel,* May, 1953, pp. 45–57.

were not made until the advent of the Belgian coal crisis at the end of the transition period. Since the Belgian difficulties warrant separate treatment, we shall confine ourselves here to Treaty measures that were called into play in connection with other situations.

One of the troublesome problems faced by the High Authority upon its assumption of its duties was that posed by scrap supplies for the iron and steel industry.[84] At the opening of the common market scrap prices varied widely within the Community, being low in the countries which could satisfy their own requirements (France, Germany, and the Netherlands) and closer to high world prices in those countries which had to rely upon imports (Belgium and, more especially, Italy). The Treaty's nondiscrimination provisions meant that steel producers in the scrap-deficit countries would be entitled to enter the markets of the other member countries and bid for scrap supplies. Even though the over-all Community deficit of scrap was small, scrap prices, which are sensitive to small fluctuations in demand, could be expected to rise sharply, perhaps to the level established by the marginal purchases of high-priced foreign (third-country) scrap. The consequence would be a rise in steel prices that both the High Authority and the governments were anxious to avoid.

As a temporary expedient, the High Authority invoked its powers to ration products in scarce supply (Article 59, 3). For the period February 9 to March 15, 1953, it allocated in

---

[84] The account which follows is based on the successive annual reports of the High Authority and upon certain issues of the *Journal Officiel* cited in those reports. See also Diebold, *op. cit.*, pp. 287–313, and Lister, *op. cit.*, pp. 59–67. It may be of interest to note that Lister provides estimates which indicate that in 1956 purchased scrap accounted for proportions of total material costs in steelmaking that varied from 10 to 50 per cent. The figure was close to 10 per cent in the Saar, a little more than 15 per cent in Luxemburg, slightly under 20 per cent in Belgium, somewhat over 20 per cent in France, more than 25 per cent in Germany, and about 50 per cent in Italy.

principle the scrap resources of each member country to that country, while authorizing certain shipments of French and German scrap to Italy. After the expiration of this period of rationing, the High Authority fixed maximum prices for various grades of scrap in nine different zones into which the Community was divided (Article 61, 1, a). To discourage speculative stockpiling, it was announced in advance that the maximum prices would decrease three months after the effective date of the initial price control. Subsequently the demand for steel declined, and the ceiling prices were reduced still further, and eventually, a year after they were first put into effect they were abolished.

At the same time that the maximum prices had been established, the High Authority had taken steps to supersede the various national groups that had been operating in the scrap markets with a Community-wide organization. It had thus authorized the establishment of an organization through which scrap consumers could negotiate jointly for imports from third countries and join in a perequation fund (Article 53, 1, a). The perequation fund, which in various forms was to be the basis of the High Authority's scrap policy for the next five years, would make it possible to divide proportionately among scrap consumers the excess costs (over low-priced Community scrap) of the imports necessary to cover the Community deficit. Only in this way, the High Authority argued, could a common market be maintained without entailing a competitive scramble for scrap that would drive its price up without benefit to the Community. However, the various consuming groups had been unable to agree upon import policy, and this voluntary arrangement had to be replaced with a plan less dependent upon the unanimity of the consumers.

Accordingly, when the price ceilings were eliminated, a

compulsory compensation fund was established by the High Authority (Article 53, 1, b). All scrap sold within the Community was subject to a levy that varied in actual practice, according to market conditions, between $3 and $13 per ton. The proceeds were used to bring down the cost of imported scrap to the Community level. (Scrap prices in the Community varied in the range of $30 to $50 per ton for the most part, and it was not unusual for the price of imported scrap to be $20 or $30 a ton higher than the Community price.)

When the 1954-55 steel boom drove scrap imports and prices up, the High Authority modified the plan so as to encourage economy in the use of scrap. Compensation payments were no longer limited to purchases of imported scrap, but were also used to encourage the substitution of pig-iron and of Thomas liquid steel for scrap by making good the difference between the cost of scrap and these substitute materials. When these incentives did not achieve the desired results, they were supplemented, over widespread opposition from the steel producers of France, Germany, and Belgium, by penalties for increased use of scrap. The penalties took the form of a surcharge in addition to the regular compensation levy; it was imposed beginning in August, 1957, on enterprises for as long as their scrap consumption exceed that of a reference period which each enterprise was free to select from any six out of seven consecutive months in the period 1953–57. An enterprise achieving a reduction in its scrap consumption per ton of output, compared to its base period or to the average Community consumption per ton, received a rebate on the surcharge.[85] Shortly after the surcharges came into

---

[85] The decision, which was made in January, 1959, provided that the surcharge would rise gradually from 25 per cent of the basic rate beginning in August, 1957, to 100 per cent in May, 1958. Since the basic rate itself varied with the need for foreign scrap and with the gap

effect, the rate of steel production slackened, and scrap requirements were reduced; at the same time, a decline in economic activity in the United States also operated to make scrap available at lower prices. Accordingly, the compensation scheme was allowed to expire at the end of November, 1958.

The High Authority felt that the relief afforded to the Community's scrap position was purely cyclical, and that a structural problem existed which could only be met in time. It followed a long-run policy of encouraging increases in the production of pig-iron and discouraging the expansion of forms of steelmaking that would have to rely on upon bought scrap. In support of this policy, the High Authority used both its lending powers (Article 54, 1) and its power to give unfavorable opinions on individual investment projects (Article 54, 5).

When the compensation program expired, the High Authority sought Council agreement on shorter-run measures to help equalize competitive conditions in different phases of the business cycle between mills with high and low scrap ratios. With the current recession, scrap prices were below pig-iron prices, and there was unused pig-iron capacity in the Community. In these circumstances, the High Authority advocated a bonus for steel mills using pig iron in order to stimulate fuller utilization of pig-iron capacity. At the same time, it wished approval for a stand-by compensation scheme for imported scrap which would become operative only if blast furnaces were operating near or at full capacity or if warranted by scrap prices. Italy, whose mills had a high scrap ratio, objected to the pig-iron bonuses, and Germany refused to approve the

---

between the prices of foreign and domestic scrap, the penalty on high scrap consumption automatically increased when the Community's need to economize on scrap rose. The rebate was five times the percentage of the reduction in scrap consumption per ton of output, to a limit of 100 per cent of the surcharge.

compensation plan without the bonuses. Thus nothing came of the High Authority proposals.

The scrap compensation scheme was plagued with administrative difficulties. As we have already noted, the complexity of the plan had to be increased in order to encourage economy in the use of scrap. In addition, a number of organizational problems were encountered. Some of the trouble could be ascribed to lack of experience and the consequent necessity to operate along empirical lines. For example, the failure to define "scrap" at the beginning encouraged both pretexts to avoid the payment of the levy and subsequent disputes about the appropriate definition. The administrative problems were compounded in mid-1958 when the Court, acting upon an appeal of steel producers against the High Authority, found that the High Authority had violated the Treaty in delegating powers to two organizations to which it had entrusted the task of operating the scheme.[86] After this decision the High Authority had to review every transaction covering either the assessment of the levy or the payment of compensation over a four-year period. Matters were made worse by the discovery of fraud in declarations claiming that certain scrap was of foreign origin and therefore eligible for compensation.[87]

Treaty safeguards were invoked also in the coal market, quite apart from the Belgian difficulties to which we will turn shortly. Given the existence of price controls over coal in all the Community countries and the tight market situation for certain kinds of coal, the High Authority found it necessary to invoke its powers to establish price ceilings (Article 61, 1, a) in order to fulfill its obligation to seek the lowest prices consistent with amortization and normal returns on capital (Article 61, 1, a, and 3, c). It sought, however, to leave some leeway to

---

[86] *Seventh Report*, p. 99.
[87] *Eighth Report*, pp. 164–165.

individual firms to make their own adjustments to the new market situations. Accordingly, it established over-all average prices for each category of coal (i. e., bituminous, anthracite, etc.) which could not be exceeded. Subject to keeping within this average and subject also to an absolute ceiling price for each category, firms were left free to set their own prices for individual grades (i. e., sizes). However, for a few grades in short supply, notably coking fines and blast-furnace coke, specific ceiling prices were fixed. After the common market had been in operation for a year, the High Authority decided that the market situation did not warrant the continuation of maximum prices. However, it feared that its withdrawal of price controls would leave coal prices to be determined by the Ruhr sales organization and the collieries of the Nord and Pas-de-Calais coal fields. It therefore kept the prices of the latter under control for another year and those of the former for two more years, by which time three independent selling agencies had replaced the single one which had existed in the Ruhr.

Another aspect of coal market policy related to price alignment. During the transition period, it will be recalled, the High Authority suspended the right of coal enterprises to engage in the general alignment of prices with competitors and used its powers to permit zonal prices (Section 24, 3, b). After the end of the transition period, the High Authority ended zonal pricing and permitted general price alignment to a limited extent (Article 60, 2, b). For any enterprise, sales at prices aligned with those of other Community collieries were not to exceed 20 per cent of its previous year's sales or, in any one sales area, the level of its previous year's sales. To protect small producers, alignment was permitted only with the delivered prices of the biggest producers or their selling agencies. The High Authority made exceptions to the quantitative limits for alignment in cases affecting "traditional" and "natural" flows of coal. While producers with high price schedules tended to take full advantage of their price-alignment privileges, others did not. Thus, three years after the decision the High Authority reported that the volume of price alignment still fell short of the permitted limit for the Community as a whole, although it had increased significantly in the last year.[88] None of the foregoing applies, of course, to price alignments with third-country coal; these were never restricted by the High Authority.

In the complex transport area, the High Authority had to determine in what circumstances it would use its Treaty powers (Article 70, 4) to give its agreement to special tariff measures in the interest of one or several enterprises. In approaching this task, the High Authority distinguished between those exceptions from general tariffs that were based upon the existence of competing forms of transport, and those that were intended as "supporting tariffs" for certain enterprises.[89] It did not consider the former as discriminatory, provided that they were properly calculated. On the other hand, it did regard the latter as discriminatory except in unusual cases; they could be consistent with the Treaty only when special circumstances required favorable transport rates in order to achieve the objectives of the Community (i. e., the aims set forth in Articles 2 and 3). For example, supporting tariffs could legitimately be established in connection with a program to alleviate difficulties affecting an entire region. Thus the problems created for certain areas by the division of Germany led the High Authority to approve reduced tariff rates

---

[88] *Ninth Report*, pp. 163–164. See also *Sixth Report,* pp. 26–27, and *Eighth Report,* pp. 181–182.

[89] *Sixth Report,* Vol. I, p. 67–70. See also Diebold, *op. cit.,* pp. 173–177 for a discussion of the problem of defining special rates and for an account of some of the important decisions of the High Authority.

for certain enterprises near Germany's eastern frontier.[90] For the most part, however, the High Authority ordered the elimination of special rates, usually providing for their gradual removal over periods ranging from two to seven years.

The Treaty's provisions regarding the impairment of the conditions of competition were called into play following the French devaluations of 1957 and 1958. Despite increases in franc prices, French steel prices became the lowest in the Community after the 1957 measures and the difference was sharply increased after the devaluation at the end of 1958. In the view of the High Authority, the necessarily sudden though legitimate French monetary adjustments could involve serious difficulties for the iron and steel enterprises of other countries by "substantially increasing differences in costs of production otherwise than through variations in productivity" (Article 67, 2). Thus, it recommended to the French Government that the latter take measures that it deemed compatible with French economic equilibrium to ease the disequilibrium that had been provoked by its actions.[91] A revival in the steel market shortly thereafter eased the situation, and the French Government never took any action in response to this recommendation.

Readaptation and redevelopment

Since trade barriers were to be dismantled immediately upon the opening of the common market, it was expected that it would soon become clear which enterprises could not hope to meet competition on a Community-wide basis. The provisions for aiding enterprises and workers who were adversely affected by the opening of the common market were therefore confined mainly to the transition period. Within this five-year period,

---

[90] *Sixth Report,* Vol. II, p. 75.
[91] *Journal Official,* March 23, 1959.

the High Authority, at the request of a government, could provide financial assistance on its own authority; for another two years it could give such aid provided Council consented (Section 23). For the permanent period, provision was made for readaptation assistance only in the event of a substantial technological displacement of labor (Article 56, which had not been used as of mid-1961).

However, in the conditions of prosperity and rapid economic expansion that characterized the transition period, there was little call for transitional (i. e., Section 23) readaptation aid. More than a year after the opening of the common market, only three requests had been received by the High Authority and favorable action had been completed only on one.[92] By the end of the transition period early in 1958, but 32 enterprises and fewer than 19,000 workers had been involved in Community assistance programs. The High Authority had allocated about $12 million for these purposes, of which only $4.5 million had actually been spent.[93] Within the next two years, however, the structural difficulties of the coal industry became clear. This, combined with the prospect of the termination of transitional readaptation assistance, brought a flood of applications from the governments. In the last month alone (January, 1960), applications were approved for nearly 100 establishments. Thus, before the readaptation powers of the Transitional Convention expired, the High Authority had approved programs involving about 200 enterprises and 115,000 workers. Nearly 90 per cent of the workers were in the coal industry, and of these over half were in German and 30 per cent in Belgian mines. Appropriations amounted to $43 million, but less than $16 million had actually been spent

[92] *Second Report,* pp. 166–167.
[93] *Sixth Report,* Vol. II, pp. 187–188. See also *Eighth Report,* pp. 282–289.

at the end of September, 1960.[94] Expenditures could be expected to lag behind appropriations because many of the programs were spread over a period of years, but it is also true that part of the funds will never actually be expended because some anticipated readaptations may not have to be carried out and because discharged workers sometimes get other work more readily than expected.

Early experience with readaptation programs was not too reassuring.[95] The first program was an attempt to move 5,000 workers from mines in southern France to those of the Lorraine over a five-year period. The plan was abandoned after a year or two when only a few hundred workers, mainly foreign, had been transferred. The scheme failed because neither the push of economic necessity nor the pull of economic opportunity was sufficient to overcome the reluctance of the workers and their families to move to a different type of countryside. While employment in the mines involved in the plan declined by 5,000, there appeared to be no severe unemployment problem in the region as a whole. In addition, the reports of the early migrants to the Lorraine reflected disappointment with housing conditions and wages. Opposition from merchants and other local sources also contributed to the unwillingness of the workers to volunteer for transfer.

There were other instances in which less than full use was made of readaptation assistance. This was sometimes due to the lapse of time between the development of the conditions requiring aid and the actual availability of the aid. To some extent, the time gap was inherent in the stages that had to be passed through before an operating program could exist; first

---

[94] *Ninth Report,* p. 274.

[95] This and the following two paragraphs relating to transitional programs are based largely upon the account of Diebold, *op. cit.,* pp. 404–426.

an enterprise had to appreciate its problem, then it had to enlist the support of its government, next the government had to work out an agreement with the High Authority, and finally the government had to make the arrangements for the actual operation of the plan. It is not surprising, therefore, that, against a background of economic prosperity and relatively little difficulty in the coal and steel industries, ordinary market forces minimized the need for planned readaptation assistance.

That problems would be encountered also at the other extreme of general unemployment was suggested by early experience in connection with Italian steel workers. The Italian Government wished to avoid according treatment to the 8,000 or 9,000 redundant steelworkers in 1954 that would be more favorable than that granted to other segments of the approximately two million unemployed workers. It proposed, therefore, that readaptation assistance take the form of advances to finance industrial expansion for firms that would promise to recruit at least half of their new workers from those discharged by the steel industry. Two and a half years after the initial request from Italy, agreement was at last reached that the Italian Government would use its share to subsidize the interest payments of the expanding firms while the High Authority's funds would provide retrospective assistance to the steel-workers. As one writer has pointed out, this amounted to a belated social security grant rather than an encouragement of adaptation.[96]

Some, but not all, of these problems could be minimized as experience accumulated. Close cooperation with trade unions made it possible for the High Authority to begin its study of a particular situation before the official request for aid reached it, and thus to shorten the period of time between the need for assistance and its provision. The High Authority developed

---

[96] Diebold, *op. cit.,* p. 417.

clearer and more consistent patterns for its readaptation programs. It stressed reemployment, and tried to design programs which, while including tide-over allowances for unemployed workers, would provide the workers with incentives to undergo retraining and to take new employment even at lower initial wages. Thus, while the programs outlined in the agreements between the High Authority and the several governments varied somewhat according to the existing social security system and the policies of the government, there were many broad similarities.

A discharged worker remaining unemployed was granted an allowance for a tide-over period usually lasting 12 or 15 months, and most often computed at a declining percentage of his former wage such as 100, 80, and 60 per cent (or 90, 80, and 70 per cent) for successive portions of the period (successive thirds of a year, for example). However, if the worker was undergoing retraining, he was frequently entitled to assistance for the entire year at the initial percentage of his past wage, and all his retraining expenses were refunded to him. Support was also provided to the retraining center itself. If a worker accepted employment at a wage below that which he formerly earned, the difference was made up to him for the duration of the tide-over period, sometimes in full and sometimes up to 90 or 95 per cent of his former wage. In the case of layoffs for plant renovation or reconversion, workers were occasionally placed on leave with full pay or near-full pay.

Travel expenses were also provided for the tide-over period for employment interviews, for the extra expenses of traveling to a more distant place of employment, and for the costs of moving a family to a new place of employment. Readaptation funds were also used to build workers' housing.

Special features of readaptation programs were sometimes designed to meet particular situations. For example, workers discharged from German mines were compensated for the loss of their entitlement to concessionary coal. The same scheme also provided for lump-sum payments to workers eligible for pensions to induce their retirement before the compulsory age so as to make room for the continued employment of younger workers. Readaptation grants in the case of Belgium included not only the usual type of aids to workers but also labor-cost subsidies to enterprises to enable them to continue to pay regular wages to workers at a pit scheduled for closure.

Almost as soon as the transitional readaptation powers expired, they were replaced by the newly adopted provision in the Treaty (Article 56, 2, finally approved in March, 1960) which empowers the High Authority to extend readaptation assistance, without any time limit, when warranted by profound changes in marketing conditions in the coal and steel industries. Before the end of 1960, these powers were utilized on behalf of 2,300 workers in three Belgian mines.[97]

The early experience of the High Authority with readaptation led it to the conclusion that the solution for redundant coal and steel workers could not be achieved by encouraging them to move to other industrial centers but rather that new economic activities would have to be developed in the localities where the excess manpower existed. For a time, however, the High Authority stressed the fact that the development and creation of new activities was the responsibility of the governments and therefore fell outside the jurisdiction of the Community's institutions. Even the financial loans and guarantees that the Community could extend under the terms of the Treaty would be insufficient unless broader programs of development, such as the provision of the necessary supporting industries and tax relief, were organized by the governments.[98]

[97] *Ninth Report,* p. 279.
[98] *Sixth Report,* p. 192.

No use had been made, therefore, of the provisions of the readaptation clauses that empowered the High Authority to aid in financing new economic activities to provide new employment activities.

However, the evidence of secular decline in the coal-mining industry, and particularly its impact upon southern Belgium, forced the High Authority to take a more active role in industrial redevelopment. At the request of the Belgian Government, it participated in studies for the redevelopment of the areas in southern Belgium (Article 46, 4),[99] and commissioned studies of employment situations in other troubled areas. It also convened a major conference on industrial reconversion at the end of September, 1960, which included delegations from the member states, now all alerted to the existence of the problem, and other interested countries and international bodies. In the careful preparatory work, the experience of European countries, including that of Great Britain with its redevelopment areas, was sifted. The conference reached a consensus on many aspects of the problem, most of which, it was agreed, fall within the jurisdiction of the individual governments. However, the need was stressed for the interchange of information between governments to avoid the formulation of mutually inconsistent programs, particularly in the energy area. Also, cooperation between countries would be necessary for the redevelopment of certain contiguous areas, such as the Borinage region of Belgium and the Nord area of France. The Community ought to assist in the development and financing of the redevelopment plans formulated under the responsibility of the individual governments, and the High Authority in particular ought to bear in mind the need for coordination of the various reconversion plans in the Community.[100] Thus, it may be anti-

---

[99] *Eighth Report,* p. 267; *Ninth Report,* p. 281.
[100] *Ninth Report,* pp. 285–287.

cipated that future lending operations of the High Authority will be directed toward regional redevelopment of the coal areas that have been suffering secular decline.

The Belgian Coal Crisis

At the time of the Treaty negotiations and for the first five years of the existence of the Community the main problem in the coal sector was the excess of demand over domestic supply. As late as April, 1958, the High Authority could still discuss the coal market in terms of the Community's "energy gap," and in Febraury, 1959, it still regarded the expected trend in coal production "as falling seriously short of requirements, notwithstanding the present marketing difficulties."[101] However, at the time of its earlier statement, the High Authority also noted that demand had eased during 1957 and warned against long-term commitments for the import of American coal beyond the level necessary to meet long-run requirements.[102] By the time it made the second statement referred to above, the decline in demand led it to describe the market situation for coal as "undeniably serious."[103] Matters subsequently grew worse. Deliveries of hard coal to consumers in the Community were 16 per cent lower in 1959 than in 1957, and pithead stocks expanded from 7 million metric tons at the end of 1957 to 31 million at the end of 1959, or from about 3 per cent of annual consumption to about 13 per cent.[104]

---

[101] The first reference may be found in the *Sixth Report,* Vol. II, p. 107; the second in the *Seventh Report,* p. 190. Earlier, in the *Fifth Report,* the High Authority had estimated that the Community's coal requirements would expand by 10 per cent between 1955 and 1960 (pp. 255–262). The estimated 1960 requirements of 300 million tons (exclusive of 7 million tons of estimated exports) may be compared with actual 1960 consumption of 251 million tons. (*Ninth Report,* p. 122).

[102] *Sixth Report,* Vol. II, p. 127.

[103] *Seventh Report,* p. 44.

[104] The figures cited in this paragraph are drawn from the *Eighth Report,* pp. 117, 118, 122.

Production which at its peak level in 1956 was about 4 per cent above that of 1952, the Community's starting year, sank below the 1952 level in 1959.

Nature of the difficulties. While all the members of the Community felt the impact of the adverse turn of events in the coal market, the effects upon them were far from uniform. Italy and Luxemburg, with negligible or no production of coal, tended to benefit from the weakening of prices. The Netherlands and the Saar, which accounted for 5 and 7 per cent respectively of Community output in 1952, are efficient producers and were able to maintain production; stocks rose between 1957 and 1960 in both places but did not become as large relative to annual production as in the other producing areas. The other areas—Germany with half the Community's productive capacity in 1952, France with nearly one-quarter and Belgium with over one-eighth—were compelled to cope with more difficult situations.

Hardest hit was Belgium, where coal production represented 12 per cent of the value of all goods produced and employed 10 per cent of the nation's industrial workers.[105] Deep pits and thin and steeply inclined seams, especially in the Borinage and other southern fields, made mechanization difficult, and placed the Belgian mines at a disadvantage relative to those of other Community countries and more especially with those of the United States.[106] We have already noted how the high-cost Belgian mines were able to market their coal as long as the demand for coal had remained high, and how Belgium had felt little pressure to achieve the cutbacks in production through the closing of uneconomical pits that had been anticipated in the Transitional Convention (Section 26).[107] With the

---

[105] *Eighth Report*, p. 152.
[106] Lister, *op. cit.*, pp. 93–95.
[107] See above, p. 217f.

end of boom conditions in the fuel market, Belgian production fell sharply and coal stocks mounted rapidly; 1959 output was 20 per cent below that of 1957, and December, 1959, coal stocks were equivalent to about 30 per cent of annual production, compared to less than 5 per cent two years earlier.[108]

Germany was sheltered from the full impact of the decline in demand by relatively low costs and by the opportunity to place the main burden of the declining sales on imports from third countries which had expanded rapidly and were equivalent to one-eighth of domestic output in 1957. Between 1957 and 1959 these imports were slashed by two-thirds, while the decline in domestic production was around 5 per cent; even in absolute terms, the 11-million-ton reduction in such imports was large relative to the 7-million-ton reduction in production. Stocks expanded from less than 1 per cent of annual production at the end of 1957 to around 8 per cent at the end of 1959.[109]

France fared better than either Belgium or Germany; indeed, French coal output actually was slightly higher both in 1958 and 1959 than in any previous year. The adjustment to the decline in demand was met almost solely by restricting imports from non-Community sources; such imports were cut even more sharply in relative terms than in Germany. Amounting to 9.7 million tons and equivalent to 17 per cent of domestic production in 1957, they were reduced to 2.2 million tons in 1959. The position of French coal on Community markets was aided by the French currency devaluation of December, 1958. Nevertheless, French coal stocks expanded from near 10 per cent of annual production at the end of 1957 to nearly double that proportion two years later.[110]

---

[108] *Eighth Report,* pp. 381, 385.
[109] *Ibid.*
[110] *Eighth Report, ibid.*

The factors that converted the scarcity of coal that prevailed in western Europe before 1957 to a glut seemed to work with great suddenness because their operation had been obscured by the rapid rate of European economic expansion and by the effects of the Suez crisis. Two main groups of long-run influences unfavorable to coal were at work. The first was the development of improved fuel utilization techniques which reduced energy requirements per unit of output. The second was the substitution of oil—and to a lesser degree of natural gas—for coal; growing supplies of oil and gas brought about a shift in relative prices that encouraged their consumption at the expense of coal. Thus the relative importance of coal as a source of primary energy in the countries of the Community declined from 72 per cent in 1950 to 63 per cent in 1955 and 54 per cent in 1959.[111] The operation of these factors was intensified by the short-run effects on demand of two years with unusually mild winters and with ample water supplies. In addition, ocean freight rates, which had been exceptionally high, declined sharply and thus worsened the competitive position of European coal *vis-à-vis* oil and foreign coal.[112]

Proposals of the High Authority. In the view of the High Authority, the impact of these changes upon Belgian mines was a Community-wide problem not only in the sense that all members of a true community are affected when one of their number encounters special difficulties but also in the sense that the Belgian troubles arose from new trends that would sooner or later bring similar problems to the other coal-producing members of the Community. In 1958 and 1959, however, the

---

[111] The percentage was 52 in 1960 and was expected to decline to 50 in 1961. See *Ninth Report,* p. 71. The 1957 forecast referred to in a previous footnote anticipated that coal would still be used to cover more than half of the Community's energy requirements in 1975. *Fifth Report,* p. 262.

[112] See *Eighth Report,* pp. 70–73, 110–111.

other coal-producing countries were not, as we have seen, as badly hurt as Belgium, and the High Authority was not very successful in leading them to regard the Belgian problem in Community rather than in national terms.

As required by the Treaty, the High Authority first tried to use the "indirect means of action" specified in Article 57, including steps intended to influence consumption and to discourage imports. The measures designed to affect consumption consisted mainly of appeals to governments to influence coal consumers, especially those in the public sphere such as power stations and railways, to take regular coal deliveries rather than to draw on their stocks, and of similar pleas with respect to the placing of steel orders, the latter being intended to support the coke market. Governments were also asked to examine the competitive conditions of coal and oil, including the taxes assessed against each.

Beyond these indirect measures, the proposals made by the High Authority to cope with the coal crisis during 1958 and 1959 centered around four main lines: (1) the reduction of imports from third countries; (2) the financing of stocks to enable the mines to continue operations rather than to throw men out of work; (3) direct financial aid to miners on short time; and (4) production quotas to limit output. More fundamental programs of reorganization of mines and readaptation of workers were advocated by the High Authority for high-cost mines, especially in Belgium, but most of the controversy between the High Authority and the governments of the large member states centered around the shorter-run lines of action. In none of the four aspects mentioned above did the High Authority succeed in winning the unanimity required in Council for the full program it proposed, and the last-mentioned and perhaps most drastic weapon it advocated, the use of production quotas, was rejected outright.

One of the first lines of defense against the decline in demand adopted by the countries and supported by the High Authority was the reduction of imports from third countries. The High Authority eased its rules with respect to price alignment so as to improve the competitive position of Community mines with respect to third-country fuel sources. After Belgium and Germany had imposed restrictions on coal imports from third countries (in February and September, 1958, respectively), the High Authority enlisted the mutual aid of the other member states (under Article 71) to enable Belgium and Germany to check on the true origin of coal coming from Community countries. Subsequently (January, 1959) when it appeared that the German Government intended to levy a duty on third-country imports in excess of a duty-free quota, the High Authority issued a recommendation to this effect. Finally, the High Authority supported efforts, particularly by Belgium and Germany, to negotiate the cancelation or suspension of import contracts with the United States, Great Britain, and other outside suppliers.

The proposals to maintain employment by helping the collieries to finance coal stocks was also advanced at a relatively early date. In April, 1958, the High Authority asked Council to consent to the establishment under Article 53 of a special levy of 5 cents a ton in order to give bonuses to the mines for stocking coal. The unanimous consent of Council was not given either in June or in October when the High Authority offered a revised stock scheme. In November, Council finally agreed (under Article 95, 1) to permit the High Authority to allocate $7 million of its own funds for this purpose. Grants of 4.33 cents or loans of 16.67 cents per ton were extended to collieries putting coal to stock after October 31, 1958, if the monthly average tonnage held exceeded the equivalent of 35 days' net production. The High Authority could not obtain the agreement of Council to increase the allocation of money for the stock program and the funds were virtually exhausted by mid-1959. German collieries received $5 million, but, unlike the enterprises of other countries aided under the plan, they obtained the funds on a loan basis. Grants of $1 million went to Belgian mines, $600,000 to French mines, and less than $40,000 to Dutch mines.[113] Stocks amounting to about $4\frac{1}{4}$ million tons were financed.

Despite these measures, the situation continued to grow worse; stocks mounted and short-time work in the pits became more widespread, particularly in Belgium and Germany. Accordingly, in February, 1959, the High Authority announced its intention of seeking Council consent to a crisis program. It proposed to invoke emergency provisions of the Treaty permitting the application of production quotas in the event of a "manifest crisis" (Article 58), the restriction of imports (Article 74, 3), and direct financial aid to unemployed miners (Article 95, 1).[114]

To implement Article 58, the High Authority proposed the imposition of a graduated levy up to $5 a ton on production exceeding a selected reference level (taken for each enterprise as the average of its 1958 production and sales). The revenues were to be used to support enterprises that operated below the reference level.

Under the authority of Article 74, which contains an escape clause for imports entering the Community in such relatively increased quantities as to threaten or inflict serious injury on Community production of similar or directly competitive pro-

---

[113] *Eighth Report,* pp. 410–411; *Ninth Report,* p. 121.

[114] Article 95, which was cited by the High Authority as the basis for this part of its program does not make reference to direct financial aid or to any other specific measure; it authorizes the High Authority to take action in cases not expressly provided for in the Treaty that is deemed necessary to fulfil one of the objectives of the Community, such action being subject to the unanimous agreement of Council.

ducts, the High Authority proposed to limit each country's imports of coal from outside sources for the year 1959 to 125 per cent of the 1954 level. This represented a reduction of about 45 per cent from the 1958 import volume.

Direct financial aid to miners affected by short-time operations was intended not only to ease the burden borne by miners and their families, but also to avoid the dissipation of skilled labor at pits thought to be eventually capable of producing coal at competitive prices.

Opposition of the large countries. Between February and May, this emergency program for dealing with coal crises was the subject of extensive negotiations. These included not only a number of regular meetings of Council, but also several special unofficial sessions with the members of Council and a series of meetings with experts representing the Council members. Although the High Authority made a number of modifications in its proposals in an attempt to meet the various and sometimes conflicting objections of the governments, it could not obtain the agreement of the three large countries and Council finally rejected the program in mid-May.

While the opposition of the large countries was based on different grounds, they were perhaps somewhat united in the feeling that they were being asked to accept sacrifices for a Community-wide solution to what was essentially a Belgian problem.[115] Furthermore, to the extent that they recognized that they too had a coal problem, the Community's two big coal-producing countries, Germany and France, preferred to find their own solutions rather than accept any under the aegis of the High Authority.

The High Authority's desire to establish production quotas

---

[115] "Problèmes posés par la réforme du Traité de Paris" (par M. Byé), Avis et Rapports du Conseil Economique et Social, *Journal Officiel de la République Française,* March 24, 1961, pp. 377–378.

seems to have aroused the strongest opposition. Certainly, it produced a proliferation of alternative suggestions with respect to the selection of reference bases, the nature and methods of imposing sanctions, and the like. In Germany, both the mining enterprises and the government were inclined to look upon the proposals as representing a *dirigist* measure. This view did not prevent the disciplined and well-organized industry from proceeding, with the help of the government, to meet the problem posed by declining demand without substantially reducing prices. Licenses for further import contracts were refused, a tariff was placed on third-country coal beyond a duty-free quota, fuel oil was subjected to higher taxation, the work week in coal mining was reduced, and an emergency association was formed to raise funds to finance the commutation of existing coal import contracts.[116]

In France, fewer special measures were necessary since the government already had effective control of the quantity of coal imported through a monopoly importing organization and it also had the means to influence oil imports. In principle, French opposition to the production quotas was based on their alleged incompatibility with the political and social responsibilities of the national governments. What would happen, the French representative in Council asked, if the quotas imposed by the High Authority produced protest strikes? "Who but the governments, one might ask, could dispatch patrols to maintain order if the Pas-de-Calais mines were closed down?"[117] Since the governments were responsible for the maintenance of public order, production quotas, if they were to be established, should be assigned to member states for the governments to

---

[116] Some of the measures have already been referred to above.

[117] This echo of the minister's question appeared in an article in *Le Monde,* the influential Paris newspaper. See Political and Economic Planning, *France and the European Community,* Occasional Paper No. 11, January 30, 1961, London, p. 25.

divide among the enterprises. Thus the French position went farther than that of Germany or any other country in opposing supranationalism *per se*.

The High Authority's proposal to assign import quotas on third-country coal to member countries foundered against the Treaty provision reserving to the individual states freedom in the area of commercial policy. A half year earlier, the representatives of the governments in a Council meeting had agreed that "there could be no question of limiting the sovereignty of the member states in matters of commercial policy *vis-à-vis* third countries."[118] Except for Italy, which wanted to be free to buy coal from the cheapest source, the disagreement seems to have been confined to the High Authority's effort to exercise power in the commercial policy area, not with its objective of shifting a substantial part of the burden of adjustment to third-country coal. The independent actions of the several countries brought Community imports down from 44.0 million tons in 1957, the peak year for imports, to 19.2 million tons in 1959. The latter figure was only 1.8 million tons over the aggregate of the quotas that the High Authority had proposed. Perhaps the discussions of imports in connection with the High Authority's proposals had some influence on this outcome.

Thus the over-all decline in the Community's demand for hard coal between 1957 and 1959 was met by a reduction in Community annual production of 13 million tons, an increase in stocks at the annual rate of 12 million tons, and a decline in yearly imports of 25 million tons. Most of the reduction in imports was at the expense of American coal, which could be delivered in Europe more cheaply than coal from many if not most local sources. It must be added, however, that coal imports since the war were subject to wide year-to-year fluctua-

---

[118] *Seventh Report*, p. 71.

tions and that their level had risen sharply between 1954 and 1957.

The High Authority's proposals for direct aid to partially unemployed miners fared somewhat better with Council. Its program for aid to Belgian miners (under the catch-all provisions of Article 95, 1) had originally been approved for a two-month period in 1959 (April and May) and was subsequently extended several times, terminating at the end of September, 1960.[119] The "ECSC allowance," as the aid was known, was calculated at 20 per cent of the worker's daily wage. Initially, it was payable for each day of unemployment, beginning with the third, in any calendar month up to a maximum of nine days. For 1960, the days of entitlement were scaled down progressively until four in the final month (September, 1960). Council agreement to these payments was forthcoming only with considerable reluctance, and Council did not approve the High Authority's proposal to extend them to miners in countries other than Belgium. Something less than $7 million was paid to Belgian miners under these arrangements in 1959 and 1960.[120]

After the defeat of its plans in Council, the High Authority sought and obtained Council approval for measures directly specifically to the Belgian coal problem. It was at this time that the ECSC allowances were first extended. In addition, the Belgian Government was authorized to pay coal subsidies beyond the end of the transition period (Section 26, 4) and readaptation assistance was extended to Belgian mines and miners (Section 23, 4).[121] The subsidies, amounting to $18.5 million, and covering 8 million tons in 1959, were to compensate for collieries' losses resulting from price reductions neces-

---

[119] Payments were reinstituted in 1961. See below, p. 254.

[120] Data in this paragraph from *Eighth Report,* pp. 131–133, and *Ninth Report,* p. 258.

[121] *Eighth Report,* pp. 130, 149–151.

sary to align Belgian prices with those of Ruhr coal delivered in Belgium. The authorization to pay the subsidies was conditional upon the execution by the enterprises of reorganization programs and upon the limitation of production (other than anthracite) in the south Belgian coal fields to 7.5 million tons. The readaptation grants included tide-over, resettlement, and retraining allowances for workers, and labor cost subsidies to enterprises in order to enable them to maintain regular wages at pits scheduled for closing. The application of each colliery for readaptation assistance was submitted by the Belgian Government and referred by the High Authority to Council for approval, the latter step being necessary since Section 23 gave the High Authority final authority over readaptation assistance only for the duration of the transition period. Council stipulated that the High Authority's contributions to Belgian readaptation should not exceed $7.5 million over three financial years ending in 1962. The funds were intended to ease the social consequences of a reorganization program that involved the closing down of 5.5 million tons of capacity.

Despite these measures taken in the summer of 1959, the Belgian coal position grew steadily worse. The Belgian Government, which had supported the High Authority in its vain efforts to take emergency action under Article 58, put great pressure on the High Authority to permit it to control coal imports from other Community countries. Under this pressure and unable to obtain Council consent to Community-wide measures, the High Authority finally decided to abandon its long struggle to prevent the isolation of the Belgian coal market from the rest of the Community. The price it extracted from the Belgian Government was agreement upon a much more drastic reorganization scheme for the Belgian coal industry than had hitherto been contemplated.

Invocation of Article 37. At this point, the High Authority decided to formulate its program for dealing with the Belgian coal crisis on the basis of a broad interpretation of the powers granted it under the somewhat cryptic language of Article 37.[122] Since the terms of this article require that the initiative be taken by a member state, the High Authority informally suggested to the Belgian Government that it invoke the article. The terms of the program seem to have been worked out in informal negotiations between the High Authority and the Belgian and other governments. Agreement does not appear to have been difficult to obtain; perhaps all concerned were tired of arguing about the coal crisis. The matter was then formally put before Council for the consultation required by the Treaty, and a conforming opinion was forthcoming.

The Belgian memorandum of November 21, 1959, supporting its invocation of Article 37 pointed to the difficulties of the Belgian coal industry, to the inadequacy of the indirect measures taken under Article 57, and to the fact that Belgium had been deprived of the assistance provided in the Treaty in the eventuality of a manifest crisis affecting the common market as a whole. It argued that Article 37 permitted the High Authority to take measures to set aside the normal rules of the Treaty when the regular application of the Treaty provokes fundamental and persistent disturbances in the economy of a member state. Such difficulties, both economic and social in character, would surely be provoked if a large and immediate reduction in coal production were to take place. To avoid this, the Belgians favored restrictions on coal imports from all sources. They also offered to extend the program for closing high-cost mines from mines with a capacity of 5.5 million tons to 7.5 million tons. Finally, they proposed a central organization to control sales on the Belgian market to make

---

[122] See above, pp. 195–200.

certain that mines scheduled for early closing did not sell easily mined coal at such low prices as to endanger the financial position of mines with good long-run prospects.[123]

The formal decision of the High Authority,[124] issued in the latter part of December, 1959, placed greater stress on the long-run factors in the situation. Because of the importance of the coal industry in the Belgian economy and because it was not adapted to its sales potential with respect either to tonnages produced or prices, the High Authority's failure to intervene, especially since recourse to Article 58 was precluded, would provoke fundamental and persistent disturbances in the Belgian economy. The decision recognized the need to safeguard the essential interests of the Community, and took specific account of the interests of Belgian consumers and of trade patterns, including those between Belgium and other Community and those resulting from the reduction of imports from third countries.

The isolation of the Belgian coal market was achieved by placing quantitative restrictions on both imports and exports of coal. Exports to other Community countries were limited approximately to the 1959 levels, thus preventing the shift of Belgian difficulties to the other countries by means of increased exports. Belgium imports from the other members of the Community were reduced by about 400,000 tons from the

---

[123] Mines scheduled for closing could sell coal very cheaply because they were freed of certain costs, such as those relating to amortization and preparatory work for further mining operation, and because they utilized their most readily available sources of easily mined coal.

The measures favored by Belgium were contained in a version of the memorandum of November 21, 1959, obtained from a Belgian source. The version of the memorandum included in the *Mémoire en Défense* in the Article 37 court case cited on page 218 differs somewhat and contains no recommendation with respect to remedial measures.

[124] Decision No. 46–59, December 23, 1959, *Journal Officiel des Communantés Européennes,* December 31, 1959.

1959 level, mainly at the expense of Germany and the Netherlands.[125]

However, the measures isolating the Belgian market were regarded merely as providing a temporary shelter under which the Belgian coal industry could be reorganized so as to enable it to compete in Community markets without any assistance or protection. Accordingly, the decision called for the elimination of 9.5 million tons of "non-integrable" capacity by the end of 1963. Furthermore, target dates were provided; 2.3 million tons of capacity was to be closed down by the end of 1959, 2.5 during 1960, 2.0 during 1961, and 2.7 during 1962 and 1963. The total of 9.5 million tons was equivalent to about 30 per cent of capacity and went considerably beyond the 5.5 million tons contemplated in the mid-1959 version of the plan or the 7.5 million tons that had been proposed in the Belgian memorandum relative to invocation of Article 37. The Belgian Government was to provide the High Authority by May 1, 1960, with the lists of mines to be closed.

The decision made no reference to a central organization to control coal sales in Belgium, but did specify that the Belgian Government was to take measures to prevent unduly rapid liquidation of coal stocks that might endanger the reorganization of the industry. Belgium implemented this provision by a decree limiting the proportion of pithead stocks which the collieries could put on the market to 20 per cent.

Belgian coal trade during 1960 remained within the limits established in the December, 1959, decision.[126] Indeed, while Belgium took the full quotas of Community coal she licensed

---

[125] As a result of the intervention of the French representative, the quotas that the High Authority placed before the Council when it requested consultation were altered so as to reduce Belgian exports to France by 50,000 tons and to raise French exports to Belgium by 50,000 tons.

[126] The figures in this paragraph are based on *Ninth Report*, p. 111 and Appendix Tables 6, 7, 8, and 9.

only 525,000 tons of third-country coal for import rather than the 600,000 ton maximum provided in the decision. Exports to other Community countries were about 240,000 tons less than the over-all quota, owing chiefly to the failure of France to buy the full amount provided in her quota. However, increased sales to Italy more than made up this difference. The advantage derived by domestic producers from the changes in coal trade thus came out to a reduction in net imports of approximately 1 million tons, a figure which may be gauged against Belgian output of 22.5 million tons in 1960.

The program of mine closing proceeded satisfactorily, though not without strains between the High Authority and the Belgian Government. Although the capacity of the mines closed down in 1959 and 1960 totaled 5.0 million tons compared to the 4.8 million tons that the December, 1959, decision had required, the Belgian Government was slow in furnishing the High Authority with the exact list of mines to be closed. The decision had specified that such a list was to be provided by May 1, 1960. The Belgians argued that it was neither socially nor economically possible to announce mine closings three or four years in advance. The social unrest that the publication of a full list of mine closings long before the actual dates would create unnecessary difficulties, and the operation of the mines scheduled for closing would be hampered in the remaining period by loss of key personnel. Also, it was often difficult to tell far in advance which mines would turn out to be the most successful in lowering their costs. Furthermore, the Belgian Government did not itself have the power to close down the mines, which were operated for the most part by private enterprises. (Its power to withhold subsidies was, however, a powerful and effective weapon.)

As 1960 drew to a close and the High Authority was faced with the necessity to decide upon the application of the Article

37 measures to the year 1961, the Belgian Government had furnished a list of closings covering only 1.7 million tons (and not all of these firm, in the view of the High Authority) rather than the 2.0 million tons called for by the December, 1959, decision. Fearful of a slowing down of the reorganization program, the High Authority was reluctant to extend the special measures for Belgium under these circumstances. It was finally agreed that the full list of mine closings covering 2.0 million tons would be presented by June 1, 1961. (Actually, the deadline had to be extended until mid-July when Belgium finally submitted the full list.) At the same time, the High Authority, stressing the temporary character of the controls on coal trade and wishing to signify its intention of arranging for their gradual abolition, established the export and import quotas for 1961 at levels 3.3 per cent above those of 1960. The increase applied also to import quotas for third-country coal.[127]

Decisions with respect to 1961 also had to be taken for the special measures for Belgian coal that had been adopted before the invocation of Article 37, namely the authorization to the Belgian Government to continue coal subsidies beyond the transitional period[128] and the payment of the ECSC allowances to miners on short time.[129]

The principle of degressivity for exceptions to the Treaty, noted in connection with the setting of trade quotas for 1961, was applied also to the Belgian coal subsidies. These subventions, which were financed entirely by Belgium, had been authorized to the extent of $18.5 million, covering 8 million tons of coal in 1959. They had been reduced for 1960, and for 1961 they were cut further to $8 million, covering 3.3

---

[127] Data in this paragraph are from *Ninth Report,* pp. 112–115.
[128] See above, p. 247f.
[129] See above, p. 247.

million tons.[130]

The ECSC allowances to Belgian miners had expired at the end of September, 1960, and even before extending them to that date Council had stressed their exceptional and temporary nature. Nevertheless, Belgian pressure and the recognition of the need to cushion the impact upon Belgian opinion of the extensive mine-closing program led to the reinstitution of the allowances for 1961. As before, the benefits were computed at 20 per cent of the miner's wage, but the payments did not begin until the fourth day of unemployment (consecutive or not) within a calendar month and the maximum number of days of entitlement was four. The High Authority set aside $1.3 million for the program.[131]

There seems little doubt that the totality of these measures eased the coal situation in Belgium. During 1960 their effectiveness was heightened, and perhaps even overshadowed, by the impact upon the coal market of an exceptionally rapid rate of economic growth in the Community, marked by increases in iron and steel production of 15 or 16 per cent.[132] The Community's consumption of coal rose by about 8 million tons, and in both Belgium and the Community, for the first time in several years, there was no significant decline in coal production. Both in Belgium and the Community, also, stocks declined by 11 or 12 per cent, again reversing a past trend. The Community's coal producers were, in addition, aided by a further decrease in imports from third countries amounting to nearly 1.5 million tons. As a result, the percentage of man-days available but not worked owing to lack of markets declined from 5.5 per cent in 1959 to 3.2 per

[130] *Ninth Report,* pp. 115–119.
[131] *Ninth Report,* p. 259.
[132] Data in this paragraph from *Ninth Report,* pp. 68, 112–132.

cent in 1960 in the Community as a whole, and from 18.6 per cent to 12.3 per cent in Belgium.

The High Authority remained fearful, however, that the improvement in the coal situation was only temporary, and pressed for the continuation of programs of modernization and consolidation not only in Belgium but also in Germany and France. However the outlook for the future of coal production in the other Community countries be assessed, there seems little doubt that a less optimistic—or more pessimistic, as the case may be—prognosis must be attached to the outlook for coal mining in Belgium.

Between the end of 1957 and the end of 1960, employment in Community coal mining declined by nearly 20 per cent and that in Belgium by more than 30 per cent.[133] Production also declined between 1957 and 1960, but by smaller amounts —about 6 per cent in the Community and 23 per cent in Belgium [134]—reflecting the fact that much of the reduction in employment was associated with the closing down of the marginal mines and the modernization of others. Productivity, measured in terms of underground output per man-shift, increased both in Belgium and in the Community as a whole. However, since the proportionate increases were roughly about the same, the relative position of Belgian coal in terms of its ability to compete on Community markets could not have been greatly strengthened. The geographical protection afforded by frieght costs would probably be of little avail when, as in 1960, underground output per man-shift was 1,318 kilograms in southern Belgium and 2,102 in the relatively nearby Ruhr.[135] Thus, it is far from clear that even the conclusion of the present programs of closing and reorganization

---

[133] Based on figures in *Sixth Report*, p. 372, and *Ninth Report*, p. 248.
[134] *Ninth Report*, Appendix Table 1.
[135] *Ninth Report*, Appendix Table 2.

at the end of 1961 will make possible the reintegration of Belgian coal into the common market.

The prospects for Belgian coal in the common market depend in no small part on the way in which the conflict in interests between various groups in the Community is resolved. Coal producers in Belgium and Germany want protection against oil as well as against third-country coal. France is willing to favor Community energy sources over external sources of supply, but is interested in finding Community markets for Sahara oil as well as in maintaining protection of French coal production. Italy and Luxemburg, and to a lesser extent the Netherlands, are consuming countries whose interests would be best served by world-wide competition for the energy markets of the Community. The closer the final policy comes to the open competition favored by the Italians, the smaller is likely to be the future size of the Belgian coal industry.

EVALUATION

The key aspects of the experience of the ECSC that are of interest from the standpoint of safeguarding mechanisms are the transition period, the attempt to solve the problem of scrap supply through market control, the working of the readaptation provisions, and the various efforts to cope with the Belgian coal problem.

Although the transition period did not proceed without some sharp struggles for positions of advantage,[136] the adaptation to the common market seems to have come about without major difficulties for any important sector of the coal and steel industries with the exception of Belgian coal mining.

---

[136] For example, the Franco-German controversy over the question of whether the turnover tax of the country of destination or that of the country of origin should be charged against goods entering intra-Community trade. Cf. Diebold, *op. cit.*, pp. 223–236.

Doubtless the strategy of avoiding injury by making changes gradually, written into the Transitional Convention, helped to ease the adjustments that had to be made. However, the apparent smoothness of the transition must be judged against a background of rapid economic expansion. Industrial production in the Community increased by nearly 50 per cent between 1953 and 1958.[137] Under these conditions, there was room for every one—even, for the time being, for high-cost Belgian coal producers.

The story might have been very different if, in the absence of rapid economic growth and with consequently keener competition for what would have been a fixed volume of business, an important sector of the French or German coal or steel industries had found itself during the transition period in a position analogous to that of Belgian coal in 1958 and 1959. If any hint is provided by the never-used technical criteria elaborated by the High Authority for the general precautionary clause for steel (Section 29), the approach that would have been followed might well have been close to the "no-injury" rule that has been applied in American reciprocal trade affairs. Indeed, there is a suggestion that protection would have been extended not only to an enterprise as a whole, but, in the case of a multiproduct enterprise, to a part of an enterprise producing a particular product. (In the parlance of American commercial policy, this represents the acceptance of the "segmentation principle.") In this event, the achievements of the Community might have been limited, to a greater degree than has been the case, to the elimination of wasteful crosshauling due to the existence of national trade barriers and transport discrimination. It is also possible that the governments of the large countries would have insisted upon

---

[137] *Eighth Report,* p. 106. The index cited excludes the building trades and the food, drink, and tobacco industries.

meeting the problems posed by Community-wide competition by means of their own rather than through the institutions of the Community.

However, speculations of what might have been are perhaps even less useful in this context than usual. In the first place, the drafting of the Treaty and its adoption by the signatories was based on the calculation that drastic differences in cost conditions did not exist. Secondly, it was based also on the notion that integration would bring more rapid economic growth.[138] Thus the framers of the Treaty placed their faith on the efficacy of gradualism against a background of expansion and small differences in competitive ability. Through correct foresight or good fortune, they turned out to be more right than wrong.

To a greater extent than in other areas subject to its jurisdiction the High Authority followed a policy of control and manipulation in connection with the market for scrap. The basic problem was to permit Italy to share in the scrap supplies of France and Germany without driving scrap prices up. While some action may have been necessary to prevent a sudden increase in French and German scrap prices upon the opening of the common market, the disadvantage of the method adopted, the compensation program, was that it made relatively cheap to consumers a raw material that was relatively scarce to the Community. In the course of successive modifications designed to correct this deficiency by providing

---

[138] The rate of economic expansion in the Community was faster than in most other Western countries during the transition years. Gross national product in real terms expanded by 29 per cent in the Community between 1953 and 1958, compared to 16 per cent in the other OEEC countries, 8 per cent in the United States (16 per cent between 1953 and 1959), and 15 per cent in Canada. *General Statistics, OEEC Statistical Bulletins,* January, 1961, pp. III, VII, and IX. Whether this was attributable in any degree to the establishment of the common market in coal and steel is not obvious.

incentives to economize on the use of scrap, the plan became more complicated. The administrative problems were further worsened by an unfavorable court decision regarding the organization of the work and by the discovery of fraud. All in all, this experience does not inspire confidence in safeguard measures that entail deep involvement in market control.

Among the Treaty's precautionary clauses, the provisions for the readaptation of workers and the development of new sources of employment represent major innovations. Here, for the first time, a frontal attack was proposed to reduce the human costs of increased international specialization. Here, for the first time, there was to be an effort to remove the injury from dislocation.

There is little doubt that the early experience was qualitatively disappointing. It is also true that the simple comparison of the number of workers covered by the projects approved by the High Authority—115,000—with the decline in the coal mining labor force over the first seven years of the common market—about 200,000—tends to exaggerate the quantitative importance of readaptation in the structural readjustments of the Community's coal and steel industries.[139] Furthermore, the readaptation provisions raised problems of equity for the Member governments which had to weigh the position of those subject to dislocation in the coal and steel industries and those suffering from displacements elsewhere in the economy.

On the other hand, it is clear that the potential of readapta-

---

[139] If the $16 million that had been spent until the end of September had all been paid out to the 115,000 workers, each would have received an average of $130. If the contribution of the worker's government had been distributed in the same manner, each worker would have gotten on the average another $130 from this source. In fact, of course, some of the 115,000 workers had received no aid as yet, and some of the money went for administrative costs and some for purposes such as training centers which would benefit the workers by means other than direct payment.

tion was obscured by the fact that there was relatively little demand for it in the early years. Even when the need became more apparent, the Belgian coal industry was reluctant to accept the necessity for contraction, and for this or other reasons the Belgian Government seems to have been slow in pressing for large-scale readaptation assistance. When the coal crisis reached the German mines, both the industry and the government seem to have acted more swiftly in mine closings and readaptation aids.

It is still too early to evaluate the efficacy of the enlarged scale of readaptation operations. At the minimum, the program has had an important psychological role in the political sphere; it has made structural adjustment without a protectionist response more feasible politically than might otherwise have been the case. Without some such effort on behalf of displaced workers, the High Authority would have been cast in the role of a remote and ruthless authority favoring mines and miners in a foreign country, and the pressures on the individual governments for intervention might have proved irresistible.

It remains true that the readaptation program was formulated mainly in defensive terms. Money was spent at least in part as supplementary unemployment allowances, and, while workers were encouraged and supported in retaining and in searching for new jobs, little or nothing was done to create new sources of employment. The High Authority was led to a more positive approach after its early readaptation experience. It concluded that jobs would have to be brought to workers since workers could be moved to other places only with great difficulty or in many cases not at all. However, the new interest of the High Authority in stimulating regional development has its own drawbacks and dangers. Not the least among these is the danger that such programs may go

too far in the acceptance of the existing patterns of population settlement despite any economic disadvantages that may
be entailed.

The most important safeguard problem in the history of the
ECSC to date is undobtedly that involving Belgian coal. The
rejection in May, 1959, of the High Authority's proposals to
cope with the coal problem on a Community-wide basis,
coming after protracted negotiations, was widely viewed as a
major setback not only for the High Authority *per se* but for
the supranational aspects of the Community and, indeed, for
the integration movement in Europe.[140] For somewhat different reasons each of the three large countries in the Community
had opposed the High Authority's program. Italy wanted to
be free to buy cheap American coal; German economic policy
was orientated against the direct controls that the High
Authority favored; and French political policy was to stress
and develop the intergovernmental character of the Community and to subordinate its supranational features.

This incident emphasizes the extent to which the governments can, through the Council, prevent the High Authority
from using some of the more extensive powers conferred upon
it by the Treaty. Despite its general policy of obtaining Council consent before taking actions even where the Treaty did
not require Council approval, the High Authority made no
secret of its feeling that the Treaty left too much leeway to
the governments in some respects. The efficacy of the Community, the High Authority argued, depends upon its
supranational character. The experience of the Community
shows that work in fields where reliance has been placed on
intergovernmental methods, such as ratemaking for road and
inland-water transport and freedom of movement of workers,

---

[140] Cf. *Economist,* London, May 23, 1959, pp. 715–716.

has not progressed very far in achieving the ends sought by the Treaty.[141]

After the rejection of its proposals for production quotas, the High Authority decided to invoke the general escape clause of the Treaty, Article 37. Without challenge from any government or from Council, it placed a broad interpretation of its powers under this provision of the Treaty. Citing only the powers conferred upon it by Article 37 and by certain general articles of the Treaty (mainly those stating objectives), the High Authority, after consulting Council, placed a maximum limit on Belgian coal imports from third countries that involved a sharp reduction from previous levels, put Belgian coal trade with other Community countries under quotas, stipulated a more extensive program of closings of high-cost mines at target dates agreed upon with the Belgian Government, and instructed the Belgian Government to avoid an unduly rapid liquidation of coal stocks. None of these powers is specifically granted to the High Authority by the Treaty, except under conditions much more circumscribed than those under which they were exercised by the High Authority in this case.

Actually, however, the program put into effect by the High Authority had been negotiated and a large measure of agreement attained with Belgian and other Governments before formal submission to Council for consultation. Nevertheless, while the over-all outcome of the case was a setback for the supranational aspects of the Community, a precedent was established—though not one that is necessarily irreversible—for the use of Article 37 as a general clause of safeguard according broad and effective powers of intervention to the High Authority. Thus a small victory, but perhaps a significant one for the future, for the supranational authority of

---

[141] *Eighth Report,* pp. 10–13, 49–50.

the High Authority was snatched at the very end from a long and frustrating struggle.

The fact that governments blocked the High Authority's original plans for coping with the coal crises does not mean that the situation was not significantly altered by the existence of the Community. In the first place, the Community tended to function in the coal crisis as something of a producers' club which often found it difficult to agree except in protecting the interests of its members at the expense of third-country producers of coal and substitute fuels, and, to a lesser degree, at the expense of the Community fuel consumers. Restrictions on third-country coal were introduced early, and imports from outside sources—largely the United States—were made to bear a larger part of the adjustment than might have been the case if the members of the Community had functioned individually. Italy, for example, would almost surely have purchased more American and less Community coal had it not been for the pressures entailed in membership in the Community. Even Belgium tended to substitute coal from other Community countries for American coal; its coal imports from third countries in 1960 were to be reduced to a little more than one-fifth of their 1957 level while the imports from the Community countries, although scheduled for some reduction from the record 1959 volume, were to be 50 per cent above the 1957 level.

There is little doubt, however, that Belgium benefited from membership in the Community. The higher cost of the Community coal over that which might have been obtained from the United States was more than offset by the financial balance between Belgium and the Community. Up to the end of 1959, the contribution of Belgian coal and steel producers under the general levy on Community production had been

$26 million,[142] as compared with Community expenditures on behalf of the Belgian coal industry of $71 million in the form of subsidies, readaptation assistance, ECSC allowances to unemployed miners, etc.[143] Perhaps in the absence of the ECSC, sales to the other Community countries would not have expanded so much in the early years (from 2.6 million tons in 1952 to 5.5 million in 1955), but that might only have brought Belgium face to face with her coal problem earlier. It is not unlikely, however, that the Belgians would have temporized much longer if not indefinitely by surrounding their coal with high protective barriers against all competing fuel sources. The competitive disadvantage of high fuel costs for Belgian steel and other industrial products could in that case have been offset only by further subsidies. In the absence of external pressure such as the Community provided, it would have been difficult and perhaps impossible for the Belgian Government to have achieved the notable (though perhaps still inadequate) progress toward the solution of its coal problem indicated by its extended program of mine closings.

For the four coal-producing countries taken as a whole the existence of the ECSC cushioned the impact of the decline in demand upon the coal industry, partly through shifting of the burden to third countries and partly through the use of funds accumulated from the special and general levies. This consequence, which is clearest in the case of Belgium, can be assessed from two different and somewhat conflicting points of view. On the one hand, the various forms of aid given to high-cost mines sometimes served to postpone the day of reckoning rather than to ease some of the burdens for the

---

[142] *Seventh Report,* p. 301; *Eighth Report,* p. 369.
[143] Bulletin du Ministère des Affaires Economiques, *Etudes,* 1961, No. 2. In addition, Belgian enterprises received loans of about $20 million from the High Authority, and some Community funds were spent for the benefit of the Belgian steel industry.

individuals involved in a reasonably expeditious contraction. The phase of the Community activity in the coal area that appears most vulnerable to criticism on this score is represented by the functioning of the compensation program under the Transitional Convention (Sections 25 and 26). Serious measures to eliminate high-cost capacity appear to have been undertaken only under the duress of declining sales, growing stocks, and the reluctance of the other members of the Community to permit the use of Community resources to shelter the Belgian industry any further.

Here, as in the case of Council's refusal to agree to the scrap control schemes advocated by the High Authority in late 1958, the better part of the argument seems to have rested with Council. If the High Authority had had its way and production quotas had been established throughout the Community, Belgian production and sales would not have been permitted to decline so sharply and the shutdowns scheduled for 1960-63 might have been less extensive.

There is, however, the social as well as the economic aspect to be considered. While the effect of the decline in imports from third countries was merely to shift some of the real burden abroad, the existence of the Community probably helped in other ways to minimize the human costs entailed in the decline of an important industry. The High Authority's emphasis on the Treaty provisions regarding continuity of employment (Article 2) and readaptation (Section 23) probably resulted in a larger total effort on behalf of the miners in the Community affected by the contraction of coal mining than would otherwise have taken place. Admittedly, conditions were favorable. Not only were mine workers being attracted away from the mines by other industries in a booming economy, but in the area most seriously affected by mine closings, southern Belgium, about half of the workers were

Italians, many of whom would return to their own country of their own volition in the course of a few years.

How, then, may the lessons of the ECSC experience as far as safeguarding provisions be summarized? In the first place, the value of gradual changes on a definite time schedule is again underlined. However, the Belgian coal case shows that this formula will not work under all conditions. The missing ingredient here, up to 1958 or 1959, was a sense of purpose on the part of the Belgian Government and perhaps even a sense of urgency on the part of a High Authority still thinking in terms of a fuel shortage. However, perhaps the most important distinction between the troublesome case of coal and the easier situation with respect to steel lies in the fact that coal turned out to be a declining industry and steel an expanding one.

Some tentative inferences may be drawn also about the nature and extent of intervention in connection with safeguarding mechanisms. On the whole, the history of the ECSC seems to suggest, in the opinion of the writer, that safeguarding mechanisms should if possible eschew direct intervention in markets in the form of controls over price, production, or allocation of supply. Simpler devices such as temporary tariffs, quotas, or tariff quotas, preferably with dates for the gradual elimination set in advance, have much to recommend them. In the setting of the ECSC, such devices seem to have worked smoothly and they have the advantage that they ease the adjustment to a new situation without obscuring the necessity or incentive for enterprises to make the adjustment. Both the scrap compensation program and the High Authority's abortive proposals for coal production quotas were vulnerable to criticism on the latter score.

The High Authority's willingness to venture into direct controls in these cases does not inspire confidence in proposals to turn safeguarding powers over to supranational authorities. On the other hand, it may be argued that the less direct methods of intervention—such as tariffs and quotas—worked well because they were used for less difficult problems and that they would have been inadequate for the scrap and coal problems that the Community faced. Certainly national governments confronted with similar problems within their boundaries have often taken analogous steps in fields such as agriculture, and, indeed, coal and steel.

Readaptation remains relatively untried, but it seems to offer the best hope for making it politically possible for authority, either at the national or international level, to obtain relief from some of the pressures for protective measures that obstruct structural adjustment to the freer flow of commerce.

Chapter 5

The European Economic Community

The extension of the common market from coal and steel to the rest of the economy, though very much in the minds of the Europeans who worked for the formation of the ECSC, did not come without some setbacks for the movement towards European integration. About six months after Schuman's famous press conference that launched the coal and steel community, René Pleven, the French Minister of Defense, suggested the creation of a European army in which the identity of the national contingents would be submerged and the entire force subject to the control of a supranational European military and political authority. The Pleven Plan, which was a response to American proposals after the outbreak of the Korean War to create 12 German divisions for the defense of Europe, was modeled upon the Schuman Plan not only in the general conception of coping with the renascence of Germany by harnessing Germany to a European movement but also in the general alignment of its institutions. The six members of the coal and steel community were able to agree upon a treaty embodying this plan in the form of the European Defense Community (EDC) in May, 1952. A second and even more ambitious proposal for a European Political Community (EPC) was put in treaty form the following year. Eventually, EPC, which was to be a full political union with a common foreign policy and a directly elected parliament, was to absorb the ECSC and the EDC. The treaties drew strong opposition, especially in France, and, in an effort to improve the chances of ratification by the French Assembly, the elements of supranationalism in both were diluted in subsequent negotiations. Nevertheless, when the EDC Treaty was put to a vote in August, 1954, after four of the six countries had ratified and a fifth was awaiting French action, French nationalism and fear of German rearmament carried the day and the Treaty was rejected.[1] This defeat also meant the abandonment of the EPC project.

The making of the Treaty

The contrast between the relative ease with which the coal and steel community had been established and the rejection of the defense community turned the advocates of integration back to the economic sphere again. There was, however, considerable disagreement on whether the proper approach was to achieve economic integration on a sector-by-sector basis or to press immediately for integration on a broad scale covering many commodities. Sector proposals for agriculture, energy, and transport were widely discussed, but so too were the difficulties in terms of the creation of vested interests and of contradictions in policy that could ensue from a series of partial integrations.

In May, 1955, the Benelux countries resumed the initiative by placing before their ECSC partners alternatives for progress toward further integration. These consisted on the one hand of suggestions for sector integration (especially in transport, electricity, and nuclear energy) and on the other hand of a revised version of a plan for the formation of a common market based on Benelux experience. The foreign ministers of the Six, meeting the next month at Messina, decided upon the

---

[1] See Ben T. Moore, *NATO and the Future Europe* (New York, 1958), pp. 37–63.

exploration of both these approaches, and also up on a new procedure. The new method consisted of entrusting the formulation of specific proposals to an intergovernmental committee of experts under the supervision of a prominent political figure. The supervisory role fell to Paul-Henri Spaak, then Belgian foreign minister. Some 60 experts, divided into specialized working groups analyzed various aspects of the problem in the ensuing months, and prepared a first series of reports outlining the alternative courses that could be chosen with respect to each point. After discussion of these reports, both in governmental circles and among private groups favoring integration, the experts drafted a second set of documents, this time proposing solutions. Out of this work was distilled a report to the foreign ministers which was submitted in April, 1956, and which came to be known as the Spaak Report.[2]

The report, which was accepted by the ministers as a basis for negotiations, favored the creation of a common market and of an atomic energy community. In March, 1957, after many uncertainties and difficulties, the Treaty establishing the European Economic Community and the Treaty establishing the European Atomic Energy Community (Euratom) were signed in Rome. This time ratification in the French as well as in the other parliaments was obtained by substantial majorities, and the treaties went into effect on January 1, 1958.[3]

The treaty establishing the Common Market (i. e., the EEC) is in many respects a more complicated document than the coal and steel treaty. The range of problems to be con-

[2] Comité intergouvernemental créé par la conférence, *Rapport des Chefs de Délégation aux Ministres des Affaires Etrangères,* Bruxelles, April 21, 1956.

[3] This account of the formation of EEC is drawn chiefly from L. de Sainte Lorette, *Le Marché Commun,* Paris, 1958, pp. 56–81; and J. Ch. Snoy et d'Oppuers, "Etapes de l'Europe," *Revue d'Economie Politique,* January–February, 1958, pp. 45–55.

sidered, the variety of interests to be protected, and the number of compromises that had to be made were greater. The treaty itself runs to nearly 250 articles and 200 printed pages, and its related documents, including annexes, protocols, conventions, and declarations of intention, take up as much space as the treaty itself.

The Treaty, which is of unlimited duration, binds France, Germany, Italy, and the Benelux countries to seek greater stability, harmonious economic expansion, and an accelerated increase in the standard of living by the establishment of a common market and the coordination of their economic policies (Article 2).[4] In many essential aspects, the framework that was set out for the achievement of these objectives was dominated by the six countries' experience with the coal and steel community. Reliance upon a transitional period for adjustment, the general outline of institutions, and juridical techniques are modeled upon the earlier community, but there are also important differences reflecting both the wider scope of the new community and the changed political climate within which it was created.

The customs union

The common market is to be established progressively during a transition period divided into three stages of four years each, with provisions for extensions that can draw out the transition period to 15 years (Article 8). This period is to be used to establish a customs union with free internal trade and

---

[4] References are mainly to an English translation of the Treaty published by the Secretariat of the Interim Committee for the Common Market and Euratom. Summaries of the Treaty may be found in Committee for Economic Development, *The European Common Market and Its Meaning to the United States,* New York, 1959, pp. 92–113; and in House Ways and Means Subcommittee on Foreign Trade Policy, *A Compendium of Papers on Foreign Trade Policy,* Washington, 1957, pp.

common external tariffs, by specified steps in each of the three stages. During the first, duties between member states are to be reduced in three steps so as to achieve an over-all tariff reduction of 30 per cent below the 1956 level; during the second stage another 30 per cent is to be shaved off. Special provisions are made for larger reductions in very high duties and to ensure that the duty for each product is reduced by a minimum of 20 per cent in the first stage and by another 15 per cent in the second stage. The timing and amounts of reductions in the third stage are left to the institutions of the Community [5] to determine, but all intra-Community duties are to be eliminated completely by the time this stage draws to its end (Article 14). Duties on exports to other Community countries are to be abolished by the end of the first stage (Article 16).

Somewhat analogous provisions are made for the establishment of the common external tariff. If a member country's duty on a particular commodity differs from that of the common tariff schedule by less than 15 per cent, the country is to adopt the common rate by the end of the first stage. For duties that differ from the common schedule by more than 15 per cent, 30 per cent of the difference is to be eliminated at the end of the first stage, another 30 per cent at the end of the second stage, and the balance by the end of the third stage (Article 23).

In principle the common tariff is the arithmetic average of the January, 1957, duties of the four customs areas in the Community (i. e., Benelux is counted as one). However, for purposes of this computation some recent tariff reductions or suspensions by Italy and France were not taken into account. (In the case of France, an annex to the Treaty, List A, indi-

---

[5] See below, p. 285f, for a description of the institutions of the Community.

cate the duties that are to replace the rates prevailing in January, 1957, for the calculation of the external tariff.) In addition, maximum levels of the common external tariff for certain products are specified in annexes to the Treaty rather than left to arithmetic calculation. Limits of 3, 10, 15, and 25 per cent are set for various lists of goods (Lists B, C, D, and E, respectively) with raw materials and semifinished products figuring mainly in the lists carrying the lower maximums and chemicals in the lists with the higher maximums. Finally, there were certain products for which the common tariff rates had to be negotiated and established individually. For some of these, including a number of agricultural products and metallic and textile materials in low stages of fabrication, agreement could be reached before the signing of the Treaty and the duties were set out in an annex—List F. For others, mainly raw materials and foodstuffs but including some manufactures,[6] agreement could not be attained before the signing of the Treaty, and the external duties for these products—placed on List G—had to be left to subsequent negotiation between the member states and, if necessary, to decision by the institutions of the Community (Article 19). List G contained 70 headings, which in 1957 accounted for about 16 per cent of imports by the Six from third countries.

The Treaty signatories declared themselves willing to enter into reciprocal agreements with third countries that would reduce customs duties below the level which the Community countries "could claim as a result of the establishment of a

---

[6] About three-quarters of the List G products were raw materials and the rest chiefly foodstuffs and a few manufactured products. Wood represented about 20 per cent of the List G imports, fats 11 per cent, aircraft and parts 8 per cent, lead and zinc 5.5 per cent, and engines for motor vehicles and aircraft 5 per cent. These figures do not, of course, reflect the protective effect of the duties of the member countries which kept the imports of other items on List G down to negligible levels or excluded them. Cf. *Bulletin of the European Economic Community*, March–April, 1960, p. 33.

customs union between themselves" (Article 18).

In order to complete the arrangements for the free movement of goods within the Community, the elimination of intra-
Community tariffs and the establishment of common external
tariff rates had to be supplemented by the abolition of quantitative restrictions on trade between member states. Restrictions
on exports are to be abolished by the end of the first stage
(Article 34); those on imports are to be done away with
more gradually (Article 33). Bilateral import quotas are to be
generalized and opened to all member states without discrimination within a year after the effective date of the Treaty. The
aggregate value of these global quotas is to be increased by 20
per cent each year and the quotas for each individual product
by at least 10 per cent. In addition, the quota for each product must equal at least 3 per cent of national output after the
first year of the existence of the Community, and a minimum
of 20 per cent of national output after 10 years. A quota is to
be abolished when it has not been filled by imports for two
successive years.

Complementing these provisions for the removal of restrictions on private trade is a requirement that the member
countries adjust the practices of any state monopoly of a commercial character which they may maintain so as to eliminate
by the end of the transition period "all discrimination between
the nationals of member states in regard to the conditions of
supply or marketing of goods" (Article 37). This means that
the market will be open to all Community suppliers and that
consumers will have free choice between domestic goods and
goods from other Community countries.[7]

---

[7] Cf. *Bulletin of the European Economic Community,* May, 1960, p. 35.
This source also states that such monopolies existed only in Germany,
France, and Italy. They affected matches and alcohol in Germany;
tobacco, matches, alcohol, explosives, petroleum, potash, and newsprint
in France; and tobacco, salt, matches, lighter flints, and cigarette paper
in Italy.

Although the common market is to extend to agricultural products, special provisions are made for agricultural trade within the Community during the transitional period while a common agricultural policy is being worked out. If the progressive abolition of tariffs and quantitative restrictions may result in prices that jeopardize common objectives in the agricultural sector, particularly those relating to the standard of living of the farm population and to the stability of markets, each country may substitute for import quotas a system of minimum prices below which imports may be reduced, suspended, or made conditional upon their price (exclusive of tariff) being above the minimum price fixed. Criteria for the establishment of the minimum prices are to be worked out by the institutions of the Community within three years of the effective date of the Treaty, and member states will have to conform to them. However, until the Community-wide criteria are established, the member states are free to fix the minimum prices in their own fashion subject to the obligation to consult about them and to ensure that they do not reduce existing Community trade or prevent an increase in it (Article 44). Another interim measure provides for the conclusion of long-term contracts between exporting and importing member states; the way is even left open for Community subsidies to offset the disadvantage that one member may encounter in buying high-cost supplies from another member if the purchase consists of raw materials for the production of export[8] (Article 45). For the longer run, a common agricultural policy and a common organization may take the form of common rules of competition, compulsory coordination of the several national market organizations, or a Community market organ-

---

[8] For another provision designed to safeguard export capacity, see Article 43, 4.

ization; the choice among these alternatives need not be the same for each product (Article 40).

Beyond the customs union

If the EEC represented merely an effort to establish a customs union, the provisions of the Treaty thus far described would have been adequate. However, the Treaty is based upon the view, advanced with particular vigor by the French, that tariffs and quantitative restrictions represented only two of the many sources of national protection and of distortions of competition. In the first place, partial integration—and integrations limited to commodities to the exclusion of labor and capital are a form of partial integration—can lead to distortions because the costs of industry are affected by nonintegrated sectors. Partial integration leads to changes in trade patterns, in the location of economic activity, in the balance-of-payments situation and in the exchange rate, but these adjustments will be based on the artificial obstacles still remaining in the unintegrated sectors. The most natural economic equilibrium can result only when integration is extended to the whole economy and includes not only all products but also all factors of production. There is also a human argument for the extension of the common market to the productive factors. The elimination of production of a certain commodity in one area owing to the operation of the common market works hardships on workers and entrepreneurs who are no less efficient or deserving than those elsewhere but suffer from the handicap of location; a common market in the factors of production gives them the opportunity to stay in the same line of work by moving to the parts of the Community that are better suited to its pursuits.

Secondly, even with respect to products, integration requires the systematic elimination of all obstacles to trade. It does not suffice merely to abolish tariffs and quantitative restrictions if the same ends would still be served by dumping, double-pricing, subsidies, the division of markets by cartels, and transport discrimination. True integration thus requires the establishment of common rules and regulation of competition. It also requires the progressive harmonization of social policies that can create artificial differences in costs, such as rules governing overtime pay, the relative compensation of male and female workers, and the burden placed by the fiscal system on taxes that directly affect commodity prices. One can allow the free play of prices internationally only if prices are established in different countries in an analogous manner.[9]

The Treaty thus has at its roots an inherently liberal philosophy which in principle would establish ideal conditions of competition among the industries of the various member countries. Perhaps this is not surprising in view of the prominence of the Benelux countries in its launching. However, the concessions to national interests and the safeguards incorporated to enable the six countries to sign and ratify the Treaty may cause the liberal character of the EEC to be compromised. In general, the commitments to end restrictions on the movements of the productive factors tend to be less sweeping than

---

[9] The line of argument given in these paragraphs may be found in many French sources. For an authoritative example see P. Uri, "L'Experience du 'Plan Schuman' et la Communauté Economique Européenne," *Quelle Europe?* Recherches et Débats du Centre Catholique des Intellectuels Français, No. 22, Paris, 1958, pp. 40–61. For a more official source see Savary and July, "Rapport fait au nom de la commission des affaires étrangères . . ." Annexe No. 5266, *Documents parlementaires,* Assemblée Nationale, Session ordinaire de 1956–57, pp. 2333–2384. Little exception can be taken to the argument that the free play of prices would not achieve an optimum allocation of resources where relative prices were affected by different social policies in different parts of the market. However, the French argument for harmonization often seemed based on the more dubious proposition that social charges placed French industry *in general* at a competitive disadvantage. Cf., for example, Savary and July, *op. cit.*

those relating to the movement of commodities, and the reservation to the national governments of the essential economic powers associated with sovereignty make harmonization in other fields depend more upon future agreements among the governments than upon compelling Treaty provisions.

With respect to the productive factors, the common market is extended to labor, capital, services, and the right of establishment. In general, freedom of movement is to be achieved by the end of the transition period. The provisions regarding the free movement of labor are, perhaps, the most explicit and least qualified[10] (Article 48). As for capital movements, the obligation to abolish restrictions on movements within the Community is undertaken only to the extent "necessary for the proper functioning of the Common Market," and there is no commitment to suppress exchange controls. On the other hand, discrimination regarding capital movements based on nationality or residence is to be eliminated and there is an outright obligation to abolish restrictions of currents payments connected with capital movements by the end of the first stage (Article 67). Programs for the elimination of restrictions on the freedom of establishment and on the free supply of services[11] are to be developed by the institutions of the Community (Articles 54 and 63).

---

[10] However, the freedom of labor to move has been interpreted, with some basis in the language of the Treaty (cf. Articles 48, 3, and 49, d), as being restricted to movements in response to actual offers of employment. In this view, the fear of an influx of unemployed workers to one country from another led to this limitation. See Savary and July, *op. cit.*, p. 2347.

[11] "Services" are defined residually as "services normally supplied for remuneration" other than those covered by the Treaty provisions dealing with movements of goods, capital, and persons. They are stated to include activities of an industrial character, of a commercial character, and those of artisans and members of the liberal professions (Article 60). For the subsequent interpretation of this definition, see *Bulletin of the European Economic Community,* August–September, 1960, pp. 37–41.

Among the other obstacles that may tend to serve protective purposes or to distort competition, the Treaty deals with transport discrimination, monopolistic practices, subsidies, and differences in social costs and in other aspects of governmental administration that may affect relative costs. Each of these will be considered in turn. It should perhaps be mentioned also that the Treaty provides for the abolition of differential taxes or rebates which afford indirect protection (Articles 95, 96, and 98).

The injunction against discrimination based on nationality is the most unequivocal of the Treaty's provisions in these areas (Article 7). This principle is repeated specifically in connection with transport, although instead of being prohibited forthwith, discrimination in rates and conditions of transport based on country or origin or destination are to be abolished by the end of the second stage of the transition period (Article 79). Other forms of transport discrimination are forbidden after the beginning of the second stage; from that time on, no state may impose rates or conditions involving any element of protection or support for any enterprise or industry (Article 80). More generally, the institutions of the Community are to develop a common transport policy (Article 74), including common rules for international transport and the conditions governing the operations of a carrier in the territory of another member state (Article 75). Unlike the ECSC Treaty, however, the EEC Treaty does not require international through rates degressive with distance, but provides only that charges for crossing frontiers should be reasonable, taking into account the costs actually incurred (Article 81).

The monopoly provisions of the Treaty of Rome are also more limited than those of the Treaty of Paris. The latter apply to all the activities of the enterprises subject to the jurisdiction of the ECSC, while the Rome Treaty's rules against monopolistic practices apply only to trade between the members."[12] Concerted practices that adversely affect trade between the member states are proscribed if they "have as their object or result the prevention, restriction, or distortion of competition within the Common Market." The practices mentioned in the Treaty, which are not intended as an exhaustive list, are price fixing; control of production, markets, or investment; market sharing; and discrimination. However, even these practices are not outlawed in every case. In instances where they are necessary to improve efficiency and promote progress while passing on to consumers an equitable share of the benefits they are permissible if they do not impose any restrictions on the enterprise that are not indispensable to achieve these purposes and if they do not enable the enterprise to eliminate competition for a substantial portion of production (Article 85).

In addition, the improper exploitation of a "dominant position" within the common market by one or more enterprises is forbidden to the extent trade between any member states is adversely affected. Among the specific practices listed in this connection are the limitation of production, markets, or technical developments prejudicial to consumers, tie-in sales, and discrimination (Article 86).

The general ban on discrimination based on nationality and the rules against concerted practices and abuse of dominant positions described above apply also to state enterprises (Article 90).

The institutions of the Community are to issue appropriate regulations or directives for carrying out the above principles (Article 87). The Treaty, in assigning certain interim tasks to the member states (Article 88) left open to dispute whether

---

[12] For an extensive discussion of the monopoly provisions of the two treaties, see S. S. Riesenfeld, "The Protection of Competition," E. Stein and T. L. Nicholson (edt.) *American Enterprise in the European Common Market: A Legal Profile,* Ann Arbor, Mich., 1960, Vol. II, pp. 197–342.

the principles were legally applicable before the issuance of the regulations or directives.[13]

The criterion of the effect on interstate trade within the Community is generally the key to the Treaty's provisions on subsidies also; state aids that distort or threaten to distort competition by favoring certain firms or products are usually banned if they adversely affect Community trade. The elaborations on this general principle and the exceptions from it that are found in the Treaty will be discussed in connection with the clauses of safeguard.

In the social sphere, the member states "agree upon the necessity to promote improvement of the living and working conditions of labor so as to permit the equalization of such conditions in an upward direction" (Article 117). In the pursuit of this objective the members are to achieve within the first stage the practice of equal remuneration for equal work as between the sexes (Article 119). In addition, the countries agree to try to maintain the existing equivalence of paid holiday programs (Article 120) and to accept the premiums for overtime pay prevailing in France in 1956 as the level which would be reached by the end of the first stage (Protocol Relating to Certain Provisions of Concern to France, II). These arrangements reflect the French preoccupation with competitive disadvantages arising from differences in social policy.

The French insistence upon the harmonization of general legislative and administrative provisions was not easy to reconcile with the retention of sovereignty by the member states. The solution was to write into the Treaty the commitment for the harmonization of such legislative and administrative provisions "as have a direct incidence on the establishment and functioning of the Common Market," but, in effect, to require the unanimous agreement of all of the countries for any Community action designed to bring about a change in the legis-

[13] Riesenfeld, *op. cit.*, pp. 329–335.

lation of one or more of the countries."[14] (Article 100). After
the end of the first stage of the transition period, however, if
a disparity between the legislative or administrative provisions
"distorts the conditions of competition" and "thereby causes
a state of affairs which must be eliminated," a state may be
required to alter its provisions whether it concurs or not[15]
(Article 101).

However far the Treaty attempts to go in the direction of
harmonization, it stops short of the establishment of a full
economic union. Economic union would require a common
currency and common policies with respect to monetary matters, price levels, and balance of payments, and obviously
would have far-reaching political consequences.[16] The general
intention of the framers of the Treaty was to remove the
restrictions to the free functioning of a common market and
not, for the moment, to go beyond this point. The governments
therefore retained their political and economic powers except
to the extent necessary to assure the establishment of the
Common Market. Nevertheless, the governments could not
expect to conduct their economic policies with the same degree
of independance that they had before the creation of the Common Market. The close economic relationships among the Six
would, of course, require the coordination of their economic
policies in certain areas, particularly with respect to cyclical
policy, monetary affairs, balance-of-payments problems, com-

---

[14] The Council must act by a unanimous vote on a proposal of the
Commission. (See below, p. 285.) The action is to be by means of a
"directive" which is binding as concerns the objective to be achieved but
leaves the means of implementation to the directee.

[15] The Council must act by means of a qualified majority upon a
proposal of the Commission. (See below, p. 285n.) In this case too, action
is by means of a directive.

[16] The more general term "economic community" employed in the
Treaty thus seems more appropriate than the term "economic union"
sometimes used by the Commission. Cf. *Third General Report on the
Activities of the Community,* pp. 30, and 231. This series of reports will
hereafter be referred to simply by number as, for example, *"Third
Report."*

mercial policy, and, as already mentioned, social policy. Under the Treaty, each member country thus committed itself to pursue the policy necessary to maintain balance-of-payments equilibrium, confidence in its currency, price stability, and a high level of employment (Article 104). Exchange-rate policy is declared a matter of common interest (Article 107) and mutual assistance may be provided for a member state encountering balance-of-payments difficulties (Article 108). Common measures may also be taken to cope with cyclical difficulties (Article 103).

In the area of commercial policy, however, the existence of a common external tariff requires not only coordination but a common policy; the Treaty provides that this is to be established in the course of the transition period (Article 111). In this connection it is stated that the member states intend to contribute to the development of world trade through the progressive abolition of trade restrictions and the reduction of tariffs (Article 110). A common commercial policy is to include uniformity in lists of liberalized imports with respects to third countries (Article 111), harmonization of measures to aid exports to third countries (Article 112) and of export policy in general (Article 113), and common protective measures including those against dumping or subsidies (Article 113). In addition, tariff and trade agreements with third countries are to be negotiated by the institutions of the Community rather than by the individual countries (Articles 111 and 113).

Common action in the international sphere is not to be confined to commercial policy alone, but is to extend to "all matters of particular interest in regard to the Common Market, within the framework of any international organizations of an economic character" (Article 116).

The relationship to the Common Market of the overseas countries and territories associated with France, Belgium, the Netherlands, and Italy formed a knotty problem because of

French insistence upon the use of Community resources for the development of these areas. The compromise is embodied in a convention the provisions of which are to be in effect for five years, subject to further renewal or revision (Article 136). The social and economic development of these areas is to be supported by a Development Fund. France and Germany are each to contribute $200 million to the Fund over the five-year period, and the other members combined somewhat less than $200 million. Nearly 90 per cent of the funds are earmarked for overseas countries and territories associated with France. (Implementing Convention Relating to the Association with the Community of the Overseas Countries and Territories, Annexes A and B). Although the overseas countries and territories will benefit from the reduction of tariffs within the Community, they may be exempted from the Community obligation to reduce internal tariffs if warranted by their developmental or fiscal requirements. However, discrimination in favor of the member state with which the overseas area has had special relations is to be eliminated (Treaty, Article 133). The overseas countries and territories are also to enlarge their import quotas and to make them nondiscriminatory as between the member states (Implementing Convention, Article 11).

The basic financial arrangements of the EEC differ in an important respect from those of the ECSC; the EEC must depend upon contributions from the member states, whereas the ECSC has the power to raise its own revenues through taxes on coal and steel output. In the EEC, France, Germany, and Italy each is to contribute 28 per cent; Belgium and the Netherlands, 7.9 per cent each; and Luxemburg, 0.2 per cent (Article 200, 1). However, it is possible that the contributions of the member countries may be replaced in whole or in part by revenues from the external tariff (Article 201).

Power relationships

This difference in the degree of financial independence corresponds to a different emphasis in the power relationship between the various institutions of the Community and the governments and the Community. If reliance is placed upon a comparison of the two treaties alone and no account is taken of actual practice, the newer Community, though much more ambitious in economic coverage, is given less power of its own and is more subject to the control of the governments.

On the face of matters, the institutions of the EEC appear to be similar to those of the ECSC. There is a Council, composed of one representative from each member state; as in the ECSC, each representative is to be a member of his government. On most important matters in the early years of the Community, the unanimity rule governs the voting of the Council. Subsequently, many decisions may be taken by a "qualified majority" in which one or two or even three countries may be outvoted by the others.[17]

The EEC Commission, like the ECSC High Authority, consists of nine members "chosen for their general competence and of indisputable independence" who are not to "seek or accept instructions from any government or other body" (Article 157). However, the description "supranational" applied to the High Authority in the ECSC Treaty does not

---

[17] Where a "qualified majority" is specified, France, Germany, and Italy each has four votes, Belgium and the Netherlands two each, and Luxemburg one. If the action of Council has to be based on a proposal from the Commission, any 12 votes constitute a qualified majority. The result is that the three large countries can outvote the three small ones, but no one large country, even if it receives the support of Luxemburg, can block action. In other instances, the 12 votes must include those of at least four countries. However the Council is able to take relatively few actions that are not based on proposals from the Commission, and in those cases in which it can act upon its own initiative, usually unanimity is required. (For some examples of such cases see Articles 75 and 93, relating, respectively, to exemptions from transport policy and state subsidies.)

appear in the Treaty of Rome. Also, the members of the Commission serve four-year terms compared to the six-year terms of the members of the High Authority, and they are always appointed or reappointed by the governments whereas the vacancies on the High Authority are filled alternately by the governments and by the remaining members of the group. Thus, the independence of the members of the Commission *vis-à-vis* the governments is a shade less than that of the members of the High Authority.

The position of the Commission relative to that of the Council is also weaker. In the EEC, it is the Council that is given the power to take virtually all important decisions. It is true that the Commission is given a significant voice in the decision-making process since, on most issues, the Council can act only on a proposal made by the Commission. Furthermore, the Council must, in these cases, either accept or reject the Commission's proposal; it can modify the proposal only if its members unanimously favor amendment. However the Commission has the right to change its proposal as long as the Council has not acted upon it (Article 149), and the Council may request the Commission to submit "appropriate" proposals to it (Article 152); thus the path is left open for negotiations between the two organs.[18]

The Commission can exercise certain powers without the need for Council approval, but these are largely technical and administrative rather than policy-making in character. In the first place, the Commission is charged with the formulation of the more detailed regulations necessary to apply the principles or rules laid down by the Treaty or the Council, particularly in the process of dismantling intra-Community trade barriers. For example, the Commission is to determine

---

[18] This system of Commission proposal and Council decision is characteristic of the Treaty and applies to most of the actions referred to in earlier pages as being left to the institutions of the Community.

the way in which duties of a fiscal character should be taken into account in calculating common external tariff rates (Article 22), to set the precise dates for the duty reductions called for by the Treaty (Article 13), and to issue directives with respect to the procedure and timing of the abolition of measures that have the effect of quotas in the trade between member countries (Article 33).

Secondly, the Commission is given certain independent powers of policing and sometimes of enforcement, particularly in connection with the rules against transport discrimination (Article 79) and monopolistic practices (Articles 88 and 89).

Third, the Commission is accorded the right to make recommendations direct to the governments particularly with respect to the more rapid abolition of barriers to trade and factor movements (Articles 15, 35, 64, and 71), and to issue opinions on a number of matters such as Community social policy (Article 118).[19]

Finally, and of greatest interest for the present study, the Commission is given the major role in the administration of the safeguard clauses in the Treaty. Occasionally, it is subject to the check of the Council in these matters, but for the most part it is left to apply the Treaty's provisions without reference to the Council.

The Council on its side disposes of certain powers that it may exercise without the agreement of the Commission. For the most part, however, these are restricted to matters involving the internal administrative affairs of the Community on the one hand and highly political questions or problems left

---

[19] The language of the Rome Treaty differs from that of the Paris Treaty in the terms used to denote the actions of the Commission and the Council. A "regulation" has the direct force of law throughout the Community; a "directive" is binding as to the result to be achieved but like the "recommendation" in the ECSC leaves open the means by which the result will be attained; a "decision," which is also binding, is directed toward a specifically named addressee; and "recommendations" and "opinions" have no binding force (Article 189).

unsettled at the time of the Treaty negotiations on the other hand. In the first category are mainly items which for one reason or another the governments did not wish to leave to the Commission; the adoption of the budget (Article 203) and the remuneration of the members of the Commission (Article 154) are examples. An illustration of a political matter in the second group is the Council's power to issue directives to the Commission which governs trade and tariff negotiations with third countries (Article 113), and examples of Council authority over matters left unsettled in the Treaty are the prerogatives of the Council to determine the future of the Social Fund (Article 126) and whether and how sea and air transport should be brought under the Common Market (Article 84).

Generally, however, the Commission and the Council are expected to collaborate closely in providing the leadership and direction for the Community. An organ reflecting the interests of the Community is thus generally given the tasks of originating proposals, but an organ representative of the governments is given the power of decision.

The Assembly and the Court of Justice, the other major institutions of the EEC, are identical with those of the ECSC as far as their personnel are concerned, but their powers are generally greater in the newer Community. Under the ECSC as it actually operated, the Assembly established a stronger position for itself than had been contemplated, and this enhanced place was accepted by the framers of the Treaty of Rome. Thus, the Assembly is specifically given the right of deliberation (Article 137); it may censure the Commission and thereby cause its resignation at any time (Article 144); and it must be consulted by the Council in certain cases including budget questions (Article 203). Another difference from the ECSC is that the Assembly's resolutions are not subject to annulment by the Court.

Generally, however, the Court has somewhat more extensive jurisdiction in the EEC than in the ECSC. This applies particularly to the Court's powers to review the actions of the Council in the newer Community. Unlike the ECSC, in which the Council can be brought before the Court only on grounds of lack of legal competence or major violations of procedure, in the EEC the Council like the Commission may be attacked in the Court also on grounds of infringement of the Treaty or of any legal provision relating to its application and on grounds of abuse of power.[20] (Article 173). The Council is also required as is the Commission, to support its regulations, directives, and decisions by reasons (Article 190). The Court is not restrained from reviewing the Commission's or the Council's evaluation of economic facts in the EEC, while it is so limited, subject to certain exceptions, in the ECSC.

The Economic and Social Committee of the EEC is the analogue of the ECSC Consultative Committee, being advisory in character and composed of representatives of various economic and social sectors (Article 193). There is, in addition, a Monetary Committee with advisory functions in connection with monetary and balance-of-payments problems (Article 105). The Council as well as the Commission is required to consult these committees before taking certain actions. Provision is made for other advisory committees also.

The balance of power among these institutions, and particularly between the Commission and the Council, reflects experience in the ECSC and hence is more realistic. Recognizing that Europe is still a "Europe of fatherlands" (to use a phrase that became current after the Treaty had been signed), the ultimate power is assigned to the Council where, in contrast to the Commission and the Assembly, national interests are more likely to predominate. Yet the power of initiative

---

[20] Cf. G. Bebr, "The Balance of Power in the European Communities," *European Yearbook,* Vol. V, The Hague, 1959, pp. 53–75.

places the Commission in a strong position, and it enjoys other advantages too. It is composed of men who devote their full time to the day-to-day business of the Community. To carry out their executive functions, the members of the Commission have the support of an extensive staff, which numbered over 1,200 persons in 1958 and grew to nearly 2,000 by 1962.[21]

The Council, on the other hand, is composed of ministers, usually of foreign affairs, who can give only part of their time to the affairs of the Community and who are unlikely to be as well versed in economic matters as the members of the Commission. The Commission can also reach decisions more readily than the Council; it can act by majority vote among nine individuals, while the Council in practice usually can act only after four, five, or six governments have reconciled their points of view.[22]

There are, however, other factors that tend to redress the balance. In the first place, domestic pressures will force ministers to use the powers that they have to protect national interests. This could, it is true, create a situation in which the Council would be cast in an obstructive role while the Commission would appear as the advocate of progress toward the Community-wide interest. There is, however, a second element, the availability of staff support, which tends to offset some of the advantages of the Commission. The ministers are aided not only by their own staffs in their national capitals but also, collectively as well as individually by staffs at the headquarters of the EEC. Each country has a permanent delegation in Brussels which serves both as a channel of communication and negotiation between the Commission and its government and as staff support for the minister's participation

---

[21] *Common Market,* March, 1962, p. 56.

[22] These factors led Professor Reuter to think that power would tend to pass to the hands of the Commission. Cf. his "Aspects de la Communauté Economique Européenne (III)," *Revue du Marché Commun,* September, 1958, pp. 310–316.

in the meetings of the Council. The heads of these delegations, usually having ambassadorial rank, constitute the Committee of Permanent Representatives, an official auxiliary body created by the Council in accordance with its Treaty prerogative (Article 115); this group is charged with the task of preparing the work of the Council between its sessions. The Commission's working relationships appear to be with the permanent delegations, and the Permanent Representatives may engage in discussions and negotiations with the Commission and with each other on behalf of their governments in order to find solutions that the ministers will be able to approve at a Council meeting. Unlike the OEEC practice, however, the Council never meets at the official level, and only the ministers may actually take the decisions. The Council and the Permanent Representatives have been aided by a large number of special-purpose advisory committees and more recently by a more comprehensive set of standing subcommittees covering virtually all of the substantive area germane to the work of the Council. The personnel for these committees is drawn not only from the permanent delegations but also from the various substantive departments of the national governments.[23] In addition there is a secretariat for the Council (numbering more than 200 persons in 1958 and more than 300 in 1962)[24] headed by a secretary-general and including five major sections.

The institutionalization of the work of the Council, and particularly the important role played by the Permanent Representatives, led to the fear, expressed in the Assembly, that this group might be usurping the preparatory role of the

---

[23] The Commission has also made extensive use of committees including experts from the various governments. This served not only to ensure that various problems would be viewed in all their aspects but also as a means of making continuing contact with the national administrations and obtaining the agreement and support of the national personnel concerned in given measures.

[24] *Common Market,* March, 1962, p. 56.

Commission.[25] However, the Commission appears to have adapted itself to the position of the Permanent Representatives with good grace. Clearly, by virtue of the Treaty and by the force of circumstance, the Commission's influence depends more on its powers of persuasion than on its legal rights.

Some policy aspects

One of the reasons often cited for the pre-eminence of the Council in the EEC Treaty is that the economic policy to be followed in the Community is not laid down at all or only in the most general terms. The broader scope of the EEC made it impossible to establish Community policy in each field to the extent that had been done in the ECSC Treaty. Since the problems and developments that would mark the path to integration could not be foreseen, the task of formulating policies and rules as the need arose had to be left largely to the institutions of the Community.[26]

Hence, the EEC Treaty is confined to a greater degree than the earlier Treaty to the provision of a framework within which these legislative or quasi-legislative functions could be carried out. By giving primacy to the Council, the governments retained the power to control the exercise of these functions. This was inevitable since the retention of large areas of national sovereignty meant that many of the policies of the Community would have to be worked out through the progressive harmonization of the economic structures and policies of the several member countries.[27]

In the broader areas of economic policy, such as agriculture, transport, economic crises, and monopolistic practices, the Treaty is either silent or offers very general principles. There

---

[25] Assemblée Parlementaire Européenne, *Débats,* January, 1959, No. 4, p. 73.

[26] Cf. Bebr, *op. cit.,* and Reuter, *op. cit.*

[27] M. July in Savary and July, *op. cit.,* p. 2381.

are thus no provisions that match those of the ECSC Treaty setting forth a regime of regulated competition. The powers of the Council and the Commission to prevent monopolistic practices and to enforce competition are much weaker than those of the High Authority and, unlike the ECSC rules, they may be invoked only if trade between the member states is affected.

The wave of mergers and business ententes that was set off by the establishment of the Common Market, much of which involved firms in two or more countries, raises important questions about the kind of economy that will emerge from the Common Market. In the first few years of the Common Market, the benefits of this movement seemed more obvious than the drawbacks. Even where businessmen contemplated reaching understandings with their competitors in other member countries, the desire for a strong bargaining position provided an incentive to reduce costs.

In some instances, this led to new investment in larger and more efficient plants; in others to mergers within individual countries which reduced costs, occasionally by shutting down small and uneconomical plants or by concentrating on a more limited range of products or models. There are probably also industries in which market-sharing agreements between producers in different member countries have smoothed the transition by avoiding sudden changes in patterns of distribution, but there are obvious limits to the extent to which this kind of arrangement can be regarded as advantageous.

In some Community circles and perhaps in the Commission itself[28] other advantages were seen in the movement towards mergers and ententes, particularly between firms in different member countries. Businessmen were led, it was argued, to think in European rather than national terms and thus the forces toward integration were strengthened. In any event, a

---

[28] Cf. *Third Report,* pp. 130–132.

vigorous anticartel policy at the beginning of the Common Market would have frightened business and prevented or dampened the burst of investment activity that occured. Furthermore, the restrictive effects of agreements, the true extent of which was difficult to judge, cannot have been so drastic; after all, trade among the Six expanded by more than 40 per cent between 1957 and 1960 compared to 15 per cent for world trade as a whole.[29] For the longer run, it seems unlikely that many of the cartel-like arrangements will survive the first slackening of economic activity in the Community, so easy and so tempting is it to violate such agreements when there is not enough business to keep all participants at full capacity.

Whatever the elements of truth in this comforting picture, it is not so certain that some of the member governments will not move to bolster the position of their own producers in order to prevent unwelcome increases in imports in a period of recession. Apparently the attitude of some of the governments, even amid the general prosperity of the early years of the Common Market, tended to restrain the Commission from acting with respect to suspected market-sharing agreements designed to protect national markets or to offset by price increases the first intra-Community tariff reductions. Thus, even though the Commission is conscious of the danger that private controls over trade may replace the governmental restrictions abolished by the Treaty, the nature and extent of future controls over concerted practices in the Common Market remains to be worked out.

This like other potential problem areas of the Common Market has been more or less thrown into the shadow by the rapid economic expansion that marked the first few years of the Community. It remains to be seen whether the Six will in the long run follow merely one or both of the twin aspects of

---

[29] GATT, *International Trade, 1960,* p. 110.

the Benelux policy of tolerance toward cartels accompanied by low tariffs on third-country goods.

CLAUSES OF SAFEGUARD

In some safeguard clauses, particularly those relating to the elimination of internal tariffs and the establishment of common external tariffs during the transitional period, the nature of the remedial measures are specified in the Treaty. For the most part, however, the safeguard clauses set forth only the grounds and procedures for authorized derogations from the Treaty, and leave the nature of the measures themselves to the Commission, the Council, or both to determine. In the language most commonly employed, the Commission and/or Council is to authorize the member state to take "measures of safeguard of which it shall determine the conditions and particulars."[30]

The measures authorized by the Commission or Council in these instances thus may include the whole arsenal of protective weapons, such as tariffs, quantitative restrictions, and other barriers or hindrances to the movement of goods and productive factors. Sometimes the duration and extent of the derogations are left entirely to the judgment of the Commission and/or Council, but in the more general safeguard clauses these bodies are admonished to limit the derogations to the minimum necessary (in degree and/or duration) to achieve the end sought or to give priority to measures of safeguard that will interfere the least with the functioning of the Common Market.[31]

Something of an exception to this tendency toward silence on the nature of the relief measures is represented by the pro-

---

[30] See, for example, Articles 37, 3; 108, 3; and 115. Slight variations of the language, to which little significance can be attached, are sometimes found; in one instance (Article 226), for example, the Commission is to "determine the measures of safeguard which it considers necessary specifying the conditions and particulars of application."

[31] See, for example, Articles 107 and 226.

visions relating to subsidies.[32] In principle, any state aid that distorts competition by favoring certain enterprises or outputs is forbidden, but the door is left open for the use of subsidies to succor various situations. Subsidies for some purposes, the Treaty states, do not violate the general principle at all; others may or may not violate it; and still others may be permitted in exceptional circumstances regardless of their compatability with it. In the first category the Treaty places social aids to consumers (provided that there is no discrimination with respect to the origin of the products concerned), relief in connection with natural calamities, and aids necessary to offset the disadvantages suffered by certain regions of Germany owing to the division of that country. Among those in the second group the Treaty mentions aids for underdeveloped or stagnating regions and relief to a seriously disturbed economy. However, this category is very broad indeed since it also includes "aids intended to facilitate the development of certain activities or of certain economic regions" provided that they do not change "trading conditions to such a degree as would be contrary to the common interest." In addition, the Council may add to this group by a qualified majority vote on a Commission proposal (Article 92). In exceptional circumstances, Council may at the request of a member state decide by a unanimous vote that a particular program of subsidies shall be deemed compatible with the common market regardless of the general principle mentioned above (Article 93).

The Commission may order the modification or abolition of existing subsidies, and new ones require its prior approval.[33]

---

[32] See also discussion of French export aids, page 305f below.

[33] Council may, however, as noted in the last sentence of the preceding paragraph, approve a subsidy program outside of the regular rules in exceptional circumstances. The Council may also, acting by a qualified majority vote on a proposal of the Commission, exempt certain categories of subsidies from the requirement of prior Commission approval (Article 94).

Since, apart from the subsidy provisions, the measures to be taken are generally left unspecified, the following review of the main clauses of safeguard in the Rome Treaty dwells mainly on the grounds and procedures for derogations; reference is made, however, to the measures to be taken when they are specified or limited in some way. Once again, it is convenient to distinguish between the clauses that are intended to ease the burden of adjustment to the Common Market during the initial period of its establishment, and those which are designed to serve the longer run needs of the Community.

In addition to the safeguard provisions of the Treaty itself, the settlement of the external tariffs of the List G items involved a number of compromises and safeguards, usually of a quite specific character that will also be discussed.

The Transition Period

A number of provisions make clear the intention of the framers of the Treaty to have the countries progress toward the establishment of the Common Market without creating serious difficulties or disturbances in the economy of any member state, or, if such untoward developments occur, to mitigate them as much as possible.

The freeing of trade between the member countries in a series of small steps, itself a precautionary measure, seems all the more conservative when compared to the immediate abolition of trade barriers for coal and steel under the Treaty of Paris. Coal and steel, it was thought, are industries characterized by highly concentrated control, and the task of avoiding a temporary disorganization of markets following a sudden end of tariffs and other restrictive devices was more manageable. While it was possible to devise specific safeguarding mechanisms for the anticipated danger spots in the common market for coal and steel, a similar undertaking for each and every industry would have been formidable indeed.[34] Thus the solution of gradual reduction of barriers with very general safeguards was favored.

Furthermore, the 12-year period contemplated for the process of liberalization may be extended to a maximum of 15 years; any country may cause the first stage of the transition period to be extended from four to five and then to six years (Article 8, 3), and the second and third stages may also be extended, through unanimity of Council on a Commission proposal is required (Article 8, 5). It is possible, in addition, that hardship cases created by the elimination of tariffs between member cases may be covered by the following passage found in Article 14 after the timing of the reductions has been specified :[35]

Any special problems raised by the application of the preceding paragraphs shall be settled by directives issued by the Council acting by means of a qualified majority vote on a proposal of the Commission. (Article 14, 5).

While the rules for tariff reductions among the member states apply also to customs duties of a fiscal nature, if the Commission finds that the substitution of an internal tax for such a duty would create serious difficulties for a member

---

[34] However, it has been argued that this drawn-out process of the removal of trade barriers was unnecessary under the conditions of full employment which prevailed when the Treaty went into effect; few if any industries in any of the member countries would have been able to achieve sufficiently large expansion or reorientation of production to make possible the flooding of the markets of another member state even if trade barriers had been cut in one fell swoop as in the case of coal and steel. Cf. R. Courtin, "L'échelonnement des mesures de libération et les clauses de sauvegarde," *Le Marché Commun et ses problèmes, Revue d'Economie Politique,* January–February, 1958, pp. 291–309.

[35] This interpretation of the cited passage is supported by the fact that when the framers of the Treaty had in mind purely technical problems incurred in applying rules, as in Article 21, they used the term "technical difficulties" rather than the term "special problems" found in Article 14.

country, the Commission is empowered, within the first year of the Community, to authorize the country to retain the duty for as long as six years after the Treaty comes into force (Article 17). In addition, each country may, within limits, remove some products on which it levies customs duties of a fiscal nature from the category of items for which the external tariffs will be determined by arithmetical averaging and place them in the category of goods for which the external rates have to be determined by negotiation among the countries (Article 22).

Further safeguards are extended also in connection with the adjustment of the tariffs of individual countries to the common external tariff of the Community. Each country is permitted to add products accounting for a total of no more than 2 per cent of its imports from third countries to the list (i. e., List G) for which the common external tariff is to be determined by negotiation rather than by arithmetic averaging (Article 20). However, since these duties are to be determined by the end of the first stage, or at the latest by the end of the second stage or the transition, this opportunity is limited temporally as well as quantitatively.

The Commission may authorize a member country which encounters "special difficulties" resulting from the progressive establishment of the common external tariff to postpone the lowering or raising of duties towards the common rates, but such authorization may be only for a "limited period" and for tariff classifications which in the aggregate do not exceed 5 per cent of the country's imports from non-Community sources (Article 26). More generally, the Commission, which is entrusted with many technical tasks entailed in establishing the common external tariff, is instructed to perform this work being guided, inter alia, by "the need for avoiding serious disturbances in the economic life of member states" (Article 29).

Special protocols are appended to the Treaty relating to tariffs on mineral oils and imports of bananas and unroasted coffee. The member states may continue to maintain their former duties against each other and against third countries on mineral oils for six years after the Treaty comes into force, after which duties among the member countries are to be abolished and duties with respect to third countries to move to the level established in the common external tariff. Tariff quotas, generally related to 1956 imports, are authorized to Germany for bananas and to Italy and the Benelux countries for unroasted coffee. The quotas are governed by provisions which permit some year-to-year fluctuation in either direction, but they are to be scaled down though not entirely eliminated during the transition period. Council will determine the final disposition of the tariff quota arrangements.

In addition to providing safeguards against difficulties that arise from the ordinary problems of adjustment to the new conditions created by the Common Market, the Treaty also seeks to forestall injury arising from dumping or certain monopolistic practices during the transitional period. In the event that a member state is injured by dumping (which, incidentally, is not defined in the Treaty), the Commission is to recommend the cessation of the objectionable practices to those engaged in them. If dumping continues, the Commission is to authorize the injured country to take such protective measures as the Commission deems appropriate (Article 91, 1). An attempt is made to minimize the possibility of dumping, either in the transition period or afterwards, by the "boomerang" technique; that is, by a provision requiring each country to readmit free of all duties or quantitative restrictions any products which it has exported to the other members (Article 91, 2). The Commission is empowered also to authorize protective measures in the event of discrimination by a state monopoly of a commercial character (Article 37), although such measures may be applied only as long as the discrimination continues.

As we have already noted, the individual countries are left with a large measure of freedom, initially at least, to continue to protect their agriculture. In addition, within the first two years after the effective date of the Treaty, the Council may by a qualified majority vote on a proposal of the Commission, expand the list of products (Annex II) to which the agricultural provisions of the Treaty apply (Article 38). Also, Luxemburg is authorized to maintain quantitative restrictions on certain agricultural products during the transitional period, subject afterwards to modification or abolition by the Council by a majority vote on a proposal of the Commission (Protocol Concerning the Grand Duchy of Luxemburg, Article 1).

France is the recipient of a special safeguard clause related to its fear of unfair competition owing to differences in social charges. The member states signing the Treaty declare that they "consider" that overtime pay rates in industry will correspond to those existing in France in 1956 by the end of the first stage of the transitional period. If this does not happen, the Commission is to authorize France to take safeguard measures for any industries "affected" by inequalities in overtime pay. The nature of the measures is left to the Commission, and they need not be taken at all if the increase in wage levels since 1956 in the other countries have exceeded the increases in France, industry for industry, by a percentage fixed by the Commission with the approval of a qualified majority of the Council (Protocol Relating to Certain Provisions of Concern to France, II).

The most general clause opening an avenue for the suspension of a member's obligations in the event of unanticipated difficulties during the transitional period is contained in Article 226. This provides that a member state may ask the Commission to authorize relief measures if there are serious difficulties in any economic sector which are likely to persist or if there are difficulties which may seriously impair the economic situation in a region. The measures, which are to be determined by the Commission, are intended to "restore the situation and adapt the sector concerned to the Common Market economy." Article 226 is in some ways more explicit than most of the other safeguard clauses to be found in the Treaty. In the first place, it states specifically that the measures may include derogations from the provisions of the Treaty, which is done in few if any other places in the Treaty. Secondly, and somewhat less unusually, the measures to be taken are circumscribed by the requirements that (1) they be limited in degree and duration to what is strictly necessary for the purpose at hand and (2) priority be given to measures that will least disturb the functioning of the Common Market. The more definite language employed here may represent an attempt to minimize the possibility that the local interests would be tempted to use this loophole to evade rather than adjust to the competition of the Common Market. Of course other safeguards not limited to the transitional period, such as Article 115 relating to diversions of traffic (see below, p. 309f) could also be drawn upon during these early years.

Safeguards Not Confined to the Transitional Period

Not quite in the category of safeguards but perhaps worth mentioning are several provisions intended to preserve the freedom of action of member states in certain sensitive areas. Thus, the rules governing the elimination of quantitative restrictions (Articles 30 to 34) are waived for controls over imports or exports which are justified on grounds such as the protection of public health, morality, or national treasures (Article 36). Again, each country is free, despite the provisions of the Treaty, to take the measures with respect to production or trade in military products that it deems necessary for its security (Article 223). In both instances, however, an effort is made to ensure that the needs in these fields are not used as pretexts to thwart the aims of the Treaty.

Most of the safeguard clauses are designed to deal with particular sources of difficulty. They may be divided into four categories, according to whether they are intended to provide relief for countries encountering (1) balance-of-payments difficulties; (2) supply deficiencies of raw materials arising out of the functioning of the Common Market; (3) the need for protection owing to unfair practices or to disparities created by the lack of harmonization of policies, particularly but not exclusively in agriculture; and (4) problems of uneven degrees of development within national boundaries. There are in addition some clauses of a more general character, and provision is made for certain institutions that may lend themselves to aid in connection with readaptation.

Balance-of-payments difficulties. Something akin to the confrontation technique of the OEEC is employed in the monetary and financial area in order to minimize the possibility of balance-of-payments difficulties. The Monetary Committee, consisting of two members from each state, is to keep each country's monetary and financial situation under review and to report its findings to the Council and the Commission (Article 105). In view of the general understaking of the member countries to pursue policies necessary for balance-of-payments equilibrium (Article 104), the Community may be able to exert pressure, aided by the *expertise* of this committee, to induce a member state to move more quickly in adopting financial measures that will forestall any balance-of-payments difficulty that is in the making.

If matters nevertheless reach a point where a country encounters or is seriously threatened with balance-of-payments difficulties, the Commission is to examine "without delay" the use that the country has made or the means at its disposal to achieve external equilibrium with high employment and stable prices (Article 108). The Commission is then to recommend to the country the measures which it considers the country should adopt; presumably these would usually involve monetary and fiscal changes necessary to establish internal financial stability. If the actions taken by the country, including those suggested by the Commission, prove inadequate, the Commission, after consulting the Monetary Committee, is to recommend to the Council that the member state be provided with mutual assistance. Mutual assistance, which is to be granted by the Council by means of a qualified majority vote, may take several forms. A concerted approach may be made to an international organization, presumably for the extension of loans to the member country in difficulty, or the other members may agree to advance credits themselves. If the state in question maintains or establishes quantitative restrictions on imports from third countries, the other members may be asked to take the measures necessary to avoid diversions of trade—that is, to obviate the possibility that third-country products will enter the markets of the country trying to restrict them via the territories of the other member states. During the transition period, before intra-Community trade barriers have disappeared, mutual assistance may take the form also of special reductions of tariffs or increases in quotas for the benefit of the member country in difficulty.

If aid is not granted or proves inadequate, the Commission is to authorize the country to take protective measures that the Commission thinks appropriate. However, the Council may by a qualified majority vote modify or revoke the authorization given by the Commission.

In the event of a sudden crisis in the balance-of-payments and if a Council decision with respect to mutual assistance is not "immediately taken," the member state may take unilateral action on a provisional basis. The measures of safeguard taken by the country are not to be greater than the minimum necessary to cope with the situation and must be chosen so as to cause the least possible disturbance to the operation of the common market. The Commission and the other member states must be informed of the measures of safeguard not later than their effective date. The Commission may recommend to the Council that mutual assistance be provided. The Council, acting by a qualified majority vote on an opinion of the Commission and after consulting the Monetary Committee, may instruct the member state to modify or abolish the measures it has taken (Article 109). Thus, the power to authorize a country to derogate its obligations for balance-of-payments reasons rests with the Commission subject to modification or veto by the Council, but the power to control unilateral derogations rests with the Council.

Special balance-of-payments provisions are included for Italy and France. In the case of Italy, the signatories agree that the measures that might be required of the Italian Government under the clauses just reviewed should safeguard the Italian program for economic expansion and the improvement of the standard of living. (Protocol Concerning Italy). The implication seems to be that neither the Commission nor the Council would be warranted in expecting Italy, in the case of balance-of-payments difficulties, to adopt restrictive monetary measures that would curb economic expansion.

The provisions for France relate to the system of aids granted to exports and special charges on imports in existence at the time the Treaty was signed. Changes in this system are to be notified to the Council and the Commission, and if the French Government does not accede to a request from these institutions to make the charges and aids uniform within each of three categories (raw materials, semifinished products, and finished products), the Council may by a qualified majority vote authorize the other members to take protective measures.

The system is to be abolished, progressively if necessary to avoid disturbance, when the balance of payments of the franc area has been in equilibrium for more than one year and reserves have reached a satisfactory level; provision is made for arbitration in case of disagreement as to whether the level of reserves is "satisfactory" (Protocol Relating to Certain Provisions of Concern to France, I).

Safeguards relating to disturbances in the functioning of the capital market owing to movements of capital are somewhat similar to the general provisions relating to balance-of-payments difficulties. Here also, unilateral action is permitted if the measures to be taken have a "secret or urgent character," but normally the prior authorization of the Commission is to be obtained and unilateral emergency measures are subject to the subsequent approval of the Commission.[36] The Council by a qualified majority vote may modify or revoke the action of the Commission in authorizing derogations (Article 73). A country may, after consulting the other member states and the Commission, take appropriate action to cope with a situation in which its exchange rules differ from those of other member countries in such a way as to make it possible for persons to use the transfer facilities of the Community to evade its transfer regulations with respect to third countries (Article 70).

Raw-material supplies. Another set of clauses is designed to keep within bounds the extent to which the common external

---

[36] The rapporteur of the French parliamentary committee that examined the Treaty seemed to consider that the provisions regarding capital movements were consistent with the desire of each country to prevent the outflow of capital. He also implies that the point of Article 72, which requires the member countries to keep the Commission informed of capital movements *vis-à-vis* third countries, was to guard against the possibility that inflows of capital from third countries might concentrate upon investment in one member country and thus create cumulative "disparities" in economic growth which would modify the political equilibrium of the Community. M. Savary in Savary and July, *op. cit.,* p. 2350.

tariff increases the costs of raw materials and agricultural products, particularly where these goods have been obtained from third countries before the establishment of the Common Market. If the Commission finds that the production of certain items in Lists B, C, and D (with duties of 3, 10 and 15 per cent, respectively) are not sufficient to meet the requirements of a member state whose supplies traditionally depended upon considerable imports from third countries, it is to propose to the Council that the member state facing the deficiency be granted tariff quotas at a reduced rate of duty or free of duty, and the Council is to act on this proposal by a qualified majority vote. However, the tariff quota may not be so large as to create the fear of a transfer of activities to the detriment of the other members (Article 25, 1).

With respect to List E, tariff quotas are to be granted by the Commission at the request of a member state where a change in sources of supply or a shortage of supplies within the Community is harmful to the member state's processing industries.[37] The relatively high duty for List E, 25 per cent, probably explains why it is made somewhat easier to obtain relief from the common external tariff for these goods (i. e., in that Council approval is not required). Here too, the tariff quota may not be so large as to endanger the trade of other member countries (Article 25, 2).

The terms relating to List E applied also to those items in List G for which the Council, by a qualified majority vote upon a proposal from the Commission, was to fix the common external duty in the event that the member states could not agree. In fact, the member countries did reach agreement on everything except petroleum in March, 1960, but the terms of their agreement for seven disputed products ran along lines

---

[37] See below, p. 321, for the Commission's interpretation of harm or injury to processing industries.

parallel to those of Article 25, 2.[38]

Finally, for the agricultural products to be included in the common agricultural policy, the Commission may authorize a member state to suspend in whole or part the collection of duties, or the Commission may grant the state tariff quotas provided that no serious market disturbances result (Article 25, 3).

In all of these cases, the Commission is periodically to examine the tariff quotas that have been granted (Article 25, 4).

It may be noted that the tariff quotas provided in Article 25 are limited to the products on Lists B, C, D, E, and G and to the agricultural products in Annex II. The large majority of tariff items are not on these lists and hence are not eligible for the quotas. Neither are the products of List F eligible by virtue of being on that list; however, a good many are to be found in Annex II and thus fall within the scope of Article 25, 3. (A fair number of the others on List F have zero or low duties).

Unfair competition. In cases of improper practices, such as discrimination, the limitation of production, or market sharing, either by ententes or by one or more dominant firms, the Commission either on its own initiative or at the request of a member state is to investigate and propose appropriate steps to end the infringement of the antimonopoly principles written into the Treaty. If the violation continues the Commission may authorize the member states to take measures, which it must specify, to remedy the situation (Article 89). This seems to make it possible for the Commission to permit the members whose trade is injured by the monopolistic practices to take defensive actions in the form of tariffs, quantitative controls, and the like.

---

[38] See below, p. 320f.

The Commission may also authorize protective measures if one of the member states alters its exchange rate in a manner which "seriously distorts the conditions of competition" and which at the same time is incompatible with an exchange-rate policy necessary for balance-of-payments equilibrium accompanied by high employment and stable prices (Article 107). The latter qualification may have the effect of removing from the purview of the clause virtually all currency devaluations except those intended for purely competitive purposes, which for a number of reasons seem unlikely to pose a real threat to relations among the Six.

The door is left open for measures of safeguard when the Commission finds that a disparity between the legal or administrative provisions of the member states "distorts the conditions of competition in the Common Market and thereby causes a state of affairs which must be eliminated." If consultation by the Commission with the interested countries does not eliminate the source of the difficulty, the Council may issue the necessary directives.[39] In addition, "The Commission and the Council may take any other appropriate measures as provided in this Treaty" (Article 101). This sentence seems open to the interpretation that the Commission and the Council may permit member states whose interests are injured to take defensive measures.

Safeguards are specifically provided when the source of the difficulty is a lack of harmonization of commercial policy measures taken under the Treaty. Article 115, which has been of great practical importance, reads in part :

In order to ensure that the execution of measures of commercial policy taken in conformity with this Treaty by any member state shall not be prevented by diversions of com-

---

[39] By a unanimous vote during the first stage and subsequently by a qualified majority vote on a proposal of the Commission.

mercial traffic, or where disparities between such measures lead to economic difficulties in one or more of the member states, the Commission shall recommend the methods whereby the other member states shall provide the necessary cooperation. Failing this, the Commission shall authorize the member states to take the necessary protective measures of which it shall determine the conditions and particulars.

In cases of emergency and during the transitional period, however, a member state may take the defensive steps upon its own initiative, but the Commission can order the state to change or abolish the measures it has taken. Priority is to be given to those measures of safeguard which cause the minimum disturbance to the operation of the Common Market and which interfere least with the early introduction of the common external tariff.

In the agricultural sphere, the possibilities for permitting continued protection include but go beyond the grounds of "distortion of competition." As a right, a member state may levy a countervailing charge on the entry of a product from another member country when the latter maintains a marketing organization or other mechanism that gives its exports of that product a favored competitive position. However, the exporting countries have a prior right to collect such a tax on their exports. The amount of the charge must be limited to what is necessary to redress the balance, and it is to be fixed by the Commission. The Commission may also authorize recourse to other measures of defense (Article 46). In addition, Council is permitted to authorize subsidies "(1) for the protection of enterprises handicapped by structural or natural conditions; and (2) within the framework of economic development programs" (Article 42).

Beyond these safeguards relating to interstate trade in agricultural products within the Community, the Treaty envisages, as has already been mentioned, that the various systems of sheltering agriculture practiced in the individual member states will be gradually replaced by a Community-wide system. Whether consisting of common rules, compulsory coordination of national marketing organizations, or of a Community marketing organization, the common system (or systems, since the same mechanism need not be used for every product) may employ "all measures necessary" to achieve the agricultural objectives of the Treaty (Article 40, 3), which include the improvement of the standard of living of farmers, market stability, and the regularity of supplies at "reasonable" prices to consumers (Article 39). Thus the entire range of instruments used for the protection and support of agriculture at the national level is authorized; price controls, subsidies for production and marketing, stockpiling, and mechanisms for the statilization of exports and imports are specifically mentioned (Article 40, 3). Agriculture is exempt from the antimonopoly rules; the latter apply only to the extent determined by the Council when it establishes the common system (Article 42). In working out the common system, due account is to be taken, *inter alia,* of the need to make adjustments gradually (Article 39, 2).

Economic development. Special provisions are included for the economic development of underdeveloped regions, stagnating areas, non-European countries and territories associated with the Community, and for large projects in the common interest. Subsidies may be authorized for all of these phases of development activity (Article 92). The Commission is also to take into account the needs of underdeveloped regions in considering transport rates that involve elements of support (Article 80). The associated countries and territories, as previously noted, are entitled to levy duties on goods from the Six to the extent justified by their developmental and budget requirements even though their exports will enter the European Common Market on equal terms with the products of the European members—i. e., eventually, duty-free. The associated countries and territories are also free of the obligation to conform to the common external tariff with respect to third countries. However, if the duties which an associated country or territory levies on third-country imports are so low that it becomes a channel through which the third-country products enter some other part of the Common Market to the detriment of one of the member states, the latter may request the Commission to propose the necessary remedial measures to the other member states (Article 134).

General clauses. Although there are many clauses providing for derogations from the obligations of the Treaty on one ground or another, the only provision designed specifically to make possible relief for a particular industry in serious difficulties is limited to the transitional period (Article 226). Perhaps this is not remarkable in a Treaty creating a common market, even though the Treaty does not allude to a more rational relocation of productive activity in its statement of objectives.[40] Neither, however, does the Treaty of Rome have a permanent clause analogous to Article 37 of the Treaty of Paris, which though not phrased in terms of a single product or industry, covers cases of "fundamental and persistent disturbances in the economy" of a member state and hence could include instances in which an important industry is seriously injured.

There are, however, several passages of the EEC Treaty which might conceivably be utilized to meet such difficulties. Perhaps the clause that comes the closest to covering injury

---

[40] A search for the rational location of *new* productive activities might, however, be inferred from the stated objectives to promote "a harmonious development of economic activities, a continued and balanced expansion" (Article 2).

to particular industries directly is found in Article 92, 3, which declares that subsidies "to remedy a serious disturbance of the economy of a member state . . . may be deemed compatible with the Common Market." While this might be invoked on behalf of an important industry and while subsidies may prove an efficacious method of protecting an industry in difficulty, the clause is in marked contrast to the general practice followed in the Treaty of leaving the nature of the remedies to the discretion of the Commission and/or the Council.

Another passage of the Treaty that may be available for the succor of particular industries does provide discretion as to means but is limited as to the sources of the difficulties. Article 103, which provides that the member countries shall consider their cyclical policy as a matter of common interest, specifies that the Council may by a unanimous vote on a proposal of the Commission decide on "measures appropriate to the situation." Similar action may be taken "in the event of difficulties arising in connection with the supply of certain products." While this rather vague language seemingly could provide the basis for almost any remedial measure, Article 103 is restrictive in that the source of the trouble must be either cyclical or a supply shortage and the consent of the Commission and of a unanimous Council is required.

A power not specifically related to the existence of difficulties in a particular industry or economic sector but nevertheless of conceivable use in such circumstances, is the right of the Council, acting by unanimous vote, to modify or suspend any rate of duty of the common external tariff.[41] After the transition period, Council may take such action by a qualified majority vote upon a proposal of the Commission, but in this procedure the change in duty must not be greater than 20

---

[41] This provision relates to "autonomous" or unilateral changes by the Community; other clauses permit changes in the common external tariff through reciprocal negotiations with third countries.

per cent nor of more than six months' duration (subject to one renewal of six months) (Article 28). Conceivably this provision may be used to succor the difficulties of an industry in one of the Six, but it might call for sacrifices from the others. The clauses could more readily be used, of course, when the tariff change was in the interests of several or all of the countries.

There is, finally, an even more general grant of power which enables a unanimous Council acting upon a Commission proposal to take any action necessary to achieve the objectives of the Community. Article 235 provides:

If any action by the Community appears necessary to achieve, in the functioning of the Common Market, one of the aims of the community in cases where this Treaty has not provided the requisite powers of action, the Council, acting by means of a unanimous vote on a proposal of the Commission and after the Assembly has been consulted, shall enact the appropriate provisions.

It seems unlikely that very free use would be made of this clause, but it could be invoked in the event that a serious disturbance loomed large in the economic and political calculus of one of the member countries.

Adaptation. Somewhat more use may be made of provisions designed to prevent injury from the changes that the Common Market brings to individuals and firms. The European Social Fund is established with the task of promoting employment opportunities, particularly by encouraging geographical and occupational mobility (Article 123). At the request of a member state, the Fund, which is administered by the Commission, is to cover 50 per cent of the expenses encountered by the state for occupational retraining, resettlement allowances, and aids to workers placed on full- or part-time leave pending the reconversion of their enterprise. Conditions are attached to the use of Community funds for each of these purposes. Before the states can be recompensed for half their retraining expenditures, the worker must have been employed for at least six months in the occupation for which he was retrained; furthermore, the Community money may not be paid out if the worker could have found employment "otherwise than in a new occupation." Resettlement reimbursements to the member states may be made only if the unemployed worker had to change his residence and after he has been in productive employment at least six months in his new place of residence. The payments for workers' leaves during conversion are also subject to the six-month rule, and in addition the conversion plan, including its financial arrangements, must have been approved in advance by the Commission (Article 125). At the end of the transitional period, the Council, acting on an opinion of the Commission and after consulting the Economic and Social Committee and the Assembly, may decide by a qualified majority to suspend one or more of these forms of aid or may by a unanimous vote assign new tasks to the Fund in the fulfillment of its broad purposes with respect to employment opportunities and worker mobility (Article 126). France, Germany, and Belgium bear somewhat larger shares of the expenses of the Fund than they do of the other Community costs, while Italy and the Netherlands bear smaller shares.[42]

---

[42] Article 200 allocates the burdens as follows:

				Per cent share in cases of	
				General Community budget	European Social Fund
Belgium	...	...	...	7.9	8.8
Germany	...	...	...	28	32
France	...	...	...	28	32
Italy	...	...	...	28	20
Luxemburg	...	...	...	0.2	0.2
Netherlands		...	...	7.9	7

The regular budget of the Community is adopted by a qualified majority vote of the Council, but that of the Social Fund is adopted by a system of weighted voting in which the weights correspond closely to the percentage shares in the budget of the Fund (Article 203).

The mission of the European Social Fund is in some respects broader and in others narrower than that assigned to the High Authority by the readaptation provisions of the ECSC Treaty. It is broader in that the promotion of employment opportunities and worker mobility is to be pursued as a general principle and not only in response to a limited set of specified conditions. This difference between the EEC and the ECSC has been reduced but not eliminated by the amendment to the Paris Treaty which extends the basis for readaptation aid to the case in which it is necessitated by structural changes in marketing conditions.[43] On the other hand, the scope of the Fund is narrower than that of the ECSC readaptation provisions because it includes only direct aids to the workers themselves and does not provide assistance to enterprise in order to create new jobs.

Although the Treaty provisions specifically mention only the occupational retraining of unemployed workers, the Commission considers that the Treaty authorizes support for the occupational training of the children of displaced workers at least in circumstances of declining employment opportunities such as those encountered in connection with the modernization of the Italian sulphur mines. This position is based on Article 128,[44] which provides that the Council, on a proposal from the Commission, is to establish general principles for implementing a common occupational training policy that can contribute to the "harmonious development both of national economies and of the Common Market."

While there is no direct provision in the Treaty of Rome for financial aids to enterprises for the purpose of easing the position of displaced workers, the Treaty creates the European Investment Bank whose activities may in part serve this function. The Bank is to use both its own resources and those

---

[43] See above, Chapter IV.
[44] *Journal Officiel,* 4th Year, No. 17, March 7, 1961   p. 449.

of the capital markets to contribute to "the balanced and smooth development of the Common Market in the interest of the Community." It may extend loans and guarantees, on a nonprofit basis, for development projects in less developed regions (apparently intended mainly for southern Italy) and for projects of common interest to several member countries which owing to their size or nature cannot be entirely financed by the means available in the member states. What is more relevant for the problem of injury, it may finance "projects for modernizing or converting enterprises or for creating new activities which are called for by the progressive establishment of the Common Market where such projects by their size or nature cannot be entirely financed by the various means available in each of the Member States" (Article 130). This language seems to leave it open to the Bank to lend its support to the creation of new employment opportunities when it deems such action necessary and feasible. Unlike the Social Fund, however, the Bank is not subject to the control of the Commission. Its credit policy is determined by the Board of Governors, composed of ministers appointed by the six member countries, and the policy is administered by the Board of Directors, consisting of 12 members, one of whom is nominated by the Commission and the others by the member countries [45] (Protocol on the Statute of the European Investment Bank, Articles 9 and 11). The capital of the Bank, subscribed by the member governments [46] is $1 billion, of which 25 per cent had to be paid up within two and a half years from the effective date of the Treaty, and the balance at the discretion of the Board of Directors to the extent that it becomes necessary to meet obligations to the Bank's creditors (Bank Statute, Articles 5 and 4). The modest means of the Bank

---

[45] Three each by France, Germany, and Italy, and two by the Benelux countries.

[46] France and Germany, 30 per cent each; Italy, 24 per cent; Belgium, 8.65 per cent; Netherlands, 7.15 per cent; and Luxemburg, 0.2 per cent.

make it likely that the extent of its activity will depend upon it ability to raise funds on the capital markets of the Community and third countries.

Other Treaty clauses. The foregoing review of the precautionary clauses of the EEC Treaty is not exhaustive. Perhaps the most notable omissions are various safeguards hedging the provisions requiring nondiscriminatory transport rates. (A permitted exception on behalf of economic development has, however, already been mentioned.) Thus account is to be taken of the effect of the application of this and other rules governing transport on the standard of living and the level of employment in certain regions, the utilization of transport equipment (Article 75), the need for subsidies for transport coordination (Article 77), and the economic situation of carriers (Article 78).

Mention may also be made of the protocol permitting France, Italy, and the Benelux countries to continue their former customs treatment of certain colonies or former colonies not associated with the Community, and of the protocol in which the member states retain their freedom to take appropriate measures in the event that difficulties arise for them from the trade of a member state (most probably Western Germany) with Communist East Germany.

The List G clauses

When most of the duties for the products on List G were agreed upon in the Accord of Rome in March, 1960, after arduous negotiations, special arrangements were required with respect to some 40 tariff lines out of approximately 225 that were involved in the agreement.[47] There were in addition, a number of compromises achieved by subdividing tariff classi-

---

[47] The Accord of Rome (March 2, 1960), may be found in the *Journal Officiel,* 3d Year, No. 80C, December 20, 1960. The body of the Accord sets out the duties for about 225 positions under the 70 tariff headings

fications so as to accord preferential treatment where the product involved was to be used for certain purposes; for example, lard and other pork fats were generally dutiable at 20 per cent, but only at 4 per cent when intended for industrial uses other than the manufacture of food products.

Some of the special provisions were necessary to compromise the divergent interests of producing and consuming member countries with respect to the level of the common external tariff. Others were designed to cushion the impact of foreign competition upon workers in one of the member countries, and still others to safeguard the interest of one of the associated countries or territories.

Since the duties of List G were, in accordance with the terms of the Treaty, settled by the member states through direct negotiation, there was no legal necessity to reply upon the safeguarding clauses of the Treaty. However, while some of the problems were in fact settled without reference to any Treaty provision, others were compromised through the invocation of one of the Treaty clauses or by provisions modeled on those found in the Treaty.

The most frequent solution of these difficult cases was to establish a tariff near the upper limit of the range under discussion but to accompany it with liberal tariff quotas.[48] The conditions under which the quotas were granted varied somewhat. For paper pulp (with a 6 per cent duty) any member

of List G and the special arrangements are contained in 17 protocols. The Accord covered all products in List G except four categories of petroleum products for which agreement still could not be reached. (Cf. *Bulletin of the European Economic Community,* March–April, 1960, p. 33).

[48] The common external duty was established in the 5 to 12 per cent range for most of the products for which tariff quotas had to be established. Even rates of this magnitude apparently caused concern, especially in the Benelux countries, about the future competitive position of export industries which had formerly purchased raw materials from third countries duty-free.

state was to be permitted to establish a quota unilaterally, being required merely to inform the Commission;[49] the quota, for which the tariff could be reduced to the zero level, was to be limited to imports that would be processed within the country concerned. For other products and for specified countries, the Commission was to grant tariff quotas on demand, sometimes up to an absolute limit stated in the Accord and sometimes up to a limit defined generally in terms of the import needs of the country's processing or utilizing industries. Settlement along these lines included salt for industrial uses for the Belgian-Luxemburg Economic Union; certain ferro-alloys for Benelux, Germany, and Italy;[50] unwrought aluminum for Benelux and Germany; unwrought lead for Belgium, Germany, and the Netherlands; and unwrought zinc for Germany and the Netherlands.[51]

For another group of products, including tropical woods, natural cork in blocks or sheets, silk yarn, imitation gems and similar articles of glass,[52] aluminum scrap, unwrought magnesium, and magnesium scrap, the Commission was instructed to grant tariff quotas upon the request of any member country

[49] Paper pulp of certain types (from cotton linters or bleached vegetable fibers) and for certain uses (manufacture of artificial textile fibers) were, however, exempted from any duty. The difficulty over the paper-pulp tariff lay in the conflict between the commercial policy of the Community and the industrial ambitions of the three large member countries. On the former score, there was a desire to avoid serious disturbance to the traditional flow of pulp from the Scandinavian countries. The argument for protection was based on the prospect of rapid expansion in Community paper consumption and the possibility that a shortage could develop. It was also felt that the development of a paper industry was particularly suitable for certain areas in the Community where little industry is to be found and where employment opportunities are scarce.

[50] Up to the end of the second stage of the transition period only; subsequently, tariff quotas are to be granted by the Commission only in the event of injury to processing industries of these countries.

[51] Italy, on the other hand, was the beneficiary of arrangements permitting it greater protection for lead and zinc. See below, p. 323.

[52] The Accord granted France and Germany duty-free quotas in specified amounts up to the end of the second stage of the transition period.

when a change in sources of supply or a shortage of supplies within the Community entailed harmful consequences for a country's processing industries. This stipulation that the tariff quota be conditional upon injury to a processing or utilizing industry, which is similar to that found in Article 25, 2 of the Treaty, was the subject of an interpretative declaration by the Commission which was included in the Accord of Rome by the member countries.[53] The Commission stated that it understood the term "harmful consequences," to involve unfavorable changes, which resulted directly or indirectly from the tariff rate in question, either on third-country markets or on the Community market. In the former category would be an improvement in the competitive position of third-country producers which could not be met by a regime of drawbacks or a similar device. Among the internal changes the Commission mentioned an increase in retail prices that reduced the sales possibilities of the Community's processing industries, financial difficulties due to the need to absorb the increased costs occasioned by the duty, inadequacy of supplies with respect either to quantity or quality, and the necessity to obtain supplies under less favorable conditions than other Community users (especially integrated enterprises). Furthermore, on the occasion of its review of existing tariff quotas or upon consideration of new requests for quotas, the Commission will take account of the changes in injury suffered by the processing industries, particularly as reflected by a growth or diminution in their activity.

The provisions for the termination on the tariff quotas vary from product to product. In some cases no provision is made for termination other than what might be implied by an instruction which is given to the Commission to review the tariff quotas from time to time (e. g., aluminum scrap, crude

---

[53] Accord of Rome, Acte Final.

magnesium, and magnesium scrap).[54] Sometimes the language calling for this review is specifically linked to the body of the protocol which sets forth the reasons and conditions for the tariff quota (e. g., cork, lead, and zinc);[55] other times it is related to developments in processing industry concerned (e.g., salt and crude aluminum).

In other cases, the end of the quotas hinge upon some future development or negotiation. Those on tropical woods are related to future negotiations in GATT, in the background being the possibility of reciprocity between the Community and the British Commonwealth in the treatment of tropical woods from their respective associated countries and territories. Those on paper pulp are to be re-examined by Council in the framework of Article 28,[56] which provides for autonomous changes in the common external tariff, after December 31, 1966; by that date, presumably, the ambitions of the three large member countries to establish a paper industry within the Community will be capable of better assessment.

Almost all of the tariff quotas were accompanied by the stipulation, again modeled upon Article 25 of the Treaty, that the quotas could not go beyond the point where transfers of activity to the detriment of other member states "becomes apparent" (e. g., lead, zinc, salt), or more commonly, "is to be feared" (e. g., ferro-alloys, cork, silk yarn).

---

[54] This provision is similar to Article 25, 4 of the Treaty.

[55] The tariff quotas for certain ferro-alloys and glass products are in this category after the end of the second stage or the transition period when they are conditional upon injury to a processing or utilizing industry; those established prior to this date, which need not be related to injury, automatically expire when the second stage ends.

[56] Another provision for a tariff quota, relating to ferronickel, also turned on the use of Article 28. It called for a review of the 7 per cent duty with a view to its autonomous reduction by the Council, and provided for a tariff quota in the event of no reduction and consequent injury to a processing industry.

Tariff quotas played a role also in the settlement of some of the agricultural products on List G. The member states took note of the intention of Germany and Italy to obtain tariff quotas for certain fish products, certain wines, ethyl alcohol, and natural cork. They included in the Accord of Rome a statement in which the Commission declared its willingness to use its powers to grant such quotas under Article 25, 3 of the Treaty when the utilizing industies in Germany and Italy were unable to obtain supplies adequate in quantity and quality under the same conditions as utilizers in other member countries or when, in the case of the fish products, traditional sources of supply can provide basic foodstuffs important to the population, especially to the less favored groups, without increases in the accustomed level of prices.[57]

For a few products, the tactic of setting high tariffs and granting exceptions was reversed. In these cases, including sulphur and iodine and certain of their derivatives, lead, zinc, and raw silk, tariffs were established at a lower point within the disputed range and exceptions were granted to Italy, the country pressing for higher duties. For these groups of products, the member states expressed themselves as favorably disposed towards the application of Article 226 of the Treaty in order to isolate the Italian market from that of the rest of the Community for six years for lead, zinc, and raw silk and for six to eight years for the other products. Since the letter of Article 226 gives neither the member states[58] nor the Council any voice in the derogations it permits, the effect of this declaration was to put the combined authority of the member states behind any request that Italy might make of the Com-

---

[57] *Journal Officiel,* 3d Year, No. 80C, December 20, 1960, p. 1871, and 4th Year, No. 17, March 7, 1961, p. 450.

[58] Of course, the member state seeking the derogation must take the initiative, but the decision to grant the request is entirely up to the Commission.

mission for escape action for these products under the terms of the article.[59] The further provisions of the compromises varied for the three different groups of commodities.

For iodine and related products, the member states simply agreed to re-examine the situation at the end of the period in the framework of Article 28; that is to consider the possibility of an autonomous change, presumably an increase in the duties (from zero for iodine and from 15 per cent for iodides and iodates).

Arrangements for two groups of products were somewhat more complicated. In connection with sulphur, there was on the one hand a guarantee by the Italian Government that sulphur would not be sold to Italian industries processing for export at prices below world prices,[60] and on the other hand agreement on certain measures designed to make the Italian sulphur mines competitive and to ease the impact of the adjustment on the workers involved. Thus, the member states expressed themselves as being favorably disposed towards aid by the European Investment Bank financing the modernization of the mines and the creation of processing industries with the necessary infrastructure. They also expressed their intention to find ways to compensate the displaced miners and to aid the program of occupational training for them and their children. Finally, they looked to the creation of a liaison and action committee to encourage private initiative and development within the framework of a regional program; the committee would be supported by the Italian Government, the Sicilian region, and the Community.

---

[59] Similar considerations are involved in the references to financial aid from the Social Fund and the European Investment Bank found in some of the settlements of the Accord of Rome, although the Treaty gives the Council and the governments somewhat larger roles in connection with these institutions than in the escape mechanism of Article 226.

[60] The Italian sulphur market is controlled by a public organism.

With respect to raw silk, a 10 per cent duty formally inscribed in the common external tariff was suspended during the six-year period of isolation of the Italian market. The member states here also indicated their favorable attitude toward intervention by the European Investment Bank, this time to help modernize sericulture and silk processing industries. At the end of the period, the 10 per cent duty is to be restored under Article 28 if Council finds that Italian production of raw silk has been maintained at least at its current level (840 tons per annum) and if its price is not more than 10 per cent above world prices for comparable qualities.

For lead and zinc, exceptions from the general duty of $1.32 per 100 kilograms [61] were permitted in both directions. Some countries, as already noted, received the right to obtain tariff quotas up to 20 per cent of the requirements of their utilizing industries. On the other hand, a provision was also included for the isolation of the Italian market for a six-year period under Article 226; this was phrased in the same terms as those used for sulphur, iodine and raw silk.

Perhaps the most elaborate set of compromises was that necessary to reconcile the desire of the Dutch to permit their KLM Airlines to continue the purchase of British and American planes and parts free of duty with the desire of the three large countries for protection to permit the development in the Community of what would, hopefully, become an aircraft industry capable of meeting foreign competition. Complete airplanes weighing more than 5 tons were to be free of duty until December 31, 1963, and those weighing more than 15 tons until December 31, 1966. After these time limits the 12 per cent duty would apply. However, in the case of aircraft in excess of 15 tons, Council might unanimously agree upon a

---

[61] Scrap and waste, however, are exempt from duty.

further suspension of the duty, for three or five years, and whenever the duty becomes effective there is to be a duty-free quota the size of which will represent the sum of the import requirements formulated by the governments of the several member states. Such quotas are to exclude any types of aircraft that are produced within the Community which fulfill all competitive requirements, but the decision to make such exclusions is to be taken by a unanimous vote of Council.

Similar provisions govern helicopters weighing more than 2 tons. The 12 per cent duty is suspended until December 31, 1963, a suspension which may be extended for three years. When the duty becomes effective, the arrangement with respect to tariff quotas comes into effect as in the case of airplanes weighing more than 15 tons.

USE OF THE SAFEGUARD CLAUSES[62]

At the time of writing only two and a half years have elapsed since the first intra-Community tariff reductions and only six months since the first movement towards the common external tariff. This limits the nature of the appraisal that can be made of the use of the safeguard clauses in the Common Market, not only because so little of the story has unfolded but also because it is too early to assess the significance of some of the things that have occurred.

---

[62] The public documentation of the use of safeguard clauses in the EEC is rather skimpy. This may be due in part to the fact that some uses of the clauses require no formal action on the part of the Commission, but even where Commission action is required the notice of the action is not always published. Often when it is published, it is only after a considerable delay, and then sometimes in laconic terms. Much of the information in this section was obtained in discussions with perhaps a score of Commission officials in two visits to Brussels and from press services of which *Europe,* published by the Agence Internationale d'Information pour la Presse, Luxemburg, was the most valuable.

There emerges, however, a fairly clear pattern with respect to the positions of the several member countries. Germany, motivated by the awkward position created for its agricultural processing industries by high domestic farm prices, sought exceptions from the Treaty obligations to reduce internal trade barriers. Germany was also desirous of maintaining its trade connections with third countries and tried to find ways to minimize the diversion of its imports from customary sources towards other member countries and associated African areas. In this connection, Germany sought first to keep down, the level of the common external tariff, and subsequently to obtain exceptions from it. France, with Belgian support, opposed the German position, taking the view that the Community represented among other things a club for the mutual benefit of the member countries at the expense of outsiders.[63]

---

[63] It is easy to understand why French support for European integration has been hailed as the abandonment of a protective policy of long standing. There has undeniably been a shift in the orientation of French industry and agriculture from a preoccupation with the domestic market to broader horizons. This has been due in part to the compulsions of growing agricultural surpluses and in part to the regeneration of French industry and to the confidence of a new generation of industrialists in their ability to meet external competition.

On the other hand, it can be pointed out that the French extracted a high price for their entry into the Common Market. The tart comment that France got a common market for her partners and a French market for herself (A. Nutting, *Europe Will Not Wait*, London, 1960, p. 87) may not have been warranted, but the French farmer was to receive for his exports to Germany the high prices Germany paid to her own heavily protected farmers, competition for French industry was to be eased by the Community-wide adoption of French wage practices regarding overtime pay and equal remuneration for men and women, and French overseas territories and associated countries were to receive substantial financial aid from Germany. Furthermore, the direction of French influence within the Community, as suggested in the text, would support the hypothesis that the shift from protectionism relates only to the other members of the Six and that the traditional French policy has not so much been abandoned as extended to the wider territory of the Community.

INTERNAL MARKET SAFEGUARDS

List G Safeguards for Italy

Italy was perhaps less prepared for open competition within the Community than any of the other members. Not as industrialized as the others, it also shared with France a highly protectionist background. Unlike France, however, its competitive disadvantages had roots that went beyond the monetary problems that were the main source of French difficulties in the years before the establishment of the Common Market. Italy feared the effects of outside competition on its efforts to industrialize and to absorb its labor surpluses, particularly in connection with its underdeveloped regions in the south.[64] Also, Italy had not been able in the course of the negotiations to bend the terms of the Treaty to its needs and fears nearly to the extent that France had. Thus, it is not surprising to find Italy prominent in the cases involving exceptions and derogations, both authorized and unauthorized.

Some of these will be treated in subsequent sections dealing with various categories of safeguards which the several member countries invoked, but it is convenient to treat as a group the exceptions made for Italy in connection with the List G products which were included in the protocols of the Accord of Rome.

In approaching the task of implementing the provisions of these protocols, the Commission took the position that it was not bound by the "favorable prejudgment" expressed therein by the member states towards the application of Article 226

---

[64] There were many references in the discussions preceding the Rome Treaty of the untoward effects of the unification of Italy upon industrialization in southern Italy. Unification, the argument ran, permitted capital to flow freely to the north which offered safety as well as good returns, and northern goods to flow to the south at prices which newly established industries would not be able to meet. See, for example, Savary in Savary and July, *op. cit.*, p. 2338.

on behalf of Italy, and that it intended to confine its authorizations to those that were actually indispensable. Furthermore, the Commission stressed the fact that the terms of Article 226 specify that the measures of safeguard are to be used not only to afford relief but also to adapt the sector concerned to the Common Market.

In keeping with this approach, the Commission authorized the isolation of the Italian market—that is, a ban on imports from the member countries—only for sulphur. The member states had contemplated similar treatment for certain sulphur compounds, iodine and certain of its derivatives, crude lead and zinc, and raw silk. However, other concessions were granted for these products. For raw silk and the sulphur compounds, Italy was allowed to maintain existing duties to other member countries despite the scheduled reductions in intra-Community tariffs. A similar exception was permitted for the minimum specific duties on lead and zinc, but the *ad valorem* duties were to be reduced according to this normal schedule.[65] No derogation of obligations within the Community was allowed for iodine and its derivatives, but concessions were made with respect to imports from third countries; the movement towards the common external tariff need only be 20 per cent rather than 30 per cent and Italy could deny Community treatment to these products even when shipped from other member states if they originated in third countries.[66] The measures of safeguard, which were authorized for one year,[67] were associated with plans for the reorganization of the industries involved. Italy was to present reorganization programs to the Commission and to submit annual reports on the progress of reorganization so that decisions could be reached about the

---

[65] Action taken under the authority of Article 226.

[66] Action taken under the authority of Article 115.

[67] As from the date of the Commission's decision at the end of March, 1961.

extension of the safeguard measures and the progressive integration of the Italian market into the normal arrangements of the Common Market. Reference was made to aid from the Social Fund for the occupational retraining of displaced workers and from the European Investment Bank for financial support of reorganization. In addition, it was stipulated that the Italian Government would ensure that the temporary measures of protection thus granted would not adversely affect the competitive position of producers in other member countries.

The main factor underlying the exceptional treatment of these products appears to have been a concern about the social consequences of Community-wide competition. In the case of sulphur, for example, the jobs of about 7,500 workers were at stake in an area of southern Italy where unemployment and underemployment were already high. Even a successful reorganization of the industry would entail a substantial reduction in the work force, and it was not clear that even the investment of substantial sums would enable the industry to remain competitive in the light of a declining trend in world prices. Thus, some suggestions were made that the mining of sulphur should be abandoned in favor of the exploitation of the potassium salts and rock salt found in the same basin. Pending the decisions about these problems, Italian sulphur was protected.

Not involved in List G, but partaking of many of the same characteristics that marked the Italian products that were provided for in the Accord of Rome, were citric acid and calcium citrate. These products are derived from bergamot, a fruit which provides an important source of income and employment in Calabria, another underdeveloped region of Italy. Unfortunately, citric acid and calcium citrate produced synthetically were cheaper than those derived from bergamot, and Italy, after failing in an effort to add bergamot to Annex II, unilaterally invoked Article 226 to avoid fulfilling its Treaty obligations with respect to tariffs and quantitative restrictions for citric acid and calcium citrate. The Commission subsequently authorized the derogation from these obligations.[68]

Agricultural products

Pending the development of a common agricultural policy for the Community as a whole, the main lines for the protection of agriculture laid down in the Treaty were (1) the right to suspend imports from other member countries or to make them conditional upon minimum prices, (2) long-term contracts between exporting and importing member states, and (3) compensatory taxes to offset agricultural price differences between the member countries.

Most of the early activity in this area centered upon the controls over imports from Community sources under the first of these safeguards, which were supposed to be invoked only when an intra-Community reduction of duties or quantitative restrictions jeopardized the agricultural objectives endorsed by the Treaty. During the first two or three years that the Treaty was in force, minimum price arrangements were operated by France for pork, lard, poultry, and a number of fresh fruits and vegetables; by Belgium and Luxemburg for most fresh fruits and vegetables; by Italy for butter, beef, and veal; and by Germany (briefly) for malt.[69] Most of these mechanisms were based on the minimum import price scheme permitted by the Treaty; that is, imports were suspended when internal prices fell below the specified minima. The Commission strongly favored the alternative system based on minimum

---

[68] *Fourth Report,* Paragraph 37.
[69] *Third Report,* pp. 92–93; *Fourth Report,* Paragraph 30.

export prices, also provided in the Treaty, under which imports are permitted to enter as long as their price is above the established minimum. The Commission's position was based on the view that the minimum export price approach represented less interference with trade.[70]

Since the "objective criteria" for minimum prices had not yet been established by the Commission and the Council, the member countries enjoyed a considerable freedom of action which in some instances was used rather broadly. There were a number of temporary suspensions of imports, including, for example, a German ban on Italian apples of a certain grade. A suspension of longer duration by Italy of the import of certain pork products—following a sharp drop in domestic pig prices early in 1961—led to the first Court case involving an allegation of a violation of the Treaty.[71] The products at issue had been notified to the Commission by the Italian Government as having been liberalized under OEEC Council decisions. The Commission held that the Treaty prohibition of any new quantitative restrictions on such products (Article 31) prevented recourse by Italy to the safeguarding provision which permits import suspensions (Article 44). Italy could, however, invoke the alternative course provided by the latter clause, that is, make imports conditional upon minimum prices. A French case also raised some difficulties but the Commission took no action pending the adoption of the

---

[70] *Fourth Report,* Paragraph 30.

[71] *Journal Officiel,* 4th Year, No. 25, April 8, 1961, p. 575. The Commission at one point rejected the Italian claim that the suspensions could be justified under Article 226 on the ground that they had been applied unilaterally without authorization from the Commission. Subsequently, when Italy did apply for the invocation of Article 226, the Commission rejected the request on the ground that Italy should employ the minimum price procedure of Article 44 to meet its problem. By the time the Court decision upholding the Commission was announced near the end of 1961, Italy had already repealed the import ban and substituted a system of minimum prices. *Common Market,* February, 1962, p. 40.

"objective criteria" for minimum prices by the Community. France established minimum prices and an import levy for eggs on the ground that other Community countries were obtaining cheap poultry feeds from external sources; however, the conditions for the establishment of a minimum price system did not seemed to be met inasmuch as the difficulties in the French egg market were not attributable to a reduction in tariffs or quantitative restrictions.

The other protective provisions for the Community's agriculture, long-term contracts and compensatory taxes, apply only to products covered by a national marketing organization in one or the other of the member states. Much to the dissatisfaction of potential agricultural exporters within the Community, only one long-term agreement, providing for the expansion of cereal exports from France to Germany and for the progressive approximation of prices towards the higher German level,[72] was concluded in the first two or three years of the Community's existence. The Commission pointed out, in response to criticism that it had not pressed hard enough for such contracts, that the Treaty gave the member countries until the end of the first stage to conclude the agreements and the Commission could not act until that period had expired.

The safeguard involving a compensatory tax was also invoked with less frequency than the minimum price provisions. The provision was used early in 1961 on behalf of Germany with respect to imports of powdered whole milk and malt from Belgium, France, and the Netherlands.[73] Germany

---

[72] *Second Report*, p. 103.

[73] *Journal Officiel*, 4th Year, No. 26, April 13, 1961, p,. 595–597, and 4th Year, No. 42, June 24, 1961, pp. 825–826. It was reported that the exporting member countries affected by the German tax on powdered milk complained to the Commission about it. France was concerned about German imports from third countries, and the Netherlands argued that Article 46 related only to distortions in competition that were created by the existence of marketing organizations and ought not to be

also requested the right to impose a compensatory tax on eggs, claiming that even if there was no marketing organization for eggs in any country, such organizations did exist for poultry feeds (i. e., secondary cereals) and thus distorted competition within the meaning of the Treaty provision. However, the Commission denied the request, considering among other factors that imports from third countries were the main source of the difficulty.

Given the existence of sizeable differences in agricultural prices from one member country to another, some form of control over intra-Community trade appears necessary at least during a transition period in which prices can be brought to a common level. Both the minimum export price system and the compensatory tax mechanism could conceivably be used for this purpose, but the Commission regarded the latter as a more flexible and hence superior device for the controlled expansion of agricultural trade during the period of price rapproachment. It therefore proposed that (for wheat and pork, among other products) all other measures for the protection of agriculture, especially quantitative restrictions and minimum prices, be replaced between Community countries by compensatory levies. The levies would be gradually reduced as progress is made towards a common price level for agricultural products and towards the elimination of other sources of distortion of competition.[74] These levies would not, of course, be limited, as are those provided in the Treaty, to situations in which the existence of a national marketing organization in one of the countries affects competition. The intra-Community levies would be related to duties on third-country products in such a way as to assure preference for EEC products.

used in cases in which the price differences were due to differences in productivity. In the case of malt, Germany had first levied a compensatory tax unilaterally.

[74] *Bulletin of the European Economic Community,* January, 1961, pp.

A special problem in the agricultural sphere was posed by the reluctance of France and Italy to conform to the Community obligations under Article 33, 2, and the acceleration decision to increase quotas for wine. France, indeed, refused to open global quotas to the other member states (except a small quota for bottled wine), basing its stand on the existence of a national marketing organization. The French system of price supports, in addition, gave rise to charges by Italy that France was dumping wine in the German market. The French fixed prices each year for the "quantum" of wine required to meet estimated demand, and the amounts in excess of the quantum were apt to be sold at very low prices since they were not eligible for support. Partly on these grounds but more because of domestic surpluses, Italy was reluctant to open wine quotas to the extent called for by the Community schedule (5.2 per cent of national production for 1961). The Commission favored the simultaneous opening of quotas of equal size by France and Italy and included this suggestion in a proposal relating to the organization of the Community wine market to the Council. Pending the decision of the Council, which under Article 43, 2 required unanimity, the Commission granted a temporary exception to Italy permitting it to open a much smaller global quota for wine, both in barrels and bottles, to the other members of the common market excluding France.[75] This action, which was taken under Article 226, was contingent upon the maintenance by Italy of an earlier global quota for bottled wine.

Industries processing agricultural products

Although the Treaty provided protection, ot least for an interim period, for the existence side by side of different

---

[75] *Journal Officiel,* 4th Year, No. 42, June 24, 1961, pp. 823–825.

agricultural price levels in the several member countries, it made no special provision for the same goods in higher stages of processing. Thus, while wheat could be sold in protected national markets at widely varying prices, bread and other products derived from wheat were subject to the rules governing the free circulation of industrial products in the Common Market. Hence, upon the dismantlement of intra-Community trade barriers, a country like Germany which maintained high agricultural prices would be at a serious disadvantage with respect to such products compared to a country like the Netherlands which had a low price policy. Of course, this problem would, it was contemplated, eventually disappear, for a common agricultural policy was to be established which would ultimately eliminate the artificial differences in agricultural prices. Meanwhile—and in view of the great difficulties encountered in elaborating the common agricultural policy, it could be a very long meanwhile—there were obvious distortions in competition. Germany was most affected, and the products involved were those processed from sugar, grains, potato starch, chicory, wine, and milk and milk powder.[76]

Three types of solutions to this problem were advocated or discussed. One proposed early in the game was the addition of a number of the semiprocessed or processed commodities to the list of agricultural products which benefited from the special safeguards (Annex II). The Treaty permitted additions to the list, it will be recalled, by a qualified majority vote of the Council acting upon a Commission proposal (Article 38, 3). The Commission did not look with favor upon this approach; it felt that difficulties peculiar to the interim period

[76] German prices for grains, pork, and sugar beets in 1959–60 ranged from 20 to 50 per cent above those prevailing in France and the Netherlands. German milk prices were 45 per cent above the Dutch, and German potato prices 55 per cent above the French. EEC Commission, *Prix Agricoles,* May, 1961.

should be met by means other than placing new products under the special regime for agriculture. However, it agreed to such treatment for a few products derived from wine and sugar on the ground that it would be difficult to carry out a common agricultural policy for the basic products unless certain of the derivatives were included. Thus, ethyl alcohol, vinegar and vinegar substitutes, and flavored or colored sugars, syrups, and molasses were added to the list of agricultural products.[77]

A second line of action, particularly pressed by Germany in search of immediate relief for certain urgent cases, was to invoke the Treaty's escape clause relating to difficulties in an economic sector during the transition period (Article 226). Two types of relief measures were actually taken under this provision. Under one, a member country was released from its obligation to reduce its trade barriers *vis-à-vis* other members. Thus, Italy was authorized to postpone the increase in quotas for citric acid and calcium citrate, products derived from citrus fruits, to the other member countries.[78]

A second type of relief measure under Article 226, preferred by the Commission, involved the establishment of special levies at the frontier in order to compensate for the differences in the costs of the basic agricultural products. This arrangement, modeled on the safeguard clause for agricul-

---

[77] *Journal Officiel,* 4th Year, No. 7, January 30, 1961, pp. 71–72; and *Third Report,* pp. 182–183.

[78] After its request for the addition of these products to Annex II had been denied, Italy announced its intention of invoking Article 226 and did not reduce duties and increase quotas on July 1, 1960, as called for by the Community schedule. When the Commission decided upon the application of the Article 226 clause nearly a year later (May, 1961), it agreed only to authorize the postponement of quota increases, not to a delay in the reduction of tariffs to community countries and in the movement towards the common external tariff towards third countries. Furthermore, it stressed that the exception was made in order to permit Italy to adapt the sector concerned to the Common Market.

tural products found in Article 46, was applied to German imports of certain bakery products from the Netherlands and confectionary products from Belgium and the Netherlands. The Commission fixed the amount of the levy on each product so as to offset the difference between the exporting and importing countries in the cost of the agricultural raw materials contained therein. The taxes were duly levied by the exporting countries, since the decision gave Germany the right to collect the levies in the event that the exporting countries did not do so.

However, the Commission was reluctant to invoke Article 226 repeatedly to cope with a whole category of actions such as was necessary owing to the close relationship between the agricultural products covered by a special regime and the semiprocessed and processed products derived from them which received no special treatment in the Treaty. Article 226, the Commission felt, should be employed only in exceptional cases and even then for limited periods of time. The Commission wanted to be able to institute the measures it deemed appropriate for the problem, namely compensatory taxes such as those established in connection with the movement of Belgian and Dutch bakery and confectionery products to Germany, on the basis of a general grant of authority specifically for this purpose rather than as a series of exceptions on the basis of Article 226. Since, in the face of the problem posed by industries processing agricultural products, the Treaty did not provide the powers necessary to promote certain aims of the Community, namely the development of Community trade in such products and the avoidance of distortions in competition, the Commission felt that it was appropriate to invoke Article 235, which in such conditions permitted the Council to arm the Commission with the necessary authority. Accordingly, at the end of July, 1960, the Commission asked the

Council to grant it the power to authorize compensatory taxes (on the model of Article 46) for about a score of tariff headings or subheadings for products derived from sugar, grains, potato starch, chicory, wine, and milk and milk powder. The taxes would not be greater than the amount necessary to compensate for differences in retail prices attributable to differences in prices of the base products. They would not be levied in a manner that would have unfavorable effects on the exports of another member country, and they might be suspended in favor of protection against imports from third countries.[79] Proposals along these lines were finally approved by the Council in January, 1962.[80]

Diversions of traffic

The most important derogations regarding the free circulation of *industrial* goods in the Common Market arose from the danger of diversions of traffic. This threat stemmed from differences among the member states in the treatment of third-country goods during the initial period when intra-Community trade barriers were being dismantled but the movement to a common external tariff had not even begun. In some instances, the difference consisted of a great disparity in tariff levels from one member country to another or of differences in the list of goods still subject to quantitative restrictions. For the most part, the Benelux countries were more liberal than the three large member countries with respect both to tariffs and quantitative restrictions. For example, a spread of 25 percentage points separated the Benelux and French tariffs on certain products. Again, Germany and Italy had not withheld the liberalization of certain imports from Japan as had France and the Benelux countries. In these circumstances the opening

---

[79] *Bulletin,* January, 1961, pp. 83–85.
[80] *Common Market,* March, 1962, p. 50.

of the Common Market would lead to the transshipment of such third-country products through to the less liberal countries unless some precautionary measure was taken. Thus, for example, in July, 1960, France suspended imports of roasted coffee from other member states; the latter maintained no restrictions on coffee, while France relied upon a strict quota system in order to support coffee prices, on behalf of associated African areas, that were 60 to 70 per cent above world prices. In this instance, the Commission directed France (in May, 1961) to substitute a compensatory tax on coffee imports from the other member states for the suspension of imports.[81]

In other cases, the possibility of the diversion of traffic arose from the existence of bilateral trade agreements, including those that provided for clearing systems with state trading countries. For example, Italy was obliged by an agreement to import certain quantities of raw cork from Spain, but, desirous of protecting its own cork production, Italy stipulated that the quotas it extended to the member countries would not be valid for cork originating in third countries (i.e., Spain). Again, France, which had a clearing agreement with certain eastern European countries, wanted to obtain on behalf of its exports to those countries the full advantage of the purchases made from them; hence, France excluded certain products originating in these countries from the privilege of Community treatment when transhipped through other member countries.

All in all action under Article 115 to exclude from customs-union treatment products shipped from third countries was taken by France for nearly 30 categories of goods including a number of animal and vegetable products, pulp and paper goods, and shoes; by Germany for fowl, string and cord, sewing machines and toys; and by Italy for 40 groups of goods

---

[81] *Journal Officiel,* 4th Year, No. 42, June 24, 1961, pp. 821–823.

including various chemicals, tiles, glass, metal, lenses, cameras, and machinery.[82]

The Commission complained that the member states followed the emergency procedure of invoking Article 115 and then notifying the Commission, whereas, since the situations which motivated their action had been long familiar, they should have, according to the terms of the Treaty, obtained prior authorization from the Commission.[83] Nevertheless, the Commission recognized the reasons given for the cases mentioned above as valid.

Article 115 was invoked in a different context in connection with a shortage of cattle hides which led several member countries to embargo exports early in 1959. The Commission pointed out that this was a violation of the Treaty's prohibition of export restrictions between member states (Article 34); furthermore, this derogation was not covered by the escape provisions of Article 115 since none of the countries involved had sought the sanction of the Commission or even notified it as required by the Treaty. The Commission, however, recognized that diversions of traffic endangered the execution of the commercial policy measures called for by the Treaty and that the provisions of Article 115 were relevant. It therefore requested the member states to suspend the re-exportation of certain cattle hides to nonmembers of the OEEC and re-exportation of certain others, if they had been imported from Belgium, France, or Luxemburg, to all non-Community countries. The member states accepted this solution.[84]

However, the Commission was concerned about the extent

---

[82] Not all varieties of the goods mentioned were included. The list of products for which the three countries had invoked Article 115 by July 25, 1960, was published in the *Journal Officiel*, 3d Year, No. 76, November 30, 1960, pp. 1463–1465.

[83] *Bulletin*, August–September, 1960, p. 35.

[84] *Bulletin*, October, 1959, pp. 30–32.

of escape actions under Article 115, and urged the member countries to cooperate with it in working out solutions that would be less harmful to the functioning of the Common Market.[85] Although not specified publicly, these solutions would seem to turn upon the development of a common commercial policy, which would then make possible such measures as the levying of a special tax upon goods originating in low-wage countries and the placing of the six countries' remaining quantitative restrictions on a common basis. There appear to have been no cases in which the Commission formally used its powers to force a member country to revoke emergency action under Article 115, but there seem to have been some instances in which a country withdrew its intention to take recourse to the article after discussion with the Commission.

Indirect protection

Apart from these formal derogations, some member states took action which in the opinion of the Commission tended to offset the effects of the reductions in tariffs. One group of measures related to the substitution of internal taxes for customs duties of a fiscal nature. While the Treaty obliged the member states to eliminate such customs duties in intra-Community trade, it left them with the prerogative of substituting internal taxes for them (Article 17, 3) subject to the proviso that the internal charges did not provide indirect protection (Article 95). Only France had no customs duties of a fiscal nature; the other countries had such duties, generally for perhaps a dozen products including such items as tobacco, spices, tea, and coffee.[86] When, at the beginning of 1959, the member states began to replace these duties with internal taxes,

---

[85] *Third Report,* p. 236.
[86] *Second Report,* p. 66.

the nature of some of the measures taken, on the best interpretation, inadvertently deprived consumers of some of the
anticipated benefits of the intra-Community reduction in
tariffs, and, on a less generous interpretation, was calculated
to afford indirect protection to other products. The most
widely noted case involved an internal tax levied on wine by
the Benelux countries. France and Italy charged that the tax
provided indirect protection for beer, but the Benelux countries claimed that their internal taxes on wines were not higher
than those on beer. Apart from the technical difficulties of
establishing the relative burdens of taxation, there was the
very troublesome problem of defining the term "indirect
protection." The Commission finally decided, with obvious
reserve, that "there was not sufficient evidence of a violation"
of the Treaty.[87]

The other danger of indirect protection arose from the
treatment of indirect taxes on commodities traded between
the member states. Following a precedent established (not
without some controversy) in the ECSC, the Treaty provides
in effect that goods will bear the burden of indirect taxes of
the country of destination. Thus, each member country may
impose internal charges on goods from other members up to
the amount levied on like domestic products (Article 95, 1),
and each country may refund internal charges on products
exported to the other members (Article 96). In other words,
each member nation is free to establish compensatory taxes on
imports and drawbacks for exports within the ceilings determined by its internal taxes. At the opening of the Common
Market, Belgium, the Netherlands, Germany, and Italy levied
compensatory taxes on imports and offered drawbacks for
exports that were for many products less than the maxima
permitted under these rules.

---

[87] *Third Report,* p. 127. Cf. also p. 82.

Several of the countries took advantage of the leeway thus afforded them to increase these taxes and drawbacks. The Netherlands imposed such levies on a substantial number of items to which they had not formally applied, and Belgium changed the rates of a number of sensitive products (particularly textiles). However, these changes were not very controversial, and they were in any case relatively minor compared to the increases promulgated by Italy in the summer of 1960 roughly doubling compensatory taxes and drawbacks on about 1,000 tariff positions. A "standstill" agreement had been concluded by the governments in the Council in June which provided that these taxes would be changed only for technical fiscal reasons and not for purposes of economic, monetary, or commercial policy. Advance notice of proposed changes was also to be provided, but Italy was exempted from this provision on the ground that her revisions were already in process. The other countries felt that the newly established rates tended to exceed the Italian taxes on comparable domestic products by 20 per cent or more, thus affording protection against imports and subsidies to exports in trade with member countries. The increases in the automobile duties[88] were particularly resented. The Italians denied that they had exceeded the limits permitted by the Treaty. Even after the Italian position had proved to be intractable, the Commission hesitated to take the issue to the Court because a decision could be expected only after a long delay, perhaps two years, owing to the burdensome nature of the case. Not only were there many

---

[88] The drawback for automobiles was increased from 5 to 8 per cent. The other countries complained also about the fact that the Italian circulation tax was payable immediately by purchasers of foreign automobiles, whereas purchases of domestic vehicles were exempted for six months. This discrimination was ended by the extension of the exemption to all purchasers early in 1961 after the Commission had informed the Italian Government that it regarded the practice as a violation of the Treaty provision forbidding state aids (Article 93, 2).

products at issue, but the Italian method of calculating the taxes was very complicated.[89] A compromise was finally worked out by which rates in excess of 5 per cent were scaled down and no rate was permitted to exceed 6.5 per cent.[90] Although the Commission felt that Italy had gone too far in this matter, it recognized that the Treaty allowed considerable leeway to the member states. In its view, a merely literal application of the Treaty would not guarantee that this freedom would not be used for protectionist purposes; this could be avoided only by means of close cooperation with the member states.[91]

Not, perhaps, in the category of indirect protection, but convenient to mention here was the action of the Commission under its Treaty authority (Article 17, 4) to permit a member country to retain duties of a fiscal nature for as long as six years after the effective date of the Treaty. The Commission authorized Germany to maintain such duties on certain petroleum products for the entire six-year period.[92]

Subsidies

The major cases in which subsidies were permitted for nonagricultural activities concerned paper pulp in France and naval construction in Italy. France had accepted the List G settlement for paper pulp (which involved a duty of 6 per cent, tariff quotas according to internal needs, and free Com-

---

[89] The calculation of the indirect tax burden accumulated by a finished product at the various stages of its production would be tedious enough. However, the matter was further complicated by the fact that Italy took advantage of a clause in Article 97 which permits the member states to establish average rates for products or groups of products.

[90] *Bulletin*, July–August, 1961, pp. 67–68.

[91] *Journal Officiel*, 3d Year, No. 32, May 11, 1960, p. 771; and *Third Report*, pp. 81–82.

[92] *Second Report*, p. 65.

munity circulation of the processed products) on the condition
that its paper-pulp subsidy be accepted. France levied a 1 per
cent tax on paper and cardboard, and the proceeds were used
partly for research and reforestation and partly to subsidize
paper-pulp producers. France considered that this subsidy
should be recognized as falling within one of the categories
specifically authorized by the Treaty—viz., aids intended to
facilitate the development of an economic activity (Article 92,
3, c). When the Commission expressed doubt that the subsidy
was compatible with the Treaty, the French Government
asked Council to grant a derogation, citing the agreement
made in connection with the List G settlement.[93] In December,
1960, the Council declared that the subsidy could be considered as compatible with the Treaty, and authorized its
continuation until 1966.[94] France was, however, to consult the
Commission each year concerning its distribution. The Council acted under Article 93, 2, which permits a unanimous
Council to declare a state aid compatible with the Treaty in
exceptional circumstances regardless of the rules other governing such aids.

The clause relating to the development of an economic
activity was cited by the Commission when it subsequently
gave approval to Italian subsidies for naval construction.[95] The
Italian aids were to support a reorganization that would
reduce the capacity and work force of the Italian yards to a
level at which they might be able to meet third-country
competition rather than a "development" of an economic
activity in the sense in which it is usually understood. However, the Italian yards were suffering from an excess of
manpower which was sharpened by unfavorable cyclical

[93] *Fourth Report,* Paragraph 55.
[94] *Journal Officiel,* 3d Year, No. 84, December 31, 1960.
[95] *Journal Officiel,* 4th Year, No. 25, April 8, 1961, pp. 582–583.

conditions, and some of their main competitors were outside of the Community. The subsidies were thus approved for the period for which the Italian Government proposed them (until 1964) on condition that the competitive position of shipyards in member states not be adversely affected and that a reorganization plan be submitted to the Commission within six months.

The Commission had not at the time of writing completed the tasks of bringing the rather large and complex field of state aids under its review and of working out its policies for applying the rules of the Treaty. However, there were already some cases in which subsidies were modified after an investigation by the Commission. France, for example, extended the privilege of accelerated depreciation for certain types of French-made capital goods to similar products made elsewhere in the Community,[96] and Germany put an end to a perequation scheme for natural and synthetic rubber that tended to favor the production of synthetic rubber.[97]

Readaptation

If, as has been suggested, the European Social Fund and the European Investment Bank are not designed to enable the institutions of the Community to play a vigorous role in bringing about the readaptation of workers and firms, their deficiencies in this respect were not keenly felt in the opening years of the Common Market. This may have been due to the rapid rate of economic expansion in the Community, to the shortness of the period and the as yet partial character of the dismantlement of trade barriers, or, as the Commission suggested, to the fact that adjustments to the Common Market seemed to involve specialization by product within industries rather than by whole industries.

[96] *Third Report*, p. 117.
[97] *Fourth Report*, Paragraph 54.

The Social Fund got off to a slow start, its governing regulations not being adopted until nearly two and a half years after the effective date of the Treaty. Its annual budget during the first few years was $10 million per annum, but since the Treaty leaves the Fund no discretion but to grant reimbursements of 50 per cent of the cost of national projects that meet the specified conditions, the budget would have to be revised upwards should the demands require it. In fact the estimates of the forthcoming requests appear to have been good ones; total requests for reimbursements for the first two years amounted to $22 million, of which two-thirds was for occupational retraining and the balance for resettlement allowances. (Since reconversion plans must be approved in advance if the Social Fund is to be used to aid workers during reconversion, the late date of the issuance of the regulations precluded grants for this purpose during this period.) The great bulk of the projects for which reimbursement was requested were carried out entirely by the national governments on purely national lines without contact with one another or the Commission. However, the Commission played a more active role in connection with a scheme for using the surplus labor of Italy to meet shortages in Germany and the Netherlands. Plans made in 1960 and carried out mainly in 1961 provided for the training of 10,000 Italian workers, over half of them for the construction industry and the others for the electrical, mechanical, transport, and hotel industries; over 9,000 of them were intended for jobs in Germany and the others in the Netherlands.[98]

The activities of the European Investment Bank were modest in size and directed mainly toward underdeveloped regions. In the first two years of its operations the Bank made 15 loans amounting to $120 million. Over two-thirds of this total was used to participate in the financing of investments in

---

[98] *Third Report,* pp. 196–199; *Fourth Report,* Paragraph 153 and 154.

underdeveloped areas of Italy and most of the rest for similar purposes in France.[99]

Tariff quotas exceptions

With the first movement of the tariffs of the individual member states toward the common external tariff scheduled for December 31, 1960, about 150 requests for quotas at lower or nil duties were submitted for some 30 or 40 different industrial products. In the aggregate the quotas requested represented less than 2.5 per cent of Community trade with third countries. The requests were about equally divided among those based on the List G settlements, Article 25, 1, and Article 25, 2.[100] Article 25, 1, it will be recalled, covers the case in which a product on List B, C, or D is not produced within the Community in sufficient quantities to meet the needs of a member state which had traditionally depended "to a considerable extent" upon supplies from third countries. Article 25, 2 deals with List E items for which a change in sources of supply or a shortage of supplies within the Community is injurious to processing industries. Towards the middle of 1961, requests were also beginning to be made for agricultural products under Article 25, 3 in anticipation of the first approximation to the common external tariff for agricultural products scheduled for the year's end. The following discussion, however, is confined entirely to the cases involving industrial products.

A sharp difference quickly became apparent in the attitudes of the several governments towards the use of tariff quotas. Germany, in particular, sought to employ the tariff quotas as

---

[99] *Third Report,* pp. 157–158; Fourth Report, Paragraph 101.
[100] *Fourth Report,* Paragraph 16; also *Bulletin,* September–October, 1961, pp. 39–45.

a means of maintaining its existing trade relations with third countries. France and Belgium, on the other hand, strongly opposed the German position. The widespread use of tariff quotas would, in their view, make the common external tariff and the customs union itself less meaningful. Tariff quotas should be used only in exceptional cases where necessary to avoid injury to processing industries or distortions of competition. In many of the instances in which tariff quotas were sought, the industries of the member countries could adequately supply the needs of the Community, and the 1 or 2 per cent tariff rate that the low-tariff member countries would have to apply in their first approximation to the Common Market could not in any case be said to endanger any Community processing industries. If tariff quotas were widely granted on the occasion of this early step towards preferential arrangements within the Community, the way would be paved for even broader exceptions as the margins of preference increased. In cases where there was, indeed, a real need for more favorable duties on third-country goods, it would be better to reduce the common external tariff for all member countries rather than to provide exceptions in favor of one or two countries that the others would not share.

On the other side, it was pointed out that the danger of the widespread use of quotas was not very great, since they were authorized only for the commodities on Lists B, C, D, E, and F, for agriculture products in Annex II, and for a limited number of products in the protocols of the List G settlement. However, the inherent logic of the Common Market arrangement seems to have favored the French and Belgian position. Nevertheless, the political settlement did not turn entirely on logic, and a good part of the German demands were satisfied, although the size of some of the quotas was less than requested. Tariff quotas were granted also to the Netherlands and Italy, which had occupied an intermediate position in the dispute, and a few to Belgium and France.

Only one of the quotas contemplated in the List G settlements—that for unwrought aluminium—was rejected,[101] but the real controversy developed in connection with tropical woods. France, acting on behalf of certain African countries and territories associated with her, asked the other member countries to waive their quota rights on tropical woods. The relevant protocol of the Accord of Rome had been designed chiefly for Germany and Italy, although the right to ask for quotas was left open to all the member states. The common tariff for the most important types of tropical woods was 5 per cent, and the duties which the low-tariff countries would have had to levy in their first approximation to the common rate would have been less than 2 per cent. In these circumstances, it might have been difficult to establish that the requirement of injury to transforming industries written into the tropical woods protocol in the Accord of Rome was really met. Nevertheless, the tariff quotas seem to have been regarded as due as of right, and when Germany refused to withdraw its request, despite the expressed willingness of Italy and Benelux to forego the quotas if Germany did, the Commission granted the tariff quotas. Nearly half of German consumption was covered by imports from non-Community sources, and Germany was probably more concerned with the maintenance of its customary channels of trade than with damage to its processing industries.[102] Later in the year (i. e., in July, 1961), a com-

---

[101] The protocol on unwrought aluminium called for a tariff quota at a 5 per cent duty (the common external tariff is 10 per cent). The Benelux countries requested a tariff quota at a lower duty since their first approximation to the common external tariff did not raise their duty up to the 5 per cent level. Although the Commission rejected their request for a tariff quota, it authorized Benelux to postpone the increase in its aluminium tariff that was called for by the first movement towards the common external tariff. (*Bulletin,* September–October, 1961, p. 43.)

[102] France and Germany were cast in somewhat similar roles in connection with the tariff quota on bananas in favor of Germany that was established in a protocol to the Treaty. The somewhat tortuous rules

promise was arranged by which the tariff quotas were waived in exchange for the suspension of the common external tariff for tropical woods of the Obéché variety.[103]

The main battle over tariff quotas, however, centered around those that were requested by member states for products on Lists B, C, or D under the terms of Article 25, 1 or for products of List E under the terms of Article 25, 2.

The Commission declared that the inadequacy of Community output, one of the conditions for the granting of tariff quotas under Article 25, 1, could be inferred, in the absence of statistics on production for some products, from trade figures and that the extent of dependence upon third-country supplies should be judged in relation to the total consumption of the product in the member state seeking the tariff quota.[104] On this basis, it recommended to the Council the granting of about half of the requests, involving more than a score of tariff quotas for over a dozen products.[105] The great majority of these were approved by the Council; for a few products,[106] however, a compromise was arranged (based on Article 28) by which duties were suspended for one year, thereby providing

---

governing this quota were intended to shift some German purchases from Latin American suppliers to African sources associated with the Community in the event of static German imports. Superimposed upon this basic division was an arrangement for the division between the two sources of supply of any future growth in the size of German imports that might occur. Of course, if the Africans could not supply the quantities demanded by the Germans, the member states agreed, the German tariff quota would be increased. At the same time, the Germans indicated their readiness to support private interests in the encouragement of imports from Africa. When the first quotas had to be established for the year 1961 on the occasion of the first approximation to the common external tariff (20 per cent for bananas), the French pressed the Germans to arrange for more imports from Africa. The Germans declared themselves willing to encourage such imports but unable to impose African bananas on consumers contrary to their preferences.

[103] *Bulletin,* September–October, 1961, p. 99.

[104] *Bulletin,* January, 1961, p. 49.

[105] Important among these products were newsprint, crude tall oil, turpentine, certain rosins, and iron and steel powders.

[106] Including sponge steel, refined tall oil, certain rosins, and resin soap.

all the member countries with equal access to duty-free external supplies rather than limiting this advantage to the countries that had sought tariff quotas.

The arrangement for the reduction of the external tariff was applied on a wider scale still in connection with the applications for tariff quotas for List E items. Since these cases all involved injury to a Community processing industry, such injury being a necessary condition for a tariff quota for a List E product (Article 25, 2), the French and the Belgians were more disposed to favor tariff reduction. About a score of the more than 50 requests were handled in this way. The Commission granted tariff quotas for about 10 cases, a number of them involving chemicals used in the manufacture of synthetic rubber.

The policy of the Commission appears to have been to limit the use of tariff quotas. It felt that tariff quotas prevented the complete realization of the customs union, and considered that the best solution to the difficulties that caused requests for tariff quotas was the adaptation of the common external tariff to the "real economic necessities" of the Community,[107] presumably through a lowering of the duties. The Commission was thus inclined to give full weight to the Treaty stipulation that the size of the tariff quotas should not exceed the limits beyond which the interests of other countries might be adversely affected. This is evident from the consultations that were held prior to the decisions, and from the terms on which the quotas were granted.

The other member countries were informed about each request for a tariff quota based on a claim that Community supplies were inadequate, and they were invited to produce evidence that there was sufficient production within the Community. In a few cases where the availability of supplies was disputed, the Commission invited the producing and utilizing

---

[107] *Fourth Report,* Paragraph 16.

firms to establish contact in order to determine whether the products in question could be supplied within the Community in the required quantities at world prices.

The first tariff quotas that were granted, including most of those under the List G arrangements and some of those under Article 25, 1, were generally based on the average volume of imports over the three prior years. Subsequently, however, efforts were made to assess the actual needs of the industries concerned and to establish the size of the quotas accordingly. The Commission established several quotas at lower levels than the countries had requested, and in a number of cases including one relating to German imports of newsprint, they were later revised upwards. Most of the tariff quotas were granted for an annual period, but a few were originally limited to six months with the intention of encouraging the processing industries to adapt themselves to new sources of supply which were expected to develop within the Community.

All in all, 69 tariff quotas were granted for industrial products in 1961, 32 of them in connection with List G, 26 under Article 25, 1, and 11 under Article 25, 2.[108] About 30 other requests were met through suspensions in the common external tariff. Over a score of requests were withdrawn after discussion, and more than a dozen were rejected. Among the reasons for the reasons for the rejections were adequacy of Community supplies (applications from the Netherlands and Germany), the dependence of all member countries on third-country supplies and hence the lack of any special handicap for the applying country (applications from Belgium and Luxemburg), and the fact that the tariff quotas could be used only to offset the injury following from an increase in tariffs in order to approximate the common external tariff (application from France).

---

[108] *Bulletin,* September–October, 1961, p. 43.

Acceleration and the external tariff

Another problem in connection with the approach to the common external tariff stemmed from the decision of the Council in May, 1960, to speed the implementation of the Treaty and to extend some of the benefits of duty reductions to third countries.[109] This decision provided that the first approximation to the common tariff would be made on the basis of the common tariff rates reduced by 20 per cent, although the resultant external duties could not go below the level listed in the common tariff. An exception was provided, however, for List G; upon the request of a member state, the Commission could decide that the approximation to the common external tariff by all the member countries would be on the basis of the duties in the Accord of Rome rather than those duties less 20 per cent. France sought to invoke this safeguard clause for a dozen products including cocoa products, various metals, paper pulp, tropical woods, salts, and machine tools, and Italy for a number of chemical and metal products. The Commission granted these requests for some products and denied them for others on the basis of the "legal, political, and economic effects" which would result.[110] In a number of the cases in which the requests were denied, the Community's processing industries had already had their interests safeguarded through the establishment of tariff quotas; in others, Community industries were heavily dependent upon outside supplies.

The decision to accelerate the approach to the common external tariff required exceptions for Germany and Benelux. These countries had signed agreements with Switzerland and also, as regards cork, with Spain and Portugal, binding duties to a date beyond the deadline for the upward movement of their tariffs under the acceleration decision. The Commission

---

[109] *Journal Officiel*, 3d Year, No. 58, September 12, 1960.
[110] *Bulletin*, January, 1961, pp. 49–50.

granted the necessary postponements under the terms of Article 26, which provides for such delays when any member state encounters "special difficulties" in adjusting its duties towards the common tariff. Article 26 was invoked also to permit the Benelux countries to levy a duty of 1.5 per cent on crude aluminium rather than the higher duty that they would have been obliged to apply during 1961 in moving towards the common external rate of 10 per cent.[111] Other requests for exceptions under Article 26, including one from Germany relating to knotted carpets, were denied.

Changes in the external tariff

After the settlement of the duties for certain raw materials on List G, the Commission and the Council used their powers under Article 21, 2 to adjust previously established rates for related semiprocessed products. Duties on molasses, vinegar, and semiprocessed aluminium and magnesium were raised to make certain that the Community's processing industries would not be placed at a disadvantage in the Common Market.[112]

At the same time (July, 1960), the Council, on the basis of Article 28 permitting autonomous changes in the external tariff, adjusted about a score of duties on fruits and vegetables and more than a dozen rates for glassware and ceramics.[113] Minimum specific duties were added to the *ad valorem* rates that had been originally established, and, for fruits and vegetables, the seasonal periods for which lower and higher duties applied were altered slightly.

---

[111] *Journal Officiel,* 4th Year, No. 42, June 24, 1961, pp. 826–828. This decision was, of course, more advantageous to the Benelux countries than the List G settlement which provided only for tariff quotas at a 5 per cent duty.

[112] *Journal Officiel,* 3d Year, No. 80 C, December 20, 1960, pp. 1886–1891.

[113] *Ibid,* pp. 1873–1887.

The authority of Article 28 was used also, as has already been noted, to reduce the common external tariff of certain products in lieu of granting tariff quotas (see above, p. 352f). There was much discussion among the member states about the use of the provision of Article 20 which permits each country to add products to List G. Germany proposed to add various food products and industrial goods. Although France made no effort to throw additional items into List G for negotiation of external tariff rates, Italy and Benelux submitted lists that they were willing to withdraw if Germany withdrew hers. Germany was finally satisfied by various arrangements, some of which involved adding certain items to the Community's GATT negotiation list and other changes or adjustments in the external tariff through other provisions of the Treaty.[114] Thus List G 2, as it was called, never really came into being.

Treaty violations

In a number of cases member countries adopted safeguard measures[115] which, in the opinion of the Commission, represented violations of the Treaty. Perhaps the most common of these concerned instances in which a country invoked a Treaty safeguard clause without the prior notification to, or authorization from, the Commission that the Treaty required. This early tendency towards unilateral action, which as has been noted was particularly evident in the case of Italy, was perhaps inevitable in view of the delays that could be expected from a Commission in the throes of organizing itself for diverse and complex tasks. The Commission appears to have been slowly

---

[114] H. Corson, "L'établissement de la Liste G," *Revue du Marché Commun*, April, 1960, pp. 136–142.

[115] See *Journal Officiel*, 3d Year, No. 84, December 31, 1960, pp. 1957–1958 for a list of 15 violations given by the Commission in response to a written question of a member of the Assembly.

and patiently attempting to bring this problem under control.

The member countries were inclined also to place their own interpretations upon the clauses of the Treaty when sensitive interests were at stake. For the most part, the member countries were willing to cooperate with the Commission in finding ways to protect the interests involved without stretching the terms of the Treaty too far, but as the Commission came into its functions more fully the probability of legal tests before the Court increased. Early in 1961 the first two cases were brought to the Court by the Commission. Both involved Italy; one related to the suspension of pork imports (see above, p. 332) and the other to increases in protective duties on certain electrical products.[116] On the other hand, the Commission appeared to avoid direct challenges when major national interests were involved, as, for example, the French failure to conform to Treaty obligations with respect to trade in wine.

The possibility of defensive safeguards arose in connection with allegations of dumping. Allegations of dumping appear not to have been infrequent, but only about a dozen complaints seemed serious enough to warrant investigation during the first two years of the Community's existence. In a number of these cases, the practices that were the subject of the complaint appear to have been altered without formal action by the Commission. In two instances, however, the Commission addressed recommendations to enterprises that were accused of dumping, but it had not been found necessary by mid-1961 to authorize an injured member country to take measures of safeguard under the dumping provisions of the Treaty.

EVALUATION

The general strategy of the Treaty of Rome with respect to safeguard clauses may be summed up in four points : (1) ample

---

[116] *Fourth Report,* Paragraph 6. Both cases were eventually decided in favor of the Commission.

provision is made for the avoidance of injury particularly during a 12 to 15 year transition period; (2) firms are in effect placed on notice that adjustment to Community-wide competition must be made, but it may be made gradually and even with the aid of temporary and progressively diminishing protection; (3) the safeguards are administered largely by the international permanent body charged with the general administration of the affairs of the Community; and (4) ultimate power, including in many ways powers over the safeguards, remains in the hands of the member states.

The intention of the framers of the Treaty to avoid injury to any economic interests is evident in the elaborate plan for a transition to a common market, characterized not only by gradualism but also by a number of additional safeguards providing for further delays and exceptions in case of need. The safeguard clauses are more numerous and more specific for the transition period than for the aftermath, presumably reflecting the assumption that they will be less needed once the transition period is over. For the longer run, powers can probably be found in the Treaty to cope with almost any kind of disturbance affecting an industry, a region, or a member state, but the specific provisions for such situations are relatively limited.

Coupled with gradualism is certainty about the eventual establishment of the Common Market. Delays are permitted, but little hope is provided for permanent protection. Gradualism is clearly intended only to permit a relatively painless adjustment to the new situation. When the gradualism automatically provided in the Treaty has to be supplemented by further safeguards invoked by administrative action, the special measures of temporary protection must usually be accompanied by steps designed to adapt the situation to the economy of the Common Market. These remarks about the inevitability of the Common Market must be qualified, however, as regards agriculture; in this area the prospect seems to be for a managed market that may or may not require adjustment on the part of individual producing countries.

The power to grant exceptions and derogations, often to specify their character, and to control their use is left largely in the hands of the Commission, an administrative or expert body charged with the daily affairs of the Community. However, this is true mainly of the safeguards relating to the transitional period; most of these—Article 226 is a notable exception—relate to derogations from rather specific obligations. The Council, which represents the governments, figures somewhat more prominently in the administration of the safeguard clauses that relate to the permanent period, such as those concerned with balance of payments difficulties, shortages of supplies of goods on Lists B, C, and D, subsidies, readaptation, and distortions due to lack of harmonization. In addition, Council action would be required to invoke some of the more general clauses which while not specifically designed for safeguarding purposes would lend themselves to such a use. Furthermore, even in the areas in which the Commission nominally has the sole prerogative, due account must be taken of the fact that it operates in an environment in which the governments have much power. At any given moment, a whole series of matters are apt to be in the course of negotiation between the Commission and the governments, and it is the latter who through the Council have the ultimate power of decision. It seems unlikely, therefore, that the Commission will take the views of the government concerned lightly even when the Treaty confers upon the Commission the sole power over a safeguarding clause.

Where, then, does the real power lie with respect to derogations from the Treaty? To what extent have the six governments transferred to an international bureaucracy the power to cope with difficult situations that may result from the obligations of the Treaty of Rome.

The greater role of the governments in the Common Market as compared to the earlier Community for coal and steel seems in large part an inevitable consequence of the basic philosophy of eliminating all sources of "distortion" of competition. Such an effort was bound to reach far and deep into the legal, social, and economic structures of the member countries. The governments either had to agree to provide continuing supervision of the policies of the Common Market themselves or to surrender broad areas of sovereignty in the economic sphere.

Since the governments in effect remain in the saddle, the diminution in sovereignty is, at least at the outset, not far beyond that entailed in a close concert of nations pursuing agreed-upon objectives and sufficiently committed so that it is difficult to turn back. It seems obvious that the EEC goes farther in limiting the freedom of action of its member states than did the OEEC at its most influential stage, when it was allocating Marshall Plan aid. But the difference, while substantial and important, may not be as great as might be inferred from a comparison of the charters of the two organizations, and the two situations are not without some parallels. The EEC is of course more ambitious in its scope and objectives, but, given the powers retained by the member states, it has to rely like the OEEC upon the commitment of policy of the governments and upon the pressures of a community of nations to bring a recalcitrant member into line. However, it has some further sources of strength. For one thing, the members may find it more difficult to remain a minority of one in a club of six than in a club of 16 or 17, especially since they will have more intimate knowledge of their mutual affairs. More important, and in the eyes of the European integrationists most important of all, as time goes

on the legal possibility of four or five of the members out-
voting the others in the Council applies to a wider number
of matters,[117] and the practice of majority voting may develop;
there are some signs that the tendency, manifested in the
experience of the ECSC to seek unanimity on all important
matters regardless of the legal voting requirements, may
wither.

Sovereignty is thus curtailed in the EEC, but it is not as a
result of turning power over to an international or supranational body of administrators as Schuman seemed to be
suggesting in his first proposal for a coal and steel community.
Sovereignty has been curtailed as a result, first, of accepting
a broad commitment to follow common policies moving
towards economic and eventually political integration. Secondly, sovereignty has been restricted by institutional arrangements that expose each member to more readily applied pressures from the others and subsequently to the possibility of
having a decision imposed by some combination of the other
member countries. Both initially and subsequently, the process
of decision-making is influenced by a body of international
administrators who may be expected to represent the interests
of the Community as a whole. In addition, any success that
the scheme enjoys may be expected to create new vested
interests which will reenforce the position of the international
administrators by offsetting some of the purely national pressures affecting the decisions of the governments; indeed, the
lively business acceptance of the Common Market promises to
bring about just this development.

In the event, the use of the safeguard clauses during the first

---

[117] A number of provisions of the Treaty call for Council decision by
unanimity in some initial period (e.g., the first or second stage of the
transition period) and for decision by qualified majority voting subsequently. See, for example, Article 87, which relates to the regulations
or directives that the Council is to issue with regard to monopolistic
practices.

two and a half years of the Common Market were confined largely to agricultural products, goods processed from agricultural products, commodities that had given special difficulty in the determination of the common external tariff (i. e., those on Lists B to G), and products which involved diversions of traffic owing to wide initial differences in tariff and quota treatment by the several member countries in their relations with third countries.

It will be seen from this list that most of the safeguards that were invoked were necessitated by divergencies among the governments in their interventions in agriculture and in international trade. This could be interpreted as supporting evidence for the French thesis of the necessity of harmonization for the establishment of a common market; on the other hand, opponents of the thesis might point to the absence of difficulties arising from lack of harmonization of labor and social policies, which after all, had been the crux of the French argument.

The moderate extent to which safeguard clauses were invoked may be explained by a number of factors. The short span of the period and the as yet partial character of trade-barrier dismantlement within the Community meant that the full impact of the free-trade provisions of the Treaty had not yet been felt. The impact that the establishment of the Common Market might have had upon competitive conditions during this short initial period was in any case cushioned by a high rate of business expansion and by widespread business agreements. Another element easing the adjustment was the nature of the pattern of specialization that appeared to be emerging; this involved the development of product specialization within major industrial sectors rather than the abandonment of whole sectors in some member countries and their expansion in others.[118] If, as the Commision seems to think, this will prove to be the course that adjustments to the Com-

---

[118]*Fourth Report,* Paragraph 71.

mon Market will follow, the need for safeguard clauses may never be great. However, the real test will come only when free trade within the Common Market has been fully established and the rate of expansion has slackened or expansion replaced by contraction.

In this initial period, there were a certain number of cases in which the member states were not to be denied protective measures on behalf of important economic interests. While the Commission was organizing itself or formulating its attitude on a particular issue, the member states were not loath to take matters into their own hands. Usually the Commission sought to negotiate the matter with the member state involved, trying to find rules or formulas consistent with the Treaty under which the desired exception would fit. This course, if it bowed to the inevitable, at least legalized the position, and squeezing the case under a rule may have avoided the creation of broader precedents for future exceptions. In some of the cases which could not be resolved in this fashion, the Commission avoided a direct challenge; only near the end of the period did it finally begin to take such cases to the Court. These instances of urgent pressures for protection within the Community—or pressures which the governments did not wish to resist—were most notable in the case of Italy, but they also appeared in Germany and France, and to a lesser degree in Belgium. Fortunately for the Community, however, they were restricted to a rather small hard core of sensitive economic areas. Infractions of the Treaty, while not unknown, could not be described as a major problem of the Community.

For the future the Commission seems to feel that a progressively declining compensatory tax, with initial rates that would offset the price differences among the member countries, offers the best instrument for coping with the problems posed by agricultural products and commodities derived from them. Problems of high-cost producers, especially in Germany, remain to be worked out. The danger is not only or not so much failure to agree among the Six, but agreement at the expense of third-country suppliers. Nevertheless, internally the Community may succeed in the future as it has in its brief past, whether due to design or good luck, in achieving gradual adjustment without extensive injury.

PART III

Lessons of Safeguard Experience

Chapter 6

The Contents of Safeguard Clauses

IT IS THE PURPOSE of this chapter to set out in a systematic way the main choices that are faced in the framing and administration of safeguard clauses. The criteria for the invocation of the clauses, the locus of control over their use, and the nature of the remedies will be examined.

In a broad way the basic principles of choice underlying each of these aspects of the subject is in microcosm the same that is confronted in the development of many institutions—the choice between customary and written law. In relation to safeguard clauses, customary law is represented by the technique of including only generally worded provisions and leaving it to the development of practice to work out rules surrounding their use. If the written-law approach is followed, efforts will be made to anticipate every problem and to provide in advance the rules for the meeting of each. Since the Anglo-Saxon tradition of customary law and the Latin tradition of written law are both represented in the membership of the four organizations analyzed in this study, admixtures of both are found in all of them.[1] The ECSC goes the farthest in the direction of prescription for every conceivable situation, and perhaps the OEEC Code relied most heavily upon the development of practice. The EEC fell short of the degree of prescription included in the ECSC and left many solutions to the institutions of the Community, mainly because there were too many problems to be solved and too many uncertainties

---

[1] Cf. Baron Snoy et d'Oppuers, *Tribune de l'Oesterreichische Gesellschaft für Aussenpolitik und Internationale Beziehungen,* January 13, 1961.

surrounding them. The other organizations that we have studied or mentioned, including GATT, EFTA, and Benelux, lean more to the side of customary law.

In an extreme version of a treaty or agreement based on a reliance upon customary law, a single general safeguard clause might suffice. However, such an arrangement would place great discretion in the hands of those to whom controls over the use of the safeguards is given. Thus, a safeguard clause designed specifically to cover a certain type of situation, such as balance-of-payments difficulties or injury to a particular industry, offers a better guarantee that it will be available in case of need than if the action has to be sought under a general clause. In the latter event the authorities who have the power of decision must first determine whether as a general principle safeguards should be given in such circumstances, and secondly whether the particular case at hand legitimately falls under the general principle which they deem it appropriate to establish. Thus if there are clearly some types of situations for which the parties to a treaty or agreement know in advance that they wish to provide safeguards, they would be well advised to include specific clauses for these purposes. On the other hand, such inclusions, even if there are many of them, do not obviate the need for a general-purpose clause to leave open the possibility of safeguard action if new and unforeseen circumstances develop.

CRITERIA FOR INVOCATION

Turning more specifically to the first broad area of choice in the framing and administration of safeguard clauses, the criteria for their invocation may be considered in terms of the definition of the difficulties, their scope, their severity, and their cause.

The existence of the difficulties

The criteria put forward to determine whether or not the difficulties alluded to actually exist in a specific situation must vary with the purpose of the safeguard clause. Balance-of-payments safeguard clauses typically cite the state of the reserves of the country concerned; this is the case with GATT (Article 12) and the OEEC Code (Article 3, c), although the EEC Treaty refers to either "over-all disequilibrium of the balance of payments or of the kinds of currency at its disposal" (Article 108, 1).

Clauses designed to safeguard particular economic sectors usually leave undefined the "difficulties" or "disturbances" or 'injury" with which they deal. However, some illustrations may be found of efforts to spell out criteria, although they tend to fall outside of the charters of our four organizations. The EEC Commission, for example, had occasion to state its understanding of the "harmful consequences" for Community processing industries which are to be avoided through the granting of tariff quotas for certain products;[2] these were, the Commission declared, "unfavorable changes" as evidenced by a weakening of the competitive position of Community processors at home or abroad, and prices, costs, and profits were all to be taken into account. Again, under the American law, the Tariff Commission is to administer the escape clause in trade agreements taking into consideration, without excluding other factors, "a downward trend of production, employment, prices, sales, an increase in imports, either actual or relative to domestic production, a higher or growing inventory, or a decline in the proportion of the domestic market supplied by domestic producers."[3] However, no indication is given of

---

[2] See above, *Chapter* V.

[3] Trade Agreements Extension Act of 1951, as Amended, Section 7 (b), U.S. House of Representatives Ways and Means Committee, *Report on U.S. Customs, Tariff and Trade Agreement Laws and Their Administration,* Washington, 1957, p. 175.

the relative importance to be assigned to the different factors on this partial list.

Little if any official recognition seems to have been given to the distinction between "displacement" on the one hand, and "difficulty" or "injury" on the other hand. The tendency in formal actions dealing with safeguard questions has been to treat the decline of an economic activity as constituting "injury" whether or not the labor and capital employed in the activity may readily find other employments. American policy in the late 1950's, under the requirement of the "segmentation" amendment, appeared to endorse the view that displacement in and of itself constitutes injury. On the other hand, government policy in a number of European countries, particularly in connection with the OEEC Code but perhaps also in relation to GATT and later to the EEC, has been to press such readily-made shifts upon industry rather than to seek to continue or to increase protection.

General-purpose clauses also are, by necessity, silent with respect to criteria for determining the existence of the difficulties except to the extent that it is almost invariably specified that they must be grave.

The scope of the difficulties

Some clauses, like balance-of-payments safeguards, obviously must be related to the whole economy, while others, such as those concerned with agriculture, serve clearly defined sectors. As has already been observed, almost every important trade treaty or agreement is apt to have balance-of-payments safeguards, and illustrations of the specific sector clauses are not hard to find; the ECSC and EEC treaties, for example, specified advance exceptions for particular industries and even for particular products in one or more clauses especially designed for each of the participating countries.

Where derogations are provided for situations that may develop in the future, the scope of the economic sector to which the safeguard applies may prove to be a matter of some importance; either it may be left open for any segment of the economy, however small, to seek relief, or an attempt may be made to confine the use of the safeguard clause to industries or sectors that have an important impact upon the economy as a whole. The OEEC Code's reference to "serious economic disturbance in the member country concerned" (Article 3, b) and the ECSC Treaty's reference to "fundamental and persistent disturbances in the economy of the said state" (Article 37) place their clauses in the latter category. On the other hand, the GATT clause (Article 19) is phrased in terms of "particular products" and the "domestic producers" thereof. The extension of safeguards to fine industrial subclassifications can easily frustrate the objectives of trade treaties and agreements by making unnecessary even those adjustments of industrial structure which would be possible without great sacrifice or difficulty. In 1955, the "segmentation" amendment to the American Trade Agreements Act took a step in this direction by requiring injury to be judged in terms of those portions of multiproduct firms that are devoted to the production of the commodity affected by import competition. Thus (to take an example from an actual escape-clause case before the change in the law), under the segmentation rule garlic producers would have had to be considered as injured when foreign garlic made inroads upon the domestic market, even though the farms growing garlic devoted only a small and easily transferable part of their resources to its production. Furthermore, producers would presumably be able to claim injury even after they had already made a satisfactory adjustment to the increase in imports. For example (to draw upon another old case), when American producers of preserved fruits lost trade in glacé cherries to imported cherries, they were presumably injured under the segmentation rule, even though their activities in connection with other fruits were sufficient to maintain their over-all employment, production, and profits.[4]

A narrow definition of the scope of the economic sector eligible for safeguard action also makes it more difficult to establish its competitive relationship with imports of a given variety. Differences in quality and design or in other characteristics often make it extremely hard to determine whether a given product turned out domestically is "like or directly competitive" with imports of given foreign goods.[5] The members of the United States Tariff Commission, for example, could not agree whether imports of tuna canned in brine and bonito canned in oil or brine were competitive with the domestic output of tuna canned in oil.

The severity of the difficulties

Criteria of severity are almost always limited to quantitative terms, the most common practice being to specify that the difficulties be "serious." This is the term used, for example, in the EEC Treaty in connection with both balance-of-payments (Article 108) and particular sector (Article 226) safeguards. The same word is employed in the GATT escape clause for particular industries (Article 19)[6] and in the ECSC provision

---

[4] For a discussion of these and other cases, some of which are mentioned below, see my paper in the June, 1954, *American Economic Review* on the escape clause cited above, and Committee on Ways and Means, *op. cit.*, pp. 68–74.

[5] Incidentally, the distinction between "like products" and "directly competitive or substitutable products" is sometimes of great significance in safeguard cases; see, for example, the references in Chapter II to the German–Norwegian dispute about the German tariffs on sprats, herrings, and sardines within GATT, and to the Australian–Chilean dispute about the treatment of different types of fertilizer.

[6] A GATT working party considering the American invocation of this clause in connection with women's fur felt hats and hat bodies concluded that increased imports had caused "some adverse effects" but it was not convinced that the degree of adverse effects amounted to "serious injury." See above, Chapter II.

dealing with measures to be taken to cope with shortages of supplies (Article 59). "Fundamental," "persistent," "manifest crisis" are other qualitative terms used.

An illustration of a safeguard which was expressed in direct quantitative terms is the provision of the Transitional Convention of the ECSC Treaty (Section 26) which stipulates that Belgian coal production will not have to bear an annual reduction of more than 3 per cent. (The reduction would be proportionately larger in the event of a decline in Community coal production as a whole.) It is interesting to note that this example, which cannot be matched by any taken from GATT or the OEEC Code and even perhaps from the EEC, comes from the structure which is, among the four, the most representative of the written-law approach.

A more striking exception to the tendency to avoid the quantification of criteria for the invocation of safeguard clauses may be found in a Benelux protocol concerning the coordination of economic and social policy, adopted under circumstances described below.[1] The protocol stated that, while the adaptation of the three economies to economic union would eventually involve the expansion of certain economic activities in some regions and their contraction in others, measures would be taken to alleviate a particularly serious and dangerous situation in which competition from one of the partners imperiled the existence of a branch of industry in another of the member countries. Safeguards could be invoked, however, only if either of two sets of statistical criteria was satisfied, one based on production and the other on imports. The first required a decline in production in the sector involved of at least 15 per cent during the course of a semester (i. e., a six-month period) compared to the average output of the corresponding semester of the two preceding years; furthermore, at least three-fourths of the diminution must be attributable to

---

[1] See below, Chapter VII.

increased imports from a partner country. The second criterion provided for relief if imports from a partner country in the sector concerned increased during a semester by 60 per cent or more above the average of the corresponding semesters of the two previous years, or, on the same semester comparison, if there was an increase in imports in an amount equal to 15 per cent of domestic production in the sector concerned. If the import rather than the production criterion was used, four additional conditions had to be met : (1) production could not have increased in the importing country; (2) no more than 20 per cent of the increase in imports could have been from third countries; (3) the rise in imports from the partner country could not have been in substitution of imports from third countries; and (4) imports from the partner country must have constituted at least 7 per cent of the consumption of the importing country.

However, the path was left open for the invocation of the safeguards by mutual consent, even if the statistical conditions were not met; on the other hand, if the application of the safeguards proved unfair to the exporting country they could be modified or withdrawn.[8] The statistical criteria, particularly the ones relating to imports, appear to have been used in the safeguard arrangements of 1952–54 described below[9] by which price agreements and export quotas were used to limit Dutch exports to Belgium.

The use of these statistical criteria must be considered against the Benelux background. Unable in the midst of war to foresee the future, and, preferring in any case to rely upon customary law, the 1944 treaty then governing Benelux was a brief document of nine articles taking one and a half pages; it adopted the principle of a customs union and left it to the

---

[8] *Protocole concernant la coordination des politiques économiques et sociales,* The Hague, July 24, 1963.
[9] See Chapter VII.

governments to work out the means.[10] As a result, as the problems and crises emerged, they were met by a series of protocols, among which was the one referred to in the present context. Thus statistical criteria were devised for a specific situation in which the problem was clearly understood, the methods for its temporary solution agreed upon, and criteria needed to separate the serious cases from the others. It is interesting to note that the subsequent Treaty establishing the Benelux Economic Union, longer than the 1944 document but still brief compared to either of the common-market treaties, did not include clauses of a statistical character but placed its reliance on more general safeguard provisions.

The cause of the difficulties

General-purpose safeguard clauses usually may be invoked regardless of the cause of the difficulties, and the same is generally true of some kinds of special-purpose provisions such as those relating to balance-of-payments difficulties. Other special-purpose clauses, however, may be invoked only when the troubles are attributable in whole or part to the obligations assumed under the treaty or agreement.

The latter tends to be the rule with respect to clauses relating to injury to particular industries. Actually, of course, the link between cause and effect is seldom so clear in actual economic events, and rigorous proof of the connection can hardly be required. In the interpretation of the escape clause in the Trade Agreements Act, for example, an increase in the import of an item which has been the subject of a tariff concession was generally regarded as having been attributable to the concession on the ground that more restrictive customs treatment

---

[10] J. Ch. Snoy et d'Oppuers, "Les débuts de l'Europe économique," *Les Aspects Juridiques du Marché Commun,* Faculté de Droit de l'Université de Liège, 1958, pp. 15–30.

could have prevented it. In some cases, however, increased imports were clearly of secondary importance among the difficulties being encountered by a domestic industry, and the issue was more controversial; Congress tried to resolve this question in 1955 by specifying that increased imports were to be considered as injurious when they "contributed substantially" toward the injury or threat of injury.[11] Incidentally, the corresponding GATT provision, Article 19, contains an additional specification with respect to causality that is not found in the American law; the GATT clause requires not only that the difficulty be due to imports that increased as a result of a tariff concession but also that the increase in imports must be the result of unforeseen developments.[12]

Difficulties may sometimes arise, in cases where the existence of an increase imports must be established, over the appropriate base period for determining whether the recent or current level of imports has "increased." This was a point of controversy in a number of escape-clause actions in the United States in the postwar period, the dispute being whether the prewar years, the war years, or the years immediately following the war should be taken as the base.

AUTHORITY OVER THE USE OF SAFEGUARD CLAUSES

The criteria for the invocation of safeguard clauses are not, of course, unrelated to the locus of the power to determine when they may be used. The more specific and detailed the criteria, the less it matters where the authority is placed to determine that the necessary conditions have been met; the more general the criteria, the more significant is the locus of

---

[11] Trade Agreements Extension Act of 1951, as Amended, Section 7 (b), Committee on Ways and Means, *op. cit.,* p. 175.

[12] The GATT case relating to hats, mentioned in a previous footnote, turned in part upon the issue of whether the increase in imports was or was not the result of unforeseen developments. See above, Chapter II.

authority. Since the safeguard clauses that are important in actual practice tend to be formulated in terms of rather general criteria of invocation, the question of authority is an important one.

The authority may rest in the hands of each country (unilateral invocation), the group of countries organized by the treaty or agreement (multilateral invocation), or a supranational body constituted by the treaty or agreement (supranational invocation).

Unilateral invocation

Unilateral invocation characterizes the safeguard clauses of the OEEC Code and the GATT. However, even where the power to invoke the clauses is unilateral, the freedom of action of the individual country is circumscribed by the existence of the treaty or agreement in some legal respects and, what is apt to be of greater practical importance, in some moral way. In GATT, for example, almost every safeguard clause may be used largely at the discretion of the individual signatory, but deterrents to the exercise of this power are built into the GATT structure. They consist of the obligation to notify, to consult, to negotiate, and to give compensation; there is also the risk of retaliation on the part of others. Finally, the need to stand before other signatories to explain and defend an action in the light of the letter and spirit of the Agreement also has its restraining influence. In the OEEC Code, where much the same techniques were employed, the homogeneity of the member countries in culture, recent experience, and current purpose greatly enhanced the moral pressures that could be exerted by the group as a whole upon a recalcitrant country. Thus there is an element of multilateral control even when invocation is unilateral.[13]

The extent of this influence varies from situation to situation. In the OEEC, it was probably greater with respect to the small countries than the large ones. In GATT, the conscience of the large countries, the close watch they keep upon one another, and the background political struggle between East and West for the allegiance of the underdeveloped countries, seem to produce the curious situation that the multilateral influence, weak though it is, is probably more efficacious with respect to the large and developed trading countries than with respect to the less powerful and underdeveloped countries. Also multilateral influence seeems less for some types of difficulties than others; in the GATT, for example, safeguards for balance-of-payments difficulties and to protect agriculture have perhaps been somewhat more immune to international pressure than protective devices to favor particular industries.

Multilateral controls

Multilateral power, as distinct from multilateral influence, may take the form of the right of veto over unilateral invocation, the requirement of prior group concurrence for unilateral invocation, or the direct authority to permit the use of the safeguard upon the application of the interested party. In a few instances the Contracting Parties of GATT were given such powers; for example, they had the right of veto over "unjustifiable deviations" from the prohibition against discrimination in case of balance-of-payments restrictions (Article 14, 1,

---

[13] In formal legal terms the OEEC Code could be classified as multilateral with respect to the nature of the authority over the use of safeguard clauses, since the Organization could, in principle, disapprove of the invocation or continued use of such a clause. In fact, however, disapproval authority rested with the Council, the decision-making body of the Organization, upon which each member was represented and could exercise a veto. See above, Chapter III.

h)[14] and their prior concurrence is required before a signatory whose economy is in "the process of development" may invoke a safeguard permitting it to take a measure to assist the development of its economy which would otherwise be inconsistent with GATT (Article 18, Section D). The Contracting Parties also have direct power over the invocation of what is perhaps the most general safeguard provision of the GATT, the waiver clause. In practice, however, waivers are seldom if ever denied, and a formal multilateral power is thus employed to a considerable extent upon the unilateral initiative of the country seeking safeguard action.

In the EEC, multilateral controls, which are exercised through the Council (upon which each member state has one representative), are somewhat more extensive. The Council has safeguard powers relating to the common external tariff, readaptation, subsidies, distortions due to lack of harmonization, and the balance-of-payments difficulties of member countries. The Council may, for example, waive on behalf of a member state the Treaty rules restricting the uses of subsidies, although unanimity is required for such action. Again, it has the right to order a member state to change or to terminate measures of safeguard taken unilaterally to cope with a sudden balance-of-payments crisis. Unlike the OEEC Council, which formally had a similar legal power, voting on this point is by a qalified majority[15] so that the country concerned cannot exercise veto power. However, in the present stage of relations among the Six, there is considerable reluctance to use legal powers for majority voting on the Council, a reluctance which might be very great indeed for a matter relating to a balance-of-payments problem. Whatever the issue involved, every avenue in search of accommodation is ex-

---

[14] This clause, which has been since replaced, related to restrictions that had been in existence on March 1, 1948, and to discriminatory relaxations of restrictions that were permitted under certain conditions (Annex J).

[15] See above, Chapter V.

plored, and in this respect matters are like they were under the OEEC Code; however, the very existence of the power of the majority to determine the issue can hardly help but influence the outcome in the EEC.

In general, however, the EEC situation like that of GATT seems to suggest that the differences in actual operation between clauses that are formally unilateral in character and those that are formally multilateral tends to be smaller than the legal gap which separates them.

Supranational powers

Supranational powers over the invocation of safeguards also are found in the EEC. The Commission, an administrative or expert body charged with the daily affairs of the Community, shares in one way or another in most of the safeguard powers of the Council mentioned in the preceding paragraph; often the Commission has the power of proposal and the Council must accept or reject the proposal in the form made by the Commission. In addition, the Commission may exercise authority over a number of safeguards completely independently of the Council, especially the safeguards that apply only during the transitional period. This is true, for example, of the general-safeguard clause applying to difficulties in any sector or region (Article 226). In practice, however, the Commission has been keenly conscious of the importance of its relations with the member governments, particularly since there are many other points in the affairs of the Community where the governments clearly hold the upper hand. Also, the governments have not hesitated to apply strong pressure on the Commission in cases in which it alone had the power of decision; on one occasion, for example, the governments formally stated their agreement that Article 226 ought to be invoked to cope with certain situations even though the Treaty gives them no role in the invocation of this article but places it entirely under the control of the Commission.[16]

In the ECSC, there is a similar sharing of safeguard powers between the Council (also composed of representatives of the member states) and the High Authority, which is the executive agency of the Community. In some import respects, however, the powers of the supranational body, the High Authority, are greater with regard to safeguards (and also in other matters) than the powers of the Commission in the EEC. To a considerable extent, the framers of the ECSC Treaty appeared to have contemplated that the High Authority would act in place of the governments in carrying out safeguard functions; thus provisions of the Treaty permit the High Authority to deal directly with individual firms in order to cope with certain basic difficulties that might conceivably affect the coal and steel industries, including a crisis owing to declining demand and the opposite difficulty of shortages of supplies of coal or steel. However, the governments through the powers of the Council were placed in a position to check the actions of the High Authority, and when the critical moment came in the negotiations over the ailing coal industry, they used this power.[17] Thus, the governments proved unwilling in the actual event to surrender their powers to succor an industry in difficulty to a supranational body, although they made provision for such a surrender in the Treaty of Paris. The EEC Treaty, concluded after some experience in the ECSC and at a different political moment, reflects a better evaluation of the balance between sovereignty and close international cooperation which the Six were willing to accept in practice. In the EEC, a supranational board has powers of initiative and administration, including certain powers over

---

[16] *Ibid.*
[17] See above, Chapter IV.

safeguards, but the governments retain the power of decision on most or all important matters. In actual operation, the EEC and the ECSC, despite the difference in the terms of their charters, have not been so far apart with respect to the relative roles of the governments. Both organizations thus come closer to multilateral control by a group of nations than supranational control.

This review of the forms of control over safeguard clauses suggests that the actual operating differences between the four organizations in this matter are smaller than the differences in the legal provisions which govern the use of the clauses. Unilateralism in the OEEC Code and GATT is pushed forward toward multilateral control, and supranationalism in the EEC and the ECSC tends to revert to multilateral control by the governments of the member countries. Perhaps multilateral control by the concert of participating governments is the logical compromise between the still strong forces of nationalism which find supranationalism unacceptable and the powerful pressures toward one world which make unilateralism less and less feasible.

Even where the governments remain in control, however, a useful role in the administration of the trading arrangements and particularly in the administration of the safeguard clauses can be played by a small expert group whose membership is at least semipermanent. To them might be given the task of sifting the facts of each case, setting out the principles at stake, and giving an advisory opinion. The work of the members of the group need not be fulltime unless tasks other than safeguard matters require their attention. They must, however, be closely acquainted with the political factors that play upon trade questions so that they can distinguish between what is possible politically and what is not. No small part of the success of the OEEC Code is, for example, attributable to just such a group—the Steering Board for Trade, an advisory committee with great prestige whose reports to the Council of the OEEC commanded great respect. The committee was composed of seven high-level officials from the service of their governments but acting in their expert capacities on OEEC trade problems at monthly or fortnightly meetings. This combination of independence, high competance, and political acuity produced prompt and expert assessments of safeguard issues and trade disputes which were consistent from case to case, equitable, and politically realistic. The obstacle to the wider use of such a device as a means of crystallizing opinion about specific issues in an organization composed of many countries is apt to be the reluctance on the part of signatories to entrust power or even influence to a body without having the guarantee of representation upon it.

REMEDIES

The nature of the remedies is sometimes specified and sometimes left to the discretion of those who have the authority to invoke the safeguard clause. The ECSC Treaty, for example, reveals a clear tendency to specify remedies, while the EEC Treaty does so only infrequently.

Nature of remedies

The list of remedies could of course include the whole range of protective devices that have been used to prevent or control international trade. Tariffs and quantitative restrictions are, perhaps, the most frequently specified remedies or the most frequently used when the choice is left open, although subsidies and tariff quotas are often employed. Subsidies have the advantage of placing a burden on the treasury and thus providing a greater incentive for their termination than exists for a tariff or import quota; where, however, there are strong political pressures for protection, as in agriculture, this deterrent has not been very effective in shortening the duration of the protective measure. Tariff quotas have been employed extensively in the EEC as a means, in effect, of permitting differences among the member countries in the actual rates of duty they levy despite the existence of a nominally common external tariff. In a more general context, they offer the advantage of placing controls over the increase in imports that will flow from a reduction in protection, and, by providing assurance against a feared flood of imports, may make the reduction possible. However, these advantages are at least partially offset by the administrative difficulties entailed in their application.

Somewhat less usual remedies involve the extension of financial aids in connection with safeguards relating to balance-of-payments problems or difficulties for particular industries or regions. In the balance-of-payments case, the aids take the form of general credits to bolster inadequate or declining reserves. In the OEEC, where the Code of Liberalization existed side by side with the European Payments Union, the availability of financial aid was made contingent upon the adoption of internal measures that would make possible the re-establishment and maintenance of external equilibrium and a planned movement towards freer trade. The EEC Treaty mentions the possibility of "limited credits" from other members in case one country encounters balance-of-payments difficulties, and also suggests the possibility of a common approach to an international organization (presumably the International Monetary Fund). The extension of such aids, the OEEC experience seems to suggest, may sometimes be an effective means of influencing the policy of the recipient country, but by the same token it also tends to alter to some degree the political position of the recipient within the group.

Financial aids for particular industries or regions are possible under the ECSC and EEC either in connection with the readaptation or with investment projects. Readaptation is clearly linked more directly with the difficulties caused for particular industries by the expansion of international trade. However, experience thus far, if not quite as discouraging as some of the early evaluations suggested, has not demonstrated that an international organization can play a major role. The question of the development of new industries is so closely bound up with the general economic plans and programs of the governments that the latter are naturally inclined to restrict the role of the international organizations. Where international bodies have funds at their disposal, as in the ECSC for example, there has been some evidence of a tendency on the part of each government to see to it that the funds it has contributed to the common pool flow back to its nationals. Apart from the problem of the division of funds among countries, a program of adjustment assistance directed specifically to workers adversely affected by imports may raise questions of equity *vis-à-vis* those hurt by changes in tastes or technology or any of the other countless influences operating in a dynamic market economy. It has been suggested that such a difference in treatment may be justified on the ground that the effects in the trade case are attributable to a reversal of a government policy of encouraging labor and capital to enter or to remain in economic activities that could not withstand open competition, whereas the general run of adjustment problems presumably flow from factors other than changes in government policy.[18] Should this distinction seem inconsequential to those

---

[18] J. Lindeman and W. S. Salant, *Assistance for Adjustment to Tariff Reductions,* Brookings Institution, Reprint No. 42, Washington, D.C., 1960, p. 272.

injured by nontrade factors, it might help to be able to point out that the funds supporting the trade adjustment program are derived in part at least from the international organization involved. Thus far, the issue does not seem to have been a vital one in the Six because the main industry which has been the focus of readaptation aid, the coal industry, has long received special treatment on other grounds. In the EEC readaptation has been limited and appears to have been almost completely integrated into the general programs of the individual governments.

Among the alternative forms of readaptation aids, it is easiest to provide workers with tide-over and resettlement allowances. In an expanding economy with readily available alternative employment opportunities these types of aid will be adequate for many workers; indeed, large numbers of displaced workers may find other jobs without any form of readaptation assistance. The latter seems to have been the case, for example, for thousands of workers in the Community's coal mines; indeed in some areas and at some times, the problem was to keep the required labor force from being drained away to superior employment opportunities. In other instances, however, it will be necessary to re-equip workers with new skills both to aid their re-employment prospects and to help them find jobs at levels of pay closer to what they had been accustomed to prior to displacement. Retraining requires somewhat more elaborate programs, but does not present major difficulties. The real rub in readaptation comes when the unfavorable impact is concentrated in a community or region which offers an inadequate supply of alternative employments. Experience in the ECSC and elsewhere indicates that a combination of local pressures and labor immobility often makes it seem desirable or necessary to bring jobs to the community or region. The ECSC Treaty made specific provision for the financial aid for job-creating investments, but the EEC Treaty did so only indirectly by providing an investment bank which could make loans for this purpose among others. Both in conception and in actual orientation, however, the bank is more concerned with underdeveloped regions than with stagnant or declining industrial areas. While the problem of depressed areas such as the Belgian Borinage is under active consideration in the Community, the basic difficulty there as elsewhere is that relatively little leeway exists for the support of industries that will be competitive in the long run. New activities that will meet this test usually do not require special financial assistance, and bribes to locate new plants in a given area may prove costly both to giver and receiver. Beyond ensuring that there is adequate infrastructure (i. e., power and transport facilities), the encouragement of investment in a particular area or region is fraught with difficulties.

The direct provision of funds for workers and for new investment are not the only means through which financial succor may be extended to an industry in difficulty as a result of foreign competition. The United States, for example, has recently announced a speed-up on tax depreciation for textile machinery in order to help the American textile industry "to modernize, meet foreign competition and provide jobs." [19] The new schedule reduced the estimated life of textile machinery from 25 to 15 or even 12 years.

The great advantage of readaptation is that it promotes the change in the allocation of resources which is the main source of the gain from increased trade. However, other safeguard remedies, which are often used for protection and to avoid the necessity for adjustment, can also be bent to the same ends.

---

[19] *New York Times*, October 12, 1961.

Restrictions on remedies

Remedies in the form of derogations, consisting of specially permitted tariffs, quantitative restrictions, subsidies and the like,[20] may serve to facilitate rather than to eliminate the necessity for adjustments if the derogations are used solely to provide the affected firms and industries with time to take the necessary measures. This requires that the derogations be granted only for a limited period of time, preferably with the expiration date specified in advance. In addition, provision may be made for the gradual abolition of the newly protective measures in specified steps to come into force automatically. Sometimes, it is specifically stipulated that derogations may be used solely to facilitate adjustments, and their availability may even be made conditional upon definite plans or actions toward this end. In some instances, the clauses containing the safeguards may be invoked only during a transitional period deemed long enough to permit the necessary adjustments to be made. Most if not all of these limitations on safeguard remedies may be found in the treaties establishing the European communities or in the actual operation of the communities.

The combination of temporary derogation and remedy is less frequent in the OEEC Code and GATT. However, the former used temporary exceptions by countries that were not yet prepared to move on to the next higher level of trade liberalization as an effective means of advancing towards its goal without delaying until the last member was ready. In

---

[20] In the United States, for example, President Eisenhower ordered increased purchases of domestic lead and zinc for stockpile purposes when he refused to raise lead and zinc tariffs in 1954 (Lindeman and Salant, *op. cit.*, p. 261). Such purchases could be linked to a program of readaptation, but they were not in the lead and zinc case. Subsequently, outright subsidies were legislated under a four-year "stabilization" program to begin in 1962 (*New York Times,* October 5, 1961).

GATT, the effort to keep exceptions and derogations on a temporary basis has met with less success.

A common provision running through the safeguard clauses of all four organizations is the requirement that the remedies employed represent the minimum deviation from the principles of the treaty or agreement that is necessary to achieve the objectives of the safeguards. Other provisions are designed to protect other signatories from adverse effects stemming from the derogations of the safeguarding country. Both in the OEEC Code and GATT, the general principle of nondiscrimination applied to remedies taken under safeguard clauses. There was, however, a significant difference in the approach of the two organizations, the former adhering to the principle of nonretaliation and the latter to the balance-of-benefits principle. In a relatively limited group with effective moral controls, the principle of nonretaliation may serve to limit the extent and duration of derogations, but in a less cohesive organization such as the GATT, where derogations have sometimes been prolonged, compensatory adjustments may be more necessary in connection with safeguard measures.

In addition to remedies that affect the flow of trade, international treaties and agreements may provide for direct market intervention by the international group or supranational agency. Some commodity agreements, for example, contain provisions for purchases in times of falling prices and sales in times of rising prices; others provide for restrictions in production, or more usually, in exports. Among the four organizations studied in previous chapters, the ECSC is endowed with most substantial powers of market intervention. The institutions of the ECSC may order output restrictions in case of oversupply of coal or steel and may arrange for rationing in case of shortages. The only actual use of powers of direct intervention thus far has been in connection with steel scrap; the Community price of this essential ingredient for steel production was kept from rising through a perequation scheme by means of which the high cost of imported scrap was spread among all scrap consumers. This scheme was plagued with administrative difficulties, and its economic wisdom was challenged.

"Voluntary" export controls

Before concluding this section on remedies, mention should be made of some instances of "voluntary" import or export quotas that were arranged outside of the framework of the four organizations studied here. In the United States, for example, under the pressure of the coal industry and domestic oil producing interests, the Government induced oil importers to accept "voluntary" quotas in 1957. However, compliance difficulties led to the conversion of the quotas to a mandatory basis the next year.

"Voluntary" export quotas have been an increasingly common feature of the current international scene during the past four or five years. Under the threat of unilateral action by the importing country, Japan has applied export controls relating to prices and/or quantities of a considerable range of goods destined for Canada, the United States, Switzerland, Denmark, Benelux, and Australia.[21] As of early 1960, the controls covered certain textile and apparel items, especially cotton piece goods, for all of the countries, as well as a number of nontextile items for the United States.[22] With respect to the United

---

[21] GATT, *Restrictions and Other Measures Relating to the Problems of Market Disruption,* Document L/1164, May 17, 1960.

[22] The nontextile items included various kinds of tuna, plywood, wood screws, iron pipe fittings, clinical thermometers, transistor radios, stainless steel flatware, porcelain and earthenware dinner sets, umbrellas, and paper cups. Other countries, such as the United Kingdom, France, and the Benelux nations did not extend GATT treatment to Japan and were

States, controls were imposed on cotton textiles, the most important Japanese export to the United States, in order to forestall escape-clause actions that had been started by American cotton interests.[23] Beginning in 1957, an over-all annual ceiling of 235 million square yards on exports to the United States was imposed for a five-year period. The total yardage was divided up almost equally between cloth and made-up goods. Within each of these two broad categories, individual ceilings were established for particular types of goods, the purpose being to prevent an undue concentration of exports upon a specific range of products and thus to avoid a source of American complaint. Near the expiration of the five-year period, a new agreement substantially along the same lines was reached by the United States and Japan which established the over-all annual ceiling at 275 million square yards and increased the number of items for which specific limits were provided.[24]

The United Kingdom cotton textile industry has also benefited from "voluntary" export quotas, in this instance exports from Hong Kong, India, and Pakistan. The United Kingdom, which maintained quantitative restrictions on most Japanese goods, was reluctant to impose limitations on Commonwealth products by government action, and encouraged the domestic industry to negotiate with the industries of the three Commonwealth sources of supply for the voluntary restriction of their cotton goods exports to the United Kingdom. Agreements were concluded for three-year periods beginning in 1959 and 1960 which, unlike the Japanese

thus freer to control Japanese imports by means other than pressing Japan to establish export controls. See above, Chapter II.

[23] Subcommittee on Foreign Trade Policy, House Ways and Means Committee, *Compendium of Papers on Foreign Trade Policy*, Washington, D.C., 1957, pp. 621–628, 934–949.

[24] *New York Times*, September 11, 1961.

quotas with respect to exports to the United States, permitted the volume of trade to expand as compared to the highest level previously reached. The agreements are implemented by export controls exercised by the Hong Kong Government, and, with respect to Indian and Pakistani goods, by import controls administered by the Government of the United Kingdom. The quotas are regarded as a temporary device to give the British industry time to restore its competitive position. The United Kingdom simultaneously adopted a program of financial assistance for the elimination of surplus capacity and for the re-equipment of the industry that would make the trade controls unnecessary in the future.

More general arrangement for "voluntary" export limitations in connection with cotton textiles were negotiated at Geneva in July, 1961. Under these proposals, if a country finds that cotton textile imports are causing or threatening "disruption" of markets, it may ask the exporting country or countries to restrain exports in any one of more than 60 categories of textiles listed in the agreement to a specified level, which may not be below that prevailing during the 12 months ending June 30, 1961. If the request is not accepted, the country making it may limit its imports to the specified level. These arrangements, which are to be used "sparingly" and only to avoid disruption from an "abnormal" increase in imports, are for the short-run only.[25] Similar arrangements were subsequently agreed upon to cover a five-year period.

---

[25] GATT, *Arrangements Regarding International Trade in Cotton Textiles,* July 21, 1961.

Chapter 7

Reconciliation Policy

THE ESSENTIAL PROBLEM AREAS FOR SAFEGUARDS

Despite the substantial number and wide variety of safe-guard clauses that exist in the four international trading arrangements discussed in the previous chapters, the essential uses of the safeguard clauses have centered around balance-of-payments difficulties on the one hand, and injury to particular economic industries or sectors on the other.

The future hope of avoiding resort to balance-of-payments safeguards in international trade treaties rests upon the formulation of new or strengthened international financial institutions which will enable countries to withstand losses of reserves when in temporary balance-of-payments difficulties. The search for such arrangements is actively engaged, but a description of the problems and prospects would carry us well beyond the trade area *per se* into the subject of international finance. Even if an advance is made as a result of these efforts, trade treaties and agreements will have to contain provisions for balance-of-payments safeguards, though it is conceivable that there may never be another time when they will be invoked by major trading countries as extensively as in the period now drawing to a close.

For the difficulties of particular industries or sectors also, the time may not be far off when more fundamental solutions will be sought, at least with respect to one major source of the difficulties bedeviling international trade. The problems of adjustment to freer trade are greatly exacerbated by the intervention of governments in certain commodity markets, particulary, though far from exclusively, in the agricultural sphere. The forms of intervention vary widely, but a common effect is the establishment of a domestic price level for the favored product(s) that differs from that which would prevail in a free market. Since the efforts of the individual governments are almost completely uncoordinated, the artificially established price level in one country is apt to differ also from the artificially established levels in other countries. These differences make trade controls inevitable unless the domestic programs are to be swamped by imports from countries with free markets or with lower government-established prices. The result is that the spirit of GATT, and sometimes its letter as well, is widely ignored with respect to agricultural products and certain other raw materials that receive similar treatment from governments. Furthermore, the problem spills over to the products which are derived from the favored commodities. Thus American cotton textile manufacturers demand government action to offset the handicap imposed upon them by the fact that they must pay the high support prices for American cotton while foreign textile manufacturers can buy American cotton at world prices. Again, in the European Economic Community safeguard clauses had to be used on behalf of Germany's industries processing agricultural products since the farm commodities were subject to a special regime that permitted Germany to maintain her high price supports for them while the derived products had to meet open competition on the Common Market. The long-run solution of these problems, if one is ever found, must surely lie in the direction pointed by the EEC; viz., the drawing together of the divergent price levels in the various countries. This is no easy task even in the relatively homogeneous group of the six EEC countries, and their success might embolden a more diversified group of countries to approach the problem.

However, even at best difficulties for particular industries created by closer international economic relations are likely to constitute a recurrent feature of the commercial policy scene for a long time to come. This chapter and the following ones are devoted largely to this general problem, although some attention is given also to balance of payments and other safeguards.

THE PRIORITY OF DOMESTIC INTERESTS

In each of the trading arrangements considered in the previous chapters the conflict between domestic interests and international obligations has been resolved in virtually every important instance in favor of the former. Perhaps this is understandable in the balance-of-payments cases, where in a sense the financial position of the whole economy was at stake, but balance-of-payments safeguards, although for the most part clearly warranted when originally instituted, were often retained longer than necessary by countries reluctant to surrender their protective effects.

The primacy of domestic interests characterized the resolution of the conflict also when the difficulties related to the position of particular industries. That the United States followed this policy in GATT was widely noted and commented upon. American actions in each of the escape-clause cases and in applying quantitative restrictions on agricultural products (both before and after a GATT waiver legalized them) have been criticized on many sides, on the whole justly, as measures inconsistent with the nation's avowed trading principles and with its position in the world economy.

What is, however, sometimes overlooked is that the purely European trading organizations—the OEEC Code, the ECSC, and the EEC—have functioned as though a "no-serious-injury" rule, although not so well publicized as its American counterpart, applied. There is little evidence that a decade of the OEEC Code and eight years of a common market in coal and steel had seriously detrimental effects upon any important industry in any country participating in either of these ventures. While it is true that some minor industries of wartime origin were permitted to drop by the wayside as trade was expanded under the OEEC Code, no well established or substantial industry was permitted to suffer injury. In the ECSC, the troubles of the Belgian coal industry could hardly be ascribed to the functioning of the common market; in any case, safeguards were invoked and the operation of the common market was not allowed to worsen the position of Belgian coal. It is, of course, premature to evaluate the EEC but the record to date hardly seems inconsistent with a "no-serious-injury" rule. Industries in underdeveloped regions of Italy, agricultural processing industries in Germany, and a number of lesser industries such as certain ones that France wished to develop were beneficiaries of special measures that involved exceptions from the principles of the common market. Special arrangements were made also to safeguard the access of Benelux processing industries to imports from third countries at low or nil duties where the common external tariff called for higher ones.

None of these three forms of more or less intimate European cooperation shows substantial evidence of bringing about or having brought about any significant shifts in the localization of European industry. Trade among the partners increased more than with third countries, but the increase in trade did not reflect greater specialization achieved through the contraction of some industrial branches and the expansion of others in each of the countries, and there does not seem to be an expectation in any responsible quarter that such shifts will occur in the future operation of the Common Market.

The record seems to indicate that the nations of Europe were hardly more willing than the United States to sacrifice domestic industries to the expansion of trade. Neither, however, did they let a fear of foreign competition play a dominating role in their commercial policy. Indeed, the European countries enjoyed great success in achieving closer trade ties and an expansion of trade with one another without entailing injurious consequences for any of their important domestic industries.

EUROPE'S INCREASED TRADE WITHOUT INJURY

Europe's success in achieving trade expansion without injury was due in part to favorable circumstances and in part to deliberate policy.

Economic expansion

Perhaps the most important circumstantial factor was the rapid rate of economic growth. In the case of the OEEC Code, low trade and production levels in the late 1940's provided ample scope for trade expansion without injury to domestic interests. Economic expansion also favored the steel industry during the life of the ECSC and industry at large during the briefer existence of the EEC. It was easy to make room for increased imports when domestic demand was booming, and in those sectors in which imports proved too competitive it was not difficult to find some other use of resources which could be profitably pursued. Firm reciprocal demands for exports also helped.

The critical importance of economic expansion in the success story is underlined by the cloud which coal cast over the European integration movement in the latter part of the 1950's.[1] In the early years of the ECSC, coal was in short supply and there were markets in the Community even for high-priced Belgian coal. When, about the middle of the decade, demand conditions changed and coal surpluses began to appear, Belgian coal was hit earliest and hardest, and after some controversy over the measures that should be taken, Belgian coal exports to and imports from the Community countries were placed under controls. France and Germany, the other major coal producers in the ECSC, insisted upon meeting the problems created for their coal industries in their own way rather than through the actions of the High Authority of the ECSC. The outcome was not of course entirely the same as if there had been no ECSC, but the differences are not all to the credit of the new organization. Belgium in effect received financial support for its miners and for a rather belated reorganization effort, and perhaps the existence of the ECSC eased the political difficulties faced by the Belgian Government in taking the necessary measures. The other main difference was that the burden of adjustment to declining demand was shifted to third-country coal more than would otherwise have been the case. Hence, Belgium's limited imports were directed away from low-cost American coal toward higher-priced Community coal, and all member countries were responsive to the urgings of the High Authority to reduce imports from third countries. Thus in case of declining demand, the trade-creating effects of the ECSC disappeared entirely and only the trade-diverting effects were operative. Economic expansion seems to be a fundamental prerequisite for a successful policy of trade expansion.

---

[1] For a more detailed account of the Belgian coal crises see above, Chapter IV.

Specialization in the fine

Economic expansion also seems to have facilitated a form of specialization which might be referred to as specialization in the fine rather than in the large. While whole branches of industry did not disappear in one country and expand correspondingly in another, within industrial branches specialization in some types of products tended to develop in one country and in other types of products in another country. This phenomenon, which was observed also in the operation of Benelux,[2] has been widely commented upon but has not been explained satisfactorily. The opening of larger market vistas has produced a movement towards larger plant size and towards the reduction in the number of product variants turned out in a plant of a given size. Given the small geographical area within which a large part of the industry of the Common Market is located, this may in itself have increased the extent of trade among the member countries to an appreciable degree.

Rationalization of distribution channels

The close proximity of industrial areas also increased trade among the Common Market countries through the rationalization of distribution channels as trade barriers declined. In coal, for example, mines near national boundaries began to serve areas determined by economic rather than political factors, with consequent reductions in over-all transport costs.

Business agreements

The development of product specialization and the avoid-

---

[2] P. J. Verdoorn, "The Intra-Bloc Trade of Benelux," *Economic Consequences of the Size of Nations* (ed. E. A. G. Robinson), New York, 1960, pp. 291–329.

ance of injury may also be explained in part by agreements or combinations between producers in different countries. The European outlook on these matters is different from that of the United States. In all of the countries of the Common Market, there is a closer working relationship between business and government, and the governments are more willing to rely upon perhaps somewhat more highly organized trade and industrial associations to achieve governmentally desired ends.

This has sometimes taken the form of explicit reliance upon business circles in importing and exporting countries to reach solutions in the safeguard area. The Benelux countries and Germany, for example, brought together representatives of the industries concerned in an effort to find a settlement for a dispute between the two countries in the framework of GATT regarding the German duty on potato flour.[3]

Again, the European Commission of the EEC, faced with demands for tariff quotas from some countries based on the inadequacy of Community supplies of certain raw materials and with claims from other members that supplies were or could be adequate, called together the supplying and consuming industries in the hope that they would come to an agreement upon the questions at issue.[4]

Business agreements in Benelux. Perhaps the most extensive reliance upon private business in connection with safeguards occured in the Benelux customs union. Since we have not devoted a separate chapter to Benelux, it may be worth interrupting the main line of thought in order to recount this incident.[5]

---

[3] See above, Chapter II.

[4] See above, Chapter V. The technique of relying upon industrial groups for aid in the solution of problems that affect industry is not, of course, unknown in the United States, but it is not so often employed as in Europe.

[5] This account is based mainly upon interviews and correspondence with officials of the Dutch Ministry of Economic Affairs and upon a

In the early 1950's, Belgium, already hit by the drop in world prices following the end of the Korean boom, found itself facing a re-equipped and modernized Dutch industry which had the advantage of a significantly lower wage level. As Dutch products, enjoying duty-free entry to the Belgian market, began to make greater and greater inroads on the business of Belgian producers, complaints rose and the value of the Benelux arrangement began to be questioned in Belgium. In response to this situation, the Belgian and Dutch Governments late in 1952 called upon the business groups in the industries concerned to make arrangements for the temporary limitation of Dutch exports to Belgium. The Governments established committees for each industry, largely with the aid of the appropriate trade associations, to work out the details of the plan; the committees were chaired by a government official and included labor representatives. Belgian industrialists had an obvious incentive for cooperation, and Dutch businessmen were led to cooperate by the knowledge that the two governments would act of their own accord if agreements could not be reached through the committees; the possibility of import quotas unilaterally imposed by Belgium was also feared by the Dutch. The agreements, which consisted of commitments by the Dutch to increase prices on the Belgian market or of arrangements to divide markets through the establishment of Dutch export quotas, covered cigars, products of the graphics industry, pottery, confectionery, round biscuits, printed cloth, cardboard, corrugated cardboard, enameled ware, hearths and stoves, woolens, carpets, shoes, wooden

---

memorandum dated December 3, 1953, explaining a Benelux protocol of July 24, 1953, relating to the coordination of economic and social policies. See also J. E. Meade, *Negotiations for Benelux: An Annotated Chronicle, 1943–1956*, Princeton Studies in International Finance, No. 6, Princeton, 1957, pp. 62–63. Another aspect of the matter is treated above, in Chapter VI.

furniture, rayon cloth, rayon knitted goods, and woolen blankets. When quotas were established, they were generally set at levels below the 1952 Dutch export volume to Belgium, and the Dutch Government enforced them through a system of export licensing. Most of the quota arrangements, which like the price agreements were concluded late in 1952 or early in 1953, ended in 1954 or 1955, but a few lasted longer. Improved business conditions in 1953 and the rationalization of some of the affected Belgian industries through new investment appear to have led to a situation in which Dutch exports were soon below the quota levels. The price arrangements were left to the industries themselves to administer, and it is more difficult to ascertain when or if the practice of price discussions and agreements was abandoned. In a few cases in which the committees could not reach agreement, the governments made their own decisions about the limitations to be placed on Dutch exports; in others they agreed that the development of Dutch exports to Belgium had not been "abnormal."

Officials of the Benelux countries feel that arrangements between business groups can play a useful role in coping with the difficulties that arise in the course of developing closer trading ties. Given their low external tariffs, they rely upon competition from third countries to prevent these business agreements from leading to unduly high prices and to the other undesirable practices of cartels. They seem inclined to believe also that such business agreements cannot be durable, particularly in the face of a recession, without the support of governments. For these reasons and perhaps also because the ties between government and business are closer and hence governmental knowledge of business arrangements greater, the Benelux countries seem confident of the ability to use business understandings as an instrument of social policy.

Business agreements in the Common Market. The formation of the Common Market produced a wave of new mergers, affiliations, and understanding.[6] Thus far the benefits of this movement are more obvious than the disadvantages. It has led to larger-size and lower-cost plants and has increased the degree of product specialization in plants of a given size; it has led also to larger firms, which are stronger with respect to research, finance, and marketing, than the smaller ones they replaced. Another result, also welcomed by the European Commission, has been the creation of business organizations with Community-wide interests. What is most relevant for our purposes is the likelihood that market-sharing arrangements or price agreements have propped up firms that might not have been able to withstand Community-wide competition, and, in this way made the acceptance of the Common Market easier. In the long run, however, the replacement of government controls on trade by private restrictions can hardly be permitted if the Common Market is to fulfill its purposes.

At the end of 1961, the Community adopted its first regulations dealing with business ententes.[7] Business understandings between firms situated in different member countries must, with certain exceptions, be registered with the Commission. The Commission has the power to declare an understanding unlawful, but if the Commission decides that an agreement serves a useful economic purpose it may find it lawful. Much depends therefore upon the policies that the Commission establishes in making its rulings. In this it will likely be influenced by the governments, some of which are at best lukewarm to a strong anticartel policy. The future of cartels in the Common Market will be affected also by the way in which the

---

[6] European Economic Commission, *Fourth General Report on the Activity of the Community,* Brussels, May, 1961, Paragraphs 70–73.

[7] *New York Times,* December 20, 1961.

Community's commercial policy develops; exposure to third-country competiton through liberal tariff and trade policies is one of the most effective ways of limiting cartels.

Restricted membership

Restricted membership was an important factor enabling the countries to go farther in the direction of freeing trade than would have been possible if trade barriers with the rest of the world as a whole had been at stake. This was true in the OEEC, but was still more important in the ECSC and the EEC.[8] Not only were the differences in price structures, and therefore in the structural adjustments that would have to be made, small among the six members of the Common Market as compared to world-wide differences, but the trouble spots could be better anticipated in advance and prospects for coping with unanticipated difficulties were enhanced by homogeneity, proximity, and small numbers. To these factors must be added the cementing influence of the appeal of European integration as a political ideal.

If this helps to explain why the countries of the Six dared go so far in their program for reducing trade barriers, another factor related to a small number of members helps to account for the lack of injury that has characterized the implementation of the plans for a common market. It is the tendency—to which reference has already been made—of the new trading groups to spare themselves injury by passing on to third parties

---

[8] The architects of the EEC were quite conscious of the advantages of small numbers in creating a common market; indeed, they deemed it impossible to establish a common market on a wider scale. Cf. Comité Intergouvernemental Créé par la Conférence de Messine, *Rapport des Chefs de Délégation aux Ministres des Affaires Etrangères,* Bruxelles, April 21, 1956, p. 14.

the burden of adjustment to untoward changes.[9] A major illustration is provided by the story of the Belgian coal crisis. Another example may be found in the maintenance of export prices for steel that were higher than the Community prices; this helped to reconcile, at the expense of outsiders, the individual governments' desires to keep steel prices from rising with the belief of the High Authority and of the steel producers that higher returns were necessary to encourage further investment. In the European Economic Community, a number of examples might be chosen but the most important one, which relates to agriculture, is still in the making; it seems likely that the export surpluses of some member countries, notably France, will be disposed of within the Common Market at the expense of the United States and other important agricultural exporters. This feature of the Common Market may be defended on the ground that the Six now constitute an entity entitled to take measures which after all are no different from those adopted in similar circumstances by, say, the United States, a nation whose territory forms a broad economic area already integrated by the fortunes of history. It may be criticized on the ground that it is wrong in principle for the Six to seek to benefit one another at the expense of third countries; it is also inconsistent with the obligations of the member countries under GATT. Whatever the moral and legal position, however, the leeway afforded by the possibility of ameliorating difficulties at the expense of outsiders helped in a number of situations.

RECONCILIATION STRATEGY : EUROPEAN INNOVATION

However, if the Six were prepared to take advantage of

---

[9] The OEEC Code was also discriminatory in that the liberalization of trade was initially applied only to trade within the OEEC group. However, the discrimination in this case seems to have consisted more in the withholding of new benefits than in the withdrawal of past advantages.

fortuitous circumstances and of the opportunities to discrimin-
ate against outsiders, part of their success in avoiding injury
was due to a well-conceived reconciliation strategy. This had
four essential points : (1) gradualism, (2) certainty, (3) readaptation, and (4) joint responsibility.

Gradualism

Gradual movement toward the new trading situation was
intended to place all concerned on notice of the new rules and
to give them time to adapt to them. If necessary, additional
protection in the form of temporary duties, quantitative restrictions, tariff quotas, or subsidies would be provided, but, in
general, only in combination with measures designed to
remedy the source of the difficulty that required such exceptional treatment.

Certainty

Thus it was made clear that the establishment of the Common Market could be expected with a high degree of certainty.

As a result, the business community reacted to the expectation of broadened markets and heightened competition by
accelerating investment. High investments in turn played a
significant part in creating and maintaining the prosperous
conditions that made the adjustment to the Common Market
easier. With less certainty—as there might have been if the
safeguard provisions of the Treaty of Rome had not so clearly
been phrased in terms of purely temporary exceptions—the
possibility that trade barriers would not really come tumbling
down or that they would be reestablished might have deterred
the new investments that were in fact made. Thus, while we
have placed economic expansion among the circumstantial

factors considered in the previous section, to a certain extent it has a claim to be included in the present paragraphs dealing with the way in which the Common Market was planned.

Readaptation

The readaptation provisions helped to disarm the fears and suspicions of labor. It is not unlikely that the economic purposes of the readaptation clauses—that is, actually easing the adjustments to changes in the location of industries—were more in the minds of the framers of the treaty establishing the ECSC than in the minds of the drafters of the EEC treaty. The passage of six prosperous years had made readaptation seem less urgent and also had made it clear that the national governments intended to discharge this task themselves. Conceivably, of course, the readaptation provisions may still be called upon to play a larger economic role, but thus far their importance has been more psychological and political.

Joint responsibility

Again and again the provisions of the treaties establishing the new European organizations make it clear that there is a common concern for the difficulties that any one member country encounters. Indeed, one can almost say that the idea that the surplus country as well as the deficit country has a responsibility for finding solutions to imbalance (a concept well accepted for some years now in the field of international finance) is being extended to the field of international trade. In the trade area, the exporting and importing countries are concerned with the disruption of particular markets in the importing country rather than with balance-of-payments problems. The cooperation between the Dutch and Belgian Governments to curb Dutch exports to Belgium, described above, is an illustration of an application of the principle of joint responsibility.

European reconciliation strategy in the postwar period has been characterized by pragmatism, imagination, and boldness. The pragmatism is evident not only in the care which was taken to avoid injury to well-established industries, but in a tendency to surrender elements of protection only when a clear advantage in commercial relations was to be obtained in exchange and in the practice of placing workable means of international cooperation above principles. European countries tended to hold on to restrictions ostensibly justified on balance-of-payments grounds after the basis for such restrictions had eased and then passed; also, within Europe, the high-tariff countries could not be persuaded to lower their levels of protection by the low-tariff countries since the latter had no inducements to offer them. The trial-and-error method of evolving European cooperation may be seen both in the OEEC Code and in the common market institutions. In the former, for example, common lists of liberalized products were tried and abandoned when they did not work; in the latter, the somewhat naive supranationalism of the ECSC was replaced in the EEC by a fuller institutional recognition of the important role which the governments in actual fact played in the ECSC anyway.

New techniques and methods of cooperation abounded in all three institutions. Liberalization in percentage tranches in the OEEC Code, readaptation in the ECSC, and the institutional arrangements of the new communities were among the more imaginative innovations.

Perhaps the OEEC Code paved the way by indicating that closer cooperation was possible without injury and could be productive of valuable results. Also, it was easier to go farther in a group of six relatively homogeneous countries than in a group of 17 ranging from Turkey and Greece to the United Kingdom and Sweden. For these or other reasons, the ECSC and the EEC reveal a degree of boldness that could never be mustered under the OEEC Code.

RECONCILIATION STRATEGY : AMERICAN STAGNATION

European innovation in reconciling domestic interests with greater international obligations in the trade field presents a sharp contrast to American stagnation in this area. Although under both Democratic and Republican administrations we have been vigorous advocates of freer trade in the councils of the nations, our own actions have fallen short of the principles we espoused to a sufficient degree to arouse cynicism in other countries and to weaken our leadership.

Our policies with respect to imports during the 15 years following the end of World War II were governed largely by Reciprocal Trade Agreements Act of 1934 as amended. This law gave the President powers to reduce tariffs below the levels set in the Tariff Act of 1930, but renewals were necessary since the powers were limited in time and extent. There were seven extensions in the forties and fifties, the last of which expired in June, 1962. Each renewal was the occasion for a political donnybrook between the supporters of freer trade and the advocates of protection. The former always succeeded in getting the law extended, sometimes with additional tariff-cutting authority for the President. The latter succeeded in limiting the duration and extent of the new tariff-cutting power. More important, however, the protectionists were able to write into the successive renewals of the law provisions which progressively limited the effective freedom that the President could exercise in making tariff reductions and in subsequently maintaining them. The key provisions that were made more restrictive over the years relate to the no-serious-injury rule that was effectuated through the "escape" and "peril-point" clauses.

The escape clause

The escape clause provided domestic industries with an avenue of increased protection after a tariff concession had been granted to another country.[10] If increased imports caused or threatened "serious injury" to domestic producers, the Tariff Commission had to recommend relief to the President. The President could reject such recommendations, but if he did he was obliged to explain his action to Congress. Between 1947 and 1961, the Commission considered about 130 cases. It recommended relief in 25 to 30 per cent of these cases, but increased protection was actually granted by the President only in 10 per cent of them.

The list of products involved includes some important ones like aluminium, lead, and petroleum, but it also includes a considerable number that are produced in small quantities like rabbit fur, pins, umbrella frames, tobacco pipes, spring clothes-pins, and garlic—to say nothing about some that are esoteric as well as small in economic importance, such as reeds and pregnant mares' urine.

The law provided no precise definition of injury, but merely set out criteria that must be taken into account—without excluding other factors—in determining the existence of injury.[11] However, changes in the law were made on several occasions that were intended to encourage more frequent findings of injury. Thus in 1955, the "segmentation" amendment to the Trade Agreements Act specified that injury determina-

---

[10] See above, Chapters II and VI, for other comments on the escape clause.

[11] See above, Chapter VI.

tions should be made in connection with the "portion or sub-division" of the firms producing products that are like or directly competitive with imported goods, the effect of this change being to bring the application of the no-serious-injury rule closer to a product-by-product basis. Another important change in the law was the "national-security" amendment which called for action against imports that "threaten to impair the national security."[12] Once again, the legislative history includes "strengthening" the clause (first introduced in 1954) from the standpoint of the protectionists. More than a score of cases were considered, but through the end of 1961 only petroleum had received additional protection.

Peril points

The advance protection afforded by "peril points" served perhaps even more than the escape clause to enforce the no-serious-injury rule. The peril points are the levels below which any further reduction of tariffs would cause or threaten serious injury to domestic producers. The peril-point concept had always played a role within the executive branch in the decision-making process about tariff reduction, but in 1948[13] Congress specified that the President had to ask the Tariff Commission to establish the peril points before he negotiated any concession with a foreign country. If the President reduced any duty below the peril point, he had to notify Congress and explain his reasons. In actual practice, it was impossible to forecast very closely what effect a given reduction in a duty would have on the level of imports. In view of this great uncertainty, it may be presumed that the Tariff Commission

[12] U.S. House of Representatives Committee on Ways and Means, *Report on U.S. Customs Tariff and Trade Agreement Laws and Their Administration,* Washington, D.C., 1957, p. 185.

[13] The peril-point provision was withdrawn in 1949 and restored again in 1951.

was inclined to err on the conservative side in estimating how far duties could be reduced without endangering domestic producers. The President ignored a peril-point finding only rarely.

The result was that the ostensible tariff-reducing powers of the President were effectively limited by high safety margins imposed by the no-serious-injury philosophy as applied through the peril-point system. By the time of the 1961 GATT negotiations, the U.S. was left with very little scope for further concessions, and the other GATT countries, especially the six countries of the Common Market, were reluctant to proceed to make the concessions that they had contemplated. A compromise was finally hammered out under the pressure felt both by the American and Common Market negotiators to avoid a failure on the eve of Congressional consideration of President Kennedy's trade expansion program which was designed to replace the trade-agreements legislation. To reach this agreement, however, the President had to breach peril points for some $76 million worth of U.S. imports.[14]

Perhaps a broader indication of the stalemate in our trade program created by the no-serious-injury rule is given by the statistics on the average rate of duty on dutiable imports. This dropped from 50 per cent, in the early 1930's when the reciprocal trade law was first passed, to 16 per cent, in the early postwar years. Much of this decline was due to the rise in prices which reduced the effect of specific duties. Nevertheless, it is significant that there was no downward movement in the average duty after 1951; it hardly moved out of the 11 to 12 per cent range.[15]

[14] *New York Times, March* 8, 1962.

[15] The average rates of duty on dutiable imports may be found in P. Kenen, *United States Commercial Policy; A Program for the 1960's,* a report prepared for the Subcommittee on Foreign Economic Policy, Joint Economic Committee, Washington, D.C., 1961, 7.

Thus, it was clear that the concentration on the avoidance of injury had brought American commercial policy to an impasse.

Reasons for preoccupation with injury

How may we explain the American preoccupation with staving off the effects of foreign competition at a time when Europeans were reaching out for closer trade ties? In part, of course, the answer lies in the difference between the two situations. At the end of the war, Europe's barriers on trade were greater, and Europe's need to find ways to break out of these restrictions was greater. Europe's need was more urgent also in that the subdivision of the continent into smaller national units —as compared to the United States—makes trade more essential. Thus Europeans were perhaps less fearful of foreign competition, or, at any rate, since the gains of trade were more obvious and important to them, more willing to take risks.

However, part of the difference may lie also in the different relationships that prevail between business and government in the United States on the one hand and in countries of western Europe on the other hand. In the United States, the relationship is more at arm's length than in Europe. This is partly a matter of the vast size of the country and partly a matter of political tradition and business philosophy. The sheer weight of numbers of decision-making persons, both in government and business, makes extensive personal working relationships between the two groups more difficult than in, say, one of the Benelux countries. In addition, political folklore casts the American government in the position of a trust buster and a watchdog over the competitive mores of business; drastic changes would have to occur before the government could assume a position of benevolent neutrality, let alone active support, for cartels or other arrangements that "stabilize markets." Even where cartels are specifically authorized by law, in the export field, the domestic environment has apparently discouraged their use. Finally, the attitudes of businessmen tend to be hostile towards government programs and towards the government's "bureaucracy." Businessmen do not hesitate to seek government intervention when the need arises, but they often seem to prefer to tell the government what measures are required rather than to accept partnership with the government in continual surveillance over the welfare of the economy, and they are inclined, perhaps, to work through elected rather than appointed officials or employees in the relevant field.

As a result of the relatively impersonal relationships between government and business, business tends to seek government action in ways that have almost become American institutions. Publicity campaigns, lobbies, and other forms of political pressure are mobilized to attain the desired end. Even administrative decisions, such as those required for the invocation of the escape clause, are characterized by advance publicity, political maneuvers, public hearings, and widely publicized decisions by the Tariff Commission and the President. If the United States wished to call maximum attention to the efforts of domestic interests to obtain increased protection, a better system for doing it would be hard to devise. Perhaps this is a price we must pay for our system of division of powers between the executive and legislative branches; other large trading countries have parliamentary systems in which differences over trade safeguards are less likely to arise between the executive and legislative functions, or at least less likely to be fought out in public.

However, there is a more fundamental disadvantage than bad publicity. Because businessmen in vulnerable industries do not feel assured of sympathetic treatment by the executive branch in the event that their worst expectations are realized, they seek to obtain security by legislation which leaves little discretion to the executive. Since the outcome of the legislative process is uncertain, the security that is sought is often much greater than necessary to avoid a flood of imports—the danger that is usually feared or alleged. Industries are thus led to divert their energies to political methods rather than to the economic measures that will enable them to meet or sidestep competition.

The real salvation of the bicycle industry, for example, may come from the reorganization of plants and the redesign of bicycles (for example, the combination of a multispeed gear with a coaster brake) rather than from the modest tariff increases that the industry netted from three escape-clause applications.

This thumbnail sketch of American commercial policy in the decade and a half following the end of World War II leaves out much that is significant, such as the quantitative restrictions we imposed on certain dairy products, initially in violation of GATT and subsequently under a waiver from GATT. Nevertheless, it should suffice to show that preoccupation with injury made further movement toward freer trade impossible. Although the U.S. broke new ground in other spheres of international relations—notably with respect to technical assistance and foreign aid—U.S. commercial policy was dominated by an industry-by-industry or even product-by-product application of the no-serious-injury rule. Europe's ingenuity in finding ways to reconcile domestic interests with trade expansion formed a rather remarkable contrast to the stagnation of American commercial policy.

Chapter 8

Implications for American Policy

WHAT IMPLICATIONS for American commercial policy may be drawn from the study of safeguard clauses in the four multilateral trade arrangements that have been analyzed? Obviously, one can hardly expect to derive from the investigation of one aspect of trade relations all the necessary ingredients for the formation of American commercial policy. Beyond this limitation, there is the further fact that the implications that are drawn from any experience depend in part upon the philosophy of the interpreter. Therefore, we begin by setting out briefly our views as the needs of American commercial policy not so much to persuade others as to establish the background against which inferences are drawn from our study.

REQUIREMENTS OF AN AMERICAN COMMERCIAL POLICY

A dominant purpose of the United States foreign policy is to maintain and further develop the cohesiveness of the noncommunist world. The commercial policy we adopt for ourselves as well as the commercial policy we advocate for others must be consistent with this basic objective. The foundation stones of the commercial policy that we have in principle espoused for a quarter of a century both for ourselves and for others—the reduction of trade barriers and nondiscrimination—meet this test. Indeed, it is difficult to see how, given our world position, we could take any other stand. The only leeway we have is to pursue this policy with more or less vigor, or with more or less consistency.

In addition to the general support of these basic principles of commercial policy, the United States must concern itself with the economic strength of particular groups of nations. Immediately after the war, we were preoccupied with the fortunes of our allies. These have now been restored, and the countries of western Europe again provide important and growing markets as well as sources of competition for third markets. The future trade policy of what will almost surely prove to be an increasingly integrated Europe will be influenced by the trade policy that the United States practices. There are already trends in European policy inimical to American exports, particularly in the agricultural sphere. We will be in the best position to counter them only if we ourselves are pursuing liberal trading policies.

We have long been conscious of the needs of the underdeveloped countries, and in recent years the economic problems of this important group of countries have moved to the center of the stage. In the noncommunist world, there are more people and more nations with underdeveloped than with developed economies. We have both a moral obligation and a compelling political interest in helping them. It is inconsistent to spend billions for aid and to close our markets to their goods. If we do not find ways to accommodate their growing power to compete in our markets with certain basic raw materials such as oil, lead, and zinc and with certain labor-intensive manufactured products, such as textiles, the political and economic advantages of our aid program will be negated.

In connection with both the underdeveloped countries and with other nations of the noncommunist world, we must try to close the gap between the trading principles we preach and those which we practice. Perhaps our practice is no worse than that of the other great developed trading countries, but our departure from the principle of reducing trade barriers have been more conspicuous. This is due in part to the fact that the world expects more of us than of the others, in part to the vigor and sometimes sanctimoniousness with which we have advocated freer trade, and in part to our perverse penchant for emphasizing our deviations from our trading principles. The readiness of American industry to seek government action against imports also appears to be in striking contrast to the much-vaunted belief of American businessmen in free enterprise and competition. In any case, leadership in world trade policy is up to the United States.

Although the European countries have made no attempt to assume leadership in trade on a world scale, they have been successful in expanding trade within Europe without sacrificing any substantial industrial interests. While there are a number of elements in this experience which are relevant to the problems that the United States faces, it is only fair to point out that some factors favorable to the European undertakings are not operative in the case of the United States.

Perhaps the most important of these is that the United States is not in a position to join a restricted group of nations that plans to expand trade internally through a discriminatory reduction in trade barriers. We are even less in a position to join in a group in which there is the slightest tendency to expand internal trade at the expense of outsiders. Our obligations to Canada, western Europe, south and east Asia, Africa, and Latin America preclude special arrangements with respect to trade barriers with any one of these areas. The reduction of trade barriers in which the United States participates must be extended to the entire noncommunist world, and that makes reduction much more difficult than when six or even seventeen countries are involved.

Similarly some of the sources of advantage in the European arrangements, such as the gains from the reduction of crosshauling of coal merely through changes in trade channels and the gains from larger plant size or through more detailed plant specialization either would not occur or would bring much smaller economies for a country with the size and quality of industrial plant of the United States.

THE INGREDIENTS OF A BOLDER AMERICAN COMMERCIAL POLICY

Yet there are some basic elements in the European experience that are relevant to the position of the United States. If American commercial policy is to break out of the impasse created by the rigidities imposed upon it by the "no-serious-injury" rule, some of the ingredients of the European methods will have to be incorporated into the American plan of attack. These may be listed as (1) security, (2) gradualism, (3) certainty, (4) adjustment, (5) safeguards, (6) joint responsibility, and (7) economic expansion.

Security

Perhaps the most fundamental change that is required before our commercial policy can serve our national interests more adequately is an alteration in the attitude of that part of the business community which feels itself exposed to foreign competition. A way must be found to end the feeling on the part of many businessmen in vulnerable industries that it is only by virtue of their own political efforts that "internationalists in the State Department" are prevented from "selling their interests down the river." If these industries can be given confidence that the government will not allow sudden disaster to befall them, and that it will not remain indifferent to their long run difficulties, perhaps some of the excessive opposition to any increase in imports will ease.

Without seeking the close relationship between government and business which does much to meet this problem in many countries of western Europe, it should be possible to find means of closer collaboration between government and business—and labor—in the management of the movement toward trade. The top business and labor groups are well aware of the problems of American foreign policy and, of course, they are cognizant also of the position and problems of individual industries. Organized business and organized labor thus have much to contribute to the program. Their advice should be sought in planning future trade barrier reductions, particularly with respect to adjustment problems. Of course, the danger is that pressures from below will force business and labor representatives to adopt a more protectionist position. On the other hand, the knowledge that business and labor representatives have a larger voice in trade matters may help to provide the essential element of security which is now lacking. If so, it might make it possible to push our trade policy out of its rut.

Gradualism

One way of easing the difficulties is to make progress slowly, thus giving the firms affected by the reduction of trade barriers the opportunity to make their adjustments to the new trading situation in a more orderly fashion. If any experience is required to demonstrate this proposition, it is available in the history of the OEEC Code, the ECSC, and the EEC. However, history indicates also that gradualism alone does not always suffice to avoid difficulty. It did not work in the case of Belgian coal, for example, and it may not work in other instances where an industry is undergoing a recession or a contraction rather than an expansion.

Certainty

It must be clear that trade barriers are really going to come down. This is inconsistent neither with security nor with gradualism. The security that the government must give to business is not a security against import competition, but a security based upon the knowledge that temporary shelter will be afforded in case of rapid and fortuitous changes in the conditions of competition, and that the long-run implications and needs can be determined and acted upon. Gradualism, it must be clear, should not be interpreted as indefinite postponement; there should be a definite time schedule for the dismantlement of trade barriers.

Once businessmen are certain about the future policy of the government, they will have a greater incentive to find ways to cope with the new conditions of competition. Adjustment to changing market conditions is after all one of the responsibilities of entrepreneurship and a main social justification for the high rewards which characterizes successful business leadership. In the past such adjustment has often included adaptation to foreign competition, but sometimes it has been delayed until it seemed absolutely unavoidable. In the watch industry, for example, American firms responded to the challenge only after increased protection obtained through escape clause action failed to prevent a further decline in the domestic production of 17 jewel watches.[1] Perhaps the new machinery, the new products, and the new marketing techniques would have come sooner if the industry had known earlier that it would have to meet foreign competition rather than nourished its hope of avoiding it.

Adjustment assistance

When, however, adjustment is made necessary by a change in the degree of protection afforded by the government (rather

---

[1] For a study of the adjustment of the watch industry, see U.S. Senate, Eighty-seventh Congress, *The United States and World Trade*, Final Report to the Committee on Interstate and Foreign Commerce, March 14, 1961, pp. 134–254.

than by some purely economic factor), there is a case for the extension of government assistance to facilitate the adjustment. The purpose of the assistance should be to remove, as far as is possible, the element of injury from the changes imposed by increased foreign competition. Of course, displacement itself —that is, the need to shift out of old lines of work and away from the production of familiar products—might be considered injurious, but if the adaption to new lines and new products occurs quickly there may be little injury in the sense of loss of income on the part either of capital or labor.

In many instances, spontaneous adjustment may take place smoothly, especially if the reduction of trade barriers occurs against a background of economic expansion which is shared by the industry concerned. Where this is not the case, however, public funds should be available for the resettlement and retraining of workers, for readaptation loans for affected enterprises, and perhaps loans also for new, employment-creating investments in areas hit by import competition.

Business-labor advisory groups could be of great aid in the management of the adjustment assistance program. Their technical knowledge and their experience should be invaluable in helping the government agency charged with adjustment assistance to determine when the need for it exists and to control the execution of the assistance program.

Safeguard measures

In addition to adjustment assistance, other safeguard measures ought to be available in case of need. In keeping with the remarks made above, measures of derogation should for the most part offer temporary relief with the degree of increased protection scaled down by a prearranged schedule. The derogations may be used to afford time for firms to make adaptations to the new trading situation through their own efforts or they may be used in conjunction with programs of adjustment assistance.

Joint responsibility

The exporting as well as the importing country should assume responsibility for avoiding the disruption of markets for individual commodities. In the past, controls over sudden and large increases in imports have largely been exercised unilaterally by the importing country. Recently, a new element has begun to be introduced : quotas governing the size of shipments have been determined by agreements between the exporting and importing countries. The arrangements between the United States and Japan with respect to cotton textiles represent the first extensive use of this technique by the U.S. In July, 1961, an international textile conference in Geneva agreed on the broader use of this method. The exercise of joint responsibility should minimize the possibility of a spiral of retaliatory restrictions on trade that might develop if import controls were unilaterally established. It should also make possible gradual adjustment to trade patterns that conform to market forces.

Economic expansion

In establishing the timing of trade barrier reductions, finally, we should bear in mind that adjustments to freer trade take place more easily during a period of rapid expansion. It would be unwise, however, to try to link the freeing of trade too closely to future cyclical conditions. The Common Market solution seems a good one here. A schedule could be established for the reduction of trade barriers which would include some flexibility for acceleration or retardation. Good economic conditions would then permit faster progress. If conditions were unfavorable, delays might be necessary.

There are many ways in which these essential ingredients could be put together to form a reinvigorated commercial policy for the United States. The following suggestions are partly illustrative of this and partly intended to apply some of the other lessons than can, in the author's judgment, be derived from the earlier chapters of this study.

The broad approach

The U.S., like Europe, can have expanded and freer trade without widespread injury to domestic industries. Such a program would require many changes, but there would have to be a sharp break with the past in four respects in particular :

In the first place, a clear and unequivocal commitment of national policy toward free trade must be made. Another compromise law giving the President the power to reduce tariffs by, say, 20 or 25 per cent in a four- or five-year period, even on an "across-the-board" basis, will merely be another in the series of dubious victories for freer trade. Such legislation would not lead businessmen to make trade adjustments; it would only result in the continuation of the dreary procession of claims for greater protection from one group after another.

Secondly, without trying to build the close relationship between government and business which helps trade adjustment in Europe, we must still find a way to establish closer collaboration among government, business, and labor in the management of the movement toward free trade.

The top business and labor groups are, of course, well aware of the problems of U.S. foreign policy, and they are, obviously, cognizant also of the position and problems of individual industries. Organized business and labor thus have much to contribute to the smooth functioning of the program. Their advice should be sought with respect to the sequence of steps that should be followed in reducing trade barriers, the identification of areas in which adjustment difficulties may be anticipated, and the extent and form of adjustment assistance that may be appropriate in specific types of cases.

Thirdly, we need a more realistic concept of injury. Under the reciprocal trade agreements legislation injury was defined in terms of a particular product without regard to the over-all ability of the industry or the firm to cope with increased imports. It is only when increased imports do have an adverse effect on the jobs of workers and the capital of entrepreneurs that they should arouse public concern. Even then, the focus of the public effort should be to remove the injury element from the adjustment process, rather than to make adjustment unnecessary.

Finally, we must be willing to surrender to some degree our power unilaterally to invoke escape clauses at will.

How, then, might these ideas, as well as the other lessons of European experience, be put together to formulate a new tariff and trade program for the United States?

Certainty through automaticity

One way which recommends itself begins by establishing the certainty of tariff and trade change in the minds of businessmen. This would be achieved through the adoption of a plan for the *automatic* reduction of trade barriers according to a predetermined time schedule. The President would be authorized to negotiate with other countries for reciprocal reductions on the same schedule. Congress might stipulate that the reductions must be spread over a period of time, perhaps as long as 20 years. Some provision ought to be made for a limited degree of flexibility in the time schedule so that the reductions may be speeded if business conditions are good, and slowed down if they are not.

Broadly speaking, there are two methods for the automatic reduction of tariffs. The simpler one calls for a certain percentage reduction in all duties at stated intervals until the desired total reduction has been attained. This method has the disadvantage that it ignores the varying degrees of vulnerability of different products to foreign competition. Thus, unless the reductions were staged very slowly over very long periods of time, it would probably involve extensive use of escape clauses. A variant of this approach that is less open to this criticism would permit different treatment for various groups of goods, either making the percentage reductions larger or making shorter time intervals for some groups than for others.

The other approach to automaticity provides still more flexibility with respect to individual commodities. Instead of "across-the-board" reductions affecting all products uniformly, it calls for percentage reductions at stated intervals in the average rate of duty collected on imports as a whole (or on each of a number of categories of products). Under this plan, some duties could be subjected to less-than-average reductions and others to more-than-average reductions, as long as the target percentage for over-all reduction was reached. (The scheme would have to be supplemented by a technique for coping with very high duties that are so effective in excluding imports that they have little influence on the average rate of duty collected; this could take the form either of a supplementary set of minimum percentage reductions for each individual duty, or of progressively diminishing ceilings on individual duties.)

A scheme of the latter type has the advantage of combining flexibility with certainty. As long as provision is made for periodic automatic decreases in the average rate of duty collected, it will matter little that each country will tend to reduce first those which they can dispense with the most readily and to avoid the reduction of those relating to industries that are more vulnerable to import competition. The knowledge that the average rate of duty has to decline will make it obvious that a given industry can at most postpone, not escape, the need to adjust to foreign competition.

Several proposals of this general type have already been made. Perhaps the most widely discussed plan was that advanced by the French in the early 1950's. As modified by discussions in GATT[2] the French plan won the approval of Belgium, Denmark and Germany, but the essential support of the United Kingdom and the United States was not forthcoming and the scheme came to naught. In its final form the proposal called for three successive reductions of 10 per cent each in the average rate of duty collected for each of 10 categories of imports. The requirement that the reduction be distributed throughout the tariff schedule was designed to ensure that the benefits of the scheme would accrue to all supplying countries. Countries with low tariffs were permitted to reduce their duties by less than 30 per cent. In order to cope with very high duties which are so effective in excluding imports that they have little influence upon the average rate of duty collected, ceilings on individual tariffs were set at 5 per cent for raw materials, 15 per cent on semimanufactures, 30 per cent on finished manufactures, and 27 per cent on agricultural products.

Adjustments: spontaneous and assisted

The adoption of such a plan could be expected to call forth spontaneous adjustment on the part of business to the prospect of freer trade. Nevertheless, government programs of adjust-

---

[2] GATT, *A New Proposal for the Reduction of Customs Tariffs,* Geneva, January, 1954.

ment assistance should be provided, partly because there will be an irreducible minimum of cases in which adjustment problems will be difficult and party for the psychological or insurance value of having assistance available. Assistance proposals have been widely discussed in recent months.

One unresolved difficulty centers around the question of equity among workers. The adjustment assistance proposals would single out for special treatment those persons unemployed because of imports. The many people continually being displaced for a variety of other causes would have to rely on unemployment compensation, the employment services, collectively bargained assistance, and their own resources to make the adjustment. Some claim that this makes it awkward for Congress to legislate the precise terms of financial aid for workers affected by increased imports.

If this were to prove a serious obstacle Congress could avoid the delicate task of establishing the terms of assistance by legislating financial support for assistance programs negotiated by unions and employers under collective bargaining. Adjustment assistance has already come within the ken of collective bargaining agreements. In the railroad industry, for example, provision is made for the retention of the full work force for a time after a merger has been completed.

The question may be raised whether adjustment assistance should be entirely a domestic matter for each country or whether a new or revised GATT should have some role in it. The argument for a GATT role is that it ensures that adjustment assistance will be available in each country and that this makes it less likely that other safeguards will have to be invoked; hence, it is in the interests of all signatories to promote such a program in each. However, the experience of the ECSC and the EEC indicates that adjustment assistance is too intimately connected with the internal responsibilities of the national states for them to be willing to delegate much of a role to an international body. Perhaps a solution should be sought along the EEC lines in which the center gives financial support to the national governments when they carry out readaptation programs that meet established criteria. This technique, not unfamiliar in federal-state relations in the United States, would require providing GATT with funds. The contributions of the various member countries might be assessed in proportion to the customs duties they collect, excluding charges that correspond to internal taxes. Whatever the manner of financing, the availability of funds from an international body might provide a justification, where one is needed, for special adjustment programs to deal with problems created by import competition.

Safeguards

In addition to adjustment assistance, other safeguards should be provided. Little harm would be done and some further flexibility might be gained by permitting countries to substitute one duty reduction for another (so long as the required reduction in the average rate was maintained) in cases in which a lowering of a particular tariff brought unexpected difficulties. The use of this safeguard could, of course, be limited in a number of ways; for example, a Common Market technique might be adapted by limiting each country's right to raise duties for imports representing no more than 5 or 10 per cent of its total imports.

It may be doubted, however, that such limitations would be necessary. Placed in a framework of the steady movement of average duties toward lower levels, freedom to make such substitutions would, unless grossly abused, facilitate the transition to free trade without creating areas of permanent protection. Another safeguard, already mentioned, is the use of agreements between exporting and importing countries to prevent market disruption; these arrangements should be designed to avoid the sudden flooding of markets, but they should not forestall the *gradual* expansion of trade. Finally, there would be a general safeguard feature in the opportunity to delay the schedule of automatic reductions, though this would not be designed to help a particular industry and hopefully would never be used.

Beyond these safeguards, it might be desirable to have a general clause in a revised version of GATT which would permit the suspension of our obligations or those of another country in case of unanticipated difficulties. The ability to invoke this clause should not, however, rest with the country involved but with the community of nations. Obviously this raises some delicate questions about sovereignty, but there are two compelling lines of argument in support of this position.

The more obvious one is that if we wish to bind our partners more firmly to free trade—so that we can be sure that our exporters will continue to enjoy access to the markets they have and the new markets they acquire—we must accept stronger bonds ourselves. So long as the invocation of the escape clauses is as permissive as it now is under GATT, other countries as well as the United States will remain all too ready to resolve conflicts between domestic interests and international obligations rather consistently in favor of the former.

It is easy to exaggerate what is involved in multilateral control over the invocation of safeguard clauses. Our reviews of the records of the OEEC, GATT, the Coal and Steel Community, and the Common Market all indicate a reluctance on the part of both multilateral and supranational groups to use power, even when they have it, to impose a course of action upon any national state whether the issue relates to a safeguard question or something else.

Of course, the existence of the multilateral or supranational power alters the psychological and political framework within which a safeguard problem is resolved, and it makes it less likely that domestic pressures will prevail as easily as when safeguards may be invoked unilaterally. There is little validity, however, in the vision that may be conjured up of exposing our domestic interests to the merciless rule of a group of foreign countries.

The degree of multilateral control that we should try to devise ought to go beyond GATT and also perhaps beyond that of the OEEC Code in its heyday, but it ought to stop short of the degree of commitment represented by the ECSC and even the EEC. One solution might be to permit the invocation of many or most safeguard clauses by unilateral action, but to subject their continued use beyond, say, a six-months period to approval by a vote of two-thirds of the member countries.

The work of the revised GATT in coping with safeguard problems would be greatly facilitated by an advisory group like the Steering Board for Trade in the OEEC which, by its competence and prestige, would have a great influence with the member countries individually and collectively. Like the Steering Board, membership ought to be limited in number (perhaps seven), semipermanent in terms of length of service, personal in character rather than representative of governments, and composed of persons both with technical knowledge and good political judgment. Such a group ought to be looked to, among other functions, for guidance in the development of a body of principles about the interpretation of the new safeguard clauses in the course of giving their advice about case after case. Thus the basic trading code would gradually be supplemented by a common law that would grow out of experience.

We have touched upon the control and remedy aspects of the administration of safeguard clauses, and perhaps a word should be added about the criteria of invocation. A country entering an international trading arrangement in a very cautious spirit and distrustful of the degree of sympathy with which its partners will regard its needs in case of future difficulties might wish, especially if it was surrendering powers of unilateral invocation, to have detailed quantitative criteria for the invocation of safeguards. In the case of difficulties for particular industries, for example, these might be phrased in terms of certain percentage declines in production and percentage increases in imports, as was done at one point in a Benelux arrangement.[3] While it might be worth a careful review of American escape-clause cases to see how quantitative criteria might have worked, the author is inclined to believe that it would be very difficult if not impossible to define in advance quantitative criteria that would be both workable and satisfactory. Even in the United States, a country rich in statistical information, data relevant to escape clause actions have often been incomplete or unavailable, and the chances that this would be the case are all the greater if an effort were made to determine the existence of injury as distinct from displacement. There are also conceptual difficulties, which are better left to judgment in the face of particular cases, rather than to specific formulation in advance; this may be true, for example, with respect to the definition of the economic sector for which the changes in production, imports, etc., are to be considered relevant. All in all, there seems to be good reason for the fact that the criteria of invocation tend to be formulated in rather general terms in all four of the trading organizations that we have analyzed.

Specific criteria of invocation may also tend to encourage domestic interests to seek safeguard action more readily than general criteria. Whether this is the case or not, an effort should be made to formulate the rules and institutions governing the trade program so as to create incentives on the part of businessmen to meet foreign competition or to adapt their

---

[3] See above, Chapter VI.

businesses to it. Perhaps the major defect of our present rules and institutions is that they create a system in which businessmen are induced not to act creatively to cope with foreign competition, but rather invited to campaign for government action to exclude imports.

A Tariff and Trade Advisory Board

In all of these aspects of the tariff and trade program—the timing of the reductions in average duties, the selection of the individual items for the various amounts of reduction, the plans for providing adjustment assistance and the administration of the program after it is devised, and the invocation of various safeguards—the close collaboration of organized business and labor should be sought.

This might be achieved through the establishment of a Tariff and Trade Advisory Board. On this Board, there might be a few public representatives, preferably with experience both in government and business. Most of the membership, however, would be chosen from businessmen and union leaders who command wide respect and support from their colleagues.

The Board would be authorized to request data and analyses from the State Department, the Tariff Commission, and other government agencies. Through its membership it might obtain information on a more informal basis from particular trade associations, firms, or unions. The work of the Board would be carried on in private; only its official reports and recommendations would be made public.

The main function of the Board would be to provide a better means of communication between government and business on trade questions than now exists. As a result of the ability of the Board to sift the claims of various business groups and to lend its authoritative support to legitimate claims, businessmen might be given more confidence than they now possess that their difficulties will receive the sympathetic and prompt attention of the government. At the same time organized business and labor might feel a great responsibility to discourage unwarranted claims for protection.

A trade program along these lines would put to work the energies and ingenuity of our businessmen in devising ways to meet foreign competition and to survive it, rather than to avoid it through political means. Unless past American history and the recent experience of Europe belie the future, no large U.S. industry will disappear as a result of such a program. Rather, U.S. industry and the Free World will emerge stronger.

Epilogue

IN THE YEAR OR MORE that has elapsed between the submission of the manuscript to the publisher for printing and the return of the galley proofs, events in the area covered by this book have for the most part provided additional rather than new experience.

Perhaps the major exception is represented by the enactment in the U.S. of the Trade Expansion Act in October 1962. While the new law carries on the broad objective of the reciprocal trade legislation which had governed American commercial policy since 1934—viz., freer trade—it constitutes a notable step forward in the formulation of more effective means to achieve the desired goal.

For one thing a new remedy—an alternative to the old one of increased protection—is provided for domestic industries adversely affected by import competition: the firms and workers in the industry may petition for assistance in adjusting to an increased flow of imports. For firms, such aid may include technical assistance, loans, and tax relief; for workers, unemployment allowances, retraining, and relocation aids.

These provisions made it possible to tighten the conditions under which domestic industries obtain increased protection. The segmentation provision is deleted and the language of the escape clause is strengthened by requiring that serious injury to the domestic industry be the result in "major part" of an increase in imports attributable to concessions granted under trade agreements. Idle capacity, profits, and employment levels are among the criteria of injury to be taken into account in the determination of the existence of serious injury. If serious injury is found to have been caused or threatened under the terms of the law, the President may increase import restrictions and/or provide that the industry concerned should seek adjustment assistance for its firms and/or workers. Increased import restrictions are subject to annual review; they are to apply for periods not exceeding four years, although they may be renewed. An Adjustment Assistance Advisory Board, constituted by representatives of the Departments of Commerce and Labor and other Government agencies, is established.

The President is also given greater scope to change U.S. duties, a major purpose being to provide him with greater bargaining power vis-a-vis the Common Market. The language of the law permits him to engage in across-the-board rather than product-by-product tariff reduction. However, he must reserve from tariff reduction negotiations products which are currently the subject of Presidential action under the escape clause and the national security clause. While the most general extension of his power to reduce tariffs takes the familiar form of authorizing him to cut duties to 50% of the prevailing level (July 1962, in the new law), he is empowered to go beyond the 50% level—indeed to abolish duties—for certain categories of goods. The most important category potentially consists of the products for which the U.S. and the Common Market together account for 80% of world trade. The aim of this provision, referred to as the "dominant supplier clause," is to enable the President to bargain for freer trade with the Common Market without exposing either the U.S. or EEC to increased competition on those kinds of products for which Japan and other low-wage countries are major suppliers. If the Common Market were expanded to include the U.K., 26 categories of exports would be covered by the dominant supplier clause, including a wide range of chemical and fabricated products; for the Europe of the Six the authority covers only aircraft, margarine and perfumes.

The passage of the Trade Expansion Act was generally regarded as a victory for the forces favoring freer trade, and this evaluation seems warranted. However, American trade policy must be gauged not only in terms of the language of the law, but also in terms of the political commitments that were made to obtain its enactment; assurances were given to several industries—including textiles, oil, and lumber—that the new legislation would not lead to sharply increased imports. In practice, these commitments will limit the President's freedom to use fully the powers conferred upon him.

The other noteworthy development of the past year has been the strengthening of the inward-looking aspects of Common Market commercial policy. The development of the variable levy system for agriculture, with its highly protectionist potentialities, and the French action in stopping the negotiations for British entry have raised new fears about the liberality of the Common Market.

The fact of the matter is that neither in the U.S. nor in Europe does there appear at this writing to be the kind of unequivocal commitment toward freer trade across the Atlantic that existed among the six countries that form the Common Market. Without such a commitment progress toward the reduction of tariff and other barriers to trade is bound to be slow.

If, however, we take a longer view, there are more grounds for encouragement. The 15 or 20 years following the end of World War II have been years of trade liberalization. Indeed, the reduction of tariffs has proceeded to a point where nontariff obstacles to trade—not only quantitative restrictions but differences in taxation, government purchase policies, health and safety regulations, and the like—are beginning to loom in importance. We may expect further efforts not only to reduce tariffs but to harmonize these national practices so as to allow trade flow more freely.

In the area stressed by this book, another portent of what is to come may be found in the current demand of the Common Market that some curb be placed on the ability of the U.S. to invoke the escape clause unilaterally. Clauses of safeguard will continue to play a major role in trade arrangements, but the pressures to bring them under international control may be expected to mount.

PHILADELPHIA   MAY 1963

Index of Names

Index of Subjects

(Italics indicate more extensive treatment)